Research Methodology in Geography

Research Methodology in Geography

Social, Spatial and Policy Dimensions

Edited by

Harikesh N. Misra
Vijai P. Singh

RAWAT PUBLICATIONS
Jaipur • New Delhi • Bengaluru • Guwahati • Kolkata

ISBN 978-81-7033-425-5

Reprinted 2024

Published by
Prem Rawat for **Rawat Publications**
Satyam Apts, Sector 3, Jawahar Nagar, Jaipur 302 004 (India)
Phone: 0141 265 1748 / 265 7006
E-mail: info@rawatbooks.com
Website: www.rawatbooks.com

New Delhi Office
4858/24, Ansari Road, Daryaganj, New Delhi 110 002
Phone: 011-23263290

Also at *Bengaluru, Guwahati* and *Kolkata*

Typeset by Rawat Computers, Jaipur
Printed and bound in India

Contents

Preface

The purpose of social science research is to understand and explain a social phenomenon or situation in its current contexts, in its relations to past events and situations and forecast the emerging scenarios. Research begins with an idea which serves as the basis for research questions, formulation of hypotheses and their testing.

The realities which social sciences deal with are of varied nature and hence the division of social sciences into several branches and sub-branches. A vast number of such realities are, however, so intricately interwoven and integrated that they cannot be successfully handled by any of the several disciplines. In fact, all real-life problems are of this nature. This calls for an interdisciplinary and integrated approach to research, often termed as multidisciplinary and interdisciplinary research.

Geography as a discipline constitutes an interface between natural sciences on the one hand and social sciences on the other, and by its very nature has to be multidisciplinary and interdisciplinary. Its subject matter is varied and cuts across a large number of disciplines; its point of departure is not a unique subject matter, but a unique perspective. Geography looks at the reality from perspective of space. This is something that no other discipline does. Joint, cooperative and collaborative research is, therefore, very common in geography.

There is no dearth of books on research methodology. But there are not many, if at all, which address themselves to the interdisciplinary research so common in geography. This book is designed to fill, even though only partially, this important gap in methodological literature. It has tried to present a set of papers which focus on contemporary methodological approaches in social and policy sciences cutting across various disciplines and pertinent to geographers. The book will, however, be equally useful to disciplines like economics, sociology, anthropology, public administration, political science, etc. The objective of the book is to present a synthetic view of theoretical analyses and empiri-derivations and observations of environmental, social and policy issues within the broad conceptual matrix of geographic research.

The volume consists of twenty-one chapters, each presenting a specific method or technique of analysis and synthesis. Chapters 2 to 6 deal with the basics of research methodology, i.e., theory of knowledge, paradigms, comparative methods, project design, report writing, hypothesis formulation and testing. Data collection, sampling, remote sensing, terrain analysis, GIS, game theory and simulation and methodological inquiry into social mobility constitute the themes of chapters 7 to 15. Chapters 16 to 21 focus on the methodological issues in the field of policy planning, essentially directed to urban and regional problems.

We are grateful to our friends who contributed papers and thus made it possible for us to bring them out in a book form. In spite of an inordinate delay in the finalization of the manuscript, some of the colleagues who were keen to make a contribution, could not do so in time. We regret the delay in respect of contributions which came as early as 1992 and also with respect to those which had to be declined because they could not come on time. Our most sincere thanks to Professor R.P. Misra, a great geographer, social scientist and visionary for encouraging this endeavour. We do hope that the volume will be of help to young researchers.

Some of the papers included in the volume were published in reputed journals, such as *Journal of Applied Systems Analysis, Annals, National Association of Geographers, India, Journal of the Indian Law Research Institute*, etc. We are thankful to their editors for allowing us to reproduce them in this volume.

Harikesh N. Misra
Vijai P. Singh

List of Contributors

Michael M. Cernea, Senior Adviser, Sociology and Social Policy, Environment Department, The World Bank, 1818, H. Street N.W. Washington, D.C., USA.

Graham P. Chapman, Head, Department of Geography and Director, South-North Centre for Environmental Policy, School of Oriental and African Studies, London University, London, UK.

Mahamaya Chattopadhyay, Centre for Earth Science Studies, P.B. No. 7250, Akkulam, Trivandrum.

Srikumar Chattopadhyay, Scientist, Centre for Earth Science Studies, P.B. No. 7250, Akkulam, Trivandrum.

K.D. Gangrade, Retd. Professor and Head, Department of Social Work, Delhi School of Social Work, University of Delhi, Delhi.

William J. Haller, Research Assistant, University Center for Social and Urban Research and Graduate Student, Department of Sociology, University of Pittsburgh, P.A., USA.

Lokesh Kaul, Professor and Head, Department of Education, Himachal Pradesh University, Shimla.

H.N. Misra, Professor and Head, Department of Geography, Himachal Pradesh University, Shimla.

Kamlesh Misra, Senior Consultant, National Institute of Public Finance and Policy, New Delhi.

R.P. Misra, Professor of Geography, University of Delhi, Delhi.

S.P. Mishra, Lecturer in Geography, Banaras Hindu University, Varanasi.
Dhirendra Mohan, Professor of Philosophy, Patna College, Patna.
Neela Mukherjee, Professor of Economics, Lal Bahadur Shastri National Academy of Administration, Mussoorie.
R. Nagaraja, Senior Scientist, Landuse Division, National Remote Sensing Agency, Hyderabad.
G.S. Sastry, Institute for Social and Economic Change, Bangalore.
Bam Dev Sharda, Professor of Sociology, University of Utah, USA.
R.B. Singh, Senior Scientist, Department of Geography, Delhi University, Delhi.
Vijai P. Singh, Director, University Center of Social and Urban Research and Professor, Department of Sociology, University of Pittsburgh, P.A., USA.
K.V. Sundaram, Development Planner and Consultant, 641, Sector A, Pocket C, Vasant Kunj, New Delhi.
Laxman Swaroop, Reader, Department of Commerce and Business Administration, University of Allahabad, Allahabad.

Chapter 1

Introduction

H.N. Misra and Vijai P. Singh

No matter how it is defined, research is referred to as the discovery of facts and/or a fresh interpretation of facts already known. The role of research is, thus, both developmental and evaluative. It endeavours to discover new horizons of knowledge as well as to utilize the existing knowledge for the benefit of society. While the former comes under the fold of fundamental or basic research, the latter is referred to as applied research. Fundamental research is purported to propounding laws and theories by seeking order and regularity among the existing phenomena. Theory building is a process which derives its base from teleological views, immanent laws and historical facts, etc. Fundamental research is basically scientific in nature and is characterized by verifiability, generality, predictability and objectivity. It is also replicable in different situations. Applied research, on the other hand, is marked by subjectivity and is not necessarily replicable. It is concerned with application and utility. But it is not necessarily ameliorative or prescriptive; it may be pathological in its approach. This is rightly so because the societal problems are complex, varied and manifold and it is practically impossible to suggest some uniform measures applicable in different conditions.

Research Process

The prime objective of research is to investigate reality and establish theories about empirical observations. The reality can be two-fold—

theoretical and empirical. Theoretical reality is assumed by the human intellect and is based on mathematical constructs. In view of the universality of mathematical constructs this may be called as theoretical totality. Empirical reality is based on observation and owing to its limited range, this may be referred to as empirical partiality (Jacobson, 1976). Research aims at bridging the gap between theoretical totality and empirical partiality through some processes which are as under:

(a) Identification of the research problem which could be descriptive, exploratory or analytical. While a descriptive problem describes the objects or cases with respect to one or more aspects of reality, an exploratory problem looks for some kind of relationships that may exist and an analytical problem involves testing of suspected relationships. This is an important step, and a researcher must be aware of the problem to be investigated alongwith its goals and contents.

(b) Formulation of hypotheses which is a set of assumptions against which reality is tested.

(c) Research design which is the blueprint or total plan of action. It entails entire research process including review of literature, sources of data, methods and techniques and organizational frame, etc.

(d) Selection of variables is an important step as variables are the characteristics of objects which keep changing with time and from object to object. This is also referred to as measurable quantity. The variables are measured on scales known as nominal, ordinal, ratio and interval.

(e) Generalizations in social science research are often based on partial data such as sample surveys. Important steps in survey research include careful sampling within the frame of random, systematic and stratified sampling, development of interview schedule or questionnaire, data collection and analysis. In addition to sampling design, special care must be taken in framing questions with appropriate content and their sequence. Questions should be framed objectively in such a way that any bias of the researcher and of the others involved in the research process can be avoided.

(f) Data analysis involves testing of hypotheses on the basis of collected data. Data are coded, tabulated, transformed and maps and graphs are prepared for interpretation. Suitable techniques are used for analysis. The techniques may be simple or complex depending upon the nature of study and degree of precision to be attained. There are many complex phenomena, such as attitudes, values, social status, power and freedom among others, that are less amenable to direct quantitative measurement. In each of these variables, several different but related elements are embedded and therefore multiple indicators are used to measure a particular variable. Scales are constructed to measure the degree of presence of such phenomena on a continuum.

Multivariate analysis involves establishing relationships between more than two variables in a study. This technique permits establishing true relationship between any two variables while controlling the third variable. It also enables the researcher to assess the degree to which this relationship will change in different contexts and conditions. Correlations, multiple regression, principal component and factor analysis, etc., are the techniques used to accomplish this research objective. The effectiveness of these techniques is largely dependent on the theory that guides the development of research hypotheses.

Qualitative methods are used in the study of institutions and social processes where quantitative measures are not applicable. Once the topic for research and the research site have been chosen, it becomes important for the researcher to become familiar with the area, people and institutions to gain insights and identify key informants. Qualitative data and observations are organized in relevant categories to identify patterns of relationship to test hypotheses. Though generalizations from such studies are limited, they still serve as the basis for testing hypotheses in other similar or dissimilar settings. Qualitative data often supplement the studies based on quantitative data and enhance the explanatory objectives of such studies.

(g) Research report is the end product of the entire research process which is prepared for formal presentation of the total finding.

Research Paradigm

Research, as a dynamic process, is heavily influenced by the changing needs and aspirations of society. It does not merely witness the change in priorities and thrust areas of research. Even epistemology, ontology and methodology—collectively called paradigm (Kuhn, 1974)—have also witnessed a great shift from time to time. The idiographic approach based on empirical-inductive logic which provides genetic explanations by treating events and phenomena as unique is being discarded as against nomothetic approach which is based on theoretical-deductive logic (Yeates and Garner, 1976). The deductive approach proceeds with a set of assumptions which are tested against real world situations to draw conclusions. This helps in generalization and prediction, and hence theory building which is the key objective of research. The quest for theory in explanation has given rise to model building, which is a process of theory building through abstraction and idealized representation of reality. The iconic, analog and symbolic models are the three-stage processes of abstracting the complex realities of world (Haggett, 1975).

The range, intricacy and ramifications of social and policy issues have also necessitated the paradigm shifts in research. The traditional descriptive paradigm was replaced by the quantitative-theoretic paradigm under the positivistic underpinnings after the Second World War. The positivistic philosophy emphasized that knowledge cannot be knowledge if it was not scientifically tested. This led to the prolific use of quantitative methods and statistic techniques—starting from simple to very sophisticated ones based on computer softwares. This paradigm remained operational during fifties and sixties and it continues to be active even today. But now it is being criticized for its mechanistic and reductionist approach. Yet another reason for the growing discontent against quantification is the fact that it fails to explain the human behaviour and value systems. Man is the key actor and real decision maker. The circumstances, in which he takes the decisions, cannot be accounted for by numbers and statistical techniques. The human mind and societal problems are so complex that they cannot be explained by any statistical measures. Even the computers and super-computers cannot understand the human mind. But, in research, it is vital to understand the processes, which can be properly explained by understanding human behaviour. This realization has re-emphasized the importance of subjective-qualitative approaches. This has resulted in the emergence of several new paradigms such as behaviouralism and structuralism. It may, however, be observed that both quantitative and qualitative approaches are complementary to each other and what is called for in research, irrespective of any discipline, is the synthetic view presenting the synergic approach for analysis, interpretation and description.

Organization of the Volume

The papers presented in this volume reflect contemporary methodological approaches in social and policy sciences. Each paper can be read independent of others, but together they form a compendium of research methods that apply to a variety of research topics from various disciplines.

The volume consists of twenty-one chapters. It starts with the introduction by editors in Chapter 1, which presents a brief resume on research methodology by briefly highlighting the research processes and paradigm shifts in social science research.

The theory of knowledge and paradigms which provide the objective base of research methodology have been discussed in Chapter 2 and 3 respectively. The paper on Indian epistemology by Dhirendra Mohan (Chapter 2) has been specially incorporated in this volume to project the Indian viewpoint on the theory of knowledge. The paper analyzes the root of knowledge and finally discusses in detail different sources of knowledge. Unlike western logic which emphasizes perception and inference alone as the chief sources of knowledge, Indian epistemology enumerates six important sources: perception (*Pratyaksa*), inference (*Anumana*), testimony (*Sabda*), similarity (*Upamana*), implications (*Arthapatti*), and non-cognition (*Anupalabdhi*), besides a few other less important sources such as tradition (*Aitihya*), presentiment (*Pratibha*) and possible entailment (*Sambhava*), etc. By describing each one of them in detail, the paper opens a much broader canvas for testing hypotheses and building theories. The paper finally comes to end by discussing the conceptions of truth and error as conceived by different schools of Indian philosophy.

In Chapter 3, H.N. Misra dwells upon the concept of paradigm and paradigm shifts as evidenced by geography in general and urban geography in particular. Paradigm is an important concept in the field of knowledge. It has built-in epistemology, ontology and methodology and provides conceptual matrix within a frame of which any discipline or sub-discipline functions. This, thus, heavily impinges upon the research process of the respective branch of knowledge. When one paradigm replaces the other, it is called 'paradigmatic shock' or 'paradigm shift'. Human Geography, or for that matter Urban Geography, has undergone several paradigmatic changes during the pre- and post-Second World War periods. The traditional paradigms, such as explorative, environmentalism and regionalism operated before the Second World War, whereas the contemporary paradigms, such as quantitative-theoretic, behavioural perspectives and structuralism have been guiding the development of researches in Urban Geography during the post-war period. The essay deals, at length, with philosophical positions, major examples, and theories and methodologies of each and every paradigm. It pleads for a unified theory based on the synthesis of different perspectives for understanding a city which is multidimensional, complex and evasive in character.

There are several sociological research methods, such as historical, comparative, structural and functional. Comparative social research is very relevant as it attempts to present a comparative analysis of societies of different kinds and in different stages. In Chapter 4, Vijai P. Singh and William J. Haller present an exhaustive review of the comparative social research by tracing the basic concepts and requirements of comparative inquiry and displaying the application of comparative methodology in the analysis of changes with special reference to regional economies of Western Europe and the United States of America. The authors discuss the logic of comparative research and raise the issues of functional equivalence and measurement. In the end, two case studies, which have used factor analysis for comparing the regional structural changes, have been reviewed.

The next two chapters (5 and 6) are devoted to research processes. Formulating the research project and finally writing the report are the processes which require special skill, dexterity and articulation in their accomplishment. R.P. Misra discusses these essential components of research in Chapter 5. In the first part of the chapter, the author dwells upon the different steps a researcher has to follow to formulate the research proposal. The second part is devoted to the art of scientific writing for presenting the final report of the research.

The research findings are said to be descriptive if there are no hypotheses. Hypothesis formulation and testing are the important steps in deductive approach as they help to propound theories. Hypothesis provides the potential answer which is tested against reality. This has been discussed in Chapter 6 by Lokesh Kaul. A detailed account of hypotheses formulation, criteria of usable hypotheses, and statement and testing of hypotheses has been presented in this chapter.

The art of data collection lies at the core of research problem. Although much depends on the aim, nature, scope and contour of the study, yet the importance of collecting primary data through questionnaires and schedules cannot be underestimated. The questionnaire is administered in a manner to be filled in by respondents whereas the schedule is referred to as a form filled in during a personal interview. The essentials of a good questionnaire and schedule are clarity, brevity, unambiguity, reliability and communicability. The whole art of collecting primary data through questionnaire and schedule, process of framing questions, question content and sequence and procedure of framing a schedule, etc., have been explained by K.D. Gangrade in

Chapter 7.

Sampling is yet another important method by which primary data from a vast array of sources may be collected. Nevertheless, it requires meticulous sampling design and appropriate sample sizes so that data so collected represent all segments of the total population. In any sampling design, however, spatial dimension is specially important because it helps to draw data from the total space matrix—points, line and area. One such exercise of spatial sampling design for urban household survey of Bangalore city has been presented by G.S. Sastry in Chapter 8. The measures for computing the sample estimates and standard errors have also been discussed.

Understanding the nature of data and their measurement scales is necessary for data processing as they determine the type of techniques to be applied. In Chapter 9, Laxman Swaroop discusses different types of scales and their feasibility in social science research. Nonetheless, the analysis of attitude scales forms the thrust of the paper which has been accomplished by demonstrating the use of some select scaling methods. These scaling methods, however, have their own merits and demerits and their utility depends upon the objectives of a researcher.

The use and applicability of remote sensing and Geographical Information System (GIS) has been discussed in the next five chapters (10-14). The natural resource management system forms the focal theme of these chapters.

Remote sensing as a science and the art of acquiring data about the earth space and its objects is the theme of Chapter 10. Various remote sensing techniques and their applications have been extensively described in this chapter by R. Nagaraja and H.N. Misra.

Terrain analysis, which forms the theme of Chapter 11, has been attempted jointly by Srikumar Chattopadhyay and Mahamaya Chattopadhyay. The basic assumption is that terrain analysis may provide the base for natural resource data management system which is necessary to plan for sustainable development. The authors discuss the principles and methods of terrain analysis and demonstrate the use of the hierarchical method for identifying the terrain of Kerala as a whole and that of Trivandrum district as a case in point.

In Chapter 12, S.P. Mishra examines the application of remote sensing data for erosion surveys. He describes the mechanics of erosion and its controlling factors and finally presents the state of soil erosion in Hissar (Haryana, India) as identified through IRS-LISS IA imagery and selective field checks. He finds the remote sensing data are quite effective in mapping the areas characterized by severe, moderate and low soil erosion processes.

There is increasing awareness and interest in geographic phenomena, such as natural resources, population distribution, land uses, etc. This has increased the pressure to develop better ways to record, store, analyze, manage, retrieve and display geographic information. In the coming decades, we will see a revolution in analytic techniques. Then, there will be need to develop human skills for adapting these techniques to very specific applications which will demand the knowledge of GIS. An overview of concepts, components and capabilities of GIS has been presented by R. Nagaraja in Chapter 13.

Environmental monitoring and developmental planning are basically information-intensive which is possible through GIS as it has immense capability of handling a variety of data or theme on a common map base. R.B. Singh, in Chapter 14, has presented a case of Chakrata tehsil of Dehradun district (U.P., India) for environmental monitoring based on GIS. Outlining the basic ingredients of GIS, he has produced the maps of forest cover change, potential soil erosion risk areas and land suitable for agriculture, which may help plan the sustainable development at the sub-micro level.

Simulation is an important technique used for understanding the processes. However, as against the conventional system of simulation, G.P. Chapman has developed two gaming simulations known as Green Revolution Game and Exaction. He discusses the use and application of these two simulations in Chapter 15. The chapter is divided into two parts. While the first part outlines the structure and analyzes the characteristics and purposes of gaming simulations by presenting an example of a game run of each of them, a philosophical interpretation of comparative utility of computer based system simulation and gaming simulations has been presented in the second part. It establishes the merit of gaming simulations over computer simulation in understanding the human realities.

Social mobility, which is defined as movement of individuals or groups between social positions, constitutes one of the most important thrust areas of sociological researches. The two basic approaches which have been followed to analyze social mobility are known as status attainment approach and mobility table approach. Bam Dev Sharda examines different methodological variants of these approaches with examples from India in Chapter 16. The status attainment approach emphasizes social origin and other background characteristics as factors in achievement, whereas mobility table examines the patterns of movement or mobility among the positions. It has been noted that status attainment approach is characterized by multivariate structural equation models while the mobility table does not go beyond the bivariate analysis. This leaves further scope for methodological improvements.

Some methodological issues related to policy planning have been discussed in Chapters 17-21.

People's participation remains at the heart of bottom-up planning but how to convert this theory into practice to ensure active community involvement in government sponsored development programmes is a pragmatic question. This obviously involves some methodology which has been explained in a series of steps by Michael M. Cernea in Chapter 17. The building blocks of bottom-up planning are based on the action-research experience of PIDER programme (*Programa Integral Parael Desarollo Rural*) in Mexico. The paper outlines the conceptual and experimental frame of community participation based on the monitoring of PIDER and suggests some key lessons for generating a social methodology for bottom-up planning, that is apt to elicit, organize, and incorporate a degree of participation of the local social actors in government-launched development programmes.

The contemporary paradigms of development lay greater emphasis on participatory development which calls for methodology of indigenous knowledge-building exercises. Neela Mukherjee describes participatory rural appraisal as a methodology for participatory development in Chapter 18. As an important variant of farming system research, it underlines the importance of participation of rural people in planning, implementing and monitoring of rural development programmes. The essay discusses the principles and a whole range of methods which may help in organization of participation.

A city performs two types of functions, viz., city-forming and city-serving. While the city-serving functions are meant for local people and are consumption-oriented, the city-forming functions are production-oriented and add to the multiplier effect of the town. The city-forming functions are the basic functions. A number of methods, such as residual, micro-cosmic, sales-employment conversion and minimum requirement, have been used by geographers from time to time to determine and distinguish the basic/non-basic ratio in the city employment structure. The minimum requirement method proposed by Alexanderson has been considered to be more appropriate. Nevertheless, this method has its own weaknesses. In Chapter 19, H.N. Misra has pointed out those weaknesses and presented a modified version of the minimum requirement method which is more logical and serves as a model to determine the basic/non-basic ratio of the city.

Analytical techniques for the study of regional structural change by Kamlesh Misra and Vijai P. Singh is the central theme of Chapter 20.

Outlining the need and importance of interdisciplinary research in urban and regional planning, K.V. Sundaram enumerates the role of different disciplines and points out the problems of multidisciplinary team work in the planning process in Chapter 21.

References

Haggett, P. (1975), *Geography: A Modern Synthesis*, New York: Harper and Row.

Jacobson, Jr. Perry E. (1976), *Introduction to Statistical Measures for the Social and Behavioural Sciences*, Hinsdale: The Dryden.

Kuhn, T.S. (1974), *The Structure of Scientific Revolutions*, Chicago: University of Chicago Press.

Yeates, M. and Barry Garner (1976), *The North American City*, New York: Harper and Row.

Chapter 2

Indian Epistemology

Dhirendra Mohan

Place of Epistemology in Philosophy

Epistemology or the theory of knowledge has acquired special importance in European philosophy in the modern period, particularly in the philosophies of Locke, Hume, and Kant. Kant thought that without a prior critical examination of the elements, sources and limits of knowledge we should not engage in metaphysical discussion. So he regarded all previous philosophy as dogmatic as contrasted with his own critical philosophy. In more recent times, however, the American neo-realists have tried to oppose the general modern European trend, initiated by Kant, that the theory of knowledge should precede the theory of reality. They have chosen to be consciously dogmatic. They are led to this position by a kind of reaction against the use of epistemology made by most modern idealists for establishing idealistic theories of reality.

But in India the position has been otherwise. From the very beginning of the different systems of philosophy until recent times, discussions on the problems of knowledge (including those of doubt and error) have formed an essential part of philosophy. The reason for this striking and continued unanimity can be found in the fact that all schools of Indian philosophy, without exception, regarded ignorance

---

Reproduced from Bhattacharya, Haridas (ed), *The Cultural Heritage of India*, Vol. III, The Ramkrishna Mission, Institute of Culture, Calcutta, 1975.

as the root cause of human suffering, so that they were all bent upon discovering the means and process of true knowledge by means of which reality could be known and life could be so lived as to overcome misery or minimize suffering. Vātsyāyana voices the feelings of all Indian thinkers on this matter when, in commenting upon the first *sūtra* of Gautama, he says that the study of the sources of knowledge (*pramāṇa*) is necessary, because through it alone can we properly know reality and thereby guide our actions so as to be able to attain desirable ends and avoid suffering.

Epistemology thus becomes closely linked with ontology and both of them again with ethics. Knowledge and moral perfection are regarded as necessary to each other in almost all systems of Indian thought. Sometimes knowledge is regarded as the means to the good life, sometimes again moral purity is regarded as indispensable for perfect knowledge, so that morality and knowledge are regarded as the two inseparable aspects of perfection.

In the course of the development of the Indian systems interest in epistemology increased and it began to claim a large share in the philosophical discussions of almost every school. The motives were sometimes theoretical, sometimes practical, sometimes simply polemical. But all led to the enrichment of epistemological thought and literature.

Analysis and Sources of Knowledge

The factors constituting and connected with knowledge (*jñātna or pramā*) are usually analyzed into the subject (*jñātṛ* or *pramātṛ*), the object (*jñeya* or *prameya*), and the means of knowledge (*pramāṇa*). But consciousness is not always regarded as the product of any relation between the subject and the object. The *Sāṁkhya*, the *Vedānta*, and the *Jaina* schools conceive the self as possessed of intrinsic consciousness, so that knowledge is nothing more than the relation of the object to an already existing consciousness of the self. The *Sāṁkhya*, the *Yoga*, and the *Vedānta* assert the possibility of the existence of consciousness even when there is no object. But the *Nyāya-Vaiśeṣika* and the *Mīmāṁsaka* hold, as do some Western thinkers, that consciousness—and so knowledge—is a product of the relation of the self, previously unconscious, to some object in some appropriate way. The Buddhists also regard consciousness, like every other phenomenon, as a momentary product of several conditions.

A distinction is maintained, however, by the *Sāṁkhya-Yoga* and the *Vedānta* between consciousness as it is in itself (*svarūpa-caitanya*) and empirical consciousness or consciousness of objects (*vṛtti-caitanya*). With the help of this distinction these schools can also maintain the common-sense notion of knowledge (as beginning in time and depending on the relation of the self to some object), because such knowledge only means empirical consciousness of some object. But they point out, like Green, that consciousness in itself is original and eternal; and it transcends time and space. In fact, such intrinsic consciousness is regarded as identical with the self (*Ātman*) itself. According to the *Sāṁkhya* and the *Yoga*, the self as the knower is real, and it is distinguished from objects as known. The relation of the self to objects is not possible, according to these schools, unless the object produces through the senses and *manas* some image of itself in the intellect (*buddhi*). This modification of *buddhi* (technically called *vṛtti*) is illuminated by the self or consciousness, resulting in the knowledge of the object. But as the *Advaita* regards the distinction between the knower and the known as a practical make-shift, untenable in the ultimate analysis, it does not hold, like the *Sāṁkhya*, the reality of even the role of the self as the knower. The knower and the known are but the two apparent aspects of one basic reality, the real Self or *Brahman*. Knowledge should not be considered therefore to be really an external relation. It is only the self-shining consciousness that is the very nature of existence, including the apparent subjects and objects. But to explain knowledge in terms of the dualistic beliefs of the ordinary man, the *Advaitin* adopts to a certain extent the *Sāṁkhya* theory of knowledge, with the important difference that he does not regard knowledge as an external relation. The object in contact with the external sense or directly present to the internal sense (*antaḥkaraṇa*) causes a modification (*vṛtti*) of the latter. This *vṛtti* only serves to remove, though to that extent and in that respect only, the illusory distinction between the knower and the known. For the Buddhist idealist, the *Vijñānavādin*, every objective knowledge is an illusory externalization or external projection of a subjective idea.

Knowledge, in the strict sense of correct cognition, is called *pramā*, and a source of knowledge is called a *pramāṇa*. Unlike Western logic that generally admits two chief sources of knowledge, perception and inference, Indian epistemology admits, in the different schools, one to six sources of knowledge. We shall briefly discuss them one by one.

Perception or Pratyakṣa

Perception, generally called *pratyakṣa*, is admitted by all the schools to be the basic source of knowledge. The *Cārvākas* regard it as the only source. According to them, inference is not reliable, since every inference, to be true, must be based upon some universal proposition containing the knowledge of an invariable relation between two phenomena; and such a universal proposition cannot be established by observations. We cannot observe, for example, whether all cases of smoke—those in the unobserved past, or in the future, or in regions beyond perception—were, will be, or are even now invariably accompanied by fire. Inference cannot therefore be relied on with certainty. About authority as a source of knowledge the *Cārvākas* point to the innumerable examples in daily life where we find ourselves deceived and misled by the testimony of other persons. Even the scriptures are not beyond doubt. The Vedas contain many meaningless words and enjoin rituals which may merely go to swell the fees of the officiating priests. They may therefore be the work of cunning priests.

Regarding the exact origin of *pratyakṣa* or perceptual knowledge, there is, however, a good deal of controversy among the different schools. The ordinary views is that *pratyakṣa* is that kind of knowledge which is generated by the relation of sense (*indriya*) to some object (*indriyārtha-sannikarṣa-janya-jñātna*). In accordance with the *Nyāya-Vaiśeṣika* view, there are six senses or *indriyas*—the five external ones of sound, sight, touch, taste, and smell, and the internal one, mind (*manas*). If the object is an external one, like a tree, the knower (the soul) directs the mind through the external sense say the eyes, to the tree, and gathers thus the visual knowledge of the tree. If the object to be perceived is internal, say a pleasure (which according to this school is a quality of the soul itself), the soul has simply to attend to it through the *manas*, which does therefore, in this case, the double duty of an organ of attention as well as that of an internal sense.

According to the *Sāṁkhya-Yoga* school also, the contact of the object with some one of the senses is necessary for ordinary external perception. But such a contact must generate some modification in the internal sense, as was mentioned in the previous section. The internal organ is sometimes considered to be a whole and called *antaḥkaraṇa* or *citta*, but sometimes distinguished by its different functions (of explication, self-reference, and determination) into the three aspects called respectively *manas*, *ahaṅkāra* and *buddhi*. The account of the origination of perception is therefore differently given by different writers of this school. But on the whole it is admitted that if the internal organ in some aspect does not assume the form of the object and present it to the self or the self-shining consciousness, there cannot be any knowledge of the object. This clue is utilized by *Yoga* when it teaches that the modification of the *citta* into the form of the object should be stopped, so that no object may appear before consciousness and tempt it into attachment and bondage. *Yoga* is thus defined as the arrest of the modification of the internal organ (*Yogaścitta-vṛtti-nirodhaḥ*).

A question often discussed in connection with the possibilities of perceptual knowledge is whether there can be any perception of entities not related to any sense. Some *Vedāntins*, who do not regard *manas* as a sense (unlike the *Naiyāyikas* and *Sāṁkhyas*), point out that internal perceptions (of pleasure, pain, etc.) prove that no sense need mediate in such cases. Moreover, they ask, 'If perception be not possible without some sense, how can the *Naiyāyikas* and others think of God as perceiving the world?' The *Yoga* system admits that there can be knowledge of external objects which are not accessible to any sense, if the mind can be sufficiently concentrated on them. The later *Naiyāyikas* agree that there are exceptional cases of extraordinary perception in which immediate knowledge of external objects, not related to an external sense, is possible; and they admit in that connection the possibility of yogic perception. Gaṅgeśa, the founder of the later *Nyāya*, states in his famous work *Tattva-cintāmaṇi* that it is not necessary to conceive and define perception in terms of sense-object relation; immediacy is the essential character of perception. This point is further emphasized and elaborated by the *Jaina* and the *Advaita* thinkers.

The Jains very aptly observe that ordinary perception in which the self knows the object through the medium of some sense cannot rightly be called immediate. It is only less mediate than inference, testimony, etc. But real immediate knowledge, worth the name, is that knowledge which the self can acquire by its direct relation to the object without the inter-mediation of any organ whatsoever. Such absolutely immediate knowledge can be gained only when the self can free itself of the obstructing influence of its many *karmas*. Everyone can attain such omniscience through the necessary moral perfection.

The *Advaitins*, the followers of the monistic *Vedānta* school of Saṅkarācarya, also hold, in another way, the potential omniscience of every man. According to his school, the self being really identical with the absolutic *Brahman*, what limits its knowledge is its ignorance of its real nature. When ignorance is overcome, what remains is the self-shining consciousness, the pure. Self or *Brahman.* Immediary is primarily the nature of this basic consciousness; only secondarily it belongs to a sense perception. Every such perception takes place by a sort of removal of the ignorance that divides the knower from the known. Perception is therefore a momentary restoration of the lost identity between the two and the flashing forth of the basic consciousness which underlies all—the knower, the known, and the entire mechanism of knowledge. The ideal of immediate knowledge is not, however, attained in sense perception or any other knowledge in the objective attitude. It is attained when the objective attitude is altogether overcome and the underlying unlimited consciousness, *Brahman*, is allowed to reveal itself.

The question is often discussed in the Indian schools as to what exactly is revealed by sense perception. The subjective idealists among Buddhist thinkers—the *Vijñānavādins* of *Yogācāras*, as they are variously called—hold that external perception is really an external projection of mind's own ideas, which emerge into consciousness by the maturation of some of the innumerable unconscious ideas that form the total mental substratum (*ālayavijñātna*) underlying the individual. The *Sautrāntika* school of Buddhism believes, however, that sense perception produces in the mind the ideas or copies of external objects, which can therefore be inferred as the originals of these copies. But the *Vaibhāṣika* school of Buddhism holds that external objects themselves, and not merely the ideas of them, are directly given in perception. The *Nyāya-Vaiśeṣika*, *Sāṁkhya*. *Mīmāṁsaka*, and *Vedāntin*, including even Saṅkarācārya, hold this last view about perception.

Consistently with its thoroughgoing realism, the *Nyāya-Vaiśeṣika* school holds that all the elements that we can find by analyzing the different perceptual judgements—in fact, all the basic categories of reality—are given in perception from the beginning, though the relation among them is established by the judging mind subsequently. The Buddhists, in general, hold that perception reveals only unique particulars—their class-characters, names, etc., are later superimposed by the judging mind. Some later followers of Saṅkara maintain, on the contrary, that perception reveals only pure Being (*sanmātra*); all particular characters are the superimpositions of the interpreting mind.

Can the self be perceived? This question is variously answered. The older *Nyāya* tries to prove the existence of the self by inferences of different kinds. But the later *Nyāya-Vaiśeṣika* writers hold that though the self as such cannot be perceived, yet it is possible to perceive it in such introspective knowledge as 'I am happy. The self as possessed of some perceptible quality (like happiness or sorrow) is the object of such internal perception. The *Bhāṭṭa Mīmāṁsakas* also think that the self is knowable as the object of occasional self-consciousness. The *Prābhākaras* strongly feel that the self, which is the subject, cannot possibly be an object of knowledge without losing its own nature. According to them, every act of knowledge reveals itself, as well as the self as the knower and the object as the known. The *Sāṁkhyas* and the *Advaitins* believe that as the self is identical with consciousness, it is self-revealing. Only it is not known in its purity, so long as it is not isolated from the empirical objects with which it is confused and mixed up in the form of objective consciousness. The self is not known objectively—not even as the object of introspection—but as the consciousness which immediately manifests itself.

Inference or Anumana

Except the *Cārvākas*, all other schools consider inference to be a valid and important source of knowledge. In reply to the *Cārvāka* objections against inference, it is pointed out (1) that even the theory that inference is invalid can be established only by an inference so the *Cārvāka* theory is suicidal, and (2) that it is not impossible to establish universal propositions (as premises necessary for deductive inference) with the help of various inductive methods (discussed below).

Gautama and his later followers of the *Nyāya* school devoted special attention to inference, which occupied these thinkers almost exclusively for centuries, particularly in Mithilā and Bengal. The views of other schools were greatly influenced by them. In the course of their intensive cultivation of this narrow field of inference, they discovered many subtleties, and developed above all a unique algebraic language for the precise formulation of ideas. This became the standard language of philosophical discussion in all schools and made all later philosophical treaties unintelligible to the general reader.

The common conception of inference—rather *anumāna*—is that it is the kind of knowledge which is derived from the previous knowledge of an invariable relation between a sign (*liṅga*) and something bearing that sign (*liṅgin*). For example, when we know the existence of fire on the distinct mountain from the smoke perceptible on it, we have an *anumāna* based on the invariable relation between smoke and fire. Such a relation is technically called *vyāpti* or pervasion (the cases of the existence of smoke being pervaded by those of the existence of fire).

This invariable relation is established by different inductive methods. The Buddhist logicians adopt the five-step method of observation (called *pañcakāraṇī*), namely, (1) cause is not perceived, effect is also not perceived, (2) cause is perceived, (3) effect is also perceived, (4) cause disappears, (5) effect also disappears. In his *Positive Sciences of the Ancient Hindus*, Sir Brajendra Nath Seal characterizes this Buddhist method of establishing induction through causal connection as the double method of difference and notes its superiority to the ordinary single method of difference adopted by western logicians.

The *Naiyāyikas*, commencing with Gautama, recognize that it is possible to have *vyāpti* or invariable connection of the 'causal as well as of the non-causal' type, e.g., all animals with horns have tails. In most cases, according to them, such a relation can be established by the observation of agreement in presence (anvaya), e.g., by observing in many cases that wherever there is smoke, there is fire, and by the observation of agreement in absence (*vyatireka*), e.g., by observing in many cases that where there is no fire, there is no smoke. This would constitute the joint method of agreement. But in some exceptional cases we may have to depend on the single method of agreement in presence only (*kevala-anvaya*), e.g., when we have to establish a relation like 'all nameable things are knowable things' (where, from the nature of the case, we cannot possibly observe any negative instance like 'this thing is not knowlable, and it is also not nameable'). In other exceptional cases, of an opposite type, we may have to depend only on agreement in absence (*kevala-vyatireka*), e.g., when we have to establish a proposition like '(of the five elements) whichever is not different from the other (four) elements (e.g. either, air, fire, and water) has no smell' (where we cannot observe any positive instance except earth since earth is the only element having smell).

To make induction more certain the *Naiyāyikas* also insist on the elimination of doubts arising from the existence of any unnoticed condition (*upādhi*) that might be responsible for the invariable coexistence of two phenomena in the cases observed. For example, someone may observe in many cases the existence of fire accompanied by smoke; and, failing to notice that in all such cases wetness of the fuel was a condition responsible for smoke, he might erroneously lay down the universal proposition, 'Wherever there is fire, there is smoke'. Only by repeated and careful observation can such errors be eliminated.

Gautama speaks of three kinds of inference, *pūrvavat*, *śeṣavat*, and *sāmānyatodṛṣṭa*. According to the common interpretation, they stand respectively for inference from cause to effect (e.g. from the gathering clouds to rain), from effect to cause (e.g. from flood in the river to rainfall up-stream), and lastly from a generally observed non-causal type of relation (e.g. from the changing position of the sun to the movement of the sun).

Later *Naiyāyikas* classify inference on another principle, namely, in accordance with the industive method on which the major premise of the inference is based. So they have the three kinds of inference called respectively *anvaya-vyatirekī*, *kevalānvayī*, and *kevalā-vyatirekī*.

Gautama lays down five steps as necessary for an inference when it is required to demonstrate a conclusion without straying from the point to be proved and without committing any formal or material fallacy. For such a purpose one should proceed as follows:

(1) State the proposition to be proved (*pratijñā*, e.g. 'That hill has fire', i.e., there is fire on the hill).
(2) State the reason in support (*hetu*, e.g., 'Because it has smoke').
(3) State the invariable relation between the sign (the reason or middle term) and the signified (the major term) supported by some concrete instance guaranteeing, material validity (*udāharaṇa*, e.g. 'Whatever has smoke has fire, as the fire-place', i.e., wherever there is smoke there is fire).
(4) Show how the above relation applies to the case in hand (*upanaya*, e.g. 'This hill has smoke which is invariably accompanied by fire').
(5) Draw the conclusion (*nigamana*, e.g. 'Therefore, the hill has fire').

It will be observed that *anumāna*, as conceived here, is not only the formally valid deductive inference of western logic, it is also, as Seal calls it, a formal-material, deductive-inductive process.

The fallacies of inference mentioned by Gautama and discussed by other thinkers after him are chiefly the different kinds of material invalidity arising from the middle term not being invariably, or at all, related to the major, or not actually existing in the minor, or leading to a conclusion contradicted by observation or by a more reliable inference. Gautama is never tired of insisting in various ways on the necessity of keeping truth as the goal of all argument and debate and the consequent necessity of desisting from all unfair use of the intellect, such as quibbling, using false analogy, arguing merely for victory, and so on.

Though the other schools do not accept in toto the *Nyāya* view of inference, their deviations are not so important as to deserve special mention in this brief essay.

Testimony or Sabda

Except the *Cārvāka* school and Kaṇāda, the founder of the *Vaiśeṣika* (who admits only perception and inference), the Indian logicians accept testimony or authority as a third source of valid knowledge. Kaṇāda thinks, like western logicians, that knowledge from authority is really a kind of inference, based on the reliability of the authority. But the *Naiyāyikas* and others point out that the process by which such knowledge is derived is so different from that of inference that it deserves a separate status. For, in order that *śabda* or verbal statement may yield knowledge, the following conditions have to be fulfilled:

(1) Each word of a sentence must carry some meaning which is by itself incomplete and raises some expectation (*ākāṅkṣā*).

(2) The meanings of the different words should possess mutual compatibility (*yogyatā*) and thereby fulfil the expectation raised by one another.

(3) The words to be construed must have mutual proximity (*sannidhi*), that is, they should not be written or uttered at long intervals.

To these three conditions some thinkers add a fourth, namely, under standing of the context (*prakaraṇa*) or the intention of the speaker of the sentence (*tātparya*).

Now, it will be seen that these conditions of verbal cognition do not involve the knowledge of *vyāpti* which is essential for inference. So knowledge derived from the words of an authority cannot be the same as inference.

Of course, it is true that only the words of a reliable person (*āpta*) can yield valid knowledge. But similarly only undisturbed perception and unvitiated inference can yield valid knowledge. In other words, the possibility of doubt and error is common to all sources of knowledge; and this should not prevent us from admitting authority as a source of knowledge. If we disbelieve authority, we have to go without so much of valuable knowledge obtainable from the statements of specialists, experts, and the scriptures. The *Mīmāṁsā* school tries to show in this connection that if we do not accept the authority of the *Vedas,* we have no other means of knowledge by which we can ascertain which ritual has to be performed for which purpose and with what result. The *Vedas* are the only source of knowledge of the various injunctions (*dharmas*).

Knowledge from Similarity of Upamāna

A fourth source of knowledge admitted by Gautama and his followers, as well as by the *Mīmāṁsā* and *Vedānta* schools, is what is called *upamāna* (literally, comparison). It is, however, variously conceived.

According to Gautama, it is that kind of knowledge which we have about an unfamiliar thing on the basis of its similarity with a familiar thing. The later *Nyāya* conceives it as the knowledge of the denotation of an unfamiliar world on the basis of a knowledge of similarity. We do not, for example, know the denotation of the word *gavaya*. An expert tells us that it denotes an animal like a cow, but without a dewlap. We go to the forest and, observing such a creature there, we know it to be a *gavaya*. This resulting knowledge is obtained through *upamāna*.

But the *Mīmāṁsā* and *Advaita* schools think that this knowledge can be said to be obtained in part by testimony and in part by inference, and does not require to be classed apart. According to them, *upamāna* is the knowledge of similarity about an absent object obtained from the perceived similarity of a present object. For example, when a man see the animal *gavaya* in the forest, he feels, 'The cow at home is like the *gavaya*'. The first judgement is derived from perception since the subject is being perceived; but the second is obtained through the knowledge of similarity contained in the first, and it is therefore called knowledge from similarity, or *upamāna*. It cannot be said to be deduced from the first, since deduction involves the knowledge of an invariable relation between some sign and something signified, a *vyāpti*, which we are not conscious of using here.

Implication or Arthāpatti

A fifth kind of knowledge, different from the four already mentioned, is recognized by the *Mīmāṁsā* and the *Advaita* schools. It is called *arthāpatti* and means the supposition of what is necessary for explaining any fact either observed (*dṛṣṭa*) or heard about (*śruta*). The stock example is: A person, Devadatta, is observed to be fasting the whole day, but growing stouter and stouter. To explain this, we are forced to suppose that he must be eating (unperceived) during the night. This last knowledge is arrived at through *arthāpatti*. Similarly, by this very method we suppose a word in a sentence where it remains understood, or we suppose the secondary, figurative meaning of a sentence where the primary meaning does not suit.

This process of knowledge is different from inference, because here do not draw a conclusion from given premises—rather we have to discover here the explanation of what is given. It resembles the method of hypothesis recognized by western logicians; but the difference is that here the supposition is not provisional but necessary.

Non-Cognition of Anupalabdhi

In addition to these five sources of knowledge, the *Bhāṭṭa* school of *Mīmāṁsā* and the *Advaita* school of *Vedānta* admit appropriate (*yogya*) non-cognition as a unique source of knowledge. The necessity of admitting this arises thus: Looking round the room we say, there is not a single jug of water here. How do we know the non-existence of the jug here? The common-sense reply would be, 'We see that it does not exist here'. But the difficulty is that we can see a thing or sense it only when it is something positive, so that it can stimulate the sense concerned. But how can non-existence stimulate the sense? The *Nyāya* school, which is the philosophical advocate of common sense, tries to get over this difficulty by holding that though non-existence itself cannot be directly related to any sense, it is indirectly related to it through its locus, say the room, which is related to the sense. Non-existence is like an adjective, a qualifying character, to its locus; and as the locus (e.g., the room) is perceived, so also is the non-existence (e.g. absence of the jug) along with it.

But this *Nyāya* view is not accepted by the *Bhāṭṭas* and the *Advaitins* who point out that any character that qualifies a thing is not necessarily perceived just because the thing itself is perceived; for instance, when we see a jar we do not perceive its weight, though it is there in the jar. So, only qualities which can be related to and stimulate the sense concerned can be perceived, and non-existence is not of this kind.

The *Prābhākaras* and *Sāṁkhyas* try to obviate the difficulty in another way. They say that non-existence is not at all an entity additional to its locus. In fact, it is a turn of expression signifying the bare locus, or the mere locus. To say that there is no jug in the room is to say that only the room is there. And when we perceive such a bare room, we say, we perceive the non-existence of the jug in it.

But even this explanation is not accepted by the *Bhāṭṭas* and the *Advaitins*. They point out that we cannot understand a bare or empty room without thinking of the non-existence of things in it. So non-existence is found to be an additional entity.

It has to be admitted therefore that non-existence cannot be said to be perceived through the senses. Nor can we infer it from anything else unless we have previous knowledge of an invariable relation of non-existence with that thing, which would presuppose some knowledge of non-existence, and thus beg the very question.

Non-existence can be said to be known, however, by non-cognition. Just as positive cognition is the source of the information about positive entities, absence of the knowledge of a thing (under circumstances in which it should have been known had it existed) yields us the information about its non-existence. That is how we primarily know non-existence, according to the *Bhāṭṭas* and the *Advaitins.*

In addition to these six sources of knowledge there are a few more like tradition (*aitihya*), presentiment (*pratibhā*), possible entailment (*sambhava*), etc., admitted by other minor schools.

Truth and Error

The conceptions of truth and error and their metaphysical outlook vary from school to school. Buddhist sceptics, who disbelieve the validity of even normal perception, hold that all such knowledge is prima facie unreliable. But still they adopt, for practical purposes, the distinction between true cognition and false cognition with the pragmatic criterion of practical utility (artha-kriyā-kāritva).

The *Nyāya-Vaiśeṣika* realist thinks that the distinction between truth and falsity is not simply a practical one, but is based on objective conditions. If a knowledge reveals something as it really is or some character as belonging to a place or substratum where it really is, it is true; and if, on the contrary, it shows the thing to be what it really is not or shows it to belong to a place or substratum where it does not really exist, it is false. Truth and falsity can be ascertained only inferentially from the soundness or defectiveness, respectively, of the condition generating the knowledge; or from the harmony (*saṁvāda*) or disharmony (*visaṁvāda*), respectively, of the knowledge with other knowledge or with the practical consequences following therefrom. Immediate knowledge under normal conditions is free from error. But illusions sometimes occur under extraordinary conditions; when, for example, a rope seen in twilight revives in our mind, by reason of its great similarity, the vivid idea of a snake perceived in the past at some other place, we have the illusion of a snake. A thing which has never been perceived in the past, however, can never appear in illusion. Illusion is only the dislocation of really perceived objects from their own locus to another. It is not the creation of something new. So this theory of illusion is called *Anyathākhyātivāda,* that is, the theory of something (previously perceived) appearing in some other place or time.

According to the *Mīmāṁsā* school and Rāmānuja, all knowledge worth the name is self-evidently valid, since whenever knowledge arises it claims belief, and we act on it without suspicion. This is know as the theory of the self-validity of knowledge (*Svataḥprāmāṇyavāda*).

The *Mīmāṁsakas* point out that if the validity of any knowledge were to depend on another knowledge, e.g., inference, then the validity of this second knowledge would require to be certified by a third knowledge, and so on. There would thus be an infinite regress (*anavasthā*).

As to illusion, the *Prābhākara Mīmāṁsakas* say that there is no positive mental state like error. When a rope is said to appear as a snake, what really happens is that we have the true perception of something long and tortuous and this revives in our mind very vividly the idea of a snake perceived in the past; and owing to a lapse of memory there is lack of discrimination (*bhedāgraha*) between the perceived and the remembered. This view is known as the theory of the denial of illusory appearance (*Akhyātivāda*). The *Bhāṭṭas* hold, however, the theory of reversed appearance (*Viparītakhyātivāda*) which maintains, like that of the *Nyāya-Vaiśeṣika*, that in illusion the elements truly perceived are presented in a distorted, dislocated, or reverse relation and cause wrong behaviour.

Ramanuja defends his theory of non-illusion (*Satkhyātivāda*) by showing that as all objects are made of the mixture of the same basic elements of matter (*bhūtas*) in different proportions, there is really something common to the rope and the snake; and it is this common element which appears in so-called illusory perception, which is therefore not illusory.

The *Advaita Vedānta* agrees with *Mīmāṁsā* that all knowledge is self-evident. But it adds that if knowledge is contradicted by any experience, it cases to be knowledge and turns into error. Truth, according to the *Advaita*, consists therefore in the uncontradicted (*abādhita*) and self-evident *(svaprakāśa*) character of knowledge. Practical efficiency is not, by itself, a safe criterion of truth, since even an illusory snake can produce fear and death. It is useful, however, as revealing non-contradiction to a certain extent, but mere non-contradiction would not suffice for truth, had not knowledge possessed also the positive characteristic of self-evidence.

But the objection may be raised that if non-contradiction be the character of truth, the most that we can say about any knowledge is that it is not yet contradicted and is provisionally true; how then can we ascertain any knowledge to be finally or absolutely true? The reply to this is that such truth can belong to knowledge, the possibility of whose contradiction is not conceivable. Knowledge like, 'This tree is green' may be liable to contradiction in future. But if the tree is considered *sub specie aeternitatis*, or from the *pāramārthika* point of view regarded as pure existence (without any specification), there is no logical possibility of contradiction, For, even if the tree turns out to be illusory, even as an appearance it possesses an undeniable 'beinghood' (though not of the specific objective character). Here we have absolute or uncontradictable truth.

Regarding illusion, the *Advaitins* hold that in every such case there is an undeniable positive appearance directly present to the mind; and it is a mis-representation of experience to explain it either as the vividly revived memory-idea of something perceived in the past or to explain it negatively as a lack of discrimination between the perceived and the reproduced. The illusory snake is as objectively present to consciousness as a real snake. Only it is momentary and contradicted by subsequent experience. It cannot be described as absolutely real, because it is contradicted; nor as absolutely unreal, because unlike such an unreality as the son of a barren woman, it can appear to consciousness. So the illusory object should be recognized as indescribable. The *Advaita* theory of error is known therefore as the theory of the appearance of the indescribable (*Anirvacanīyakhyātivāda*). Moreover, it is admitted that the illusory object is the temporary creation *(sṛṣṭi)* of ignorance (*avidyā*) which is responsible for all errors.

Chapter 3

Traditional and Contemporary Paradigms of Urban Geography

H.N. Misra

Any discipline, or subdiscipline thereof, always functions and proceeds within a framework of some conceptual matrices, called paradigms. Paradigms focus the philosophical perspectives and methodologies that have been in vogue and which continue to provide the theoretical feedback for the new researches. The paper discusses the concept of paradigm and underscores the paradigmatic changes which urban geography has undergone before and after the second World War. While the pre-war developments have been grouped under the traditional paradigms, the post-war trends have been examined under the contemporary paradigms.

The Concept of Paradigm

The term "paradigm" is not new to social sciences. But as a dynamic concept it was developed by Thomas Kuhn in his classical book, *The Structure of Scientific Revolutions*, published in 1962. It is defined as "the entire constellation of beliefs, values, techniques, and so on shared by the members of a given community" (Kuhn, 1970a, 175). Kuhn uses the terms "disciplinary matrix" as an alternative to paradigm; "disciplinary because it is common to the practioner of a specified discipline, matrix because it consists of ordered elements

Reproduced from *Annals of the Association of National Geographers of India*, Vol IX (1), 1989, pp. 49-58.

which require individual specification" (Kuhn, 1970b, 271). The paradigm, thus provides the basic framework, a broad based model or a general body of knowledge within which a discipline functions. To Harvey, paradigm is conceptual apparatus (Harvey, 1979). Philosophy, theory and methodology are built into paradigm. Paradigms are sometimes referred to as super theories as theories form only a part of it. The three major attributes of paradigm are: (a) exemplar, (b) image of the subject matter and (c) theory and methodology (Ritzer, 1975). Kuhn is of the view that continuous sedimentation and accumulation of anomalies in the growth of normal science lead to a stage of "crisis" which eventually results into "revolution". The "revolution" gives birth to a new paradigm. When the new paradigm comes into being and attempts to replace the old one, it is called "paradigmatic shock" or, "paradigm shift". However, there is no "paradigm lost" as old ones cannot be completely rejected or discarded. According to this dynamic concept, thus, paradigms have life which may be either evolutionary or cyclic. Kuhn has used this term in 21 different ways which have been aggregated into three categories by Masterman (1970). These are (a) metaparadigm which presents a global view of science in a discipline, (b) sociological paradigm which is based on universally recognized scientific achievement and (c) construct paradigm which may be some classic work or instrument. All the three are nested with each other in such a manner that construct paradigm forms the central point and Kuhn prefers to call it as "problem-solution paradigm".

A discipline may be non-paradigmatic if it is not able to differentiate its subject matter from allied disciplines. It moves from this stage to dual paradigmatic stage when two paradigms compete with each other and finally to single paradigmatic stage when one paradigm replaces the other. This is known as "paradigm shift". Social sciences are, however, characterized by multiple-paradigms. "In a multiple-paradigm science, many paradigms are competing for hegemony in the field" (Harvey and Holly, 1983, 14) "but in such a situation" supporters of one paradigm are constantly questioning the basic assumptions of those who accept other paradigms "(Ritzer, 1975,12). The Kuhnian concept of paradigm was first introduced in geography by Haggett and Chorley in their book *Models in Geography*, published in 1967 (Billinge et al, 1984). They foresaw the emergence of a model-based paradigm as the traditional school represented by the Hartshornian concept of areal differentiation was under severe stress (Haggett and Chorley, 1967). However, the use of this word became quite popular in geography with Harvey's paper on revolution and counter revolution in 1972 (Harvey, 1972). The exemplars such as those of Ratzel's environmentalism, Vidal's possibilism, Sauer's cultural landscape, Hartshorne's areal differentiation and Schaefer's exceptionalism or spatial interaction have all the attributes of being treated as paradigms (Harvey and Holly, 1983). During the last two decades some new trends have emerged which have influenced the philosophy and methodology of human geography in general and urban geography in particular. These trends have set in pace the growth and development of some new paradigms.

Paradigms and Urban Geography

Urban geography is one of the most rapidly expanding subdisciplines of geography. Deriving its sources from land economy and urban ecology, it has acquired a firm footing and opened new vistas of research in the area of urban problems, planning and policies. The critical role played by a city in the social, economic and political spheres of contemporary society has aroused an increasing interest among a wide range of researchers who have been busy building up an adequate framework of knowledge to understand its different dimensions. However, it is the emphasis on the spatial dimension which distinguished urban geography from all other allied disciplines. It studies the city both at intra-urban and inter-urban scales. "Urban geographers are concerned to identify and account for the distribution of towns and cities and the spatial similarities and contrasts that exist within and between them" (Clark, 1982, 2). The rural-urban relationship and the processes shaping the urban landscape form an integral part of urban geography. "Urban geographic investigations are concerned primarily with the areal variations within and among cities including the relationships between urban and non-urban areas, and the forces that are shaping the urban landscape" (Mayer, 1965). A perusal of the growth of literature in urban geography would reveal that it does not merely imbibe and focus the fashionable paradigms in geography, urban geographers have been among the leaders in suggesting alternative philosophy and methodology (Johnston et al. 1986, 509). Having a modest beginning with only a slow change urban geography had major breakthrough only after 1955. "Before 1950", Johnston observes, "very few members of the academic world would have called themselves urban geographers, and it was only a change of emphasis in geography as a whole after about 1955 that made urban place a major focus of academic research" (Johnston, 1984, 14). It has experienced some important paradigmatic shocks since then. The ecological and neo-classical approaches have given way to behavioural and structuralist approaches. Similarly the level and scale of analysis have also changed. Whie traditional pattern process and response studies continue to occupy an important place, they are nevertheless treated as consumption level studies. The emphasis has shifted now towards studying the production (social formation) and distribution (allocative) systems (Herbert, 1982, 24).

Traditional Paradigms of Urban Geography

The traditional paradigms are those ideas which guided the growth of the discipline from the classical period until the second World War. Although urban geography is comparatively of recent origin, it has deep roots. It is not hard to discover the influence of early paradigms in this subdiscipline of geography. A few of them that can be easily identified are as follows.

(a) *Exploration Paradigm*: This is a classical paradigm which formed the foundation of the subject and remained in operation prior to the beginning of twentieth century. In fact, in recent centuries geography began with exploration. The basic approach was to explore unknown places and people, and to know more about the objects distributed on the earth surface. Many expeditions were financed by geographical societies for this purpose (Freeman, 1961, 1980). Although it was quite useful for mercantile activity, yet its educational value could not be ignored (Johnston, 1983). It was basically impressionistic with a descriptive approach and had no theoretical base. However, it introduced the map-making tradition which has been so very crucial in the growth of this discipline. Hence, exploration has attained the status of a paradigm.

As mentioned earlier, urban geography had a very late beginning and the first systematic book on this subject appeared only in 1949 (Taylor, 1949). But there are several examples of gazetteer type of approaches which presented descriptive accounts of people, location and architectural styles of buildings of some towns and cities in England. The geographical magazine of Martyn of 1793 and the modern geography of Pinkerton of 1807 may be cited as good examples of urban geographic descriptions based on the exploration paradigm. (Clark, 1982, 8).

(b) *Environmentalism*: This paradigm was a very important intellectual apparatus during the 1920s and played vital role in the early development of urban geography. The basic theory behind this paradigm was that human activities are controlled by nature and this theoretical assumption influenced the study of towns and cities as well. A great emphasis lay on the study of site and situation elements. The physical elements such as soil, water, terrain and climate etc., were considered to be important attributes to describe the genesis and growth of towns and cities. The growth of a city and the form it assumed were viewed as an expression of location and situation. The pioneering works of this period were those of Hassert (1907) and Blanchard (1911) who not only discussed the importance of site and situation elements, they also gave direction to development of this newly emerging sub-discipline. The first doctoral thesis, which was submitted in United States of America examined the relationship of site to the development of New York city (Emerson, 1908). The work of Salisbury and Alden (1920) is yet another example of one of the earliest works of this type. This paradigm dominated the scene of urban geographic researches for a pretty long period. Several scholars have attempted to classify towns based on their site and situation and emphasized the importance of physical environment. There was a relative neglect of socio-economic and historical factors which was redressed by some German geographers of that time. They discussed the general layout, and build of towns and cities. Thus the study of morphology based on ecological approaches of the Chicago School of Sociologists became yet another important theme in urban geographic studies during this period.

(c) *Regionalism*: This may be easily referred to as a modern paradigm. While site and situation approach continued, regional relationship of towns and cities became the focal theme of study during 1930s and 1940s. The basic philosophy of this approach was that there was symbiotic relationship between city and its surrounding region, and this functional linkage ought to be examined to explain the socio-economic changes in the urban areas and their countrysides. Thus while identification of morphological regions continued to be studied at the intra-urban scale, the delimitation and mapping of sphere of influence became a very common theme for study at the inter-urban scale. Needless to emphasize that this has been a very important theme in promoting the theoretical base of urban geographic research and a number of scholars have made studies of city-region, umland or hinterland. The work of Dickinson (1947) is however worth mentioning for its emphasis on the study of city-region as a functional region. The urban geographic research in India was greatly influenced by the regional paradigm. The first work that came to light was that of Singh (1955) which draws heavily from the elements which form regionalism as conceptual matrix. In fact this marks the beginning of urban geography in India as several researchers engaged themselves in delimiting the sphere of influence of one or the other city by using different qualitative criteria (Misra, 1984).

It may be pointed out that the thematic contents of this paradigm continued to command respectable image even during the 1950s. They provided the background for the theoretical and deductive methodological developments during the contemporary period (Misra, 1984).

Contemporary Paradigms

The mid-1950s may serve as a period of great change, almost a great divide in the historical development of geography in general and urban geography in particular. It has witnessed several significant changes in its epistemology, ontology and methodology. There has been an emergence of a new geography whose paradigms have been heavily influenced by the reputation of physical sciences in the field of technological developments and also by the success of some of the social sciences such as economics, psychology and sociology in dealing with the socio-economic crises prevailing in the society. Interestingly, urban geography became central to this new geography and the city became the laboratory to test the applications of these new paradigms. The paradigms underpinning the development of urban geographic research during the post-war period have been critically examined here.

(a) *Spatial system paradigm*: This analytical paradigm developed as a critique of earlier paradigms which were caricatured as descriptive type. It was an important paradigm during 1950s. This was the time when some of the young researchers of the United States rejected the conventional methods and approaches. They developed the spatial system and spatial organization approach based on neo-classical economics and location theories. The philosophy behind this approach has been positivism, and quantitative methods based on statistical techniques have been employed to derive generalizations and formulate theories and models based on generalizations. There have been several scholars who have pioneered urban geographic research based on this paradigm; but B.J. L. Berry must be specially mentioned. "Urban geography proved especially amenable to the impact of this move towards increased quantification, and the role of Brian Berry, who promoted the analysis of settlement patterns and sought spatial order in size and location of towns and cities, villages and hamlets, neighbourhood and regional centres, was considerable",

(Herbert 1982, 23).

There have been two types of approaches to study a city. The first concentrated on a system of cities in which the cities and towns were treated as points on space, and spatial pattern, city size, hierarchy and functional classification of urban settlements in a region were studied and analyzed at the inter-urban scale. The Central Place Theory of Christaller (Baskin, 1966) and its modification by Loscha (Losch, 1954) were extensively applied to measure the departures and to seek the general laws and principles. The second approach treated the urban settlement or city as a region by itself. This was a study at the intra-urban scale in which land-use patterns, factorial ecology and social area analysis were carried out by using quite sophisticated statistical techniques just as it was the case with the first approach. The land-use models developed by the Chicago School of sociologists served as a great stimuli for the second approach. The methodology and philosophy remained the same in both the approaches and so was the case with some of the models and theories. The major research trends summarized by Berry are: system of cities, correlates of city size and urbanization, models of city size distribution, relations between patterns and metropolitan system, spatial structure of land-uses within cities, and simulation models as the means of conducting urban laboratory experiments (Berry, 1965). These studies were used for the purposes of urban planning as well. It is, however, significant to mention that empirical studies have revealed a great anomaly between the observed and the expected patterns. The location and planning of social and economic services based on transport-cost minimization approach, have failed to meet the desired objectives of planning. The models and theories have not been able to predict human spatial behaviour. However, "the most significant is the fact that many workers have learned the advantages and disadvantages of the new techniques, and in turn have discovered the need for more and better theory and concepts" (Berry, 1965). The spatial system approach has been criticized for being mechanistic, aggregative and for its reducing the space into geometric abstraction (Ley, 1977). In spite of the criticism levelled against the positivist approach, the researches based on the spatial paradigm using highly sophisticated quantitative techniques such as multiple regression analysis, factor analysis, discriminant analysis etc., continue to dominate the urban geographic literature. Indian urban geography also follows this tradition but the techniques of analysis in most of the cases are very elementary mainly due to poor access to computer software as well as the hardware.

(b) *Behavioural Perspectives*: This is not a paradigm by itself; rather this is one of the many strands of subjective imperatives such as phenomenology, idealism, humanistic geography and *verstehen* which were developed against the growing discontent of the grand generalization of spatial paradigm. The major objective of the subjectivists was to re-emphasize the importance of human values and human agency in studying the place and space. The behavioural approach within the broader framework of subjectivism was developed in mid-60s to provide an inductive base for building theories and models. The important assumption of this approach is that the spatial phenomena are manifestations of decisions taken by individuals under different conditions. A study of the human spatial behaviour is, therefore, important to understand the processes responsible for understanding the spatial outcomes. Merely studying the spatial outcomes, which was the emphasis of the spatial paradigm, was not considered to be adequate to explain the socio-economic structure of a city. Behaviourists believe that the examination of decision making helps the geographic understanding of the processes that produce spatial phenomena (Amedeo and Golledge, 1975). There are several studies which examine the spatial behaviour of consumers and retail traders studies and decision of migrants and house builders etc. Some of the important contributors which set the tradition for this type of research in urban geography were those of Wolpert (1965), Pred (1967, 1969) and Rushton (1969). Stimuli for this type of work came from social psychology. The pioneer work of Lynch (1960) on the image of the city introduced the study of spatial imagery and cognition mapping as one of the local themes in urban geography as well. As a part of behavioural approach, this type of research concentrates on how people perceive and restructure the image of a city in decision making. Studies based on perception and mental maps are categorized as (i) structural such as that of Lynch who introduced the concept of path, edges, nodes, district and landmarks to study the image of a city, (ii) evaluative in which individuals evaluate the quality of a place and space in terms of being safe, dangerous etc., and (iii) preferential which seeks to assess the level of desirability or preference for a place and attempts to define reasons for it (Gould and White, 1974). The concepts such as urban neighbourhood and urban environmental awareness are the outcome of these types or work.

The goal of the behavioural approach has mainly been to seek general principles of human spatial behaviour and quantitative techniques have been extensively used to arrive at a conclusion. Ley (1981) considers the behavioural approach as an appendage to the positivist tradition, yet it has moved well beyond its positivist underpinnings (Cadwallader, 1988, 237).

(c) *Structuralism*: This developed as a reaction and also as an alternative to quantitative-theoretical and subjective-humanist approaches. The quantitative theoretical or spatial system paradigm is considered as ahistoric and static which is unable to account for the evolution of the patterns or for the ways that they will change in future. The location theories which formed the bases for this kind of approach did not consider the laws of capitalism which governed economic decision making and created inter-class conflict by way of unequal distribution of resources and income. Likewise the behavioural or subjective-humanistic approach investigates the individual's choice and decision making without taking into account the social, economic, spatial and environmental factors which impose constraints on optimal choices. This perspective was, thus, rejected as being reductionist for it treated urban phenomena as separate from the societal matrix. A major shift that occurred in paradigm during 1970s is know as structuralism or also sometimes loosely referred to as radicalism or political economy approach. Structuralism is defined as a method of enquiry based on the concept of totality, self regulation and transformation. Its concern is to grasp the meaning of underlying structure (Herbert et al. 1982, 41). The underlying assumption is that there is a hidden structure beneath the surface structure which needs to be explained and analyzed to understand the patterns which are apparently the spatial outcomes of the processes underpinning the hidden structure. This emphasizes that the study of spatial system must be set within the context of the total milieu. Johnson (1984, 25) observes, "Creative change can be achieved only by understanding how society operates to structure space within the urban system and then producing programmes which will effect the operations not just the outcomes." Structural imperatives have opened new dimensions in urban geographic research by way of introducing the concepts of symbolism and culture, conflict and power, and historical specificity to the realm of urban geography. There are many branches of structuralism, often each associated with a particular host discipline. It is not intended to go into the details of these. It may however, be pointed out that one of the most influential schools of structuralism derives its position from linguistics and linguistic philosophy; and Gregory (1978) demonstrates how this concept has evolved and has been adopted by human geographers. The common denominator that allows one to include this diversity within the term 'structuralism' is the position that generality is not to be found in surface (i.e., superficial in the literal sense) observation, but in deeper and concealed generative mechanisms that underlay or underpin the observed phenomena. With this broad illustrative approach, an example will be given here of the use of the distinction between idiosyncratic appearance and underlying structure in the analysis of 'western' and Indian urban forms.

The structural analysis of the 'western' and Indian urban forms may be examined by using the concept of primary contact and secondary or role-playing contact. While primary contact is based on complete familiarity (almost taking familiarity literally), the secondary contact is role-playing contact in which behaviour is conditioned not by knowledge of personality (personality becomes an unwanted intrusion, i.e., role players can be too familiar) but by expectations associated with depersonalized role, e.g., the bus driver, the customer, the bank clerk etc. The stylized morphology of a 'western' city (see Fig. 1A) shows two types of areas: (a) the unshaded areas or the residential areas are the areas for primary contacts outside the working hours, (b) The shaded areas are the areas of urban role-playing which function during the working hours. In this case, people divide their lives between urban role-playing and primary social relations. Most people carry out all urban role-playing in specified "urban" areas beyond their social area. The town functions by daily displacement (daily flow of people from residential areas, see Fig. 1B) which activates the arenas of urban role-playing namely Central Business District (CBD) commerce, CBD retail and industry. The stylized diagrammatic morphology of an Indian city has been shown in Fig. 1C. Unlike a 'western' city, it consists of *mohalla* bazars which are places of manufacturing, trade and retailing besides being residential. Most retailing and most manufacturing is in small-scale enterprises in which primary contacts predominate. Most managers and workers live in, over, or near 'the shops'. Daily displacement to activate 'urban role-playing arenas' is not necessary. In other words the city seems to be a loose aggregation of independent and self-sufficient *Mohallas*. But it exists as an urban area because there is also exchange between specialist *Mohallas* organized by city traders who fulfil the 'urban role-playing' required. It would seem that these are two types of cities having superficially different forms of organization but at the structural level they are the same.

These examples underline the importance of hidden structure to explain the urban forms in specific contexts. The hidden structure is

FIGURE 1

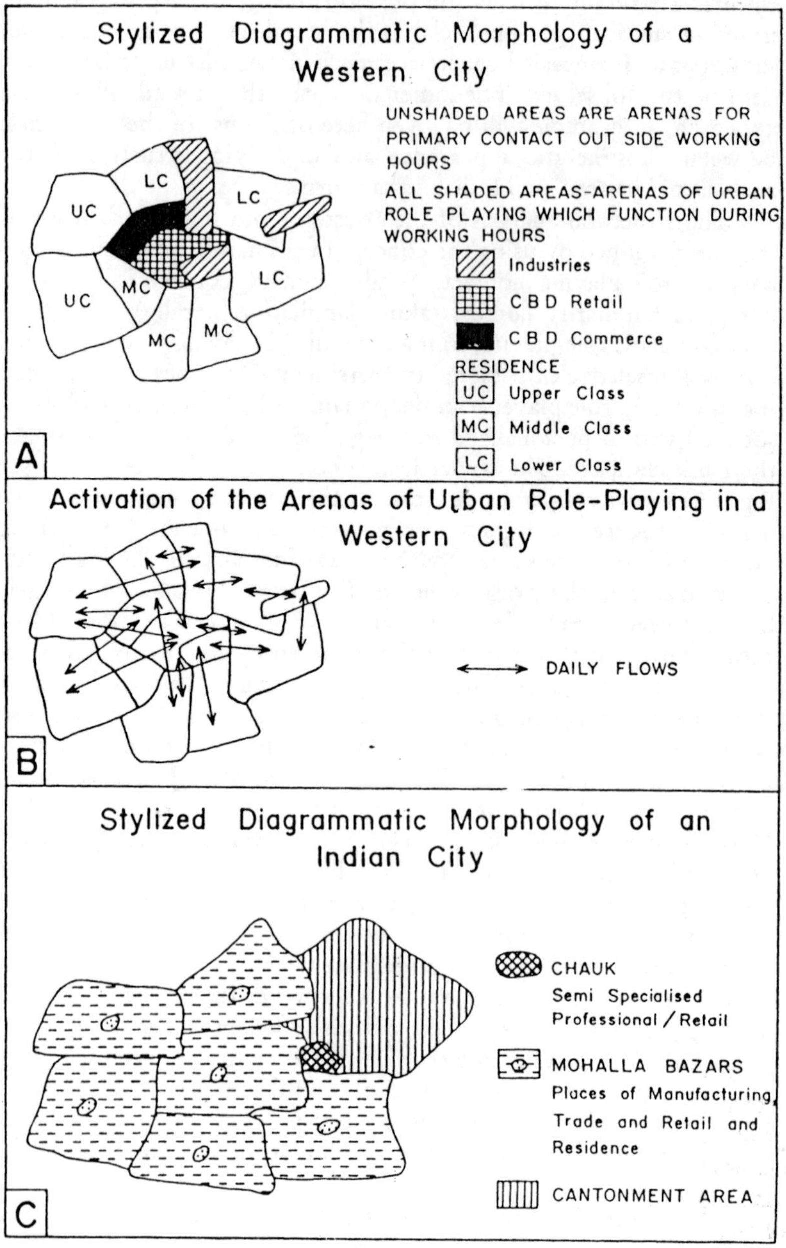
Stylized Diagrammatic Morphology of a Western City
UNSHADED AREAS ARE ARENAS FOR PRIMARY CONTACT OUT SIDE WORKING HOURS
ALL SHADED AREAS-ARENAS OF URBAN ROLE PLAYING WHICH FUNCTION DURING WORKING HOURS
Industries
C B D Retail
C B D Commerce
RESIDENCE
UC Upper Class
MC Middle Class
LC Lower Class
A
Activation of the Arenas of Urban Role-Playing in a Western City
DAILY FLOWS
B
Stylized Diagrammatic Morphology of an Indian City
CHAUK
Semi Specialised Professional / Retail
MOHALLA BAZARS
Places of Manufacturing, Trade and Retail and Residence
CANTONMENT AREA
C

represented by an axiomatic set which relates to urbanization in general. The axioms are:

(i) Cities exist because proximity has value for urban function.

(ii) Urban functions require urban role-players and the development of secondary relationships.

(iii) All persons need primary relationships; the number of people developing secondary relationship can be variable.

These axiomatic conditions do not uniquely specify the form a city has to take; they limit the range of possible forms. Actual forms can vary according to specific contexts. The relationship between hidden structure and surface forms which has been diagrammatically presented (Fig. 2) shows three important surface forms: The Indian city, American city and Soviet-socialist city. They are different from each other in the organization of urban forms because of different historical-social contexts. But they are based on the same underlying structure.

Figure 2

Relation between Hidden Structure and Surface Forms

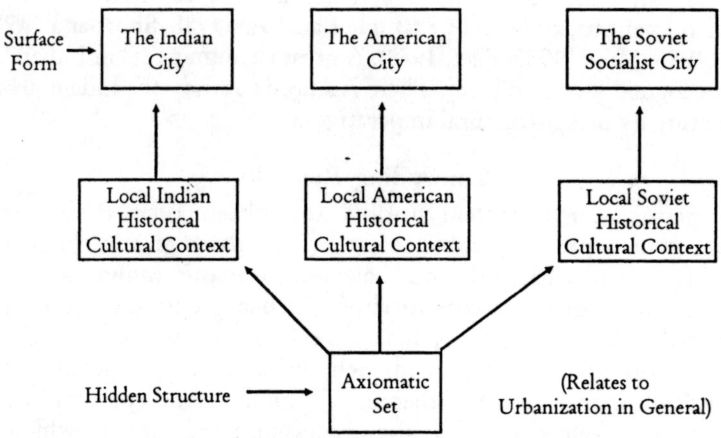

The two important variants of structural imperatives which directly influence the urban geographic research are known as the political economy approach and urban managerialism. The political economy approach examines the roles of government policies and private capitalism to the extent they affect the growth and development of city structure. Needless to emphasize that the degree of investment and political interests heavily influence the socio-economic structure of a city. Harvey (1973) pioneered this concept in his book *Social Justice in the City*. He brought a kind of revolution in urban geographic research by arguing that social injustice is the characteristic feature of the capitalistic societies, and private ownership and its monopoly on land need to be abolished to achieve social justice. Similarly the concept of urban managerialism underlines the importance of urban management and class conflict in studying the social formation and allocation of resources in a city. This assumes that there is an intermediate level between the bottom and top structures.

This intermediate level is represented by the urban managers and gatekeepers who contribute enormously to the intra-urban disparities by way of production and distribution of already scarce resources. "Managerialism provides useful way of penetrating the complex relationship that structure urban areas at the points of contacts between consumers and allocators of scarce resources; it may help both to expose the allocative processes and rationalities on which they are based" (Herbert et al., 1982 48). The urban managers (planners, private and public institutions and bureaucrats etc.) and gatekeepers such as housing societies, estate agents and financiers are the key actors, and analysis of their role forms the major area of research in a built environment today (see, for example Larkham, 1988, Short et al. 1987 and 1986, Moor, 1983, Peet, 1978). A great vacuum exists in Indian urban geography on this front. There is a need to study the Indian urban structure by using structural imperatives.

Concluding Remarks

The period after the second World War has been crucial in the development of urban geographic research. The paradigmatic shifts that urban geography has undergone have improved our knowledge of different dimensions of a city structure. Urban geography has moved forward in its epistemology, and methodology by way of continuing debates on spatial system approach, behavioural perspectives and structural imperatives. The theoretical pluralism and epistemological debate have helped to refine the process-oriented theories which in turn provide better explanation of urban phenomena today than ever before. The decision-making variant of behavioural approach, and the institutional and political economy variants of structuralism underline the importance of key actors in a built environment, factors which are so very significant in understanding and explaining the processes operating in the socio-economic structuring of a city. However, "each perspective is only able to provide a partial explanation of urban phenomena (Cadwallader, 1988, 228) and each one of them is only complementary to others. There is a need to develop a unified theory by synthesizing the approaches of different perspectives. This unified theory based on the synthesis of different approaches may help in understanding a city which is multi-dimensional, complex and evasive in its character. Beauregard (1987, 372), while underlining the objective of urban planning remarks that the city is more than a two dimensional arrangement of land values. It is a socially created, spatially dynamic reality sensitive to historical shifts in political, economic and cultural forces. It has been rightly observed that an understanding of a city is a difficult prize to attain which is not won by any single line of attack (Short, 1984, 4).

References

Amedeo, D. and Golledge, R., (1975), *An Introduction to Scientific Reasoning in Geography*, New York, John Wiley.

Baskin C.W., (1966), *Central Places in Southern Germany (translation of Christaller*, New Jersey, Prentice-Hall.

Beauregard R.A., (1987), The Objective of Planning, *Urban Geography*, 8.

Berry, B.J.L., (1965), Research Frontiers in Urban Geography, In Hauser, P.M. and Schnore, L.F. (edit), *The Study of Urbanization*, New York, John Wiley, pp. 403-430.

Billinge, M. Et al. (eds) (1984), *Recollections of a Revolution: Geography as Spatial Science*, London, Macmillan Press.

Blanchard, R., (1911), *Grenoble, Etude de Geographie Urbane*, Paris.

Cadwallader, M., (1988), Urban Geography and Social Theory, *Urban Geography*, p. 9.

Chorley, R.J. and Haggett, P., (1967), *Models in Geography*, London, Methuen.

Clark, D., (1982), *Urban Geography*, London Croom Helm.

Dickinson, R.E., (1947), *City Region and Regionalism*, London, Routledge and Kegan Paul.

Emerson, V.F., (1908), A Geographic Interpretation of New York City, *Bulletin of American Geographical Society*, 40, 587-612, 726-738.

Freeman, T.W., (1961), *A Hundred Years of Geography*, London, Gerald

Duckworth.
—, (1980), The Royal Geographical Society and the Departments of Geography, In Brown, E.H (ed), *Geography, Yesterday and Tomorrow*, Oxford: Oxford University Press.
Gould, P.R. and White, R., (1974), *Mental Maps*, Penguin: Harmondsworth.
Gregory, D., (1978), *Ideology, Science and Human Geography*, London: Hutchinson;
Harvey, D., (1969), *Explanation in Geography*, London, Edward Arnold.
—, (1972), Revolutionary and Counter Revolutionary Theory in Geography and the Ghetto Formation, *Antipode*, 4,2,1-12.
—, (1973), *Social Justice and the City*, London, Edward Arnold.
Harvey, M.E. and Holly, B.P. (Ed.), (1983), *Themes in Geographic Thought*, London, Croom Helm.
Hassert K., (1907), *Die State Geographic Betrachtet*, Leipzig: Veit;
Herbert G.T. and Thomas C.J., (1982), *Urban Geography: A First Approach*, New York: John Wiley.
Johnston, R.J., (1983), *Geography and Geographers*, second edition, London, Edward Arnold.
—, (1984), *City and Society*, London, Hutchinson.
—, et. al. (Eds.) 1986), *The Dictionary of Human Geography*, Oxford: Basil Blackwell.
Kuhn, T.S., (1970a), *The Structure of Scientific Revolutions*, second edition, Chicago: University of Chicago Press.
—, (1970b), Reflections on My Critics, In Lakatos, I. (Ed it), *Criticisms and the Growth for Knowledge*, Cambridge: Cambridge University Press.
Lakham, P.J., (1988), Agents and type of change in the conserved townscape, *Translations, Institute of British Geographers*, 13(2), pp. 148-164.
Ley, D., (1977), Social Geography and the Taken-for-granted World, *Transactions, Institute of British Geographers*, 2, 498-512.
Losch, A., (1954), *The Economics of Location*, translated by W.H. Wolgom and Stopler, W.F., New Haven: Yale University Press.
Lynch K., (1960), *The Image of the City*, Cambridge (Mass), MITP Press.
Masterman, M., (1970), The Nature of a Paradigm, In Lakatos, I., (Ed.), *Criticism and the Growth of Knowledge*, Cambridge: University Press.
Mayer, H.M., (1965), A Study of Urban Geography, In Hauser, P.M. and Schnore, L.F., *The Study of Urbanization*, New York: John Wiley.
Misra, H.N., (1984), *Urban System of a Developing Economy*, Allahabad, IIDR and In (1988) New Delhi: Heritage Publishers.
Moor, N., (1983), *The Planner and the Market: An Examination of the Role*

of the Planner in the Development Market, London, George Allen and Unwin.

Peet, R., (1978), *Radical Geography*, London, Methuen.

Pred, A.R., (1967), *Behavioural and Location Foundations for a Geographic and Dynamic Location Theory*, Part I. Lund: C.W.K. Gleerup.

—, (1969), *Behavioural and Location: Foundations for a Geographic and Dynamic Location Theory*, Part II, Lund: C.W.K. Gleerup.

Ritzer, G., (1975), *Sociology: A Multiple Paradigm Science*, Boston, Allan and Bacon.

Rushton, G., (1969), Analysis of Spatial Behaviour by Revealed Space Preference, *Annals, Association of American Geographers*, 59, pp. 391-400.

Salisbury, R.D., Alden W.C., (1920), The Geography of Chicago and its Environs, *Geographic Society of Chicago, Bulletin 1*, Chicago, University of Chicago Press.

Singh, R.L., (1955), *Banaras: Study in Urban Geography*, Banaras, Nandkishore Publishers.

Short, J.R., (1984), *An Introduction to Urban Geography*, London, Routledge and Kegan Paul.

—, Witts, S.C. and Fleming, S.C. (1987), Conflict and Compromise in the Built Environment; House Building in Central Berkshire, Transactions, Institute of British Geographers, 12, (1), pp. 29-42.

—, (1986), *Housebuilding, Planning and Community Action: The Production and Negotiation of the Built-Environment*, London; Routledge and Kegan Paul.

Taylor, T.G., (1949), *Urban Geography*, London, Methuen.

Wolpert, J., (1965), Behavioural Aspects of the Decision to Migrate, *Papers and Proceedings of Regional Science Association*, 15, 159-169.

Chapter 4

Comparative Social Research: Some Limited Applications in Regional Analysis

Vijai P. Singh and William J. Haller

This paper consists of two parts: one, outlining basic concepts and requirements of comparative inquiry, with special reference to sociological traditions and two, demonstrating the application of comparative methodology in the analysis of changes in the regional economies of western Europe and the United States. It should be noted that some of the strictest principles of comparative research presented in this paper are difficult to apply in many policy areas because they transcend disciplinary boundaries in which relevance takes precedence over rigor. However, it is still important to understand the logic behind the principle of comparative research so that intelligent choices on particular methodologies are made by the researcher if and when adjustments in these principles are dictated by the issue area under investigation.

Logic of Comparative Research

According to Zelditch (1971) the logic of comparative inquiry must be based on the following rules:

(i) Two or more instances of a phenomenon may be compared if and only if there exists some variable, say V, common to each instance.

(ii) ... no second variable, say U, is the cause or effect of V, if it is not found when V is found.

(iii) ... No second variable U is the cause or effect of V if it is found when V is not.

(iv) ... No second variable U is definitely the cause or effect of V if there exists a third variable, say W, which is present to absent in the same circumstances as U.

The comparison can be descriptive or explanatory. But much of the comparative research is latter in nature by choosing "similar" or "dissimilar" cases or units of comparison. The cases are usually "societies" or "nations" but sometimes other geographic units within a nation are compared over time with respect to a particular phenomenon. For example, a region or a state may be compared with other regions and states within a nation over time on a variety of social, economic and demographic phenomenon. In addition to such political or administrative units, there may be "functional regions" such as labour market region, industrial sector region and health region that cut across political boundaries. Such functional regions are most appropriate to understand the dynamics of a particular phenomenon, but it is difficult to obtain data consistently over a period of time for comparative purposes, especially when such regions encompass more than one political or administrative boundary. Sometimes it is difficult to compare a labour market or a particular industrial sector which is proximate or intertwined with another region or regions which do not share similar characteristics. Inferences developed by comparing regions may not be generalized to the higher levels of aggregation such as state or the nation because of internal heterogeneity in that the state or the nation contain regions that exhibit differing trends. Sometimes at the high level of aggregation the meaning of variable itself may change (Zelditch 181-81).

The choice of "region" as the sub-national unit of comparison is appropriate even though it has not been a part of dominant society and tradition, because the economic development decisions and impacts are readily absorbable at that level. The region may consist of several political or administrative units, but as long as they share the context of policy decisions or actions, it is appropriate to group them into a single unit of comparison. The units of comparison must share economic, social and political characteristics before inferences based on comparisons are developed. For example, regional comparisons of Gross National Product (GNP), unemployment or income should not be undertaken unless all regions measure these variables in ways that are comparable. As Zelditch had noted, subject matter knowledge, purpose of comparison, and finally understanding of the nature of inferences drawn from such comparisons are necessary (Zelditch

187-88). In principle, dissimilar regions can also be compared, provided the main purpose is to develop or test a particular social theory. However, such comparison in the context of policy analysis is problematic.

In spite of recent critical re-examination of its advantages and limitations, the comparison of a few purposefully selected cases for intensive study remains the dominant general paradigm for comparative social research.[1] One main advantage of comparative research is that it allows theory to be constructed and tested outside the limited scope of a single case, be it defined geographically, culturally, or however. Marsh (1967) indicated that, "Many of the 'general' principles and theories of sociology and anthropology are in fact culture-bound" (Marsh vii). Therefore, statistical inference without cross-cultural comparisons provides no support for any notion that generalizations based on such inferences are truly general social theory. If a theory holds firm in the face of evidence gathered from different societies, on the other hand, there can be greater confidence in its generalizability. this reasoning has been labelled the "parallel demonstration of theory" (Skocpol and Somers 1980: 176-78).

Skocpol and Somers also identify two additional uses of comparative research: "contrast of contexts", and "macro-causal analysis" (ibid, 175). Contrast of contexts is used to underline the uniqeness of distinct historical trajectories and, thereby, call widely held views into question. Thus, the use of contrasting of contexts is opposite to that of parallel demonstration of theory.

Macro-causal analysis is a mode of comparative research which rests on the logic of experimental method though it can never attain the rigor. Macro-causal analysis actually encompasses two distinct principles of comparison: the "method of agreement" and the "method of difference" (John Stuart Mill, cited in Skocpol and Somers 1980: 183). These principles were also incorporated by Zelditch in his second and third rules for intelligible comparisons (see above). Zelditch's fourth rule is also implicit in Mill's "method of agreement", though to have it stated explicitly is useful to promote stringency in comparative analysis and interpretation. The selection of cases according to the criteria of Mill's methods can serve in practical applications to provide cases for comparison between which the range of differences is either minimized or maximized. "Where 'most similar systems' designs posit... that closely comparable units offer optimal samples for comparative enquiry, 'most different systems' strategies assume (at least initially) that systemic factors play no substantive role in explaining outcomes of immediate interest" (Gayle 1988: 527-58).

The comparative paradigm is flexible. Both quantitative and qualitative methods can be used to investigate the empirical detail within the cases regardless of the choice of methodological approaches.

Functional Equivalence and Measurement Issues

Though highly flexible, there are limitations to this paradigm which must be understood for comparative research to be carried out successfully. First, it is sometimes criticized on the basis that the cases for comparison are strategically selected and, therefore, do not constitute an unbiased sample. This can be true for the parallel demonstration of theory if the researcher advances insufficiently substantiated or unqualified generalizations, however, such criticism is misplaced for macro-causal analysis and for contrast of contexts. The causal inference of macro-causal analysis is not based on probability but on selecting cases with conditions which mimic experimental control to the greatest extent possible. Probability presupposes the possibility of variability, but causal relationships are invariant. This criticism would be equivalent to arguing that control introduces bias to the results of an experiment. Contrast of contexts is a strategy used to challenge rather than to establish theoretical generalizations; therefore, again, the criticism of bias is not applicable.

The main liability of comparative research is that the equivalence of evidence among the cases to be compared must be established. First, if findings of dissimilarity between any of the cases are discovered when the evidence was not gathered consistently for each case, then it is impossible to tell whether the apparent differences across cases resulted from actual differences in the properties under investigation or whether they are merely research artifacts.[2]

Though there recently has been a considerable resurgence in the discussion about comparative research, perhaps the most complete treatment of measurement issues in comparative research was in Przeworski and Teune's (1970) work. As these authors indicated, comparative analysis is sound when it rests on measures which are "reliable across systems (i.e., cases) and valid within systems" (Przeworski and Teune 1970: 114). The problem of reliability, can arise in situations where either direct measurement or inferred measurement is used. The problem of validity, however, arises only when inferred measurement is attempted. The distinction between direct and inferred measurement and the associated problems of reliability and validity, however, are common to all quantitative measurement.

Direct measures measure only observable "surface" phenomena. Przeworski and Teune state, "Direct measurement is based on definitions by fiat... In direct measurement the operations are synonymous with the concept [and therefore] the results of these operations will necessarily be valid..." However, reliability remains a concern simply because errors in measurement during the collection of the data may have been made (ibid. 95-96).

Inferred measures are measures of phenomena which are assessed to be valid indicators of more pervasive, but less tangible, concepts.[3] Przeworski and Teune indicate that inferred measures are generally more useful than direct measures. Concepts which bear on social theory are usually too broad to be estimated by direct measurement, therefore inferred measures are typically preferable (ibid, 95).

There are three requirements to be met in direct measurement, some of which apply only in comparative research. "Direct measurement requires that the language of measurement be common to all observations, reflect relationships among the phenomena observed, and be consistently applied" (ibid. 97). The language of direct measurement also "must express the relationships between classes of phenomena" in order to achieve comparability. "Once the definitions of [the] concepts [have] been stated in terms common to all systems, the grammar of the language must be chosen" (ibid). The grammar of definitions must be sufficiently inclusive so as to not proscribe the possibility of comparison (i.e:, a grammar which provides a 'common denominator' for comparison must be derived). The particular grammar is determined partially by the type of data and also in part by the rules of interpretation of the language of measurement (ibid. 98). The third requirement is the consistent application of the rules of empirical interpretation. Different (i.e., case-specific) rules of interpretation, however, may be applied in each of the respective cases as long as the definitions and grammar used in the language of measurement are broadened to provide a common denominator for comparability (ibid).

At issue in comparative research is the ability to conduct equivalent measurement of common properties between cases which are distinct. Equivalent measurement in comparative research is measurement which is valid within cases and reliable across cases. Reliability in the context of comparative research means not only that indicators produce the same results repeatedly within a case, but that indicators produce the same results repeatedly for their respective cases and can be transformed into common, comparable terms. This implies the use of equivalent measurement instruments.

The major concern to establish equivalency is to minimize all doubts as to the case-specific validity of measurement, rather than to carry out identical measurement procedures in each of the cases under investigation. "... System-specific propositions that provide greater accuracy should be the dominant focus of measurement..." (ibid, 106). Because measurement of the property under investigation is of concern and because a property can embody itself differently in different systems, different measures may be needed to uncover the magnitudes of a property within different cases. Differences among cases are acceptable provided that the same property in each of the respective cases is measured in such a way as to maximize the probability of accuracy.[4]

Though this principle is most obvious in the context of cross-cultural comparative research, where system interference is most salient, it carries implications for reliable and valid measurement of any social phenomena. One additional instance of system interference is where identical observable surface phenomena in different cultures have underlying causes unique to each (ibid. 104).

Reference to the particular social system as a whole may be necessary to understand the contextual influence on the behavior of specific inferential indicators, and thus to interpret their meaning. Prezeworski and Teune state,

> Social systems influence the behavior of indicators, and therefore inferences made from indicators to concepts must be modified according to the system in which they were observed... [Moreover] It is necessary in comparative measurement to vary the propositions used for inferences so that the validity of measurement statements is maintained in each system. This can be done only by reference to the systemic context of observations used in an inferred measurement statement (ibid. 104-05).

Understanding system interference and its implications for inferential measurement is essential for understanding how to establish cross-case measurement equivalency. Though system interference and the use of inferential measurement together provide the necessary condition for equivalency across cases to be problematic, equivalency is always a concern in comparative research. One implication of the principal that inferential indicators are case-specific is that they are best viewed as hypothetical constructs. Given their hypothetical basis, inferences should be framed in probabilistic rather than invariant terms. Even in cases where criterion validity (i.e., observational verification) holds, an indicator so validated does not encompass the property with which it is associated. Unlike direct indicators, inferential indicators do not define the concept to be measured, therefore there is still room for an error component.[5]

There is a useful but unattainable theoretical ideal for the generation of inferential indicators which carries implications for both the development of indirect indicators with the most desirable properties at the practical level, and for further procedures to assess equivalency in inferential measurement. What should come into consideration is the domain of the concept to be measured. While the definition of the full domain of a concept might not be possible, the ideal is to arrive at the total population of inferential indicators for a given concept from all empirical cases. Naturally, only a proportion of all these indicators will adhere for any given case. Thus, for the cases under study, that proportion of the total population of indicators which adhere for each of the respective cases can be partitioned from the rest. This would yield both the full empirical domain of the general concept under study and all the indicators which adhere for each of the empirical cases. Though the total population of indicators can never be known, research can start with specific cases and samples of indicators for properties in each of the cases can be determined (ibid. 108-09). Accurate measurement from a random sample of the total population of indicators for a general concept in a case will give an unbiased measurement of that concept as it is manifest in that case.[6] Moreover, out of total population of indicators relevant for each case, some will be shared across cases, others not.

It is important to be able to find which indicators are shared across cases and which are case-specific because separate procedures of varying strength for determining equivalency are available for the situation where all indicators are shared among cases, that where some indicators are shared among cases, and that where no indicators are shared among cases.

The inter-changeability of results as the logical basis for assessing equivalency implies the necessity of specific transformation rules which permits scores from an instrument developed to measure a concept in one case to be shown in the same terms as scores on a measurement instrument developed for the same concept in another case (ibid., 111).[7]

If common indicators can be shown to behave identically across cases, then measurement instruments based on the common indicators expressed in a standard language will be equivalent. Such a situation would imply the absence of system interference. Thus, the procedure to determine if common indicators only are sufficient for comparative analysis to proceed is based on the hypothesis that no system interference is present.

If a certain degree of system interference is found and the research has been committed already to the use of common indicators, Przeworski and Teune (122-23) suggest two possible remedial measures: either "to adjust the indicators so that system interference is minimized," or to "adjust the scores of some systems so that they will be 'like' the scores of the systems to which they are to be compared."[8] Because the options of mixing common indicators with case-specific indicators is also available and because an inordinate amount of effort may be needed to compile an adequate set of common indicators,[9] this path to establishing equivalency may simply not be worth the effort (ibid. 126).

The lack of any common indicators between cases for a general concept to be studied need not obstruct the progress of comparative research. As long as the equivalency of measurement instruments can be demonstrated, it does not matter whether the indicators which compose the measurement statements are the same or different. Indeed, Przeworski and Teune hold that "it is generally simpler to develop measurement instruments if the indicators are initially conceptualized in system-specific (case-specific) terms rather than in system-free terms (i.e., in terms of indicators common among all cases)" (ibid. 126). Furthermore, much information that is valuable for comparative research is generated from the systems (of the cases) themselves, and therefore cannot be defined in a standard measurement language (ibid). What is needed are "procedures to evaluate the equivalence of measures based entirely on system-specific indicators" (ibid). Przeworski and Teune outline "three versions of a procedure to establish the equivalence of measurement statements based on measuring instruments composed of entirely different indicators" which "vary in their stringency" (ibid. 126).

The weakest version of the three grants equivalence when the mutual inter-dependence of the indicators within cases are approximate and the reliability of the sets of indicators within their respective cases is also approximate. "In practice what would be done is to inter-correlate the indicators within each system and select those that are most reliable. The system in which the indicators have the highest level of reliability would then become the standard for evaluating the equivalence of the measurement statements in other systems" (ibid, 126). Ideal conditions are a degree of reliability for the sets of indicators which is equal and high within each of the cases (ibid).

However, by assuming that the properties to be investigated are multi-dimensional, a stronger version of the procedure to establish equivalency where the cases share no common indicators becomes available. First, the indicators adhering to each case are determined and, then, the specific dimension of the concept with which each indicator is associated is hypothesized (ibid. 126-127).

It is also possible for factor analysis to reveal dimensions of a concept which were not previously hypothesized (ibid: 128). "The criterion for inferring the equivalence of measurement statements is the similarity in the structure of the indicators. The indicators, structured into these clusters by the factor loadings, compose the measurement instruments" (ibid).

> These measurement instruments, providing equivalent measurement statements across cultures, make it possible to seek explanations of particular scores... As long as intrasystem scores are used for explanations of relationships within systems rather than for comparison of populations across systems, it is possible to talk about the same properties for all cultures in which this structure of individual responses was found... However, [such a procedure produces]... only an overall measure of similarity of the structure rather than a precise statement of the similarity, not only of the factor structures, but of each indicator in those structures (ibid.).

The strongest version of the procedure to establish cross-case equivalence where no common indicators are shared among cases is to, first, hypothesize the indicators specific to each case for the general concept under study; and, next, to state explicitly which dimension of the concept in each case with which each indicator is hypothesized to be associated. "If there is a precise set of statements on the one-to-one correspondence of indicators and on the nature of the similarity of the dimension of the indicators, two criteria for inferring the equivalence of measurement statements across [cases] become available" (ibid. 129).

The first criterion is exactly the same as that for the relatively weaker version presented immediately above: "whether the selected indicators form the factors that were predicted" (ibid. 129). The second criterion is whether the corresponding indicators "fit into the overall factor structure."[10]

Reliable cross-case measurement instruments are demonstrated [by inference] when the indicators have been secured and have been shown to be interacting with each other in similar ways within each system (ibid. 130). However, Przeworski and Teune warn that with the rate of social change worldwide, relationships among indicators cannot be presumed to remain constant for long. Though they admit that the strongest test for equivalence of indicators among cases which share no indicators in common rests decisively on theoretical assumptions, Przeworski and Teune point out not only that it is better for scientists to be aware of and be explicit about their theoretical assumptions, but that "Observations acquire meaning only within a theory; hence, the more explicit and the stronger the theoretical assumptions, the greater the confidence that can be placed in an instrument" (ibid. 131).

Comparing Regions: Two Examples

These discussions point out that social scientists must be familiar with these rules of comparative research and apply them where they are necessary and practical. What follows now is a brief description of applying comparative methods in studying economic distress in the selected regions of the European communities. As we will see, variables selected involved comparable definitions and direct measurements. It is possible because the regions in European communities fit the "most similar cases" approach.

The European communities have maintained relevant social, economic and demographic data to address relevant economic and social policies for the member states. One of the areas in which European communities have paid a great deal of attention is to analyze policy consequences of global industrial re-structuring at the regional levels within the community. The European communities are comparable with respect to economic development, social infrastructure and political culture. It permits comparison of regions across member states and allows inferences applicable to the units under comparison to be drawn with appropriate caveats. Some of the principles that govern comparative research are embedded in what follows. We present the logic and basic methodology used in a study conducted by the commission of the European communities (EC 187-219).

Productivity and employment were used to compare European regions with respect to impact of economic re-structuring. A synthetic index was constructed to combine these two elements which took into account only structural factors and ignored the cyclical changes.

It is assumed that productivity is related to technological innovations, availability of labour force and infrastructure, all of which help businesses produce goods and services efficiently. Productivity and employment are related in that lower levels of productivity produce higher unemployment rates. Equal weights are attached to both variables. The index measuring the level of regional distress uses averages for the years 1977, 1979 and 1981. Comparable data were not available for periods prior to 1977 and therefore, an index based on a longer period could not be constructed.

It is important to note that the definition of unemployment used here is the same as used by the International Labour Organization (ILO). According to this definition, anyone seeking paid employment is unemployed irrespective of whether they are registered. It thus excludes underemployment. Since comparable data on unemployment were not available for the regions in Greece and Greenland which also happen to be least developed in the European community, these were excluded.

The synthetic index was computed by calculating arithmetic averages of the variables for the three years and since indices had different range, it was necessary to standardize them using the following formula (ibid. 193):

$$Y = (Y - \bar{Y})/\sigma Y$$

where,

$\bar{Y}$ = weighted average of the series, and

σY = weighted standard deviation of the series.

By inverting the sign of standardized value of unemployment rate, the direction of change of both variables was made consistent. Now the values of both variables can be added. The synthetic index provides relative place of regions with respect to intensity of economic distress. The grouping of regions that fall within a certain range of unemployment and productivity was great. It shows the regions that reflect low productivity and highest unemployment and vice versa. It allows analysis of the process of economic development and evaluation of whether a region suffers from unemployment even if productivity levels are reasonably high.

Since the number of regions is large and shows a substantial degree of diversity with respect to population, labour force, productivity, capital investment and development potential, factor analysis was used to identify a few factors that capture the inter-relationships among them. A principal component analysis was chosen and the method is elaborated in the report (ibid. 211). Thirteen variables, namely migration rate, dependency ratio, demographic pressure, unemployment, youth unemployment rates, structural unemployment rate, agricultural employment, share of independent workers, gross domestic per head, gross domestic product per person employed at current prices and exchange rates, productivity, industrial capital, investment and centrality and peripherality were chosen to reflect relevant aspects of distress (ibid. 215). Measurements of these variables were based on the availability of data for the three time periods and consistency of onverage in the regions included in the study.

Rotated Factor Matrix (3 factors)

		Factor 1	*Factor 2*	*Factor 3*	*Communalities*
1.	Migration rate	0,07338	0,61730	0,01996	0,38685
2.	Dependency ratio	-0,35931	-0,21456	-0,69706	0,66102
3.	Demographic pressure	0,00025	-0,27615	-0,83900	0,78018
4.	Unemployment rate	-0,03037	-0,91926	-0,22359	0,89596
5.	Youth unemployment rate	-0,43824	-0,80549	-0,14510	0,86192
6.	Structural unemployment rate	-0,19038	-0,90511	-0,26587	0,92615
7.	Agricultural employment	-0,71222	0,06741	-0,49073	0,75261
8.	Share of independent workers	-0,80830	-0,02099	-0,12805	0,67019
9.	GDP per head in ECU	0,87397	0,27062	0,15890	0,86232
10.	GDP per head in PPS	0,77,832	0,20097	0,32545	0,75209
11.	Productivity	0,88161	0,19292	-0,03425	0,81562
12.	Industrial capital endowment	0,76393	0,15886	-0,10288	0,62872
13.	Centrality/peripherality	0,76004	0,14494	0,32730	0,70580
	% total variance	37,17	23,29	14,15	
	% cummulated variance	37,17	60,46	74,61	

Source: Commission of the European Communities. *The Regions of Europe*; Luxembourg: Office for official publications of the European Communities, 1984: 217.

Three principal factor developed through the factor analysis, explaining 75 per cent of variance of the thirteen variables included in the analysis. The three factors were economic structures, labour market and demographic structures. These are the factors that determine the differences in the levels of distress between the regions. Ameliorative policies designed to address the economic distress must be responsive to these factors.

In another study, Bergman and Goldstein (1986) analyzed changes in economic structure between regions in the USA using factor analysis. It shows the degree to which an area's economy conforms or deviates from average structural changes at the national level. For each metropolitan area Bergman and Goldstein included sixteen variables that included changes in relevant industrial sectors, productivity, economic performance and local fiscal burden between 1972 and 1977 in 202 metropolitan regional economies. A factor analysis produced six factors namely, corporate headquarters, price-productivity, economic distress, market centre, manufacturing multiplier and residentiary. These six factors accounted for 60 per cent of variance in the sixteen variables included in the study. The scores show the degree and duration of structural change in a particular regional economy, in comparison to national trends.

A careful review of scholarly comparative studies shows that they are too infrequent to have a firmly established systematic understanding of societies beyond the narrowly defined subject areas and well-known geographic regions. The rates of comparative research vary according to level of theory, clarity of concepts and availability of empirical measurements. This makes research relatively easy for some disciplines such as economics and demography, more difficult for others such as psychology and sociology, and most difficult for inter-disciplinary efforts. Many policy areas are inter-disciplinary and involve different types of variables which must be used in the analysis. The example from the European communities clearly demonstrates that there are economic, sociological and demographic variables that can be directly measured. Studies utilizing such approaches respond to particular policy issues but do not provide the bases for developing or testing theories.

Notes

1. A full review of the literature to support this assertion would be cumbersome. It should be sufficient to note that one recent commentator depicts case-based methods as the "classical comparative methods" (Region 1987: (2), that more recently another referred to this general

paradigm as his "own preferred strategy' (Kohn 1989: 53), and also that this same paradigm is implicitly assumed in the majority of the articles in a still more recent volume on comparative research (Qyen [ed.]: 1990). Ragin (1987), however, provides a notable exception.

2. Kohn (1989: 85). Kohn also advises to "...try to establish damage control... to present whatever evidence one can that methodological incomparables are not so great as to [be able to] explain [any of] the differences in findings" (ibid).
3. Socio-economic development is a classic example of such a multidimensional concept which can be evaluated only by inferred measurement. "Development is now seen as a seamless web, without clear linear demarcation between interwined economic, political, and socio-cultural strands" (Gayle 1988, 262).
4. Prezeworski and Teune provide the following example: "In a questionnaire it is not relevant whether the stimuli were the same or whether a question was well translated from one language to another. What is important is whether this question as asked allows for a valid inference to the same underlying properties regardless of the social system. Stimulus equivalence is an important problem only if measurement does not involve inference. In inferred measurement, stimulus equivalence is of secondary importance. The focus must be placed on the equivalence of inferences made from observations... Thus, in our view, the customary emphasis on equivalence of stimuli is misplaced. Interviewer training, time, and manner in which the interviews are conducted and even the formulation of questions need not be identical. Stimulus equivalence should be viewed solely from the point of view of equivalence of the resulting measurement statements" (ibid., 108 and 108n).
5. Przeworski and Teune explain that, "Propositions used for inference should be viewed in probabilistic rather than in deterministic terms... If observations are accurate, the error is a function of the probable truth value of the social law on the basis of which the inference is made. If agreement with a question is assumed to indicate an attitude but it also reflects acquiescence, then measurement will contain error. Although inferred measurement recognizes inferential error, the language of measurement does not express this type of error. A response to a question is treated as a precise measure, but what that response indicates can be stated in probabilities" (ibid: 102).
6. This proposition is based on the following assumption: "The indicators hypothesized for each system are assumed to be a sample of indicators for each system, and each of these system-specific samples is assumed to be a sample of the total population of indicators" (Przewor-

ski and Teune 1970: 109).

7. Przeworski and Teune indicate that in strict terms, the development of such transformation rules demands prior knowledge of the properties of the measurement instruments; in particular, the intervals between scores on the instruments and the origins of the instruments. However, they state that these can be extremely restrictive conditions. Therefore, these conditions are normally circumvented in comparative research by assuming that "the intervals are the same in all systems and the origin of the scales, if unknown, is common to all systems... [They continue so as to clarify that] It is important to recall that comparative analysis of relationships within systems does not require a knowledge of common origin or size of intervals. This is necessary only for descriptive comparisons. Thus, comparative analysis of relationships within systems demands less powerful measurement instruments than those disarming pieces of descriptive information that compare within system parameters" (ibid. 111).
8. Przeworski and Teune concede that in practice this procedure is quite rare, but maintain that it can be a promising course: "Although this strategy is not often followed, it could further comparative analysis between systems when the influence of some specific systemic factors were known. Generally what is done, however, is to examine the influence of these factors when testing theories across systems... But the measurement option is also open. By following it we could identify a common set of indicators that are identical in all systems under study when systemic influences [i.e., the intervening case-grounded historical factors] are removed" (ibid, 123-24).
9. Przeworski and Teune pointed to the likelihood that "in attempting to obtain similar correlations within systems, many common indicators will have to be discarded, and those retained will not be the ones most highly correlated within each system" (ibid. 122).
10. Przeworski and Teune also note that "One way of expressing this correspondence would be to correlate their factor loadings on similar factors across all systems. What we want is a measure of the 'congruence' of factor structures." It is also recommended that researchers be thorough to compare all the factors (ibid. 129).

References

Bergman, Edward M. and Harvey A. Goldstein, (1986), "Dynamics, Structural Change, and Economic Development Paths", pp. 84-110 in Edward M. Bergman (ed.), *Local Economies in Transition: Policy Realities and Development Potentials*, Durham: Duke University Press.

Commission of the European Communities, (1984), *The Regions of Europe*, Luxemburg: Office for Official Publications of the European Communities.

Gayle, Dennis John, (1988), "Applying 'Most Different Systems' Designs: Comparing Development Policy in Alabama and Jamaica," *Comparative Political Studies*, Vol. 21, No. 2: 257-80.

Kohn, Melvin L., (1989), "Cross-National Research as an Analytic Strategy", pp. 77-102 in Melvin L. Kohn (ed.), *Cross-National Research in Sociology*, Newbury Park: Sage Publications.

Marsh, Robert M., (1967), *Comparative Sociology: A Codification of Cross-Societal Analysis*, New York: Harcourt Brace, and World, Inc.

Przeworski, Adam and Henry Teune, (1970), *The Logic of Comparative Social Inquiry*, New York: Wiley-Interscience.

Qyen, Else (ed.), (1990), *Comparative Methodology: Theory and Practice in International Social Research*, Newbury Park: Sage Publications, Inc.

Ragin, Charles C., (1987), *The Comparative Method: Moving Beyond Qualitative and Quantitative Strategies*, Berkeley: University of California Press.

Skocpol, Theda and Margaret Somers, (1980), "The Uses of Comparative History in Macro-social Theory, *Comparative Studies in Society and History*, Vol. 22, No. 2: 174-97.

Zelditch, Morris Jr., (1971), "Intelligible Comparisons", pp. 267-307 in Ivan Vallier (ed.), *Comparative Methods in Sociology: Essays on Trends and Applications*, Berkeley; University of California Press.

Chapter 5

Research Project and Report Writing

R.P. Misra

Formulating the Project Idea

Researchers interested in taking up research have the initial difficulty of picking up a problem worth investigating. At times they waste considerable amount of time in just thinking about the pros and cons of problems suggested by different persons. This indecision usually results from certain misunderstandings about "What is research?" The usual notion about research is that it must result in something spectacular; it must come up with a new discovery or theory.

It must be pointed out here that a study which brings forward new facts, or generalizations or which demolishes or establishes a hypothesis or a theory or a principle already in vogue, or which puts a variety of information into an order or system, or which prepares grounds for further research is as valid a research as one which ends with a new discovery or theory.

Research can be of two types: (1) fundamental and (2) applied. The latter is done to understand the processes through which a certain constructive programme can be successfully applied, whereas the former is solely devoted to the understanding of the basic principles underlying a phenomenon and is not directly concerned with its application and usefulness. In actual practice the two are, however, not always separable. Whether a researcher should engage himself in fundamental or applied research, will depend solely upon his research interest, orientation, and training together with the purpose of his research.

The best problem for research is one which arises from the researcher's own curiosity. He can handle a topic in which he is really interested better than the one suggested by someone else. This has, however, to be qualified by an equally important element. The researcher must know the tools which can handle the problems he proposes to take up.

Before choosing the problem for research one should therefore ask the following questions to oneself:

(1) Is this problem really of interest to me?
(2) Is it significant in the sense that it extends the frontiers of knowledge or fills an important gap in knowledge?
(3) Can I handle this problem within the constraints of resources of (money, time and others) available?
(4) Has this problem not been investigated by someone else?

After the problem has been identified, it should be put in the form of a proposal which should cover the following:

A. Describe problem situation or problem area
   (1) Indicate conditions which give rise to the problem.
   (2) Indicate individuals or groups which are affected.
   (3) Indicate specifically how each individual or group is affected.
   (4) Briefly, describe previous work in this area. Point out the extent to which satisfactory solutions exist, shortcomings in methodology, etc.

B. State the problem to be investigated in clear and concise terms. These may be called specific objectives of this project.

C. Present the justification of these objectives by:
   (1) Relating specific objectives to problem area.
   (2) Indicating the manner in which "users" could apply answers in making decisions.

D. Collection of data
   (1) Indicate the kinds and amount of data needed to solve the problem, accomplish the objectives, or test the hypotheses.
   (2) Indicate where and how the data will be obtained. If data are to be obtained from survey, develop a questionnaire.

E. Analysis
   (1) Describe the manner in which data will be analyzed:
      (a) Indicate what relationships will be tested.
      (b) Indicate criteria for establishment of relationships. (For ex-

ample, what conditions must exist to support the conclusion that variable A is or is not related to variable B.).

General Comments

Research projects vary so widely in nature and scope that it is difficult to develop a specific outline to serve all purposes. Therefore, this general outline should be modified and adapted for the particular project. The above outline could be stated as follows:

— Development of theoretical framework.
— Statement of hypotheses.
— Justification.
— Collection of data.
— Analysis of data and test of hypotheses.

Defining the Problem

In order to maximize their research results, students must be clear about the purpose, the objectives and the scope of their research projects and must be sure of the research methods they are likely to use. It is, therefore, important that these initial steps be planned and thought out carefully before a research project is taken up for study.

There are various purposes for which research is done. Generally speaking, a post-graduate student has to conduct research in order to fulfil an assignment given by his professor or to meet the requirements of a post-graduate degree. At times research is conducted to satisfy one's own curiosity and interest, while at other times it is done as a commercial venture. No matter what the purpose, the end product of all researches is either a new insight into the problem under investigation or a new method of approaching the problem or a new order or system of data hitherto available only in a haphazard way. The prior and clear understanding of the purpose for which research is proposed to be done, enables the researcher to formulate his objective and research design more specifically and appropriately.

The success of a researcher is largely determined by his ability to meet the objectives of his research project. It is, therefore, important that the objective or objectives of a research project be stated unambiguously and at the very outset. While stating the objectives, the researcher is expected to state "what he wants to find out" and what he means by "what he wants to find out." More often than not, it is not difficult to define one's objectives in a theoretical sense but it is difficult to define them operationally. Let us take the example of a student who wants to find out the impact of culture on the land use pattern of an area. He may state his objective in the following term: "To find out the impact of culture on the land use pattern of X area." It seems as if the objective has been very clearly stated. But it is not so. It is really very ambiguous. The student has not yet given the theoretical and operational definition of the terms "culture" and "land use". Culture may mean different things to different people. After giving the theoretical meaning of the term "culture", he will have to state how he is going to measure it in order to determine its impact on the land use pattern of the area in question. In other words he will have to back his theoretical definition of the term 'culture' by its operational definition. He will have to do the same thing with regard to other terms.

In addition to the clear understanding and statement of the purpose and objectives of research, students should also know the scope of their research and the methods which can be used to meet the objectives of the project. All these preliminaries should be so stated that the reader is not left in doubt about the intentions of the researcher.

Preparing a Tentative Outline

The next step in the process of research is to prepare a tentative outline, which can be used as a framework for collecting research data. A well defined outline should clearly reflect the purpose, objective and scope of research and the order in which the contents of the report are to be presented.

An outline may be divided into parts, chapters and sub-headings. The structure of the outline will be determined by the nature of research output one is aiming at. A long report will consist of several chapters. But a research paper to be published in a professional journal will have only sub-headings. Ordinarily the first chapter should be an introduction which contains statements of purpose, objectives, scope and methods of research and the organization of the report. The order in which the chapters and sub-headings are placed in the outline should be logical and rational so that the flow of thought is orderly. The sub-headings should not deviate from the main objective of the chapters under which they appear (Fig. 1).

After the preparation of the outline, one should look for sources of information relevant to the research project.

Data Sources and Data Collection

After the project idea has been settled, one should begin a serious search for the sources of information. Usually there are two main

Figure 1
Sample of Contents

CHAPTER 1. INTRODUCTION

Purpose, Objective and Scope

Methods of Research

Organization

CHAPTER II. THE LAND AND THE PEOPLE

The Land
  Land forms
  Climate
    Temperature
    Rainfall
    Others

Soils

sources of information:
(a) Field Investigation, and
(b) Library Research

Which of the two sources should be tapped by a researcher, will depend upon the nature of his research project. If it involves field work, he will have to chalk out a programme and the methods of investigation. If it is based on library research and desk work, he will have to concentrate on secondary sources of information. Most projects involve both field investigation and library research. Researchers should therefore know the methods of handling both.

The first step in any research is the picking of the general sources of information for basic understanding of the problem.

The Literature Search

One can get a number of relevant and useful references in the encyclopedia, index to periodicals, and a few professional periodicals. A suggested list of such sources is given below:

1. Encyclopedia Britannica.

2. Encyclopaedia of Social Sciences.
3. International and national indices to periodicals.
4. Bibliographies.
5. National and international journals, and
6. Library catalogue.

Most of these sources are available in almost all university libraries including the one of the University of Mysore.

The nature of the research project will, of course, influence the kind of literature the researcher will look for. If his project concerns an aspect of physical planning, he would choose a different set of sources than would be the case if he were considering an aspect of economics. If the project concerns a small area, an encyclopaedia may not be of much help and he may have to depend on official reports, occasional publications and, of course, on his own field investigations.

How to Look into Encyclopaedia and Indices

Selecting Key Words

In order to save time, it is better to write down a set of key words on a 5"x 8" card. If a paper is entitled "Land Use in South-east Asia—Problems and Prospects," the key-word card may at first, look like Fig. 2.

One may add other terms like Thailand, rice, soils, tropics, monsoon and so on. While looking into one of the references found under

Figure 2

Sample of a Key-word Card

Key Words:

Asia

South-east Asia

Land tenure

Land utilization

China

Japan

Indo-China

Cambodia

a key word, one can easily pick up other terms which can be potentially useful.

The researcher should look for these key words in the encyclopaedia of index he examines. He should add to and eliminate the words from the list of key words as his knowledge of the sophistication on the topic increases. He should note down the references given at the tail end of the articles and also read the articles wherever they appear to be relevant to the topic.

Preparing a Check List

One cannot make a systematic search for literature unless one keeps a complete and accurate record of the sources consulted. It is, therefore, essential to keep a running account of such sources. How to do it, is shown in Fig. 3. The check list should give the date on which a particular source was consulted, and the pages consulted. It should also indicate whether references were listed there.

Figure 3
The Check List

			Check List
Britannica	1958 ad. Feb. 10.		
	Japan	-	Industry, population, government, administration, agriculture, defence (no bibliography)
	Indo-China	-	Feb. 11.
			Land use, (bibliography)

It is definitely desirable to check out the most recently published materials first because such materials will send to additional materials published earlier.

Preparing a Bibliography Card

Each time one comes across a reference—book, articles, report, etc., useful to the research project, one should copy down all the information needed for the bibliographic reference in the final draft of the research report. Each bibliographic item should be put on a separate 5"x8" card in the form shown in Fig. 4.

At times it is possible to have a look at the reference. In such a case it is better to put a short abstract on the bibliography card to remind oneself what to expect of the source when one looks it up later. If it is not available readily, the abstract can be prepared at the time of preparing notes from the reference. Enough space should be left in the right hand corner of the bibliography card to write the library accession number. For his own convenience, the researcher should set up some sort of style of his own, putting each different item of information at a different place in the card. He should perfect his style the first time he writes down the reference for bibliography. This will save a lot of time later on.

Figure 4

A Bibliography Card

Graham, Edward H. Library
Accession No....

Natural Principles of Land Use
London: Oxford University Press, 1944
The book is written upon the premise that biological concepts can contribute importantly to the wise use and management of land.

In case a researcher is planning to do a sample study requiring interviews with a number of persons, he can write the name of persons, their addresses and their relevant characteristics in the card. For efficiency sake it will be better to keep these address cards separate from the bibliography cards.

The bibliography cards should be filed alphabetically under relevant alphabetic index cards,- a set of which every researcher is supposed to have and a form of which is give in Fig. 5.

Figure 5

Sample of an Alphabetic Index Card

S	T	U	V	W	XYZ
M	N	O	P	Q	R
G	H	I	J	K	L
A	B	C	D	E	F

Preparing Notes

Systematizing the Procedure

Before starting the preparation of notes, the researcher should transfer the essence of his outline to the index tabs and attach these tabs to 5" x 8" cards (Fig. 6). It is also possible to buy ready made index cards without alphabets.

A researcher has the choice of using either the 5"x8" cards with index tabs affixed, or the ready made index cards available in the market. In any case, he should write down the outline of his report on the tabs of the cards as shown in Fig. 6 and arrange these cards in the same order as the outline. This will form his outline file.

Figure 6

Sample of an Index Card

Chapter 1	Chapter 2	Chapter 3	Chapter 4	Chapter 5	Chapter 6

Using the Scratch Pad

After these cards are put in order, he is ready to prepare notes from the references he has noted on the bibliography cards. As he checks his actual bibliographic sources, he should keep one of his 5"x8" scratch pads in hand. On the left of the top sheet of the pad he should write down the name of the author and the year of publication. As he peruses the sources he should make his notes on these sheets. He should identify the location of each note by writing the page number(s) next to the note (Fig. 7).

Figure 7

Sample of a Page from the Scratch Pad

Boeke, 1953	
3	Boeke defined a dual economy as one where "Simultaneously two or more social systems appear... and each dominate a part of the society."

The researcher should make it a point to put only one idea on a sheet of the scratch pad. And each time an idea is put, it should be identified by noting the last name of the writer and the page number of the book (Fig. 7). After the notes are completed, they should be filed under the appropriate section in the outline file. And as soon as a source has been consulted, a mark should be made on the relevant bibliography card as a reminder that particular reference has already been consulted.

If during the process of preparing notes, a researcher comes across additional references for his key-words card and additional ideas for his outline, he should continue to include them at appropriate places. He should not, however, forget his original objective in this process by looking for ideas not so useful for his project, although very interesting and valuable otherwise.

While going through the preparation of notes and the field work, the researcher may get some ideas from his associates, professors, colleagues or friends. He himself may think of something while sitting alone and meditating. He should immediately note down these ideas on the scratch paid and file them at the appropriate place in the outline file.

If there is considerable amount of facts and figures that need to be analyzed, the researcher should complete the analysis and file the results in the outline file. If there are certain maps or diagrams to be included in the paper they should be noted on the scratch pad and filed.

Field Work

Field work provides the primary data for research. Researchers without adequate background, often neglect the preparatory work necessary before any field work can be conducted. One must decide precisely the nature and type of data needed, the procedure of gathering the data, the format of the data and the analytical tools to be utilized for the data analysis.

There are two basic procedures for data gathering: (i) census, and (ii) sample. In the case of census, information is gathered from all the units of the "population" or "universe". Whereas in the case of sample, only selected units are observed. It is rarely that a researcher uses census method unless his objective/problem of the research is too localized and micro and he can handle all the units without difficulty. This may be the case when the study of a single village is done.

Scientific Writing

Sometimes, a researcher considers his research complete when the project has been completed and regards the writing of the report as a nuisance. As Charles Darwin expressed it, "We naturalists' life would be a happy one if we had only to observe and never to write."[2] Nevertheless, the work of a scientist must be recorded. The completed manuscript is the end product, the enduring proof that something has been uncovered and offered for the use of society.

"Scientific writing" has been defined as that writing which is directed to scientists outside the author's speciality and to the general public.[3] Scientific writing has a broader scope than technical writing. Technical writing includes only the writing a scientist does in addressing fellow specialists or in connection with technological applications of scientific principles.[4] In both scientific and technical writing the writer should strive always for an accurate, logical, comprehensive, and smoothly readable expression of facts and ideas.

Organizing the Writing

Writing procedures differ naturally, according to the subject matter and the personality of the writer. Three methods for organizing facts and ideas for scientific writing are suggested.

(1) The separate card method utilizes a card for each fact and idea. On a distinguishable set of cards are listed the main structural parts of a manuscript such as introduction, purpose, procedure, etc. Then the fact cards are sorted and placed in their appropriate category. With this material in front of the writer the first draft is merely a process of connecting the facts and ideas.

(2) For the more experienced writer there is the total recall method. Mentally, the prospective author recalls in general terms what he was trying to find out, what he did, and why, and when. From this mental outline he writes down a series of general statements. (a) I asked the question... (b) To find an answer, I adopted the method of... (c) Using this method I obtained the following observations... (d) From these data I conclude... The first draft is written directly from this outline. In this method the emphasis is placed on thinking through the entire report in order to assemble logically the facts and ideas.

(3) Called the relaxed method, the manuscript itself, plus the author's original unformalized plan, serves as the outline. In practice, this is a process of writing a few paragraphs, stopping for a period of time; upon beginning to write again, the writer revises the text and composes anew until he has completed the report. This method is recommended only for the experienced writer.

The preliminary outline should be planned carefully in order to ensure that all facts are considered logically. It is easier to shift sections in an outline than to shift paragraphs in the written copy.

Drafting the Manuscript

The first draft is written directly from the outline. Begin the writing in a systematic manner with a relaxed frame of mind. Write rapidly; if you have trouble, leave a blank for words that do not come readily to mind. In addition, write only on alternate lines, thus leaving room for later changes. While writing, if you get tired or bored, take a break. You should always try to finish a given segment at one sitting because a break in your train of thought might mean losing a good idea. Finally, leave time in your schedule for putting your completed first draft aside for at least a day before beginning to revise it. This will enable you to take a more critical view of it.

When writing the first draft certain aspects should be covered in the introduction, body, and conclusions of the manuscript. The introduction should include enough of the history of the problem to show how the new data relate to earlier work or to the science in general. If the author can sketch in the relevant points of earlier studies, even briefly, he will help both the beginner in his own field and the scientist in a related field. The introduction should point out the basic assumptions, if any, underlying the arguments. Many reports, especially those of an interpretative or theoretical nature, are based on certain hypotheses that may seem to the author to be implicit in the discussion. Nevertheless, he should state them clearly and concisely, for the benefit of less sophisticated readers.

The body of any piece of writing is the meat of a writer's ideas. Here you give all your facts and substantiate them. You develop your major and minor points and tie them together into a clearly comprehensible whole. The case with which you develop your subject in the body of your text depends upon the adequacy of your research, prior thought and outline. Gathering a multiplicity of details before you begin to write and then pruning them down to essentials is a better practice for most of us than gathering a sparse quantity of details and trying to build them up to a tightly woven argument or description. Above all, the body of the exposition should leave no gaps in your reasoning. Here is where you test every statement and substantiate it by detailed explanations or proof.

The conclusion may be a brief re-statement of the principal ideas covered in the paper; it may be a re-statement of the purpose of a described object; in the research paper it may be a statement of conclusions reached through the research study. The conclusion may also include a prophecy, such as, "Future research may prove that..." or "A later study will be attempted to learn whether the relationship between..." Whatever form the conclusion takes, it should so summarize the main idea of the study that it sharpens and solidifies that idea in the mind of the reader.

Writing for the Reader

Before undertaking writing, it is essential to have in mind the educational level of the reader to whom it is addressed, as this will govern the whole approach to the style and treatment of the material. Writing, in essence, is a conversation between people, not a monologue into the void. The writer sets down his comments and the reader answers by his acceptance or rejection of the ideas. "The golden rule in scientific writing is, therefore, to put yourself constantly in the place of the reader."[5] If there are no readers, the labour of writing is wasted and it is, therefore, in the writer's own interest to secure and hold the reader's attention.

Style

The selection of words, the choice of sentence structure, the ideas to be expressed, the point of view, the audience addressed, all help to form the style of a composition. What are the essentials of a scientific style? It is generally agreed that the qualities of greatest importance in a good scientific style are clarity, precision, conciseness, directness and objectivity.

Clarity and precision are to a great degree interdependent. Clarity results when the writer is successful in making his communication understandable to the reader. Precision represents the attainment of an exact correspondence between the matter to be conveyed and its verbal expressions.

Writing that is concise—that expresses its meaning in the fewest possible words—saves the time and energy of the reader and contributes to readability. Directness also serves these ends and facilitates communication through the avoidance of circumlocutions and awkward inversions and of excessively numerous "there is" and "it is" constructions in which the appearance of the subject is delayed. In general, directness is the foe of verbiage, which impedes a simple, straightforward approach.

It is expected that the scientist's style should reflect the objectivity of his attitude toward the problems he investigates and toward his results. This emphasis on objectivity as a quality of scientific style implies that in subordinating subjective considerations, scientific style should be more formal and more impersonal than is prose style in general.

Two factors work against the scientist in his writing. The journals plead for brevity, and custom urges him to write impersonally. The style of much of the resulting prose reflects a writer under restraint.

Here is an example:

> In order for us to understand the details of the history of our attempts to interpret the complicated phenomenon of heat in its evolution from the now extinct caloric concept to the accepted kinetic theory, there are several alternative approaches all of which we must pursue if we are to understand the nature of the phenomenon.[6]

The style of this long, complex sentence, carrying its burden of unnecessary words, almost buries the author's thought. With enough patience, however, a reader can finally recover it:

> Heat is a complicated phenomenon. Physicists have now discarded the idea of a caloric fluid and have generally adopted the kinetic theory. A review of the earlier concepts, however, will help us to understand the nature of heat.[7]

The original version was difficult to understand, not because of the grammar but because of the style.

A more or less deformed style inevitably develops when a writer accepts the convention that the scientist must write impersonally. Avoiding the first person does not necessarily produce grammatical mistakes, of course, but it does encourage indirect statements. In addition, the need to use passive verbs increases the probability of errors in grammar. Passive verbs start long trains of prepositional phrases; they foster circumlocution; and they encourage vagueness. A writer will almost automatically improve his style if he shifts from passive to active construction.

In general, short, simple sentences make the clearest exposition. A very long sentence strains the reader to understand what it says. Sometimes a good explanation requires a long sentence; the author should then help the reader as much as possible. The predicate should follow the subject, closely and modifying clauses should appear close to the words they modify. The experienced writer will vary the length of his sentences as a short sentence placed among longer, complex structures provides emphasis as well as relief.

Thus, to achieve a good style in scientific writing an author needs only a few principles; write simply, avoid long sentences, choose plain words, and use active voice.

Functional English and its Use

The style for presenting facts and instructions is known to scientific writers as functional english. Its mood, person, and tense may be varied to suit particular documents, but it remains essentially the presentation of exact reasoning with mathematical precision. Sentences are confined to the function they are required to serve. They deal with a single topic and give their message in crisp, direct phraseology.

Chief among the hazards confronting the scientist preparing a manuscript is his unconscious blunders in English. The majority of grammatical errors are caused by carelessness in writing and can usually be found by the writer when he checks his first draft. Most common errors are likely to be:

(i) Faulty agreement: Faulty agreement is the incorrect agreement of verbs with their subjects and of pronouns with their antecedents.

(ii) Incomplete constructions: Two types of incomplete constructions are more common than the sentence fragment. (a) When two verbs have the same subject or object, an error may occur in the omission of a necessary auxiliary verb. Such omission causes fragmentary construction within the sentence. (b) Comparisons—a sentence is not complete unless all comparisons and implied comparisons are expressed and proper conjunctions used. A common error is to omit the second part of a comparison or to omit a word needed to make a sentence of comparison grammatically correct.

(iii) Dangling constructions: Dangling constructions the participle, the gender, the noun, and even the adjective may hang loosely from the wrong hook or from no hook at all.

When a writer suspects that one of his sentences seems unaccountably vague, puzzling, or confusing, he should look for the possibility of one of the above-mentioned errors. Various devices can serve to correct the dangling phrase. Sometimes a simple shift in the position of the words will do the trick; a simple change from the passive to the active voice will correct some danglers; sometimes a prepositional phrase will correct the mistake. Anyone who can plan and carry out a research project should learn to recognize common blunders in writing and to correct them.

The following references are useful guides to assist the writer when he is in doubt. Therefore, it is suggested that the following books or ones of a similar nature be available to the writer:

Webster's New Collegiate Dictionary.

The Concise Oxford Dictionary (for its many examples of correct use of words and phrases).

Soule's Dictionary of English Synonyms.

Roget's Thesaurus.

The Perrin Writer's Guide and Index to English, or other good handbooks of English composition.

Revision and Completion of the Manuscript

Once the first draft is on paper, the hard work of composition begins. Revision, often complete rewriting of three or more drafts, is necessary. For simple changes in phrasing use the space between the lines. If it is necessary to rearrange paragraphs or blocks of text, use scissors and scotch tape, or staples.

During the first revision, give attention to the order and development of the larger divisions of the paper—sections and paragraphs. The order of the topics may have to be shifted. If the paper is long, the first part may have to be rewritten to make it consistent with the last part. Irrelevant parts should be eliminated. If a vital point has been omitted, put it in the text where it belongs, not in a footnote. The footnote irritates many readers who regard it as an unwelcome interruption to the argument.

With the second revision, focus your attention on the sentences, study and revise the sentences in groups, rather than singly. Make each group of sentences develop the exact idea you wish to express. There should be only one possible meaning, and this should be easily understood by the reader. A useful test of clarity is to see whether the writing is understandable when it is read rapidly aloud.

In reviewing the technical content, try to adopt a detached point of view, read over the entire text and give particular attention to the material in (1) the introduction, (2) the observations, and (3) the conclusions. The following topics should be considered in the introduction: Reasons for undertaking the investigation or for writing the article, brief history of recent work of a similar nature, possible outcome, or advantages which may accrue from the work described, and any special restrictions which might apply in reading the account of the work.

The observational or experimental data usually occupy the central part of the manuscript. In revising, consider whether you have presented all the necessary evidence and whether you have given it the proper emphasis. Irrelevant details and vague descriptions easily creep into the first draft, but they should not be allowed to survive in the revision. On the other hand, a too-condensed explanation may need expansion. To produce a well-balanced account you need perspective; you will get the most helpful advice, as a rule, from sympathetic and informed colleagues.

Evaluate the conclusions with special care. Have you adequately discussed the evidence you presented earlier? Have you pointed out how the evidence relates to your original problem? Have you stated your conclusions in definite terms? The reader should be able to understand exactly what this particular investigation accomplishes and what it means.

With the manuscript written and revised, the main task has been completed. One important consideration is the selection of a title. The title selected should be brief and as a rule it should not occupy more than one printed line. The title should indicate the subject of the manuscript but should not attempt to summarize the content. A good, brief title gives a general rather than a detailed description of the contents.

The summary consists of few paragraphs stating succinctly the problem or subject and the main conclusions reached by the writer. It provides a predigested abridgement of report so that the busy reader can tell at a glance whether the subject is one that interests him. More than that, the summary is a discipline for the writer, forcing him to test his thesis to see if it has one central idea or conclusion that can be stated in capsule form.

The author alone must decide how many drafts of a manuscript are enough. The complexity of the material as well as the care in writing will determine when one can stop revising and pronounce the most recent draft the last.

Format for Scientific Reporting

Before starting the writing task the researcher should see that the following steps have been taken.

(i) Outline is completed and if needed revised;
(ii) Notes written on the scratch sheets are properly filed under various sections of the outline file; and
(iii) Bibliography is alphabetized in the alphabetic index cards file.

If these steps have been taken the remaining thinking and writing tasks will seem easy.

After its completion a research report will have three main divisions. These are;

— the preliminaries
— the text and
— the reference materials.

The Preliminaries

The Title and Half-title Page

The first element of the preliminaries is the title page. A title page should indicate the title of the report, institution or organization which published it, the name of the author/editor and the time and place of publication. In what order all these should come depends on individual taste, but in most cases the date and place of publication come last.

The title page may be followed by a half-title page. The half-title page should ordinarily give more information about the title, the writer and the publisher. For example it may also give the sub-title if any and the designation and qualification of the writer. This page should be paginated as the first page of the preliminaries indicated by small Roman numbers but the page number should not appear on it.

Preface and Acknowledgment

The half-title page is followed by a preface. A preface includes such matters as the writer's reasons for conducting the research, and the scheme or programme under which the study was conducted. A preface is also a suitable place to mention the assistance given by the organizations or individuals in the process of research. If a student does not wish to mention anything except the assistance he received, then he may do away with the preface and replace it with "Acknowledgment".

Table of Contents

After preface comes the "Table of Contents". A table of contents shows the main headings including the chapter headings in capital letters. The chapter heading is preceded by chapter number in capital Roman numerals. On the left hand side of the page the word "chapter" in small letters is typed above the column of chapter numbers and on the right hand side the word "page" above the column of page numbers.

The chapters in the text are usually divided into sub-headings of first, second or sometimes even third orders. Whether all subheadings should appear in the table of contents or not will have to be decided by the writer himself. If they are given, the following should be the system. The sub-headings of the first order are typed in capital and small letters. The first letter of the first and the last words together with that of all nouns, pronouns, adjectives, adverbs and verbs should be capitalized. The sub- headings of the second order should contain only the first letter of the first word capital and while that of the third order should not have any capital letters unless, of course, they happen to be proper nouns or proper adjectives. Each author should develop his own style.

The spacing between the chapter headings should be double. It should also be double between the chapter heading and the subheadings of the first order. The spacing between the sub-headings should be single.

At times the sub-headings are also numbered. In the case of numbering, the sub-headings of the first order should be numbered in capital letters, i.e., A-Z, those of the second order in Indian numerals, i.e., 1, 2, 3, ... those of the third order in small letters i.e., a-z, and those of the fourth order in small Roman numbers i, ii, iii...

The table of contents should incorporate all sections of the report including the preliminaries and the reference materials. The preliminaries, however, are paginated in small Roman numerals.

List of Tables and Illustrations

Table of contents is followed by the list of tables which shows the table numbers in Indian or Roman numerals and the titles in capital and small letters. In order to avoid repetition, the word "table" in small letters is typed above the column of table numbers, and the word "page" above the column of page numbers, as in the case of table of contents.

The 'List of illustrations' is placed after the list of tables. It is advisable to designate all illustrations as figures and to number them in Indian numerals. The title of the figure in the list of illustrations should be the same as it appears with the figure. It can be shortened only in very exceptional cases.

With the list of illustrations, the preliminary part of the report is over and the next part, i.e., the text begins.

The Text

Chapters and Sub-headings

The text of a paper begins with an "introduction". An introduction can be the first chapter of the report or if it is short, it may be referred to as "Introduction" without chapter number.

Ordinarily an "Introduction" contains the objectives, methods of research, and the organizational structure of the report. Other chapters follow the introduction.

Introduction as well as the other chapters can be divided by sub-headings of various orders as pointed out earlier. The problem naturally arises as to what should be the location of various order of sub-headings in the text... Supposing that three orders are used, the following scheme will be most appropriate.

Centre heading, underlined;
Side heading, underlined;
Paragraph heading, underlined.

If it is required to have as many as six orders of sub-headings the following system may be used;

Centred heading, underlined;
Centred heading, not underlined;
Side heading, underlined;
Side heading, not underlined;
Paragraph heading, underlined;

The Paragraph heading should be followed by a colon and a dash. The system of using the capital and small letters is the same as discussed earlier under "Table of Contents". The last chapter of the text should be the "Summary and Conclusions" or only "Summary".

Quotations

Wherever it is necessary to quote a passage or a verse from a publication it can be put in the text. As far as possible the quotation should correspond with the original in wording, spelling and punctuation.

If the quotation is a small one i.e., a sentence or two, it may be incorporated into the text of the report and enclosed in quotation marks. Wherever a quotation is incorporated within the text, one should see that it fits in the sentence grammatically. But if it is a long one containing more than two sentences, it should be put separately from the text in single spacing. It should be located four spaces to the left of the left hand margin. In this case it is not necessary to put quotation marks.

At times one comes across such quotable passages which contain certain sentences which are irrelevant to the subject. In such cases the authors are free to delete the irrelevant portions. This is done by substituting each of those portions by three dots. This process is called elipsis. If after the elipsis there is a full stop, the number of dots will be four. In case a whole paragraph or a line or more in a verse are omitted, the elipsis should be shown by a full line of spaced dots.

It sometimes so happens that a quotation contains an error. If it is given in a text without any warning, the reader may feel it to be the mistake of the writer of the report. To assure the reader that the mistake was in the original, one should put sic (underlined) within parenthesis, soon after the faulty word.

Use of Numerals, Abbreviations and Foreign Words

In general no abbreviation except Mr. Messrs, Mrs., Dr., St., Rev., Hon., should be used in the text. Ordinarily all foreign words used in English should be underlined. The exceptions to this rule are very few.

Footnotes:[8]

1. To cite the authority for the statements made or the passages quoted;
2. To make side remarks;
3. To make cross references;
4. To make acknowledgments;
5. To explain a term or a point or an idea. It is done when it is felt that incorporation of the explanation in the text will obstruct the flow of ideas; and
6. To further elaborate a point.

Whenever a footnote is given, the place in the text at which a footnote is needed is marked by an Indian numeral elevated less than one space above the line.

There are three systems of numbering the footnotes. Under one system there is only one set of numerals in the whole text. Under the other system there is one set of numerals for each chapter. And under the third system each page has its own set of numerals, each time beginning with one. Amongst these, the last system is most convenient.

All footnotes should be arranged in numerical order under a line typed at the foot of the page. The footnote numbers at the foot of the page should correspond to the footnote numbers in the text. A reference footnote should contain the following information.

For a book:

1. The name of the author showing the initials first and the family

name last, followed by a comma.

2. The title of the book, underlined; put a comma after it, if step 3 follows.
3. Name of editor or translator, if any.
4. Facts of publication, within parenthesis, showing:
   (a) Place of publication;
   (b) Name of the publishing agency; and
   (c) Date of publication.
5. Volume number.
6. Page Number.

For example:

Ralph H. Brown, *Historical Geography of the United States*, (New York: Harcourt, Brace and Co., 1948), p. 96.

If the details of the edition of the book are also to be given the footnote will take the following form:

T.C. Chamberline and R.D. Salisbury, *Geology*, Vol. I, *Geologic processes and Their Results*, (II ed., rev.; New York; Henry Holt and Co., 1969), p. 155.

For articles:

The form of footnotes for articles published in professional periodicals is different from that for the books. The author's name is given in the normal order, i.e., the initials are followed by the family name. The next item is the title of the articles within double quotation marks. The title is followed by the name of the periodical (underlined). The volume number, the month and the year of publication and the page numbers referred to are given after the name of the periodical. The basic form looks as follows:

R.S. Ecksus, "Factor Proportions in Under-developed Countries", *American Economic Review*, XXXXV (September 1955), pp. 539-65.

William E. Moore, "The Social Framework of Economic Development", in *Tradition, Values and Socio-Economic Development*, edited by R. Braibanti and J. Spengler (Durham; Duke University Press, 1961), p. 69.

If there are more than three writers, the name of the first writer followed by the abbreviation et al., (underlined) should be given. If the writer happens to be an editor and not an author, the abbreviation (ed.) in parenthesis should be put after his name. If the work has been translated by someone, the abbreviation 'trans' followed by the name of the translator should appear after the title of the work.

If a publication belongs to a series, it may be footnoted as follows:

Marcel J. Lemeirleir, *Manufactured Occupance in the West Central Areas of Chicago*, Department of Geography Research Paper No. 11 (Chicago: Chicago University Press, 1950), p. 11.

William Burge, *Theoretical Geography*, Lund Studies in Geography, Series C. General and Mathematical Geography, No. 1, (Lund: Royal University of Lund, Sweden, 1962), p. 8.

If the publication happens to be a report without an author, the name of the author may be omitted. The rest of the form stands. If it is a newspaper, only the name of the paper followed by the date and year of publication together with the page number referred to should be given.

Indian Express (Bangalore), August 29, 1965, p.5.

If the reference is unpublished such as a dissertation the citation should appear as follows:

R.P. Misra, "Agricultural Development in a Traditional Society—A Theoretical and Empirical Analysis of the Process of Agricultural Development and Change in Lancaster Country, Pennsylvania" (Unpublished Ph.D. Dissertation, Department of Geography, University of Maryland, College Park, Md., U.S.A., 1964), pp...

If a reference cited before has to be cited again, the following system should be adopted; (i) If the references to the same work follow each other without any other intervening reference, even though separated by several pages, the reference in question should not be repeated. Instead the abbreviation "ibid" should be used. It is, however, not permissible to use 'ibid' if the work cited is different although the author is the same. (ii) In case the second reference to the same work is intervened by other references, the last name of the author together with the page number under reference should be noted. There is no need to repeat the full form of the footnote.

Tables and Illustrations

Tables: Usually a table is put immediately after it is first mentioned in the text. But in case it cannot be accommodated within the space left out in the page, it should be placed in the following page. The table number in Indian numerals must be put at its appropriate place in the text to indicate the exact position to which it belongs. If the table is too wide to be accommodated length-wise in a page, it can be put broad-side.

The caption of the table should be preceded by the word "Table" in capital letters and table number in Indian numerals. A colon is placed after the table number. The caption of a table should be centred in the page by leaving five to seven spaces on both sides of the caption.

There are, of course, several styles of writing captions for tables. Only one of them is given above. Writers are free to use any other style if they so prefer. What is important, however, is that the style used once should be consistently used all through the report.

The footnotes to the tables should be put immediately below the tables and not at the foot of the page as in the case of the footnotes to the text. To avoid confusion, it will be desirable to indicate the footnote mark in the table by symbols or small letters (a,b,c,...,z). Table having more than two columns of facts should have their columns separated by vertical lines.

Illustrations: A research report may include graphs, pictures, plans, maps and diagrams as illustrative materials. Such illustrations should, as far as possible, follow their first reference in the text. Each illustration must have a caption and should be numbered in Indian numerals. As the illustrations form part of the text, they should be paginated consecutively with the textual matter.

Pagination

Every page of a report, including the blank ones, but excluding the blank sheet following the title page should be paginated. In the preliminaries the page numbers are indicated by small Roman numerals typed at the bottom of each page. The rest of the report should be numbered in Indian numerals centred at the top of the page. The page numbers can also be placed at the right hand corner of the page if so desired. A page, containing a major heading i.e., chapter, will, however, bear its number only at the bottom of the page. Unless it is a small paper of informal nature, all major headings should be started on a new page.

Preparing Scientific Papers for Publication

In a small scientific paper prepared for a professional periodical, preliminaries are not important. In such cases, one should come immediately to the subject matter. It should, however, be divided into different sections. The whole paper should be typed in continuation putting the main and the sub-headings of various orders in their appropriate places.

References

Appendix

In the process of preparing a research report, a researcher may come across lot of information which, although useful otherwise, tend to detract the attention of the reader from the main theme of the paper if included in the text. This may include the details of the methodology used in the research process, lengthy tables giving facts and figures, derivation of mathematical formula, etc. Such materials can usefully be put in Appendices.

Each item of information should be kept in a separate appendix. The appendices may be numbered in capital letters or in capital Roman numerals.

Bibliography

Bibliography is the last important part of a research report. A bibliography lists the sources used in the preparation of the report. These may be:

(i) Books,
(ii) Articles in periodicals,
(iii) Reports and documents issued-by official or unofficial agencies,
(iv) Interviews,
(v) Lectures, and
(vi) Radio and television talks.

If a bibliography is not a very long one, it can be put in alphabetical order by author. But if it is a long one and the references included are diverse, it should be according to types of publication. It can also be classified chapter-wise.

The forms of entries in the bibliography are different from that of the entires in the footnotes. Authors must keep this in mind. The usual forms are given below. These should be supplemented with the references given in the bibliography of this monograph and other publications.

Chamberlin, T.C., and Salisbury, R.D., *Geologic Processes and Their Results.* 2nd ed. rev. New York: Henry Holt and Co., 1906.

Hettner, Alfred, "Ferdinand von Richthofons Bedeutung fur die Geographic," Geogr. Ztechr., 12 (1906), 1-11.

Friendman, Milton, *Essays in Positive Economics*, Chicago: The University of Chicago Press, 1953.

If the bibliography is not an exhaustive one, the writer may call it "Select Bibliography", Selected References' or "References Cited".

Index

If a research report is to be published, the writer may like to give an index at the end of the report. An index is given to assist readers to instantaneously spot the information they want to get. For example, a researcher may like to know whether there is any information in the report about the economic development of Africa. He can find it out easily if there is an index listing all important terms used (such as "Congo" and "Zambia") in the report in alphabetical order with the page numbers at which they appear in the text.

The Final Touch

One can easily spoil all the good work done for several months or even years by publishing the report in such a hurry, that it is full of mistakes, that it follows no format, and that it is not well organized. It is therefore necessary that a researcher earmarks an adequate amount of time for final touches.

One should follow any of the several manuals for writing dissertations, reports and papers. The manuscript should be edited before it is sent for typing. The illustrative materials should be mounted, folded and inserted at appropriate places.

Editing is a time consuming and at times very frustrating work. It should be attempted in several ways so that all possible errors are eliminated. As suggested by Durrenberger "it should be done section-by-section so that internal consistency can be achieved, and word-by-word, sentence-by-sentence, and paragraph-by-paragraph in great detail. It is a good idea to edit selectively for spelling, punctuation, and word usage. Check to see that all spelling and usage are correct and consistent. Go over sentence construction to see that verbs are in agreement with their subjects, that pronouns are in agreement with their antecedents, and that it is always clear what the antecedents are. Be sure that you do not have any incomplete sentences. In doing this final job of editing seize every opportunity to improve the language of the report and to improve the transition from one thought to another. Finally, have some competent relative or friend look your manuscript over. Often, someone else with a detached eye will catch errors or unclear statements that may have escaped you.[9]

Notes

1. Based on a monograph on the topic-prepared by Phillip Foster, Professor, Dept. of Agricultural Economics, University of Maryland, U.S.A., 1963.
2. S.F. Trelease, *How to Write Scientific and Technical Papers*, Baltimore: The Williams and Wilkins Company, 1958, p.v.
3. M.R. Emberger and M.R. Hall, *Scientific Writing*, New York: Harcourt, Brace and Company, 1955, p. xi.
4. M. Norgaard, *A Technical Writer's Handbook*, New York: Harper and Brothers, 1959, p. 1.
5. D.H. Menzel, H.M. Jones and L.C. Boyd., *Writing a Technical Paper*, New York: McGraw-Hill Book Company 1961, pp. 73-74.
6. Ibid.
7. Menzel, Jones and Ibid.
8. There exists wide variations in the systems of footnoting. Only one of the systems is given here.
9. R.W. Durrenberger, *Geographical Research and Writing*, New York: T.Y. Crowell Co., 1971, p. 80.

Chapter 6

Hypothesis: Formulation and Testing

Lokesh Kaul

Introduction

Hypothesis helps to explain facts. It's derivation, thus, forms the most important step in the research process especially after the selection and definition of the research problem have been accomplished.

Etymologically hypothesis is made up of two words, "hypo" (less than) and "thesis", which mean less than or less certain than a thesis. It is the presumptive statement of a proposition, or a reasonable guess, based upon the available evidence, which the researcher seeks to prove through his study. The terms hypothesis, theory, and conclusion occur frequently in research literature and need some clarification. The hypothesis is precisely defined as a tentative or working proposition suggested as a solution to a problem, and the theory as the final hypothesis which is defensibly supported by all the evidence. The final hypothesis which fits all the evidence becomes the chief conclusion inferred from the study. According to Hilway (1964, p. 123):

> From the research scholar's point of view, the hypothesis may be conveniently considered as a tentative or working assumption, and the theory as the surviving or final hypothesis which is most defensibly supported by all the evidence, But since knowledge arrived at through the scientific method is subject to revision in the light of new data, a theory is in only one sense always only a working assumption, so that the conventional distinction between hypothesis

and theory (on the basis of increasing adequacy of evidence and hence of greater certainty) is a relative one. For all practical purposes, the duality of the term hypothesis need not concern the research scholar except to serve as a salutary reminder that no conclusion reached by the scientific method is necessarily a fixed and final truth.

The hypothesis is a powerful tool in research process to achieve dependable knowledge. It helps the researcher to relate theory to observation and observation to theory.

Hypotheses are formulated only as the suggested solution to the problem, with the objective that the ensuing study may lead either to its rejection or to its retention. They enable the researcher to locate and identify the variables involved in the study and suggest methodological procedures that are to be employed.

Importance of the Hypotheses

The importance of hypotheses is generally recognized more in the studies which aim to make predictions about some outcome. In experimental research, the researcher is interested in making predictions about the outcome of the experiment or what the results are expected to show and therefore the role of hypotheses is considered to be of utmost importance. In the historical or descriptive research, on the other hand, the researcher is investigating the history of a city or nation, the life of a man, the happening of an event, or is seeking facts to determine the status quo of some situation and thus may not have a basis for making a prediction of results. A hypothesis, therefore, may not be required in such fact-finding studies. Hillway (1964, p. 130) too too is of the view that "when fact-finding alone is the aim of the study, a hypothesis may not be required."

Most historical or descriptive studies, however, involve not only fact-finding but interpretation of facts to draw generalizations. If a researcher is tracing the history of a school or making a study about the results of a coming assembly poll, the facts or data he gathers will prove useful only if he is able to draw generalizations from them. Whenever possible, a hypothesis is recommended for all major studies to explain observed facts, conditions, or behaviour and to serve as a guide in the research process. If the hypotheses are not constructed, a researcher may waste much time and energy in gathering extensive empirical data and then find that he cannot state facts clearly and detect relevant relationships between variables as there is no hypothesis to guide him. The importance of hypotheses may be summarized as under (Ary *et al.*. 1972, pp. 73-74):

1. Hypotheses facilitate the extension of knowledge in an area. They provide tentative explanations of facts and phenomena, and can be tested and validated. Such explanations, if held valid, lead to generalizations which help significantly in understanding a problem and thereby extend the existing knowledge in the area to which they pertain.
2. Hypotheses provide the researcher with rational statements, consisting of elements expressed in a logical order of relationships which seek to describe or to explain conditions or events, that have not yet been confirmed by facts. Some relationships between the elements or variables in hypotheses are known facts and others transcend the known facts to give reasonable explanations for known conditions. The hypotheses enable the researcher to relate logically known facts to intelligent guesses about unknown conditions.
3. Hypotheses provide direction to the research. They represent specific objectives and thus help the researcher to determine the type of data needed to test the proposition. The hypotheses tell the researcher specifically what he needs to do and find out in his study. They help in the selection of relevant facts and variables that the researcher needs in his study. Hypotheses provide a basis for selecting the sample and the research procedures to be used in the study. The statistical techniques-needed in the analysis of data, and the relationships between the variables to be tested, are also implied by the hypotheses. Furthermore, the hypotheses help the researcher to delimit his study in scope so that it does not become broad or unwieldly.

   For example, a researcher is interested in studying the effect of test anxiety on the academic achievement of sixth grade children. He hypothesizes: "There is a negative relationship between test anxiety and academic achievement of a sixth grade student." It is clear from the statement of the hypothesis that the researcher would use an experimental method in which he may compare the academic achievement of a group of sixth grade students with high text anxiety with the achievement of a similar sample of students with low test anxiety. The significance of the difference between the mean academic achievement scores of the two groups could be analyzed by using t-test or analysis of variance technique.
4. Hypotheses provide the bases for reporting the conclusions of the study. The researcher will find it very convenient to test each hy-

pothesis separately and state the conclusions that are relevant to each. On the basis of these conclusions, he can make the research report interesting and meaningful to the reader.

Formulation of the Hypotheses

Hypotheses are guesses or tentative generalizations, but these guesses are not merely accidents. Collection of actual information alone does not lead to successful formulation of hypotheses. Hypotheses are the products of considerable speculation and imaginative guess work. They are based partly on known facts and explanations, and partly conceptual. There are no precise rules for formulating hypotheses and deducing consequences from them that can be empirically verified. However, there are certain necessary conditions that are conducive to their formulation.

1. Richness of background knowledge. A researcher may deduce hypotheses inductively after making observations of behaviour, noticing trends or probable relationships. For example, a classroom teacher daily observes student behaviour. On the basis of his experience and his knowledge of behaviour in a school situation, the teacher may attempt to relate the behaviour of students to his own, to his teaching methods, to changes in the school environment, and so on. From these observed relationships, the teacher may inductively formulate a hypothesis that attempts to explain such relationships.

Background knowledge, however, is essential for perceiving relationships among the variables and to determine what findings other researchers have reported on the problem under study. One finds limitless knowledge in almost any area of human pursuit which has accumulated in the form of literature as a result of the painstaking efforts of various researchers. New knowledge, new discoveries, and new inventions should always form a continuity with the already existing corpus of knowledge and, therefore, it becomes all the more essential to be well versed with the already existing knowledge. The researcher may be led astray, if he does not have thorough acquaintance with and mastery of the existing knowledge.

Relevant to a particular problem, various researchers may have different hypotheses but the soundness of the hypotheses will depend upon the quantum of knowledge that one possesses in the area of investigation. Significant researches have not taken place accidentally and if it be a mere accident to come across some important discovery, the researcher must have the rich background knowledge which may enable him to perceive that important discovery. Closed minds tend to see problems from a narrow and biased view point but liberal and objective educated minds look at them from multiple points of view suggested by their multiple experiences. Hypotheses may be formulated correctly by persons who have enriched experiences and academic background but they can never be formulated by those who have poor background knowledge.

2. Versatility of intellect. Hypotheses are also derived through deductive reasoning from a theory. Such hypotheses are called deductive hypotheses. A researcher may begin a study by selecting one of the theories in his own area of interest. After selecting the particular theory, the researcher proceeds to deduce a hypothesis from this theory through symbolic logic or mathematics. This is possible only when the researcher has a versatile intellect and can make use of it for restructuring his experiences. Creative imagination is the product of an adventure, a sound attitude and an agile intellect. In the hypotheses formulation the researcher works on numerous paths and he may be led to blind alleys and only rarely he may be led to the right path. The researcher, therefore, has to exercise great restraint and command considerable patience. He has to make a consistent effort and develop certain habits and attitudes. Moreover, the researcher has to saturate himself with all possible information about the problem and then ponder liberally over it and proceed further in the conduct of the study.

3. Analogy and other practices. Analogies also lead the researcher to clues that he might find useful, in the formulation of hypotheses and for finding solutions to problems. For example, suppose a new situation resembles an old situation with regard to a factor X. If the researcher knows from previous experience that the old situation is related to other factors Y and Z as well as to X, he reasons that perhaps a new situation is also related to Y and Z. The researcher, however, should use analogies with caution as they are not fool proof tools for finding solutions to problems.

Sometimes, conversations and consultations with colleagues and experts from different fields are helpful in formulating significant hypotheses.

Criteria of Usable Hypotheses

It is essential that hypotheses be carefully formulated. Travers (1978, pp. 76-78) has suggested seven criteria to which they should conform:

1. Hypotheses should be clearly and precisely stated. When hypotheses are clearly stated they usually avoid the use of general terms

such as personality, intelligence, social class, etc., in their statements. On the other hand, the researcher may use "personality as measured by the Sixteen Personality Factor Questionnaire," Intelligence as measured by Raven's Progressive Matrices," or "social class as defined by socio-economic status scale by Jalota." The clear statement of hypothesis generally involves concise technical language and definition of terms that are better defined than those in common language.

2. Hypotheses should be testable. Hypotheses should be formulated in such a way that they can be tested or verified. Such hypotheses enable the researcher to determine by observation whether these consequences that are derived deductively, actually do or do not occur. It the hypotheses are not testable, it would be impossible either to confirm or contradict them and therefore they do not help the researcher to draw conclusions. For example, the hypothesis: "The N.C.C. programme promotes the all-round adjustment of the high school students" would be hard to test because of the difficulty of defining and measuring "all-round adjustment". Moreover, it would be difficult for the researcher to isolate other factors that might contribute to the adjustment of high school students.

Since hypotheses are predictors of the outcome of the study, they must relate variables that are capable of being measured. It is essential that the tools or instruments should exist (or can be developed) which will provide measures of the variables involved. If no tools or means are available for measuring the variables, then it would be impossible for the researcher to collect the data necessary to test the validity of the hypotheses. A hypothesis, therefore should define the variables operationally by stating the operations or procedures necessary to measure them. For example, the hypothesis: "There is a negative relationship between neuroticism and achievement in mathematics of fifth grade students," meets the criterion of testability because the variables involved in the statement can be defined operationally. Neuroticism might be defined as "the scores made on the neuroticism stability scale of Maudsly personality inventory" and achievement in mathematics defined as "marks obtained in mathematics by the fifth grade students in their annual examination."

3. Hypotheses should state the expected relationship between variables. A satisfactory hypothesis should state explicitly an expected relationship between the variables. Let us consider two hypotheses:

(i) High school students who attend N.S.S. programmes show greater moral growth than students who do not.

(ii) Extroversion, as measured by the Maudsly Personality Inventory, will be related positively to achievement in social studies of seventh grade students, as measured by standardized test X.

The first hypothesis is not usable because the term "greater moral growth" does not refer to a variable that is measurable at the present time, or likely to be measured in the near future. On the other hand, the second hypothesis refers to the variables 'extroversion' and 'attainment in social studies' that can be measured by Maudsly Personality Inventory and the standardized test X respectively. Moreover, the relationship posited is that the personality variable and the attainment variable will be related positively.

4. Hypotheses should be limited in scope. Hypotheses of global significance are not usable as they are not specific and simple for testing and drawing conclusions from. A novice researcher, however, is overly ambitious in his initial efforts and formulates hypotheses of global significance. It is partly because of his earnestness and partly because it takes maturity of viewpoint to realize how little can be accomplished in a specified period. It is desirable to formulate hypotheses that are simple to test, and yet are highly significant. Sometimes it is, of course, possible to state a rather broad research hypothesis and derive a number of operational hypotheses from it.

5. Hypotheses should be consistent with most known facts. Hypotheses should not be inconsistent with a substantial body of established fact. They should be grounded in the well established theories and laws. Consider the hypothesis: "There is no relationship between the self concept of adolescent male students and their rate of physical growth." This hypothesis is not worth testing because the preponderance of evidence supports the relationship between self concept and rate of physical growth.

Hypotheses, however, cannot be consistent with all known facts because in so many areas the facts themselves contradict one another. In such cases it is worthwhile to formulate hypotheses that resolve the contradiction.

6. Hypotheses should be stated as far as possible in simple terms. Stating the hypotheses in simple terms not only makes their meaning clear to others, but also helps in their testability. Moreover, the simplicity of statement provides a basis for a clear and easily comprehended report after the completion of the study.

Hypotheses should not make use of the vague terms or constructs. It is quite useless to formulate a hypothesis that makes use of the terms or constructs which do to convey the intended meaning to the reader. The researcher should make use of such terms that are generally accepted for naming a phenomenon.

7. The hypotheses selected should be amenable to testing within a reasonable time. The researcher should not select a problem which involves hypotheses that are not amenable to testing within reasonable specified time. He must know that there are problems that cannot be solved for a long time to come. These are problems of immense difficulty that cannot be profitably studied because of the lack of essential techniques or measures.

Statement of the Hypotheses

A research or substantive hypothesis must be stated in a testable form for its proper evaluation. As already stressed this form should indicate a relationship between the variables in clear, concise, and understandable language.

Research hypotheses are classified as being directional or non-directional. The hypotheses which stipulate the direction of the expected differences or relationships are termed as directional hypotheses. For example, the research hypothesis: "There will be a positive relationship between individual's attitude towards high caste Hindus and his socio-economic status," is a directional research hypothesis. This hypothesis stipulates that individuals with favourable attitude towards high caste Hindus will generally come from higher socio-economic Hindu families and therefore it does stipulate the direction of the relationship. Similarly, the hypothesis: "Adolescent boys with high IQ will exhibit low anxiety than adolescent boys with low IQ" is a directional research hypothesis because it stipulates the direction of the difference between groups.

A research hypothesis which does not specify the direction of expected differences or relationships is a non-directional research hypothesis. For example, the hypotheses: "There will be difference in the adaptability of fathers and mothers towards rearing of their children" or "There is a difference in the anxiety level of adolescent girls of high IQ and low IQ" are non directional research hypotheses. Although these hypotheses stipulate there will be a difference, the direction of the difference is not specified.

A research hypothesis can take either declarative form, the null form, or the question form.

When the researcher makes a positive statement about the outcome of the study, the hypothesis takes the declarative form. For example, the hypothesis: "The academic achievement of extroverts is significantly higher than that of the introverts," is stated in the declarative form. In such a statement of hypothesis, the researcher makes a prediction based on his theoretical formulations of what should happen if the explanations of the behaviour he has given in his theory are correct.

In the null form, the researcher makes a statement that no relationship exists. The hypothesis, "There is no significant difference between the academic achievement of high school athletes and that of non-athletes," is an example of null hypothesis. Since null hypotheses can be tested statistically, they are often termed as statistical hypotheses. They are also called the testing hypotheses when declarative hypotheses are tested statistically by converting them into null form. This often happens in educational research.

A null hypothesis challenges the assertion of a declarative hypothesis and denies it altogether; it says that even where it seems to hold good it is due to mere chance. It is for the researcher to reject the null hypothesis by showing that the outcome mentioned in the declarative hypothesis does occur and the quantum of it is so much that it cannot be easily said to have occurred by chance. The criteria for rejecting the null hypothesis may differ. Sometimes the null hypothesis is rejected only when the quantity of the outcome is so big that the probability of its having occurred by mere chance is one time out of 100 or .01 time out of one. We consider the probability of its having occurred by chance to be too little and we reject the chance theory of the null hypothesis and take the occurrence to be due to a genuine tendency. On other occasions, we may be more bold and reject the null hypothesis even when the quantity of the reported outcome is likely to occur by chance five times out of 100 or .05 times out of one. Statistically the former is known as the rejection of the null hypothesis at .01 level of significance and the latter as the rejection at .05 level.

It may be pointed out that if the researcher is able to reject the null hypothesis, he cannot directly uphold the declarative hypothesis. If an outcome is not held to be due to chance, it does not mean that it is due to the very cause or effect relationship asserted in the particular declarative statement. It may be due to something else which the researcher may have failed to control. However, inferentially the case of the declarative hypothesis becomes quite strong. The less plausible the null hypothesis the more plausible the declarative one. Hayman (1968, p. 23) is of the opinion that null hypothesis should not be used as an alternative to the declarative hypothesis but should be used in combination with it for statistical purposes.

In the question form hypothesis, a question is asked as to what the outcome will be instead of stating what outcome is expected. Suppose a researcher is interested in knowing whether programmed instruction has any relationship to test anxiety of children. The declarative form of the hypothesis might be: "Teaching children through the programmed instruction material will decrease their test anxiety." This statement indicates that programmed instruction is related to test anxiety. The null form would be: "Teaching children through programmed instruction material will have no effect on their test anxiety". This statement shows that no relationship exists between programmed instruction and text anxiety. The question form puts the statement in the form: "Will teaching children through programmed instruction decrease their test anxiety?"

A novice in research finds it relatively easy to state a hypothesis in question form. It seems easy for him to write down all of the questions that he wants to answer in his study. On the other hand, he often experiences some difficulty in predicting the outcome of the study and stating the hypothesis in declarative form. However, it must be noted by the researcher that the question form is less powerful than the declarative or null form as a tool for obtaining valid information.

Testing of the Hypotheses

Hypotheses are possible explanations which account for the factors, events, or conditions that the researcher attempts to understand. After they are formulated according to the criteria discussed, they are subjected to empirical as well as logical testing:

1. Some hypotheses are simple and they can be tested directly. In most situations, however, they are complex and therefore cannot be tested directly. They have to be tested in terms of their deduced consequences. In scientific thinking process, the hypotheses involve deduction of consequences. Suppose a researcher wants to test the hypothesis: "Affluence leads to immorality"; he cannot test this hypothesis directly and he has to proceed indirectly. He might deduce the consequences emanating out of the situation of affluence, e.g., great consumption of liquor, thereby leading to loss of reason, giving rise to greater crime rates, adultery, fast driving, etc. It would then be considerably convenient to test the hypothesis in terms of its deduced consequences. Indirect method of handling research problems involve intricate and complex procedures. Intellectual and disciplined effort is needed for the deduction of consequences. In this way the researcher does not test the hypothesis but tests the deduced consequences of the

hypothesis. Once all the deduced consequences, after testing, come out to be true, the hypothesis is confirmed. If some of the consequences are true and certain others untrue, then the hypothesis will have to be examined afresh.

In order to test the hypothesis in terms of deduced consequences it is necessary to collect evidence by selecting or developing data collecting instruments, to analyze the data, and then to interpret results in the light of the hypothesis and its deduced consequences. Any hypothesis then will be confirmed if the evidence agrees with the deduced consequences.

The necessary conditions for confirmation are:

(a) All factual evidence collected through tests or other means should correspond with the deduced consequences.
(b) The test situation or data collecting tool should take into account all factors and conditions that are suggested by the consequences.
(c) The consequences are logically deduced from the hypothesis.

2. The absence of conflict with the other satisfactory proved generalizations lends support to the correctness of a hypothesis.

3. A hypothesis is also confirmed to be correct if the predictions made on its basis prove to be successful.

It is important for the researcher to formulate hypotheses before data are gathered. This is necessary for an objective and unbiased study.

References

Ary, D., Lucy C. Jacobs and Asghar Razavieh (1972), *Introduction to Research in Education* New York, Holt, Rinehart and Winston.

Beggas, Donald L. and Ernest L. Lewis, (1975), *Measurement and Evaluation in the Schools*, Boston, Houghton Mifflin Company.

Best, W. John, (1977), *Research in Education*, New Delhi, Prentice-Hall.

Gephart, William J and Robert B. Ingle, (1969), *Educational Research: Selected Readings*, Columbus, Ohio, Charles E. Merrie Publishing Co.

Good, Carter V., A.S. Barr and Douglas E. Seates (1941), *Methodology of Educational Research*, New York, Appleton-Century Crofts.

Good, Carter V., ed, (1959), *Dictionary of Education*, New York, McGraw-Hill, p. 149.

Good, Carter V., (1966), *Essentials of Educational Research: Methodology and Design*, New York, Appleton-Century Crofts.

Hillway, Tyurs, (1964), *Introduction to Research*, Boston: Houghton Mifflin Company.

Travers M.W., (1969), *An Introduction to Educational Research*, New York, The Macmillan Company.

Travers, M.W., (1973), *The Handbook of Research on Teaching*, Chicago, Rand McNally.

Travers, M.W., (1978), Introduction to Educational Research, New York, Macmillan Publishing Company.

Tuckman, B.W., (1972), *Conducting Educational Research*, New York, Harcourt Brace.

Chapter 7

Methods of Data Collection: Questionnaire and Schedule

K.D. Gangrade

Introduction

The heart of any research design is the collection of data. There are two sources of collecting data-the primary and the secondary. In the first, are the data directly collected from the respondent, whereas in the second the main source is published and unpublished material. This is often called library research as well. Most of the studies have found these sources very beneficial. Several devices are employed to collect primary data. In this paper we shall confine our discussion mainly to two tools and techniques: questionnaire and schedule. The specific preparation, construction and use of these tools will largely depend on aim, nature, scope and contour of the study.

Definitions

Questionnaires and schedules are designed to collect data from a group of people coming under the purview of the study. The questionnaire is designed to collect data from large, diverse and widely scattered groups of people. Thus, it is a device for securing answers to questions by using a form which the respondent himself fills in. This is usually mailed to the respondents or is administered to a group of people at the same time by giving them appropriate forms and collecting them later.

Reproduced from *Journal of Indian Law Institute*, 24 (4), 1982.

The schedule is referred to as a form filled in during a personal interview in which both the interviewer as well as the respondent are present. It contains a set of questions which are asked and then the columns are filled in by an interviewer in a face to face situation.

The two forms have much in common, particularly the fact that in both the cases the wordings of the questions are the same for all the respondents. However, at the same time there are important differences between the two methods. One distinction is based upon the predominant method of collection of data. The questionnaire is usually mailed to the respondents whereas the schedule is referred to as a form filled in during a personal interview. The impersonal nature of a questionnaire necessitates standardized wordings to ensure uniformity. It is much more rigid and less flexible than the schedule. Both the methods have their own advantages and disadvantages.

Advantages

Questionnaire

The questionnaire is likely to be a less expensive procedure than the interview as it is simply mailed to the respondents with a minimum of explanation. Further, the questionnaire can often be sent to a large number of individuals simultaneously; an interview, on the other hand, usually calls for questioning each individual separately. With a given amount of funds, it is usually possible to cover a wider area and obtain information from more people by means of questionnaires than by personally interviewing each respondent.

The impersonal nature of a questionnaire—its standardized wording, its standardized order of questions, its standardized instructions for recording responses—ensures some uniformity from one measurement situation to another. Another advantage of the same is that respondents may have greater confidence because of their anonymity, and thus feel more free to express views which they fear might be disapproved of or might land them into trouble. Sometimes, the questionnaire places less pressure on the subject for immediate response. When the subject is given ample time for filling in the questionnaire, he can consider each point carefully.

Schedule

A questionnaire requiring extended written responses can be used with only a very small percentage of the population as even many college graduates have little facility for writing, and of those who do, few have the patience or motivation to write as fully as they might speak. On the other hand, the schedule can be used with almost all segments of the population. Surveys conducted through personal interviews have an additional advantage over surveys conducted through mailed questionnaires in that they usually yield a much better sample of the general population and many people are willing and able to cooperate in a study where all they have to do is to talk. The proportion of returns in questionnaires is usually low, varying from about 10 to 50 per cent. Another advantage of the schedule is its greater flexibility. In a questionnaire, if the subject misinterprets a question or records his responses in a baffling manner, there is usually little that can be done to remedy the situation, whereas in the schedule, there is possibility of repeating or rephrasing questions to make sure that they are understood.

In addition, the interviewer is in a position to appraise the validity of reports. He is in a position to observe not only what the respondent says but also how he says it. Interview is a more appropriate technique for revealing information about complex, emotionally laden subjects or for probing the sentiments that may underlie an expressed opinion. In the interview situation, the "social atmosphere" can be varied in other ways. Behaviour in real life occurs in situations that are seldom free from social pressures. The interviewer can, for example, point out objections to the position taken by the person being interviewed, and observe how the latter responds. This flexibility has advantage, especially if the ultimate objective of the measurement is to predict behaviour in varied situations.

Choice of Instrument of Data Collection

The choice of a particular instrument of data collection will depend on the characteristics of the respondents as well as the field situation. Of course, the constraints of resources—trained personnel, funds and time—will continue to operate all along. In fact, every item in a questionnaire or a schedule constitutes a hypothesis or a part of a hypothesis in itself. It is, therefore, essential to decide which data are and which are not relevant. This judgment requires critical thinking, guided largely by past study and theory. For example, in a study of social background and social values of judges, one would be required to consider the information about climate or atmosphere as relevant. The hypothesis of the study will suggest the type of data needed, and the framework of argument will indicate the form they shall be in. The most important task for us to reach our cherished goal is to develop an instrument which would yield reliable and accurate data and be economical as well.

Types of Schedules and Questionnaires

The vast variety of questionnaires and schedules can be classified on the basis of their structuring. Structured questionnaires are those in which there are definite, concrete and preordained questions. The form of the questions may be either closed or open; the important point is that they are stated in advance, not constructed during the interview. They are used in a wide range of projects, both to initiate a formal inquiry and also to supplement and check data previously accumulated. The purpose of the inquiries may be to obtain social or economic information, to assess opinion on public issues or events, to study administrative policies and changes, and so on.

For some research problems, a still more flexible approach than that provided by a standardized interview with open-ended question is appropriate. Such interviews take various form and are under various names such as the "focused" interview, the "clinical" interview, the "depth" interview and the "non-directive" interview. They are commonly used for a more intensive study of perceptions, attitudes and motivations, etc., than a standardized interview. The flexibility of the unstructured or partially structured interview, if properly used, helps bring out the effective and value-laden aspects of the subjects and responses, and determine the personal significance of their attitudes. Ordinarily, no schedule is used for this purpose. In other words, the non-structured interview is an open situation in contrast to the standardized structured interview. This does not mean that an unstandardized interview is casual. It should be carefully planned as the standardized one. However, it is recognized that many research problems may, and often do, require a compromise type of interview in which the interviewer is permitted leeway to use alternate questions that he considers appropriate in respect of particular respondents and particular question.[1]

Essentials of a Good Instrument of Data Collection

The ingredients of a good questionnaire and schedule are: (a) clarity, (b) brevity, (c) unambiguity, (d) reliability, and (e) communicability. Direct questions should be avoided as far as possible. The language should be simple and easy to grasp. Too many ideas should not be put into one question. The best and correct information can be elicited by having one idea in one question. The sequence of the question should be logical and to the point. There should be adequate checks and balances in the question to ensure reliability and validity of the responses. Annoying questions must be avoided at all cost. The researcher and his sponsoring organization should be able to win the confidence of the respondents by establishing a good rapport, credibility and communicability with them.

The answers to questions are attitudinal and opinions are situational. They do not reflect values directly. An opinion may run counter to what a person is predisposed to believe because of pressures in the immediate situation. An opinion is often the complex resultant of many attitudes. For example, a large majority of the respondents were in favour of capital punishment when a survey was conducted immediately after the murder of Chopra children in Delhi. This was contrary to the opinion of a majority which was earlier in favour of abolition of the capital punishment. Similarly, attitudes derived from the value of personal integrity may call for rejection of wire tapping. But a belief that the community is in danger may bring other attitudes into play. The resultant opinion may accept wire tapping with some reservations. Where opinions reflect situational pressures, they may be held weekly as in the case of legislators or leaders who respond to group threats or to shifting climates of opinion. The legal system must safeguard itself from such pressures.

It must be remembered that public opinion is relatively unstable and fluctuates with changing situations. For instance, "Do you approve or disapprove the way Mrs. Indira Gandhi is handling her job as prime minister?" This type of question tends to reflect immediate pressure. Despite its instability, public opinion develops within a social setting. The more the setting is understood, the less arbitrary the shifts in opinion appear. Though, opinion emerges from day to day interaction, people have social background and group affiliation; they are not separate entities moving about at random. In any study, knowledge of the group structure of society is indispensable to proper understanding of public opinion. Opinions are affected by social experience, and the interaction of groups, varying in strength and activity, determines the weight and direction of public sentiments.

Studies on prediction of election returns have been considered an important achievement of modern social science. The polls have helped demonstrate that the behaviour of a large population can be studied through the sophisticated use of sampling techniques. This method and technique can be gainfully employed to ascertain as to how a small nation-wide sample can accurately reflect certain characteristics of the population as a whole. The implicit assumption here is that each respondent understood the question and answered it precisely from the same point of view as that of the person conducting the study. It is, therefore, very essential that words and concepts involved in the questions should be very clear and explicit. Questions having double meaning and a variety of interpretations must be avoided.

Process of Construction of Questionnaire

The entire process of construction of questionnaire can be divided into the following six steps:

(a) deciding what information should be sought,
(b) deciding what type of questionnaire should be used---structured or unstructured,
(c) writing the first draft,
(d) re-examining and revising questions,
(e) pre-testing, and
(f) editing the questionnaire and specifying procedures for its use.[2]

Question Content

In both questionnaire and interview schedule information is obtained by asking questions. Questioning is particularly suited to obtaining information about what a person knows or expects, feels or wants, intends or does or has done, and about his explanations of reasons for any of these. These major types of question content are discussed below. It is essential to remember, however, that questions do not always fall really into one or the other content type. The distinction among types are a matter of custom and convenience.

For Ascertaining Facts

Often the simplest and most economical method of obtaining facts is to go directly to the people who are in a position to know them and to ask for the desired information. It is reasonable to assume that people who have access to information, who are sufficiently intelligent to absorb it and who are motivated to acquire and retain it, are able, if they are willing, to provide the investigator with reports of many interesting and valuable facts. We may expect, for example, that the people who are responsible for the execution of a policy know what it is. Questions about the person's age, education, religion, income, nationality, marital status, occupation etc. are of this type.

For Ascertaining Beliefs about What the Facts Are

Instead of asking question to find out the objective facts from people, the investigator may wish to learn what people believe to be the facts, for example, in asking a respondent to indicate whether the following statement is true or false: Child marriages are taking place in spite of the Child Marriage Restraint Act 1929. Here the respondent's answer is not used to establish what is objectively true but to provide a picture of his beliefs.

For at Ascertaining Feelings

A person's belief about what the facts are, will often give clear indication of his feelings and desires. In questionnaires and schedules, perhaps the most common method of investigating feelings is to include items that bear directly on various possible emotional reactions like fear, distrust, disgust, contempt, hate, envy, sympathy, admiration etc.

For Ascertaining Standards of Action

An individual's definitions of appropriate behaviour in various social situations are of interest both as a reflection of the prevailing climate of opinion and as a basis for predicting his probable behaviour in such a situation. Definitions of appropriate action frequently have two components—ethical standards of what should be done, and practical considerations of what it is feasible to do. Questions may be directed towards either of these issues.

For Ascertaining Present or Past Behaviour

The present or past behaviour of any person is a type of fact that he himself is in a uniquely favourable position to observe. How a person has behaved in the past in a certain type of situation is, in the absence of contradictory evidence, an indication of what his future behaviour will be in a similar situation.

For Ascertaining Reasons for Beliefs, Feelings, Policies or Behaviour

Finally, the question may be aimed at obtaining the reasons the respondent is able to offer for his beliefs, feelings, policies or behaviour. In this the investigator is interested in finding out "why".

Question Sequence

Developing a questionnaire is moving from the "inside" outward.

What is meant by this is that the researcher should first lay out tentatively the logical implications of his problem and then draw upon his own experience and the literature for questions which are relevant to those logical implications. At this stage the researcher may consult his colleagues and others for their opinions. This would enable him to have a list of areas to be covered and perhaps some rough formulations of some of the areas. This total process is one of obtaining an even larger number of questions and of progressively uncovering omissions, biases and ambiguities.[3] The draft questionnaire---whether highly structured or unstructured—must be pre-tested.

Reported facts must always be evaluated in terms of credibility. The rules of evidence that have developed through the centuries in judicial procedure are a good source of insight into factors affecting credibility. It is always pertinent to raise such questions as: "How did the respondent obtain knowledge of the 'fact'—through direct observation, through inference, through hearsay, etc.? What motives may the respondent have in reporting the 'fact'? How accurate is the respondent's memory of the 'fact' likely to be"?[4]

Interview Schedule

Interviewing itself is an art, but the planning and writing of an interview schedule is all the more so. It is difficult to produce a good schedule without considerable prior study and practice. There are several reasons for this, the main one probably being the multiple meaning and ambiguity of words, the lack of sharp and constant focus on the problems and hypotheses being studies, a lack of appreciation of the schedules as a measurement instrument, and a lack of necessary background and experience.

The purpose of a schedule is to provide a standardized tool for observation or for interview in order to attain objectivity. By schedule every informant has to reply to the same question framed in the same language and the researcher cannot get the desired reply by asking a different question or changing the language of the same question. The order of the questions is also the same and thus the whole interview takes place under standardized conditions and the data received is easily comparable. The other purpose of the schedule is to facilitate the work of tabulation and analysis. In fact, the questions are formed while keeping the tabulation plan in mind.

Procedure for Framing a Schedule

While framing a schedule, the first question to be asked is, what are the different aspects of the problem? The problem under study should first of all be split up into its various aspects. The determination of these aspects will depend upon a clear understanding of the problem under study. The next question to be decided is, what information is necessary? For this purpose each aspect has again to be broken up into a number of sub-divisions. These sub-divisions should be exhaustive enough to give a full and complete picture of the aspect under study. The third step is the framing of actual questions. This part deals with the form and wordings of the questions. More than one question may be asked to get complete information about the particular aspect. When information cannot be secured through direct questions, indirect questions may be resorted to. This part is the most vital part of the schedule and any error in it may invalidate the whole enquiry through biased, incorrect, incomplete or irrelevant information. The fourth step is the general layout of the schedule and arrangement of questions. Once the questions have been given a definite form, the next problem is to arrange them in proper form. The last step is testing the reliability and validity of schedule. After the schedule has been prepared, it has to be tested on a sample population to find out if any discrepancies have crept in. Ultimately it may be amended in the light of the experience thus gained.

Contents of Schedule

The whole schedule may be divided into three parts according to the nature of contents: (1) Introductory part, (2) Main schedule, and (3) Instructions to the interviewer or observers.

(1) *Introductory Part*—This part contains introductory information about the schedule, investigation and respondent. It is more or less common to all the schedules and is called an identification data which deals with general information about the interviewee e.g., his name, address, age, sex, post held, education etc.

(2) *Main Schedule*—After the preliminary part comes the main portion of the schedule. It is the most vital part and has to be prepared with great care. The schedule consists of questions as well as blank tables where information to be supplied by the interviewee has to be filled in.

(3) *Instructions to Interviewers*—The schedule generally contains exhaustive instructions for the interviewers. Although they are personally instructed and even practically trained in the work, instructions in writing are necessary.

Type of Questions

The type of questions to be included in the schedule is the same as that of the questionnaire except for the fact that the frequency of open-ended questions may be increased. However, no hard and fast rule can be laid down for selection of the nature of questions to be asked. It all depends upon the individual nature of study—type of respondents, quality of field workers and other means of verifying the information.

The questions should be few, short, clearly worded, simple and easy to reply. They should be within the information scope of the respondent. While framing the questions, tabulation plan should be kept in mind. At places, indirect questions may be asked to get a correct reply. Interrelated questions may be asked to act as cross-checks. When questions seeking the degree of intensity of feelings or convictions are asked, questions beginning with why, what, when and how should also be included; but they must be properly rated or ranked to avoid confusion in later stages.

While framing questions for the interview schedule too, long, complex, personal, suspicious and leading question or questions should be avoided. Moreover, there should not be any embarrassing question or questions that are likely to yield inaccurate response.

Conclusions

The heart of any research design is collecting data. There are two sources of collecting data—primary and secondary. Primary data is collected mainly through questionnaire and interview schedule. The questionnaire is designed to collect data from large, diverse and widely scattered groups of people. This is usually mailed to the respondents or is administered to a group of people at the same time by giving them appropriate forms and collecting them later. The schedule is referred to as a form filled in during a personal interview in which interviewer as well as the respondent both are present and it contains a set of questions which are asked and filled in by an interviewer in a face to face situation. The two forms have much in common, particularly the fact that in both the cases, the wording of the questions is the same for all the respondents. However, at the same time there are important differences between the two methods. In a nutshell, both have their own advantages as well as disadvantages.

The choice of a particular instrument of data collection will depend on the characteristics of the respondents as well as the field situation. Both of these can be classified on the basis of their degree of structuring—structured having fixed alternatives of replies and unstructured having open-ended question. The essentials of a good questionnaire and schedule are clarity, brevity, unambiguity, reliability and communicability.

Notes

1. Fred N. Kerlinger, *Foundations of Behavioral Research* 481 (1973) (Surjeet Publication, Delhi).
2. Claire Selltiz, Marie Jahoda, Morton Deutsch, Stuart W. Cook, *Research Methods in Social Relations* 347 (Revised one-volume ed. 1964) (Holt, Rinehart and Winston, New York).
3. William J. Goode and Paul K. Hatt, *Method in Social Research*, 135-36 (International student ed. 1952) (McGraw-Hill Book Co., Inc., New York).
4. *Supra* note 2 at 244.

References

Deuold T. Campbell and Julian C. Stanley, *Experiment and Quasi-Experimental Designs of Research* (1966) (Rand McNally and Co., Chicago).

Edward A. Suchman, *Evaluative Research*, (1967) (Russel Sage Foundation, New York).

Ernest Nagel, *The Structure of Science: Problems in the Logic of Scientific Explanation*, (1961) (Harcourt, Brace and World, Inc., New York).

Gee Wilson, *Social Science Research Methods*, (1950) (Appleton-Century-Crafts, Inc., New York).

J.H. McGartle, *Research Methods and Designs for Education*, (1970), (International Text Book Co., Scranton Pa.).

Leonard Broom and Philip Selznick, *Sociology* (1973) (Harper and Row, New York).

Matilde White Riley, *Sociological Research I: Case Approach* (1963) (Harcourt, Brace and World, Inc., New York).
M.S. Gore, *Urbanization and Family Change*, (1968), (Popular Prakashan, Bombay).
Pauline V. Young, *Scientific Social Surveys and Research* (1968), (Prentice-Hall of India Pvt. Ltd., New Delhi).
Vimal Shah, *Research Designs and Strategies* (1972) (The Agricultural Development Council, New York).

Chapter 8

Spatial Sampling Design for an Urban Household Survey

G.S. Sastry

Introduction

With the increasing recognition of the importance of the spatial dimension in urban planning for optimum location and allocation of amenities and services to ensure better socio-economic life to the ubranites, necessitated the need for the data base at the urban spatial units level like wards, blocks, division or zones. It has been found that the available secondary data through census and city institutions is scanty and out-dated for any rigorous planning exercises that are being taken up by the urban planning authorities. Hence, the need for primary data, specially of the household sector at the urban spatial units level proved of vital importance for such new tasks of ecological nature. The complete enumeration of all households at the urban spatial units level for any urban area as a whole has proved almost impossible due to several constraints like time, cost and the availability of trained personnel, and hence the need for sampling techniques which assures data on the required characteristics for any required period at the urban spatial units level in the form of precise estimates was stressed upon. Thus the spatial sampling techniques acquired special significance in urban research and planning.

Bangalore, the capital and primate city of Karnataka, also a prominent city in the national system ranking second in airline connectivity, fifth in metropolitan functions and commercial activities, seventh in population, and a leading industrial, administrative and research centre has acquired special significance to study the structure and future thrust of its growth for efficient future planning purpose. Hence in 1973 an interdisciplinary urban research project of ecological nature was sponsored to identify the structure (social, economic, demographic and ecological), growth and other relevant characteristics of the city. For the study, the urban households formed the unit of study and hence, the obvious choice for the primary data collection was the well designed spatial sampling technique.

The present paper details the sampling design used for the urban household data collection, such as sampling frame, sample size, sampling technique used, vitality of the independent interpenetrating sub-sampling and self-weighting design techniques at the drawing up of samples and estimation stages, problems of urban household data collection and precautions to the future urban researchers, precautionary measures taken to reduce the non-sampling errors, non-response obtained by types and an attempt to reduce it by recall method, preliminary and final estimates of the selected household characteristics with the respective standard errors both at the spatial units level and at the study area as a whole respectively.

Sampling Frame

It is needless to mention that one of the main requirements for efficiently designing a sample survey is a well constructed sampling frame which is either a list of sampling units with identification particulars of map(s) showing the spatial boundaries of the sampling units. As the sampling frame forms the basic material from which the samples are drawn, it should be ensured that the frame is up-to-date and free from omissions and duplications. Normally such an usable frame is not readily available for any study area, and Bangalore city is not an exception. Preparation of such an usable frame is not customary due to time, cost and personnel constraints. At the time of the survey though the households lists were available from the census departments, the election commissioner and the food and civil supply departments were not used as they were not up-to-date.

The National Sample Survey Organization, Bangalore (NSSO, B) had just completed a survey, called "Urban Frame Survey" for Bangalore Urban Agglomeration (Bangalore city + CITB layouts + Townships) with an aim to prepare an up-to-date sampling frame spatially. In this survey, Bangalore urban agglomeration has been divided into 144 investigators' units (IV units) based on the number of households (one IV unit = 3,000 households on an average). These IV units are arranged contiguously and numbered in a spiral fashion starting from the north-west corner of the city periphery (Jalahalli) towards the city centre (Chikpet). Again these IV units are divided into 2,956 blocks called urban frame survey blocks (UFS blocks) based on the number of households (one UFS block = 150 households on an average). The number of UFS blocks in different IV units varied from 48 (IV unit No. 8, HAL Sanitary Board) to 1 (IV unit No. 23, Industrial Estate). The UFS blocks in each IV unit are also arranged contiguously and numbered in a spiral fashion starting from the north-west corner. The UFS blocks so designed by the NSSO was up-to-date and spatially arranged to provide even spatially distributed samples and hence, the estimates on the required characteristics at the spatial units level, was found to be the most ideal sampling frame for the envisaged urban household survey.

Sample Size

In surveys, normally, the optimum sample size is fixed by striking a balance between the precision and representation on the one hand, and time and cost constraints on the other. Thus the most important determinants of sample size for any survey are: (1) the time and cost availability, and (2) the degree of precision required for the estimates of the required characteristics. Though several methods like cost and precision functions are designed by many scholars: McHugh (1961), Thompson (1961), Murthy (1963), Mace (1964) and others, normally simple cost and time balancing method will be used keeping in view the representativeness for the fixation of the sample size.

In the present survey, the time available for the fieldwork was 150 man-days and had budget provision for 10 full time investigators. This worked out as 1,500 man-days for field work. Based on the pilot listing of households, it was decided to select 150 UFS blocks as first stage units (5% sample) which would take 500 man-days for identification, listing and scrutiny of JFS blocks and households respectively. With the remaining 1,000 man-days, it was decided to select a sample of 2,000 households (0.67%) with an aim to cover two sample households per man-day. Thus a sample of 150 UFS blocks and 2,000 households were fixed at the first and second stages respectively.

Two-Stage Systematic Sampling

Systematic sampling, a more frequently used design in large scale surveys due to its operational convenience, specially when the sampling units are arranged in some order, was found to be the most suitable design here due to the contiguous circular spatial arrangement of the first stage units (UFS blocks), which would provide even spatially distributed samples, an important requisite for ecological study, and workability and operational convenience. In the present study, the same sample design has been used separately, for the two planning areas: (1) the city corporation area and CITB layouts, and (2) the townships for planning implications.

Selection of UFS Blocks

The corporation areas—CITB layouts and the townships had 2,754 and 202 UFS Blocks each from which 134 and 16 blocks had to be drawn systematically in the form of two independent interpenetrating sub-samples of 67 and eight blocks each respectively, in order to keep an over-all check on the estimates, reduce sampling and non-sampling errors, and specially to simplify the estimation procedures of mean and variance.

As the sampling interval (K) and the random start(r) completely determine the sampling units of the study, the same were derived (Table 1).

Table 1

Sampling interval and random start by sub samples and planning area

Planning Area	*Sub-sample 1*		*Sub-sample 2*	
	Sampling Interval	*Start*	*Sampling Interval*	*Random Start*
Corporation Area-CITB Layouts	41	18	41	2
Townships	25	5	25	11

With the chosen random starts, two sets of interpenetrating sub-samples of 67 and 8 UFS blocks each were chosen by selecting every 41st and 25th units systematically. All the selected UFS blocks were identified (Fig. 1) using the maps provided by the NSSOB, and the listing of all the households in each of the selected UFS block was done starting from the north-west corner.

Selection of Households

In the multi-subject surveys like the present one, there will be several parameters to be estimated by inflating the respective sample totals by

FIGURE 1

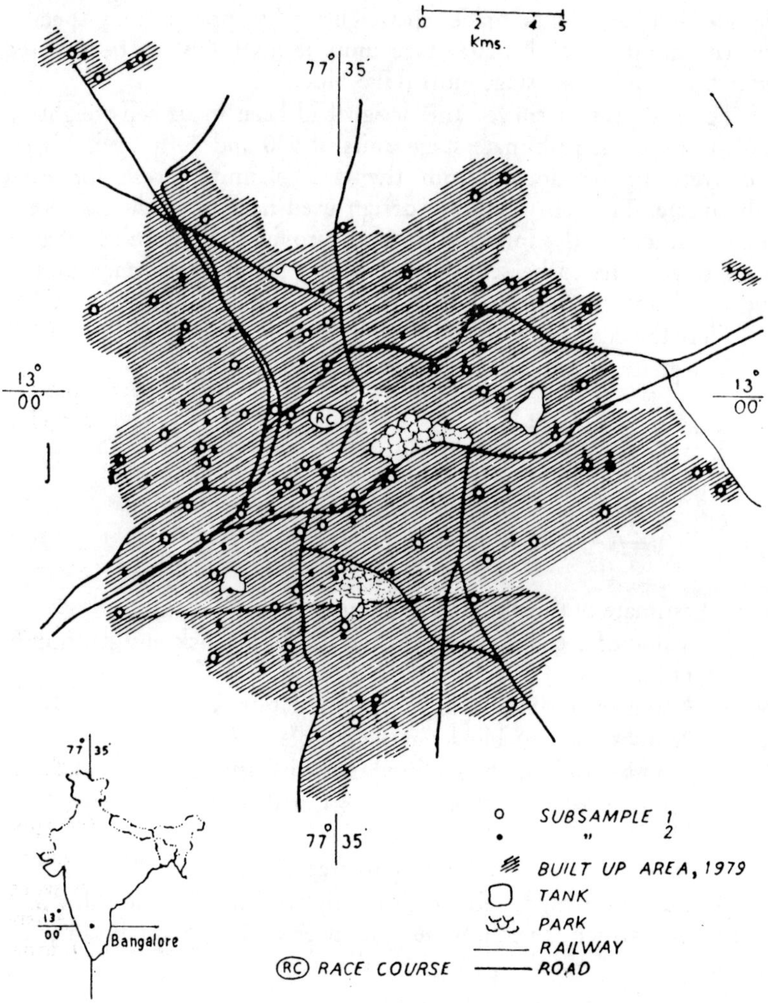
0 2 4 5
Kms.
77° 35'
13° 00'
13° 00'
RC
77° 35'
77° 35'
13° 00'
Bangalore
SUBSAMPLE 1
" 2
BUILT UP AREA, 1979
TANK
PARK
RAILWAY
ROAD
RC RACE COURSE

some weight which depends on the selection and estimation procedures of the design. As the inflation process at the estimation stage becomes heavy, time consuming and costly, a design which can take care of the problem of weighting by supplying a single common weight for all the sample units is the need of the hour. The multi-stage design used here can be made self-weighting by appropriately specifying the number of ultimate stage units (households) to be selected from the penultimate stage units (UFS block).

For the present survey the design had been made self-weighting with the specified ultimate stage units of 930 and 70 households respectively to be drawn from the two planning areas for each sub-sample. The self-weighting design used here, in addition to the simplification of the inflation process, provides the number of ultimate stage units to be selected from each penultimate stage unit, a special advantage of the design.

Here the design is made self-weighting as follows:

The general estimator for the two-stage sampling is

$$\underline{\hat{Y}} = \frac{N}{n} \sum_{i=1}^{n} \frac{M_i}{m_i} \sum_{J=1}^{mi} y_{oj}$$

$$\underline{\hat{Y}} = \lambda \sum_{i} \sum_{j} y_{ij}$$

$\underline{\hat{Y}}$ = estimate of the population parameter $\underline{Y}$

y_{oj} = Value of a characteristic in the *i*th UFS block and jth household.

N = Number of UFS blocks in the population

n = Number of UFS blocks in the sample

M_i = Number of households listed in the ith selected UFS block

m_i = Number of households to be selected from ith selected UFS blocks

λ = Inverse of the overall sampling fraction

The design is made self-weighting by working out the value of λ in advance, which is nothing but the inverse of the overall sampling fraction i.e.,

$$\lambda = \frac{\text{Total households in the population}}{\text{Total sample households}}$$

The self-weighting design worked out for the two areas are tabulated (Table 2).

Table 2

Self-weighting design by planning area

Planning area	*Weighting factor*
Corporation area CITB Layouts	320
Townships	705

Having made the design self-weighting, the number of households to be selected from each UFS block was computed from the formula:

$$m_i = \frac{1}{\lambda} \frac{N}{n} M_i$$

At the second stage, the number of households from each selected UFS block were drawn using simple random sampling without replacement.

The sample number of first stage units (UFS block) and the second stage units (households) derived using the self-weighting design by sub-samples are detailed in Table 3.

Table 3

Distribution of sample UFS blocks and households by sub-samples

Planning Area	*Sub Sample 1*		*Sub Sample 2*		*Total*	
	UFS blocks	*House-holds*	*UFS blocks*	*House-holds*	*UFS blocks*	*House-holds*
Corporation area-CITB Layout	67	970	67	980	134	1950
Townships	8	55	8	95	16	150
Total	75	1025	75	1075	150	2100

Problems of Urban Data Collection

The problems of urban data collection especially primary data are becoming very acute due to rapid changes in urban life style, time conscious respondents and pseudo-investigations etc. Our field experience clearly revealed some salient features of the respondents' behaviour.

The respondents were normally suspicious in nature due to the surprise visit of our investigators, though the latter were equipped with the proper identification letter from the project director, and a covering letter addressed to the respondent detailing the objective of the survey and the co-operation solicited. Even then some investigators were not even allowed to enter the household premises due to their earlier pseudo-investigation experiences. In some households, though the respondents were willing to respond positively, did not do so, due to the paucity of time, and hence resulted in partial non-response. The earlier pseudo-investigations experienced by the respondents of a sample UFS block, has resulted in the most severe consequences to one of our field staff and hence the whole UFS block of about 25 households ended up with non-response. Later it was ascertained that these 25 households do not affect in any way the final estimates of the selected characteristics. The other problem faced by us was the wrong identification of a sample UFS block by an investigator which was immediately identified and rectified by the senior project member to avoid the possible effects on the final estimates. Another routine problem in surveys is, of course, non-response which is dealt with separately in the next section.

The problems of urban primary data collection detailed above thus warrant for the following precautionary measures to be taken by future urban researchers like

(1) The project director has to undertake an extensive publicity of the project through mass and informal media, and also by meeting the local leaders before the commencement of the project. This would definitely improve the response rate due to the awareness and authenticity,
(2) The project director has to take special care in designing the schedule or questionnaire to suit the time conscious urban respondents to get precise and 100 per cent information, and
(3) The project director has to train the field staff thoroughly, so that the investigator can explain the purpose and the type of data needed under each item of the questionnaire to the respondent in a convincing manner without any ambiguity.

Measures Taken to Reduce Non-Sampling Errors

The non-sampling errors which can creep in at any and every stage of the project, needs tighter control measures to minimize them. In the present project the measures were taken at all the stages—questionnaire designing and training, field work, and the data processing.

Questionnaire Designing and Training

While designing the questionnaire, many questions were precoded to avoid the possible delay and response errors. The field staff were given thorough orientation about the objectives of the project, and the purpose, and the type of data required under different headings in the questionnaire. The field staff were taken to the households by the senior project members to demonstrate the method of data collection and its recording before entrusting the full responsibility of the required data collection from the urban households.

Field Work

For the urban household survey, the sample of 2,000 households fixed were to be drawn in the form of two independent interpenetrating sub-samples of 1,000 households each to carry out the survey more efficiently under the supervision of two independent field teams. The questionnaire filled by the investigators were immediately scrutinized by the senior project members using some built in controls and were sent back to rectify the inconsistencies found there on. Thus the number of visits made by the investigators to the respondents varied from 1 to 4. Meanwhile the senior project members used to conduct tighter field supervision followed by the surprise visits and random checks to the sample households to keep track of authentic data base. After the completion of the field work, the household data were checked for consistency and authenticity based on the 5 per cent post enumeration check. The household questionnaire designed for the survey contained 629 items covering various aspects of the urban households, and the time taken to fill in also varied from 20 minutes to 4 hours 15 minutes with the modal time of one hour.

Data Processing

As the errors are more likely in the data processing stage, it needs tighter control measures to minimize them. Here, the scrutiny procedures were designed at the following three stages;

(1) scrutiny of data transferred from questionnaires to code sheets,
(2) scrutiny of data transfers from code sheets to computer cards, and
(3) scrutiny of data on magnetic tapes by computer programmes written for the various checks.

In the first two cases scrutiny was carried out by checking the data and using the verifying machine. But these methods did not eliminate the errors totally. Hence, about eight computer programmes were written to check alpha characters, to avoid the duplicate data sets, to correct the mistakes that occurred while correcting to check the valid range of code in each column and finally to identify the inconsistencies using the built in controls in the questionnaires. After the correction the data was stored in magnetic tapes for easy access.

Non-Response

One of the main visible source of errors in survey is incomplete coverage due to many reasons like refusal to answer, not-at-home, not-located, and wrong identification. Incomplete coverage specially from a particular group as a whole (high income, certain caste groups etc.), will have serious impact on the final estimates and hence rigorous attempts are required to reduce it. Though Hanson and Hurvitz (1946), Polintz and Simmon (1949) and other scholars have developed some techniques to reduce its rate, it still persists.

Here, household survey resulted in 11 per cent non-response, which was well distributed over the population. Though there is no safe limit to the non-response, its rate depends on the chosen characteristics and their distribution. The different types of non-response by size and sub-sample is detailed in Table 4.

Table 4

Distribution of non-respondents by types of non-response and sub-samples

Non-Response Type	*Number of Households*		
	Sub-sample 1	*Sub-sample 2*	*Total*
Refused to answer	46	71	117
Not-located	40	16	56
Not at home	13	7	20
Locked/vacant house	12	7	19
Others-vacant site, hostel/ashram/ shop (converted after the listing)	11	4	15
Total	122	105	227

From the reported non-response types, the category 'others' had been excluded, and a sample of size 15 per cent was fixed for re-survey. The re-survey was conducted by the senior project member and separate estimates were computed.

Estimates

To test the efficiency of the design, and also to get the estimates on some selected household characteristics, a series of estimates was computed at different levels.

Preliminary Estimates of Households

Based on the listing of the households in the selected UFS blocks the total number of households in the two planning areas were estimated using the estimator.

$$\hat{\underline{Y}}_k = \frac{\underline{N}}{\underline{n}} \sum_{i=1}^{\hat{}} \underline{M}_{ik}$$

$$\hat{\underline{Y}} = \frac{1}{\underline{K}} \sum_{k=1}^{2} \hat{\underline{Y}}_k$$

k = 1, 2

Relative Standard Error is given by

$$SE\ (\hat{Y}) = SQR\left[\frac{(\hat{\underline{Y}}_1 - \hat{\underline{Y}}_2)^2}{4}\right]$$

$$RSE\ (\hat{Y}) = \frac{SE\ (\hat{Y})}{\hat{\underline{Y}}}$$

Table 5

Preliminary estimates of households by planning area

Planning area	*Estimates*	*RSE*
Corporation area CITB layout	298,366	0.38
Townships	22,599	0.41

The preliminary estimates provided by the design was more precise and hence, the design was found to be an efficient one.

Estimates at the Spatial Units Level

To provide greater insight on the structure of the different parts of the city to the city planning authorities, estimates of some selected characteristics like population and occupation by broad service groups were worked out (Table 6).

Table 6

Zonewise estimates of population and workers by type

Zone	Population (in '000)	Basic	Neighbourhood	Local	Metropolitan	Total
1.	41	3,258	340	5,114	170	8,882
2.	170	13,940	5,270	16,830	3,074	39,114
3.	65	3,102	170	1,530	340	5,142
4.	118	9,886	1,374	8,810	170	20,240
5.	145	5,624	2,734	10,100	538	18,996
6.	183	6,134	5,780	12,410	2,890	27,214
7.	157	28,914	3,060	16,150	5,950	54,074
8.	159	12,240	1,530	5,440	510	19,720
9.	249	18,034	2,380	15,640	850	36,904
10.	320	53,904	10,200	46,948	9,520	120,572
11.	214	41,224	4,930	27,256	8,854	82,264
12.	35	30,590	354	1,586	170	32,700
13.	12	19,418	170	184	0	19,772
14.	58	28,196	524	3,284	0	32,004

It was found that these estimates were very close to the parametric values.

Estimates at the City Level

The following households and persons characteristics like number. of persons by sex, number. of couples, migrants by types, literacy by types, workers by types, households in different income groups and house tenure were selected to get the estimates. The estimates and standard errors for the selected characteristics were given by the estimator:

Total:

$$\underline{\hat{Y}}_1 = \lambda \sum_i \sum_j y_{ij1}$$

$$\underline{\hat{Y}}_2 = \lambda \sum_i \sum_j y_{ij2}$$

$$\underline{\hat{Y}} = \frac{\underline{\hat{Y}}_1 + \underline{\hat{Y}}_2}{2}$$

Standard Error

$$SE\ (\hat{Y}) = SQR \left[\frac{(\hat{Y}_1 - \hat{Y}_2)^2}{4} \right]$$

$$RSE\ (\hat{Y}) = \frac{SE\ (\hat{Y})}{\hat{Y}}$$

The final estimates were derived by pooling the primary and non-response estimates. The estimates worked out for all the selected characteristics were precise as their respective relative standard errors were low (Table 7).

Table 7

Estimates of selected urban characteristics

Characteristics (Persons/Households)	*Estimate*	*Relative Standard error*
Persons:		
Male	922,080	0.96
Females	874,480	0.93
Total	1,796,560	0.04
No. of couples	312,245	7.95
Residential status of household head:		
Resident	114,070	1.04
Rural migrant	88,910	5.93
Urban migrant	93,160	3.28
Outside the country	2,210	23.08
Total	294,610	1.67
Unemployed persons by education:		
No education	3,230	26.31
Upto Secondary/PUC/Inter or less	27,710	12.88
Graduate and above	8,840	26.92
Total	39,780	17.09
Workers:		
Professional	54,570	21.49
Administrative	24,990	12.92
Clerical	78,540	14.72
Sales	58,140	4.67
Service, production and related	260,100	10.98
Total	476,510	1.03
Household in the income classes:		
Less than 299	71,740	15.64
300-749	145,180	7.02
750-999	27,030	16.98
1000+	50,660	23.48
House tenure:		
Owned	107,270	0.79
Rented	187,850	0.27

Notes

1. The interdisciplinary project was sponsored by the Indian Council of Social Science Research, New Delhi and the Government of Karnataka jointly in 1973.
2. The grid sampling which does not require a formal household lists in an up-to-date form and which provides tighter spatial control had been attempted first, but due to the non-availability of the standard procedure to get the optimum grid size, it was discarded.
3. The stratified two stage sampling based on the ecological stratification (core, intermediary, periphery) was attempted, but the stratification based on the ecological grouping found inefficient for an inter-disciplinary multi-subject survey like this, and hence discarded.

References

Cochran, W.G., (1953), *Sampling Techniques*, John Wiley and Sons, New York.

Deming W.E., (1960), *Sampling-Design in Business Research*, John Wiley and Sons, New York.

Hansen, M.H. and Hurwitz, W.N., (1946), "*The Problem of Non-response in Sample Surveys*", *JASA* 41, r517-528.

John, Holmes, (1967), "Problems in Locational Sampling, *AAAG*, 57, 757-780.

Mace, A.E., (1964), *Sample Size Determination*, Chapman and Hall, London.

McHugh, R.B., (1961), "Confidence Interval Inference on Sample Size Determination," *American Statistician* 15(2), 14-17.

Murthy, M.N., (1963), "A Note on the Determination of the Sample Size," *Sankhya* 25(A), 381-382.

Murthy, M.N., (1967), *Sampling Theory and Methods*, Statistical Publication Society, Calcutta.

Politz, A and Simmons, W., (1949), "An Attempt to Set the Not-at-home into the Sample Without Call Back, *JASA*, 44, 9-31.

Prakasa Rao, V.L.S. and Tewari, V.K., (1969), *Structure of an Indian Metropolis: Bangalore*, Allied, New Delhi.

Roger, A., (1974), *Statistical Analysis of Spatial Dispersion*, Pion limited, London.

Tewari, V.K., (1978), "A Model of Bangalore Metropolis", mimeographed, Institute for Social and Economic Change, Bangalore.

Thompson, Jr. W.A. (1961), "The Required Sample Size when Estimating the Variances", *American Statistician*, 15(3), 22-23.

Chapter 9

Measurement Through Scaling Methods

Laxman Swaroop

In general, measurement can be defined as the assignment of a class of numerals to a class of objects (Large, 1951). In the usual case this is simple enough. For example, the class of individual persons who reach the same point on a ruler may be called six feet tall. Those coming on certain distance below it are placed in a different class. The classes here are defined in terms of height. The numerals assigned to each class have certain relationships with each other that are crucial in speaking about height and that allow us to make certain statements, for example, to the effect that A is twice as tall as his son, or that he is taller than his wife to the same extent that she is taller than the son. Obviously, such properties do not always apply in the case of measurement. Thus, it does not make much sense to say that A is twice as adjusted emotionally as B.

Although there is little doubt that quantification facilitates the establishment of scientific laws, it should be recognized that measurement exists in a variety of forms. Sometimes, measurement has been defined so as to exclude methods of data collection that permit only qualitative discriminations. For example, McGregor (1955) defined measurement as "the process of assigning numbers to represent qualities." Other writers, such as Weyl (1949), Stevens (1946,

---

Reproduced from Tandon, B.C. (ed) *Research Methodology in Social Sciences*, Chaitanya Publishing, Allahabad.

1951), and Coombs (1953), have included in their concept of measurement any empirical procedure that involves the assignment of symbols, of which numerals are only one type, to objects or events according to rules.

The purpose of measurement is to make the events or objects being analyzed amenable to mathematical description and analysis.

Definition should tell us the conditions or circumstances under which we should make observations. Measurement is the way we get symbols to represent the properties of objects or events. In a restricted sense, it involves the use of a constant unit of measurement.

In measurement, there are four critical properties of relations between variables: reflexivity, symmetry, transitivity, and connectivity. A relationship is reflexive if it holds between a thing and itself, for example, if we can use the = sign in case of real numbers, if we can state as to human beings that A resembles B or if we can say 'is similar to' regarding geometric elements such as planes. A relationship is symmetric if, in relating one thing to another, it similarly relates the second to the first, as is true of 'is married to' in a monogamous society. A relationship is transitive if, where it holds between the first thing and a second and between the second and third, it also holds between the first and third. A relationship is connected if it applies to every pair of elements whether taken in one order or another order.[1] Unless we are careful we shall make unwarranted assumptions as to the status of the variables in our research with respect to these four critical properties.

Measurements, whether nominal, ordinal, internal or ratio, are of little significance unless there is some knowledge of the accuracy of the measurement. With such knowledge it is possible to employ controls to keep the margin of error within predetermined limits. The range of uses for a measurement increases with the exactness of the measurement.

Principles of Measurement

Let us examine, for a moment, what is involved in the instruction and evaluation of any measurement tool. We shall take as our example an ordinary ruler.

(i) *Unimentionability*: This means that the scale should be about one thing at a time, as purely as possible. Thus, the ruler should measure length, not temperature or viscosity. In the case of attitude scales, problems arise because the manifest contents of the items may be a poor guide to what the items actually measure. We need correlation techniques to find out how the items 'hang together' and which of them are 'purest'.

(ii) *Linearity*: This means that the scale should follow the straight line model and that some sort of scoring system should be devised, preferably one based on inter-changeable units. Such units are convenient to handle statistically, though they may be psychologically dubious. With a ruler, it is relatively easy to make sure that it is straight rather than bent and that it is marked in equal units of inches or centimeters. Attitude scales assure the straight line model (though this may not be adequate), but the creation of scoring units is difficult, and they are, at best, of doubtful inter-changeability. An inch is an inch, whether it lies at one end of the ruler or at the other, but numerically similar attitude scale differences may represent very different psychological distinctions. Also, how can we ensure comparability of units from one attitude to another? For both these reasons, ranking is often preferable when constant scale units are hard to come by.

(iii) *Reliability*: This is the indispensable attribute of consistency. If the same measure were applied to the same object today and next week, the results should be near-identical (unless a real change in the object has meanwhile taken place). A ruler can be applied, say, to the leg of a table and the results, for all practical purposes, will be quite consistent over time. The greater length and diversity of attitude scales make them more reliable than single questions, but even so, complete consistency is difficult to achieve; people are bound to react somewhat differently to a scale when they are confronted by it a second time. Nevertheless, reliability coefficients of 80 or higher are quite common.

(iv) *Validity*: This tells us whether the scale measures what it is supposed to measure. We may have obtained unidimensionality by keeping only those items which inter-correlate highly, yet the scale may not measure what we want it to measure. Instead of measuring authoritarianism, for instance, it may just be a measure of acquiescence. Sometimes, it is possible to correlate the new scale with an older, well established one. At other times, it may be possible to use criterion groups, such as membership in religious congregations or political parties, between which the scale should be able to distinguish but behaviour is often not a simple manifestation of an underlying attitude, and so there is no way of making sure that an attitude scale is valid.

(v) *Reproductibility*: When we say that a man weighs 150 pounds, we meant that the pointer on the scale will move from 0 to 150, but will cover none of the remainder; in other words, the figure of 150 refers, not to just any odd 150 pound units, but to the first 150 pounds on the scale. From the 'score' of 150, we can reproduce exactly which units on the scale were covered and which were not. This is not an essential requirement when we are dealing with constant and interchangeable units, such as pounds or inches; but if we are dealing, say, with the symptoms of the different stages of an illness it would be helpful if they could be ordered or scaled in terms of their degree of seriousness in such a way that the presence of symptom D would mean that the patient also must have symptoms A, B and C. Similarly, a score on an attitude scale might show us, by means of a single figure, which statements the respondent agreed with and which he disagreed with, thus telling us his place on the attitude continuum. This is a requirement that in practice is difficult to achieve, for many attitude pools are not amenable to this kind of cumulative or progressive scaling partly because they may not be unidimensional.

Apart from these main requirements, there may be others. For instance, it is helpful to have norms or standards derived from the scores of large number of respondents, so that we can compare an individual's score with those of others and interpret its meaning.

Scale Score

For a given population of objects, the multivariate frequency distribution of a universe of attributes is called a scale if it is possible to derive from the distribution a quantitative variable with which to characterize the objects such that each attribute is a simple function of the quantitative variable. In this definition, the 'population of objects' refers to a class of objects of an investigation. The 'universe of attributes' refers to a class of qualitative variables associated with these objects that is defined to study. These variables may be any type of qualitatively recorded observations, not necessarily restricted to attitudes. The quantitative variable that is derived in this manner is called a 'scale score'.

Various researchers have classified the scales into various groups. S.S. Stevens has mentioned four types of scales, namely, the nominal, the ordinal, the interval and the ratio scales.

Nominal Scales

One of the dictionary definitions of nominal is "of, pertaining to, or consisting in a name or names." A nominal scale is one that consists of two or more named categories into which objects or individuals or responses are classified. The basic requirement of a nominal scale is that one should be able to distinguish two or more categories relevant to the attribute being considered and specify criteria for placing individuals, etc. in one or another category. The only specified relationship between the categories is that they are different from each other; there is no implication that they represent "more" or "less" of the characteristic being measured. The empirical operation is the decision that a given object, individual, or response belongs to a given category or that it does not; in other words, it is the determination of equivalence or non-equivalence, with respect to the attribute in question, between the given object and other objects placed in a given category[2]. Classification of individuals according to nationality, for example, constitutes a nominal scale.

For convenience, numbers may be used to identify the categories in such a scale, but they are used only in the way that letters or words would be; there is no empirical relation among the numbered categories that corresponds to the mathematical relation between the numbers assigned. Therefore, statistical techniques that make use of mathematical relations among numbers (such as the computation of means or correlation coefficient, for example) are inappropriate; one may use only such statistics as are appropriate to counting; for example, the number of cases, the mode, the coefficient of contingency and the chi-square.

Use of Nominal Scale: Use of nominal scales is characteristic of exploratory research, where the emphasis is on uncovering a relationship between two characteristics rather than on specifying, with some degree of precision, the mathematical form of relationship; or where the focus of the study is on the pattern of relationship among several characteristics of the person. However, if the data permit the ordering of people in terms of a characteristics, it is uneconomical to use a nominal scale, since such a scale severely limits the nature of the conclusions that can be drawn. Evidently, a good deal of data can be handled by means of the nominal scale. The predictions of many political opinion polls, such as the Gallup Poll, are often made on the basis of contingency tables constructed in this way. The nominal scale is thus a useful type of measurement, although it is limited in comparison with other scales.

Ordinal Scales

One of the most commonly used scales in psychology and behavioural sciences is the ordinal or rank order scale.

An ordinal scale defines the relative position of objects or individuals with respect to a characteristic, with no implication as to the distance between positions. The basic requirement of an ordinal scale is that one should be able to determine, for each individual or object being measured, whether that individual has more of the attribute in question than another individual, or the same amount, or less; in other words one must be able to determine the order of position. This pre-supposes that one must be able to place each individual at a single point with respect to the attribute in question. If the attribute or the measuring procedure is such that one can say, "In some respects A has more of this attribute than B, but in other respects he has less", the two men cannot be placed in relation to each other on a single ordinal scale. Difficulties of this sort are not uncommon in the social sciences. The ability to place a given individual at a single position is a prerequisite for the more powerful scales as well.

An ordinal scale is like an elastic tape measure that is being stretched unevenly; the scale positions as indicated by the numbers of the tape are in a clearly defined order, but the numbers do not provide a definite indication of the distance between any two points. With ordinal scales we are limited to statements of greater, equal or less; we cannot undertake to state how much greater or how much less.

An example of an ordinal scale in the physical sciences is the Moh's scale of hardness, which is applied to minerals. The empirical relation in this case is the ability of minerals to scratch one another. A diamond is ranked highest on this scale, since it can scratch all other known minerals but none can scratch it; however, the scale does not assert anything about how much harder a diamond is than other minerals.

When the operation by which objects or individuals are placed on scale involves direct comparison of the individuals in terms of the extent to which they possess the attribute in question, it is easy to see that the scale reflects only the order of positions and not the distances between them. This is the case, for example, in a spelling bee, or in a teacher's ranking of children in terms of cooperativeness or in the judgment of the relative desirability of applicants for a job.

However, when the data needed for placing the individual are gathered by an instrument that yields a numerical score, the fact that one may still be dealing only with an ordinal scale is sometimes obscured. Suppose that three individuals taking a spelling test or an attitude questionnaire receive scores of 100, 80 and 60, respectively.

Our knowledge of mathematical relations may dispose us to think that the person who scores 100 is as much higher than one who scores 80 as the latter is above the one who scores 60. But unless we have reason to believe that the distance between 80 and 100 represents the same amount of the attribute being measured as does the distance between 60 and 80, these scores indicate only that the first person ranks higher than the second and the second higher than the third.

The rank order scale has two properties—asymentry and transitivity. By asymentry we mean that we can make the following types of statements:

$\underline{A} = \underline{B}$ or $\underline{A} > \underline{B}$ or $\underline{B} > \underline{A}$

By transitivity the following types of statements can be made:

If $\underline{A} > \underline{B}$
and $\underline{B} > \underline{C}$
then $\underline{A} > \underline{C}$

It is important to note that transitivity does not always hold true.

The statistics applicable to data that permit only rank ordering are limited. It addition to those applicable to nominal scales, one may, strictly speaking, use only such statistics as medians, percentiles, and rank order correlations. During recent years there has been a rapid expansion of statistical tests appropriate to data that are simply ranked or ordered.

Interval Scales

On an interval scale, not only are the positions arranged in terms of greater, equal, or less, the units or intervals of measurement are also equal. In other words, the distance between the positions labelled one and two on the scale is equal to the distance between positions two and three, etc. The basic empirical operation for the establishment of such a scale is a procedure for determining that intervals are equal. The fahrenheit and centigrade thermometers are examples of interval scales; the units represent equal amounts of change in the volume of a column of mercury under a certain pressure.

For many of the attributes with which the social sciences deal, procedures have not yet been devised to give reasonable certainty about the equality of intervals. Attempts, however, have been made, particularly in connection with the measurement of attitudes. The most frequent approach to determining the equality of intervals has made use of the judgments of large numbers of people about the location of various positions. Intervals between adjacent positions have been considered equal either on the basis of a consensus of judgments that they appeared equal, or on the basis of statistical calculations based on the distribution of judgments about the location of various positions.

Ratio Scales

A ratio scale, in addition to having the characteristics of an interval scale, contains an absolute zero. The empirical operations necessary to establish a ratio scale include methods for determining not only equivalence, non-equivalence rank order and equality of intervals, but also the equality of ratios. Since ratios are meaningless unless there is an absolute zero point, it is only with this type of scale that one is justified in making assertions such as "A is twice as heavy as B", or "I spent half the amount that you did.

This type of scale, often called 'fundamental measurement', is most commonly found in physics. Measures of weight, time intervals, length, area, angles, etc., all conform to ratio scales. So does the scale for cardinal numbers itself—the scale we use when we count people, rupees, dollars, eggs, etc.

For most of the subject matter of the social sciences, we are far from having devised procedures that satisfy the requirements of a ratio scale. However, attempts have been made to construct such scales in connection with the judgment of psychological attributes such as loudness and pitch (Stevens 1951, 1957). As in the case of attempts to construct interval scales for the measurement of attitudes, the judgments of people have been used as the basis for determining positions on the scale. For example, a tone of a given magnitude is sounded, and subjects are asked to select a tone that is half as loud.

If one's data conform to the criteria for a ratio scale, all the relations between numbers in the conventional system of mathematics obtain between the correspondingly numbered positions on the scale. Thus, as in an ordinal scale, an individual, object, or event which is placed at the position labelled 10 on the scale ranks higher on the attribute being measured than does one which is placed at the position labelled five; as in an interval scale, the individual, etc., at position 15 is as much higher than the one at 10 as that one is above the one at position five; and, in addition, the one at position 10 can be said to possess twice as much of the attributes as the one at position five. With such a scale, all types of statistical procedures are applicable.

Rating scales and attitude scales have the same purpose: to assign individuals to numerical positions in order to make distinction of degree possible. The scale positions generally indicate only the order of position with respect to the characteristic being measured. Although there have been attempts to construct interval scales, most rating scales and attitude scales do not provide more than ordinal measurement.

Several types of rating scales have been employed; the distinction and the names given to them tend to vary with the measurement theorist.

One feature is common to all types: the rater places the person or object being rated at some point along a continuum or in one of an ordered series of categories; a numerical value is attached to the point or the category. Scales differ in the fineness of the distinctions they permit and in the procedures involved in assigning persons or objects to positions.

Graphic Rating Scales

Perhaps the most widely used is the graphic rating scale. In this type, the judge (the subject himself, the interviewer, observer, coder, etc.) indicates his rating by simply placing a check at the appropriate point on a line that runs from one extreme of the attribute in question to the other. Scale points, with brief descriptions, may be indicated along the line; their function is to serve as a guide to the judge in localizing his rating rather than to provide distinct categories. This scale is relatively easy to use with certain precautions like avoiding the use of end statements that are extreme, and making the descriptive statements as close as possible to the numerical scale.

One of the major advantages of graphic rating scales is that they are relatively easy to use. Guilford (1954) has pointed out that "the graphic scale provides opportunity for as fine discrimination as that of which the rater is capable, and the fineness of scoring can be as great as desired." Yet for the effective use of graphic rating scales, experience has shown that certain precautions must be taken in their design and use: end statements so extreme that they are unlikely to be used should be avoided; descriptive statements should be placed to correspond as closely as possible with numerical points on the scale, etc.

Itemized Rating Scales

Itemized rating scales have also been referred to as "specific category scales" (Krech and Crutchfield, 1948) and "numerical scales" (Guildford, 1954). In this type of scale, the rater selects one of a limited number of categories that are ordered in terms of their scales position. The number of scale positions or categories used has varied depending on the research problem and the kinds of judgments required. Scale with five or seven categories are most frequently employed, but many investigators have used as many as nine or eleven points.

In general, the more clearly defined the categories, the more reliable the ratings are likely to be. How much definition is needed depends on such considerations as the nature of the material, the familiarity of the coders with the concepts involved, the fineness of distinctions required for the study, etc.

The problems involved in the construction and application of itemized rating scales are for the most part similar to those that characterize other types of rating scales.

Comparative Rates Scales

In using graphic and itemized rating scales, the rater makes his judgment of the individual without direct reference to the positions of other individuals or groups with which he might be composed. On the other hand, comparative rating scales, as the name suggests, clearly imply such relative judgments. The positions on the rating scale are expressly defined in terms of a given population or social group or in terms of people of known characteristics.

Rank Order Scale

Another comparative or relative rating procedure is the rank order scale. Here the judge is required to rank individuals specifically in relation to one another; he indicates which person is highest in terms of the characteristic being measured, which is next highest, etc., down to the one who is lowest. Ranking in this fashion is used only when the investigator is concerned with a limited group of individuals. The ranging an individual receives indicates simply his relative rank or position in the group being studied; it would not necessarily be of any use apart from the specific group whose members are being compared.

Self-rating versus Rating by Others

All these types of scale may be used to secure an individual's rating of himself or someone else's rating of him. Self-ratings have the same advantages and limitations as self-reports. It seems reasonable to assume that the individual is often in a better position to observe and report his beliefs, feelings, etc., than any one else is. This assumption is valid, however, only if the individual is aware of his own beliefs and feelings and is willing to reveal them to others. If the individual is unaware, for example, of the fact that he has hostile feelings towards a particular minority group or if he is aware of such feelings but is afraid of the consequences of revealing them, then the self-rating procedure is of little value. Another difficulty arises from the fact that even if the individual is capable of reporting his beliefs or feelings objectively, his conception of what constitutes a moderate or an extreme position may be quite different from that of others making comparable self-ratings.

Despite the hazards involved, self-ratings have proved useful in the measurement of social attitudes. For beliefs and feelings that the individual can be expected to be aware of and willing to report, self-ratings are a useful source of information with respect to certain attributes of attitudes, for example, intensity, importance, etc. Self-ratings have so far proved to be the only satisfactory source of information.

Attitude Scales

The analysis made so far gives an idea of the different types of scales and their feasibility for social science research. Most of these attempts of scaling have contributed to the development of scales for the measurement of attitudes towards social issues. This attempt was to devise procedures whereby the individuals could be placed on an attitude-continuum. The attitude scales differ in the method of construction, method of response, and the basis for interpreting scores. Since the assessment of the attitude is a primary concern among social scientists, the remaining part of this chapter devotes itself to a discussion of the attitude measurement in terms of the different types of attitude scales as developed by L.L. Thurstone, R. Likert and L. Guttman, etc.

We will discuss the four best-known methods of attitude scaling. One might well ask why we need more than one method. This has come about because, over the past three decades, different research workers have developed methods of scale-building in which they have laid particular stress on one or the other of the above requirements. One method has concentrated on unidimensionality, another on finding equivalent scale units, a third on obtaining reproducibility, and so on. There does not seem to be a method that combines the advantages of all of them. It is, therefore, important that we understand their respective aims and the differences between them.

It follows that, for the present, it is impossible to say which method is best. Each of these methods has important desirable features, but each of them is also open to criticism. For our own inquiry, the best method is the one which is the most appropriate to our particular problem. If we wish to study attitude patterning or explore theories of attitudes, then probably the Likert procedure will be the most relevant. If we wish to study attitude change, or the hierarchical structure of an attitude, then Guttman's method might be preferable. If we are studying group differences, then we will probably select the Thurstone procedures, and so on. Each type of scale does one thing rather well.

Fundamentally, scaling methodology is much the same in all fields. The differences that exist are of content and emphasis. The sociologist, for example, is much more concerned with the development of instruments to measure institutions and other cultural phenomena than is the psychologist and psychiatrist. On the other hand, psychologists, sociologists and the management experts manifest great interest in attitude scales. In this introduction we shall limit our discussion mainly to scales designed to measure attitudes.

Attitude measurement consists of assessing an individual's response to a set of social objects or situations. This is done by observing a sample behaviour from an attitude universe. Each behavioural element in the attitude universe is the response to a particular situation or object. The particular situation or object that evokes the response together with the specified set of response categories is called an item. An item is a manifest variable. A number assigned to an individual's item response is an item score. A collection of items is called a questionnaire. The questionnaire is free from some of the connotations of the other terms like test, inventory or scale. A questionnaire may contain items from different attitude universes although usually a single universe is represented. A number derived from item response which represents a position on the latent variable is called a scale score or simply the score. The score forms the attitude scale. The scale implies a system for obtaining a score from individual's item responses. The term scale is also occasionally used to refer to the scoring system.

Scaling always implies the existence of a continuum of some kind. Its nature must be inferred from the character of the items selected to make up the scale. The first step, therefore, in scaling procedure regardless of the technique employed is a thorough knowledge of the subject matter. It is also necessary to assume that every scale is composed of items which are only a sample of the possible universe of the items. Therefore, the scale construction requires a high degree of consciousness of the logical problem surrounding the twin assumptions—the existence of the continuum, and the representation of the responding continuum achieved by the particular scale. The question of representativeness is checked by tests of validity and the existence of a continuum can be empirically verified through various attitude scaling techniques. The reliability of the scale is also very important as its pre-requisite before the scale is administered to a larger population for any purpose.

A unidimensional scale measures a single variable. In general, the property of unidimensionality means that people with the same score have the same attitude. Operationally, unidimensionality and homogeneity have essentially the same meaning. In general, if the items on a scales are highly interdependent, then the items are homogeneous and the scale is unidimensional. A homogeneous scale is, in general, a reliable scale. If a scale is reliable and homogeneous, it measures some variable. The problem of validity is to discover what it measures. The first problem in validation is to delimit and define this attitude universe. It is helpful to distinguish at least three kinds of attitude universes, namely, elicited verbal attitudes in terms of respondents' opinion to a statement, spontaneous verbal attitudes like the opinions expressed by individuals in normal conversation, and action attitude like the verbal and non-verbal behaviour expressed in a particular situation. Although most of our attitude scales measure elicited verbal attitudes, other scales are equally possible. This description will facilitate the assessment of the validity of the scale or the attitude universe. There are various known methods for assessing validity of attitude scale which are not discussed here.

Judgment Methods

The judgment methods of attitude measurement are all variants of a technique developed by L.L. Thurstone and E.J. Chave. The technique requires dichotomous, non-monotone items having operating characteristics with single maximal. There are two major aspects of the judgment methods. First, the items must be scaled, i.e., each item must be given a scale value that represents its degree of favourableness towards the issue. Secondly, the respondents must be scored on the basis of their responses to the items.

There are several methods of determining the scale values of items. If only a few items are to be scaled, the method of paired comparisons is appropriate. Here each one of the several judges (preferably 25 or more) is presented with every possible pair of items and is asked which of the paired items is more favourable to the issue in question.

For each pair of items, the proportion of times one item was judged to be more favourable than the other is obtained. Therefore, if we have "n" statements and each statement is compared with every other statement, then the total number of pairs will be given by the formula:

$$nC_2 = \frac{n(n-1)}{2}$$

Several methods may be used as short-cuts in the situation including the rank order. The method of rank order or order of merit method is seldom used. In this method, each judge places the items in rank order of favourableness towards the issue in question. The scale value of an item is the weighted or unweighted average of the ranks given to the item by a group of judges. Alternatively, a paired comparison analysis can be used following the procedure developed by Thurstone.

The law of comparative judgment assumes that for a given stimulus, there is associated a most frequently aroused or model discriminal process on a psychological continuum. A discriminal process is a theoretical concept and represents the experience or reaction of an individual when confronted with a stimulus and asked to make a judgment of some attribute. Thurstone also makes an assumption that the distribution of all discriminal processes aroused by stimulus is normal about the modal discriminal process. The mean or median discriminal process associated with a stimulus is taken as a scale value of the stimulus and the standard deviation of the distribution of discriminal process is referred to as discriminal dispersion. The modal discriminal process and the discriminal dispersion for any given stimulus will, therefore, depend upon the particular attribute that is being judged. In the case of comparison between any two statements about the psychological object, the subjects are required to make comparative judgments as to the extent of favourability of a particular statement in relation to the other. In case there are two statements, A and B, for which comparative judgments are to be obtained by a number of judges, where 50 per cent of the judges say that A is more favourable than B and another 50 per cent say the reverse then the proportion of favourable judgment for each of the statements would be .50 which is the modal discriminal function. If we find more than .50 of the judges say that statement A is more favourable than B, then the modal discriminal process will be higher for a in relation to B. On the basis of the comparative judgment obtained, it is possible to arrive at the frequency corresponding to the number of items a particular statement is judged more favourable than the other. Based on the preferred frequency, it is possible to obtain the proportion of a particular statement being judged more favourably than the other. These proportions thus obtained can be expressed as unit normal deviate by means of the table of normal deviates. By adding up the unit deviations, and dividing by the number of statements in each row and adding a constant, the scale values are obtained for each one of the statements.

For large number of items, the method of rank order or the paired comparison becomes unwieldly.

The method of equal appearing intervals is the most widely used of the judgment methods. It is much simpler in application than the method of paired comparisons since it requires only one judgment per item. The procedure for developing the scale is as follows. The investigator gathers several hundred items conceived to be related to the attitude being investigated, that is, the items must elicit responses that are psychologically related to the attitude being measured. It also requires that the scale differentiates among people who are at different points along the dimensions being measured. Secondly, a large number of judges (who could range from 50 to 300), working independently, sort the items into fixed number of categories (usually 7, 9 or 11) that are arranged in the order of favourableness. For example, the judge places statements which he considers most favourable in the first pile, the second most favourable in the next pile and the statement which he considers most unfavourable in the 7th, 9th or 11th pile as the case may be. The 4th, 5th and 6th positions depending upon the number of categories used, serve as a neutral position at which there is neither favourableness nor unfavourableness. The judge is usually asked to sort the items in such a way that the intervals between categories are subjectivity equal. However, there is no way of determining whether in fact the intervals are subjectively equal which, by and large, remains an assumption of the experimenter. Now the scale value of a statement is computed as the median positions to which it is assigned by the group of judges. Statements that have too broad a scatter as revealed by Q value are discarded as ambiguous or irrelevant. The final selection is made taking items that are spread out evenly along the scale from one extreme position to another. It is often possible to construct duplicate forms of the scale from items not used for the original form. Usually it is preferred that the final scale should contain around 20 items. The subjects in filling up the scale are either asked to check statements in the scale with which they agree or to check two or three items that are closest to their attitude position. The median of the scale values of the items the individual checks is interpreted as indicating his position on a scale of favourable-unfavourable attitude towards the object.

In preparing statements for a scale of this type the following precautions should be observed. The statement should be as brief as possible so as not to fatigue the subjects. It should be such that it can be endorsed or rejected according to one's opinion. Every statement should be such that acceptance or rejection of the statement does indicate something. Double barreled statements should be avoided. One must ensure that at least a fair majority of the statements really belong to the attitude variable to be measured.

There are some objections to this scale. First, the amount of work involved in constructing it is cumbersome and time-consuming. However, in view of the recent developments in time saving techniques, the amount of time and labour involved in constructing a scale by this method is not substantially different from other scales. Second, it has been mentioned that the scale values of statements are not independent of the attitude of the judges doing the sorting. There are several studies which revealed that the scale values assigned do not depend on the attitude of the judges. However, it has been found that judges of superior and low intelligence differed due to the interaction of attitude and intelligence bringing about some effect on the scale position of the items. Third, it has also been pointed out that the individual score is the mean or median of the scale values of the several items checked by the respondent. This results in essentially different attitudinal patterns being expressed in the same score. For example, if items, let us say, one and two having scale values of 8.6 and 8.4 are checked, the median value will be 8.5. But in the case of an individual who checks items 1,2,3 and 4 with scale values of 8.6, 8.4, 10.3 and 3.8, the median value again will work out to 8.5. This suggests that basically both the individuals have a similar attitude in the favourable-unfavourable attitude dimension but the median score is constituted of different attitude patterns by virtue of the different types of items marked by the individual. Although this score has some of these defects, it has been found to be more useful in attitude assessment as it constitutes a reasonably satisfactory ordinal scale and provides a basis for saying whether one individual is more favourable or less favourable than the other.

The method of successive intervals was designed by Thurstone to overcome some of the difficulties inherent in the method of equal appearing intervals. Here also the procedure to obtain the scale values is the same as that for equal appearing interval scale, except that the latter does not require the judges to discriminate between statements placed within the same category. If a judge encounters a statement that he regards as extremely unfavourable early in the judging process, he will undoubtedly place that statement in the extreme category. Subsequently, if he encounters another statement that is more extreme than the first, then he may not have a category beyond the one previously used and hence he sorts the second statement in the same category as first. He is not forced to discriminate between the two statements as would be the case in paired comparison. This method of successive intervals takes care of the possible inequalities in the widths of the intervals on the psychological continuum of a scale. Like the method of equal appearing intervals this method requires a single judgment from each subject for each statement to be scaled. As mentioned, the procedure followed to obtain judgment and arrive at the cumulative frequencies is similar to the method of equal appearing intervals. The scaling problem in this method is to determine estimates of the widths of the intervals making up the psychological continuum from the cumulative proportion distributions for a given set of statements. After obtaining the cumulative proportions for each of the statements, they are converted into the unit normal deviate by using the table of unit normal distribution. After obtaining the unit normal deviates, the differences between the successive entries (between 2 and 1, 3 and 2, 4 and 3, 5 and 4, 6 and 5, etc.) are obtained which indicates the estimates of the various interval widths. It is assumed that the best estimates in the widths of the various successive intervals are the arithmetic means of the entries in each of response categories for all the subjects. These means are the estimates of the widths of the various intervals on the psychological continuum. The cumulative widths of the various intervals are obtained in order to achieve the psychological continuum. Once the knowledge of psychological continuum is achieved, it is a simple matter to find the scale values of the various statements. The scale values of the statements may be taken as the medians of the corresponding cumulative proportions of this continuum. the medians may be calculated by using the relevant formula. This will give the scale value for each one of the statements. However, this procedure does not permit us to obtain an estimate of the width of either of the two extreme intervals. It is because no estimate can be obtained for the lower limit of the first intervals or the upper limit of the last interval as the widths of these two intervals are indeterminate.

Thurstone Scale Construction (Calculation of scale and Q values)

The judgments from various judges were obtained on three statements and data were obtained from large number of judges. The data obtained from a large number of judges can be arranged in the form shown in Table 1. Three rows are used for each statement. The first gives the frequency with which the statement was placed in each of the 11 categories. The second gives these frequencies as proportions. The proportions are obtained by dividing each frequency by N, the total number of judges or, more simply, by multiplying each of the frequencies by the reciprocal of N. The third row gives the cumulative proportions, that is, the proportions of judgment in a given category plus the sum of all of the proportions below that category.

Table 1

Summary Table for Judgments Obtained by the Method of Equal Appearing Intervals

State-ments												*Scale Value*	*Q Value*
	f	2	2	6	2	6	62	64	26	16	18	4		
1	p	.01	.01	.03	.01	.03	.31	.32	.13	.09	.04	.02	6.8	1.7
	Cp	.01	.02	.05	.06	.09	.40	.72	.85	.94	.98	1.0		
	f	0	0	0	10	40	28	50	26	28	14	4		
2	p	.00	.00	.00	.05	.20	.14	.25	.13	.14	.07	.02	6.9	2.8
	Cp	.00	.00	.00	.05	.25	.39	64	.77	.91	.98	1.0		
	f	0	0	0	2	8	6	26	44	56	44	14		
3	p	.00	.00	.00	.01	.04	.03	.13	.22	.28	.22	.07	8.7	2.0
	Cp	.00	.00	.00	.01	.05	.08	.21	.43	.71	.93	1.0		

Note: The Table has been taken from Techniques of Attitude Scale Construction by Allen L. Edwards, pp. 86-89.

If the median of the distribution of judgments for each statement is taken as the scale value of the statement, then the scale values can be found from the data arranged in the manner of Table 1 by means of the following formula

$$\underline{S} = 1 + \frac{.50 - p_b}{p_w}$$

where

$\underline{S}$ = the median or scale value of the statement,

l = the lower limit of the interval in which the median falls,
pb = the sum of the proportions below the interval in which the median falls,
pw = the proportion within the interval in which the median falls,
i = the width of the interval and is assumed to be equal to 1.0.

Substituting in the above formula to find the scale value for the first statement in Table 1, we have[3]:

$$\underline{S} = 6.5 + \left(\frac{.50 - .40}{.32}\right) 1.0 = 6.8$$

The other scale values shown in Table 1 are found in the same manner.

Thurstone and Chave used the interquartile range or Q as a measure of the variation of the distribution of judgments for a given statement. The interquartile range contains the middle 50 per cent of the judgements. To determine the value of Q, we need to find two other point measures, the 75th centile and the 25th centile. The 25th centile can be obtained from the following formula:

$$\underline{C}_{25} = l + \left(\frac{.25 - \underline{p}b}{\underline{p}w}\right) i$$

where
$\underline{C}_{25}$ = the 25th centile,
$\underline{l}$ = the lower limit of the interval in which the 25th centile falls,
$\underline{p}b$ = the sum of the proportions below the interval in which the 25th centile falls,
$\underline{p}w$ = the proportion within the interval in which the 25th centile falls,
$\underline{i}$ = the width of the interval and is assumed to be equal to 1.0.

The 75th centile will be given by

$$\underline{C}_{75} = l + \left(\frac{.75 - \underline{p}b}{\underline{p}w}\right) i$$

where
$\underline{C}_{75}$ = the 75th centile,
$\underline{p}b$ = the sum of the proportions below the interval in which the 75th centile falls,
$\underline{p}w$ = the proportion within the interval in which the 75th centile falls,
$\underline{i}$ = the width of the interval and is assumed to be equal to 1.0

For the first statement in Table 1, we have

$$\underline{C}_{25} = 5.5 + \left(\frac{.25 - .09}{.33}\right) 1.0 = 6.0$$

and

$$\underline{C}_{75} = 7.5 + \left(\frac{.75 - .72}{.13}\right) 1.0 = 7.7$$

Then the interquartile range or $\underline{Q}$ will be given by taking the difference between $\underline{C}_{75}$ and $\underline{C}_{25}$. Thus

$$\underline{Q} = \underline{C}_{75} - \underline{C}_{25}$$

or for the first statement in Table 1, we have

$$\underline{Q} = 7.7 - 6.0 = 1.7.$$

The interquartile range is a measure of the spread of the middle 50 per cent of the judgments. When there is good agreement among the subjects in judging the degree of favourableness or unfavourableness of a statement Q will be small compared with the value obtained when there is relatively little agreement among the subjects. A large Q value, indicating disagreement among the judges as to the degree of the attribute possessed by a statement is, therefore, taken as an indication that there is something wrong with the statement. Thurstone and Chave regard large $\underline{Q}$ values primarily as an indication that a statement is ambiguous.

$$\underline{S} = 1 + \left(\frac{.50 - \underline{p}b}{\underline{p}w}\right) i$$

$$= 6.5 + \left(\frac{.50 - .39}{.25}\right) 1$$

$$= 6.5 + \frac{.11}{.25} \times 1$$

$$= 6.5 + .44$$

$$= 6.94 \text{ or } 6.9$$

Scale value

$$\underline{C}_{25} = \underline{1} + \left(\frac{.25 - \underline{p}b}{pw}\right) \times \underline{i}$$

$$= 4.5 + \left(\frac{.25 - .05}{.20}\right) \times \underline{i}$$

$$= 4.5 + \frac{.20}{.20} \times 1$$

$$= 4.5 + 1$$

$$= 5.5$$

$$\underline{C}_{75} = 7.5 + \left(\frac{.75 - .64}{.1}\right) \times 1$$

$$= 7.5 + .8$$

$$= 8.3$$

$$\underline{Q} = \underline{C}_{75} - \underline{C}_{25}$$

$$= 8.3 - 5.5 = 2.8$$

$$\underline{S} = l + \left(\frac{.50 - \underline{p}_b}{\underline{p}_w}\right) \times 1$$

$$= 8.5 + \left(\frac{.50 - .43}{.28}\right) \times 1$$

$$= 8.5 + \frac{.07}{.28} \times 1$$

$$= 8.5 + .2$$

$$= 8.7$$

$$\underline{C}_{25} = l + \left(\frac{.25 - \underline{p}_b}{\underline{p}_w}\right) \times \underline{i}$$

$$= 7.5 + \left(\frac{.25 - .21}{.22}\right) \times 1$$

$$= 7.5 + \frac{.04}{.22} \times 1$$

$$= 7.5 + .1$$

$$= 7.6$$

$$\underline{C}_{75} = l + \left(\frac{.75 - \underline{p}_b}{\underline{p}_w}\right) \times \underline{i}$$

$$= 9.5 + \left(\frac{.75 - .71}{.22}\right) \times 1$$

$$= 9.5 + \frac{.44}{.22} \times 1$$

$$= 9.5 + .1$$

$$\simeq 9.6$$

$$\underline{Q} = \underline{C}_{75} - \underline{C}_{25}$$

$$= 9.6 - 7.6$$

$$= 2.0$$

Method of Summated Ratings

The summated scale consists of a series of items to which the subject is asked to react. The type of summated scale most frequently used in the study of social attitudes follows the pattern devised by R. Likert and is referred to as the Likert type of scale. In this scale, the respondent indicates his several degrees of agreement or disagreement with each item that constitutes the scale instead of indicating his agreement for only a few items. Each response is given a numerical score, indicating his degree of agreement or disagreement based on a three point or five point response category. The sum of the scores of the individual responses to all the separate items gives his total score which is interpreted as representing his position on the scale of the favourable and unfavourable attitude towards the object. Thus one would expect an individual with a favourable attitude to respond favourably to some and unfavourably to others and an individual with an unfavourable attitude to respond unfavourably to many items.

The procedure for constructing the Likert type of scale is as follows. The investigator assembles a large number of items considered relevant to the attitude being investigated, either clearly favourable or clearly unfavourable. These items are administered to a group of subjects representative of those with whom the questionnaire is to be used. The subjects indicate their response to each item by checking one of the categories of agreement or disagreement. The response to the various items are scored in such a way that a response which is indicative of a most favourable attitude is given the highest score. It makes no difference whether five is high or one is low in a five point response category or vice-versa. The important factor is that the responses should be scored consistently in terms of the attitudinal direction they indicate. Each individual total score is computed by adding his item scores. The responses are analyzed to determine which of the items discriminate most clearly between the high scores and low scorers on the total scale. The items which do not discriminate as measured by the discrimination power of the item between low and high scores in the scale, or items that do not shows a substantial correlation with the total score are eliminated to ensure that the scale as a whole is internally consistent. That is, every item is related to the same general attitude. Sometimes it is also necessary to find out the inter- relationship among each of the items on the scale to assess the extent of homogeneity of the items that constitute the scale. This scale has certain advantages over the Thurstone scale.

It permits the use of items that are not manifestly related to the attitude being studied. This scale is generally considered simpler to construct and likely to be more reliable than a Thurstone scale of the same number of items. The range of the responses permitted to an item given in this scale provides a more precise information about the individual-opinion on the issue referred by a given item. However, some of the disadvantage of the Likert type of scale are: It does not claim to be more than an ordinal scale, i.e., it makes possible the ranking of individuals in terms of the favourableness of their attitude towards a given objects but it does not provide a basis for saying how much more favourable one is than the other nor for measuring the amount of change after some experience. Another disadvantage of the Likert type of scale is that the total score of an individual has little clear meaning since many patterns of response to the various items produced the same score. This is also true in the Thurstone type of scale but the extent of its occurrence is much more in this scale. Despite the lack of theoretical rationale for scalability the scores on the Likert type of questionnaire provides the basis for classification of people based on the characteristics measured. The selection of items, format of the items, etc., are similar to that already mentioned while discussing the Thurstone's scale.

Cumulative Scale or Scalogram Analysis

In a cumulative scale, the items are related to one another in such a way that ideally an individual who replies favourably to item two also replies favourably to item one, one who replies favourably to item three also replies favourably to items one and two. Sometimes, the items as they appear in the scale are arranged in the order of favourableness; sometimes, they are randomly arranged. Ordinarily, no attempt is made to determine whether the intervals between items are equal. Thus, in practice, cumulative scales are ordinal scales.

The general procedure for determining whether or not the responses of subjects to items form the scale is knows as scalogram analysis. It is based on an analysis of the response patterns of the subjects to a set of items where a response pattern denotes the set of response to items given by a subject. In practice, scalogram analysis can perhaps be most accurately described as a procedure for evaluating sets of statements or existing scales to determine whether or not they meet the requirements of a particular kind of scale as described by L. Guttman. For items of this "cumulative" type of scales as mentioned earlier, acceptance of one item implies that the person possesses enough of the attribute to accept all items of a lesser magnitude. When responses to a set of attitude statements meet this requirement that set of statements is said to constitute a unidimensional scale. Therefore, the first task in analyzing cumulative scales is to ascertain the degree to which the initial set of items represents a single dimension which is inferred from the degree to which subjects respond with the admissible answer patterns (scale types). It is assumed that any non-scale pattern reflects one or more response errors. The number of response errors counted is the minimum number of changes required to convert a non-scale response pattern into a scale type. The total number of response errors (e) made by a sample of subjects is divided by the total number of all responses they make (nk, where n is the number of subjects and k is the number of items). This ratio is subtracted from unity minus (1) to yield the coefficient reproducibility, R : ($R = 1 - e$ nk). The value of R may be used as a measure of the degree to which the set of items is scalable, that is, it represents a unidimensional attribute. An arbitrary value of .90 is, sometimes, taken as the minimum acceptable coefficient of reproducibility. Generally the reproducibility or scalability of a set of items can be increased by eliminating certain items which account for a disproportionate number of errors.

The procedure involved in constructing a scalogram is briefly as follows. First, it involves the selection of a small number of statements from a large number of possible statements representing a universe of a content, which, by and large, should have the most homogenous content. For each statement, weights of 0 and 1 are assigned for two response categories of agree and disagree. Usually, Guttman's techniques can be best illustrated for two response categories though there are methods to apply this technique for more than two response categories. These weights are so assigned that one is always given to the response category that indicates more of whatever it is that is being measured in terms of favourable attitude getting 1 and unfavourable attitude getting 0. These statements are given to a sample of hundreds of persons. They are asked to respond to these statements in terms of agree and disagree. A score is obtained for each individual by summing the weights assigned to the response categories he had selected. The total score of each subject is arranged in rank order from high to low.

From this point, there are several procedures to evaluate the scalability of the set of items. There are techniques like the Cornell technique and techniques suggested by Goodenough H.H., etc. In the Cornell technique, the important task would be that from a person's rank position based on the total score, it must be possible for us to reproduce his response to each of the items in a simple fashion. That means if an individual has indicated his agreement for four items, his total score should be 4, implying that he has agreed with each of the items. If an individual's total score is three, then it implies that he has agreed with three items and disagreed with one. Similarly, if the individual has disagreed with all the items, his total score would be 0. Thus, it would be possible to reproduce the responses of individual to the various statements based on the total score alone. Since perfect reproducibility based on the knowledge of the total scores is not to be expected in practice, it become, a matter of some importance to measure the degree of reproducibility present for any given set of responses to attitude statements. This is accomplished by setting cutting-points for the response categories of each statement. A cutting-point marks that place in the rank order of the subjects where the most common response shifts from one category to another. Guttman suggests two rules in locating cutting-points: the cutting-point should be located as to minimize the error; no category should have more error in it than non-error. On the basis of a cutting-point, the errors in each category of response are located for each of the statements and they are summed up. The total number of errors is expressed as a proportion of the total number of responses and this value is subtracted from unity. This gives the co-efficient of reproducibility. In another method, as suggested by Goodenough, the score matrix is prepared with rows corresponding to the subjects and columns to statements. The responses of the subjects to the various statements are recorded in the row of matrices in terms of 0 and 1 weights.

The response patterns are recorded having subjects with the higher score assigned to the first row and the next row will correspond to the subject with the next higher score and so on. The scores for each one of the rows are summed up down the rows and across the columns which gives the frequencies with which the 1 response has been made to each of the various statements. The sums for each column of the matrices is divided by the total number of subjects to obtain the proportion of subjects giving the 1 response to each of the statements, and the proportion giving 0 response is found out for deducting the obtained proportion from the unity. A bar-chart is prepared for each statement where part of the chart indicates the proportion of subjects giving 1 response to a statement and the lower part represents the proportion giving 0 response. The point of division is indicated by the solid lines and each point of division is extended to charts of other statements in terms of dotted lines. For example, in a four statement scale, the possible range of scores is 0 to 4. The bar-charts are used to find out the predicted patterns of response to the statements corresponding to each total score. The errors can be located in the observed patterns of response based on the predicted pattern of response for each of the subjects. The response errors are summed up and recorded, and the coefficient of reproducibility as mentioned earlier is found out.

Another simple method to find out the coefficient of reproducibility is based on the total frequency of the responses for each statement. The predictive patterns of response for each of the statements for a set of, say, four statements with a total score of 4 or 0 can be easily assumed. The predictive patterns of response for the remaining total scores of 3, 2 and 1 for a set of four statements can be worked out as follows: The distribution of total frequencies for each of the statements is examined and the lowest frequency is given 0 response for a total score of 3. Similarly, among the remaining total frequencies, the lowest is given 0, and the next two, 1 each which gives the predictive response for a total score of 2. Thus, the predictive response pattern is found for a total score 1 also using the same procedure. On the basis of this, the predictive pattern of response for each total score is obtained and the response errors are calculated for each subject to arrive at the coefficient of reproducibility.

Though cumulative scales like summative scales are composed of monotone items, the additional property of item magnitude is taken into account by the scoring procedure. Clearly this procedure is cumbersome, arbitrary and difficult to specify analytically. There are other reasons besides analytical complexity for rejecting cumulative scaling procedure. Whether items are retained or discarded depends more on variation in item popularities than on degree of inter-correlation or functional equivalence. The ideal modal of scalogram analysis assumes unidimensional items which probably do not exist. The kind of items retained are typically those which are widely spread in popularity. Generally, cumulative scales are not recommended for attitude measurement.

An attempt was made in this paper to briefly sketch some of the major scaling methods for attitude measurement which are in use. Each one of the methods has its own advantages—refineness of the procedure, scoring and analytical nature but each of them has its own disadvantages in terms of time consumed, feasibility for certain measurements and complexity involved through cumbersome scaling procedure. The use of any particular technique very much depends on the nature of research and the type of data that an individual researcher would seek to examine. As pointed out in the beginning, it is a question of whether the interest is in the response or in the individual, which by and large decides the approach to be followed and the scaling methods to be used. This paper only gives an outline in a descriptive way.

In conclusion, we should note that attitude scales have been developed for many subjects, and that a researcher may be able to employ an existing scale in his enquiry. But before adopting an existing scale, he must ensure that it is applicable to his population, and this may necessitate some pilot work; if he can use an established scale, he not only saves on the construction of the scale and on the testing of its reliability and validity, but also has the results of other studies with which to compare his own results.

Notes

1. For more precise definitions see Hussell L. Ackoff, S.K. Gupta and J. Sayre, *Scientific Method: Optimizing Applied Research Decisions* (New York: John Wiley and Sons, Inc. 1962).
2. The relation of equivalence (or equality) has the logical characteristics of being transitive and symmetrical. See Jahoda, p. 18.
3. The interval represented by the number assigned to a given card or category is assumed to range from .5 of a unit below to .05 of a unit above the assigned number. Thus the lower limit of the interval represented by the card assigned the number 7 is 6.5 and the upper limit is 7.5.

References

Edwards, A.L., *Techniques of Attitude Scale Construction*, (1969), Bombay, Vakils, Feffer and Simons Pvt. Ltd.

Goode, W.J. and Hatt, P.K., *Methods in Social Research*, 1952, New York, McGraw Hill Book Co.

Lindzey, G., *Handbook of Social Psychology*, 1954, London: Addison Wesley Publishing House.

Muthayya, B.C., 'Scaling Techniques' in Unpublished Material of N.I.R.D., Hyderabad.

Oppenheim, A.N. *Questionnaire Design and Attitude Measurement*, 1968, London: Heinemann.

Sellitz, C., Jahoda, M., Dentsh, M. and Cook, S. W., *Research Methods in Social Relations*, 1969, W.S. A. Methuen and Co. Ltd.

Torgerson, W.S., *Theory and Methods of Scaling*, 1958, New York: John Wiley and Sons.

Young, Pauline V. and Schmid, Calvin F., *Scientific Social Surveys and Research*, 1961, Bombay: Asia Publishing House.

Chapter 10

Remote Sensing Techniques and their Applications

R. Nagaraja and H.N. Misra

Remote Sensing (RS) is the science/technology of making inferences about material objects from measurements made at a distance without coming into physical contact with the objects under study. When viewed in this context remote sensing covers various disciplines from astronomy to laboratory testing of materials. However, remote sensing is currently used more commonly to denote identification of earth features by detecting the characteristic electromagnetic radiation that is reflected, emitted or scattered by the earth's surface. Electromagnetic radiation extending from the ultraviolet to the far infrared and microwave regions provides the greatest potential in the context of earth resources survey. For collection of remotely sensed data the first requirement is the sensor. The different sensors available in different remote sensing platforms and their spatial sensitivity are shown in Figure 1 and Table 1.

Characteristics of Satellite RS Data

Satellite data is available in the digital form and is normally supplied on computer compatible tapes (CCTs) which can be used on standard tape drive units. The way in which information is stored on the tapes will differ from sensor to sensor and also will depend on the standards adopted by the agency or receiving station supplying data.

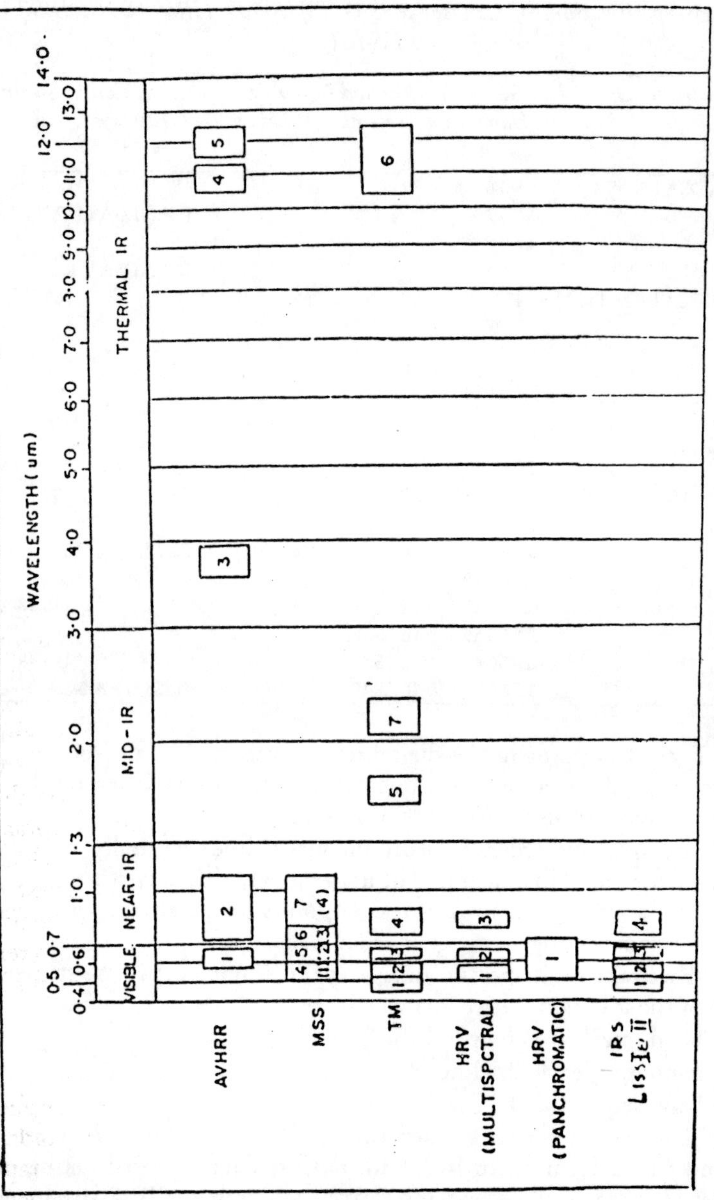

Figure 1: Summary of Spectral Sensitivity of **NOAA**: *AVHRR, LANDSAT-MSS&TM SPOT-HRV and IRS-LISS-I&II*

Table 1

Major Specifications of Landsat MSS & TM, SPOT HRV 1&2 & IRS-IA, LISS-I&H

Satellite Sensor	*Spectral Hands in Micrometer*	*Ground Res.(m)*	*Quantization Levels*	*Repetition Cycle(days)*	*Swath (Km)*
LANDSAT MSS 4	0.5-0.6	79	128	18	185
5	0.6-0.7			(LANDSAT1/2/3)	
6	0.7-0.8			16	
7	0.8-1.1			(LANDSAT 4/5)	
LANDSAT TM 1	0.45-0.52	30	256	16	185
2	0.52-0.60				
3	0.63-0.69				
4	0.76-0.90				
5	1.55-1.75				
6	10.5-12.5	120			
7	2.08-2.15				
SPOT 1&2 PAN HRV	0.51-0.73	10	256	26	60
	0.50-0.59				
	0.61-0.68	20	256	26	6
	0.79-0.89				
IRS-IA & IB	0.45-0.52	72.5	128	22	148.48
	0.52-0.59	(LISS-I)			
	0.62-0.68	36.25			145.48
	0.77-0.86	(LISS-II)		(LISS-II A&B combined)	

Each data point in the digital image is termed as a pixel (picture element) and has a density value called "grey value" for each band. These values are also referred to as DN (Digital Number).

The spatially ordered nature of images leads naturally to a data storage format. Thus each line of image pixels is usually stored as a record. So a record is a stream of data points (or pixels). A set of such records constituting an image is called a file.

If we take multispectral images as the example, they are stored in one of the following three formats.

(1) band interleaved by pixel (BIP)
(2) band interleaved by line (BIL)
(3) band sequential (BSQ)

There is however some variation in the BIP format, known as BIP 1 and BIP 2 formats. In BIP 1 format the data is stored taking one pixel from each waveband interleaved whereas in BIP 2 the format consists of pairs of pixels from each waveband interleaved within each record.

Each of these formats is particularly suited to certain types of processing.

Satellite data is also available in large photographic form both in colour (different band combination), and black and white (single band) after certain preprocessing.

Digital Image Processing Systems

Digital image processing involves the manipulation and interpretation of digital images with the aid of a computer. This form of processing began in 1960s. However, it was not until the launch of Landsat 1, in 1972 that digital image data became widely available for land remote sensing application. At that time, not only was the theory and practice of digital image processing in its infancy but also the cost of digital computers was very high and their computational efficiency low by today's standards. Now, access to low cost, efficient computer hardware and software is common in developed and some developing countries. The digital data from a range of commercial earth resources satellite and meteorological satellites is being processed and analyzed using the image processing techniques.

As compared to the visual or electro-optical methods of image analysis, digital processing has the following distinct merits.

1. Digital processing has the greatest potential for preserving the correct radiometry and the maximum resolution of the images.
2. Digital processing is fast and accurate and yet flexible to cater to the analysis requirement.
3. The general availability of computer permits different investigators to perform repeatable and quantifiable analysis on common imagery.

The central idea behind digital image processing is quite simple. The digital image is fed into a computer. The computer is programmed to insert these data into an equation or series of equations and then store the results of the processed data. These results form a new digital image that may be displayed or recorded.

Integrated hardware components complete with software constitute an image processing system.

Components of an Image Processing System

1. Digital computer to process the image data.
2. Mass storage devices such as tape drives and disks to store and re-

trieve large volumes of image data.

3. An image workstation to have a visual look at the contents of both the input and process imageries.
4. Plotters.
5. Printers.
6. Software.

Multispectral Classification

One of the most widely used and accepted applications of pattern recognition techniques to digital image processing has been the assignment of picture elements (pixels) to various categories through multispectral classification. It is nothing but assigning the decision-making process to the computer with or without the help of a prior information. The intention of multispectral classification is to replace the subjective interpretations of the analysis by more quantitative and repeatable processes. The process of classification makes use of multiple images of the same scene, obtained from several spectral regions as input, and products as output display or images of scene content on a pixel by pixel basis and statistical summaries of scene content in tabular form. Hence, the process is known as multispectral classification. Multispectral classification has found wide usage in agricultural, forest management, mineral, land use mapping, urban planning, ecological monitoring, water resources studies etc.

The initial step involved in any classification procedure is to first "train" the computer (classifier) to recognize the class signatures of interest. There are two methods in which this can be done—'Supervized' and 'Unsupervized' training. In supervized training the analyst uses prior knowledge derived from field surveys, photo interpretation, topographic map information and other sources in giving sample information about different features to be classified by the computer. Using the feature signatures defined by the analyst, each pixel with similar characteristics is grouped and assigned into respective classes defined by the analyst.

In unsupervized training the analyst employs a computer algorithm which locates and groups the naturally occurring concentrations of similar feature vectors from any given heterogeneous sample of pixels. This is called 'clustering'. Each cluster represents feature class(es) in the image and is used to calculate class signatures. Using these clusters any decision criteria can be adopted to classify each pixel to the computer-derived classes. These computer-derived classes remain to be identified. They may or may not correspond to classes of analyst's interest. The resulting classification is known as unsupervized classification.

Classification Algorithms

To simplify the graphical portrayal the presentation of various classification techniques is illustrated here for two band data. But for numerical implementation these procedures may be applied to any number of bands.

The two dimensional digital values or measurement vectors attributed to each pixel may be expressed graphically by plotting them on a scatter diagram.

Figure 2

Pixel Observations from Selected Training Sites Plotted on Scatter Diagram

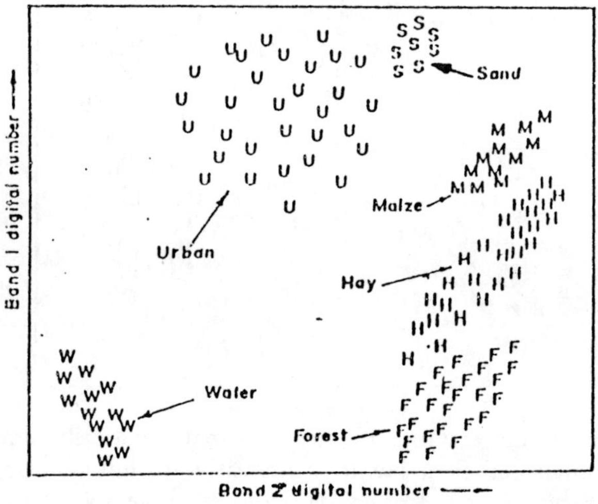

Each pixel value has been plotted on the scatter diagram (fig. 2) with a letter indicating the category to which it is known to belong. Note that the pixels within each class do not have a single repeated spectral value. These clouds of points represent multidimensional descriptions of the spectral response patterns of each category of cover type to be interpreted. The following classification strategies are used by which pixels of unidentified cover type are categorized into their appropriate classes.

Minimum-distance-to-means Classifier

Figure 3 illustrates one of the simpler classification strategies that may be used. First, the mean spectral value in each band for each category is determined. These values comprise the mean vector for each category. The category means are indicated by '+' in Figure 3. By considering the two channels pixel values as positional coordinates, a pixel of unknown identity may be classified by computing the distance between the value of the unknown pixel and each of the category means. In Figure 3 pixel 1 is classified to maize while pixel 2 is classified to sand.

Figure 3

Minimum Distance to Means Classification Strategy

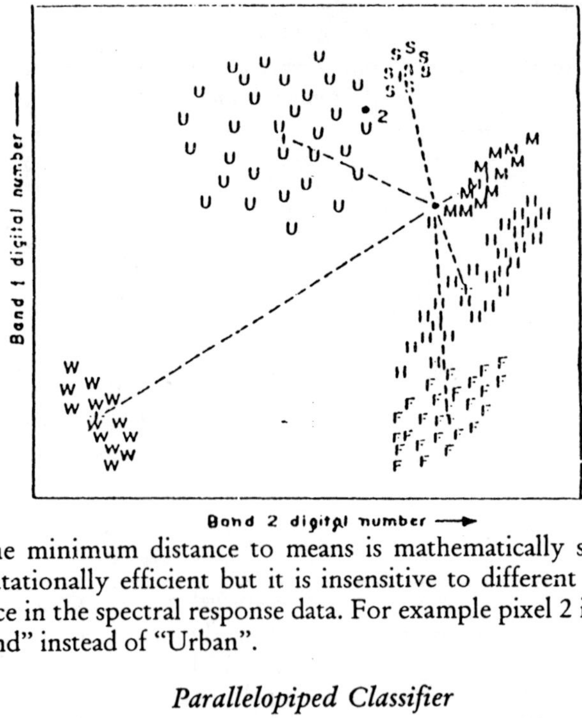

The minimum distance to means is mathematically simple and computationally efficient but it is insensitive to different degrees of variance in the spectral response data. For example pixel 2 is classified to "Sand" instead of "Urban".

Parallelopiped Classifier

The sensitivity to category variance can be introduced by considering the range of values in each category training set. The range may be defined by the highest and lowest digital number values in each band, and appears as a rectangular area in the two-channel scatter diagram (figure 4). An unknown pixel is classified according to the category range, or decision region, in which it lies, or as unknown if it lies outside all regions.

Here pixel 2 will be classified to Urban class while pixel 1 will be

Figure 4

Parallelopiped Classification Strategy

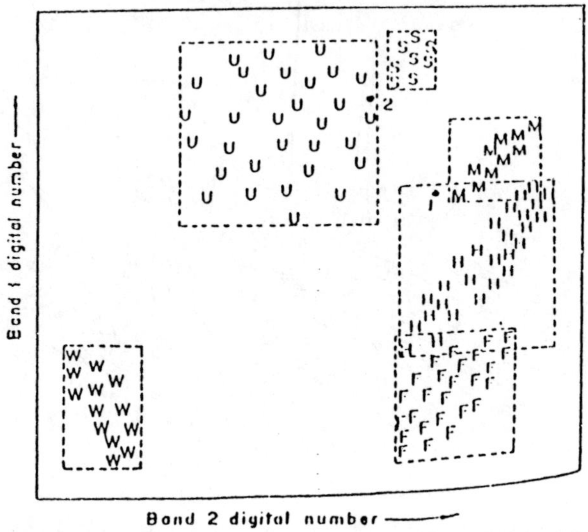

classified to Hay.

This method takes care of variance but not of covariance. In the presence of covariance, the rectangular decision regions fit the category training data very poorly. For example, the insensitivity to covariance would cause pixel 1 to be classified as "hay" instead of "maize".

Gaussian Maximum Likelihood Classifier

The maximum likelihood classifier quantitatively evaluates both the variance and covariance of the category spectral response patterns when classifying an unknown pixel. To do this an assumption is made that the distribution of the cloud of points forming the category training data is Gaussian. Under this assumption, the distribution of a category response pattern can be completely described by the mean vector and covariance matrix. With these parameters, the statistical probability of a given pixel value being a member of a particular land cover class can be computed. Figure 5 shows the probability values plotted in a three-dimensional graph.

The probability density functions are used to classify an unidentified pixel by computing the probability of the pixel value belonging to each category. That is, the computer would calculate the probability of the pixel value occurring in the distribution of class "maize", then

Figure 5

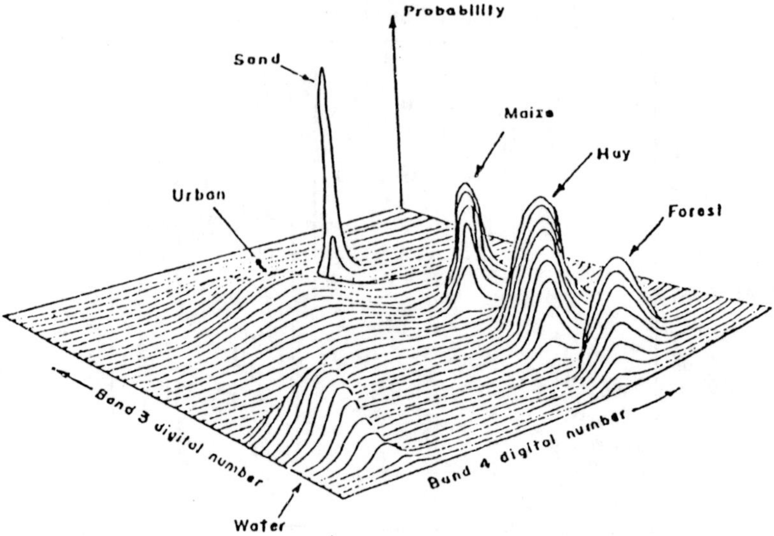

the likelihood of its occurring in class "sand", and so on. After evaluating the probability in each category, the pixel would be assigned to the most likely class or labelled unknown if the probability values are all below a threshold set by the analyst.

In essence, the maximum likelihood classifier delineates ellipsoical eqiprobability contours: in the scatter diagram, the shape of the equiprobability contours expresses the sensitivity of the likelihood classifier to covariance. For example, because of this sensitivity, pixel 1 would be appropriately assigned to the "maize" category (Fig. 6).

Supervized Classification

There are a number of classification algorithms in use in the supervized classification. The choice of algorithm depends on the nature of input data and the desired output. Here we are considering one of the classification methods namely, the Maximum Likelihood Classification, which is commonly used.

Training Area Delineation

Ground truth collection is necessary for checking and ascertaining some the ground features about which the analyst has doubts. This can be done by using topomap and imagery as reference. The analyst will be in a position to train the computer to recognize the grey tones

Figure 6

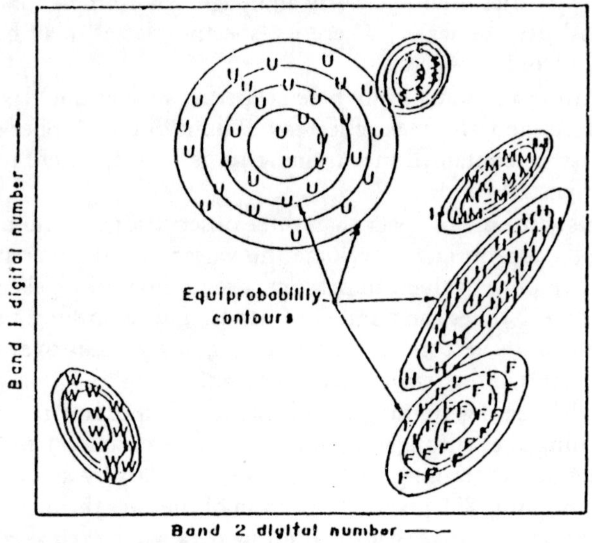

corresponding to a particular class using the ground truth information. For example, an analyst is interested in studying land use categorization. He has already made ground truth data ready with the help of topographic map, interpreted image and a few sample ground checks. It is now possible for him to correlate the reflectance data with the ground check information, i.e., he can now say that a feature on the satellite imagery represents a particular land use class. Now, it is possible for the analyst to give training areas on the image data using a special program for training area delineation. Using this program it is possible to delineate the training area in any shape he wants. The minimum area which can be enclosed by the polygon should not be less than 5 pixels in size. It is possible for the analyst to spread out his training areas throughout the image using the available sample data. The computer will be able to recognize similar features anywhere else on the image based on homogeneity.

The quality of the training process determines the success of the classification and therefore the value of information generated from the entire classification effort. The overall objective of the training process is to assemble a set of statistics that describes the specific spectral response pattern for each land cover type to be classified in an image.

The point that must be emphasized is that all spectral classes constituting each information class must be adequately represented in the training set statistics used to classify an image. An example for 'information class' may be water, where its 'spectral classes' may be clear water, very turbid water etc.

When using any statistically based classifier such as the Maximum Likelihood Method, the Theoretical lower limit of the number of pixels that must be contained in a training set is n + 1, where n is the number of spectral bands.

Obviously the use of fewer than three observations would make it impossible to appropriately evaluate the variance and covariance of the spectral response values. In practice, the number of pixels chosen is from 10 to 100 times the number of bands. This is so since the estimate of the mean vectors and covariance matrices improves as the number of pixels in the training sets increases.

When delineating training set pixels, it is important to analyze several training sites throughout the scene. For example, it would be better to define the training pattern for a given class by analyzing 20 locations containing 800 pixels. Dispersion of the sites throughout the scene increases the change that the training data will be representative of all the variations in the cover types present in the scene.

Maximum Likelihood Classifications

This method has three steps namely (a) statistical analysis of training sets (b) reliability test of training sets and (c) classification state. A brief description follows:

(a) Statistical Analysis of Training Samples: The first step is to calculate the multispectral statistical parameters on the training sets. It is always mandatory to statistically analyze the characteristics of the training areas so that more refinement can be performed on the training areas for better classification. Using the training area as a mask subscene over the original scene, mean vector, variance-covariance matrix or correlation matrix and optional histogram are calculated for each spectral class. Studying these parameters one can infer about the spectral dependency of one band data over the other and also spectral separability of classes.

(b) Reliability Test of Training Sets: A measure of the statistical separation between category response patterns can be computed for all pairs of classes, and represented in the form of a matrix. One statistical parameter commonly used for this purpose is confusion matrix. This matrix gives the number of pixels correctly classified in the corre-

sponding class verses number pixel classified in other classes. Using this matrix the training sets can be altered 80 that the misclassification can be minimized.

(c) Classification Stated: In Maximum Likelihood Classifier, an assumption is made that the distribution of the pixel values are Gaussian (normally distributed) in each class. This assumption of normality is generally reasonable for common spectral response distributions.

The computer would calculate the probability of the pixel value occurring in the distribution of all the classes. After evaluating the probability in each category, the pixel would be assigned to the most likely class (highest probability value), or labeled "unknown" if the probability values are all below a threshold set by the analyst.

The principal drawback of maximum likelihood classification is the large number of computations required to classify each pixel. This is particularly true when a larger number of spectral classes must be differentiated.

The reject threshold is defined as the minimum probability for which a pixel is classified. The value entered in the command is a percentage probability. The allowed values are 1, 2, 5 and 10. A pixel which has a lower probability of belonging to all the classes is assigned to reject class.

After the classification is completed to the user's satisfaction, the file can be saved and colour coded film and photographic outputs can be generated. Also the statistics can be generated automatically for each class.

Case Study

Land Use/Land Cover Analysis Using Two Season IRSLISS-II Data

Operational methodology of land use analysis was not available in digital domain, particularly for large area coverage involving two seasons data. Pilot studies were therefore carried out by Department of Space and a viable methodology using IRS LISS-I data has been developed. The methodology comprises the following seven steps (Figure 6):

1. Data acquisition, loading, merging and geo-referencing.
2. Ground truth collection.
3. Demarcation of district boundary and transfer of administrative and cultural features.
4. Stratified classification of the two seasons data.

Figure 7

Methodology of Land Use/Land Cover Mapping using Digital Techniques

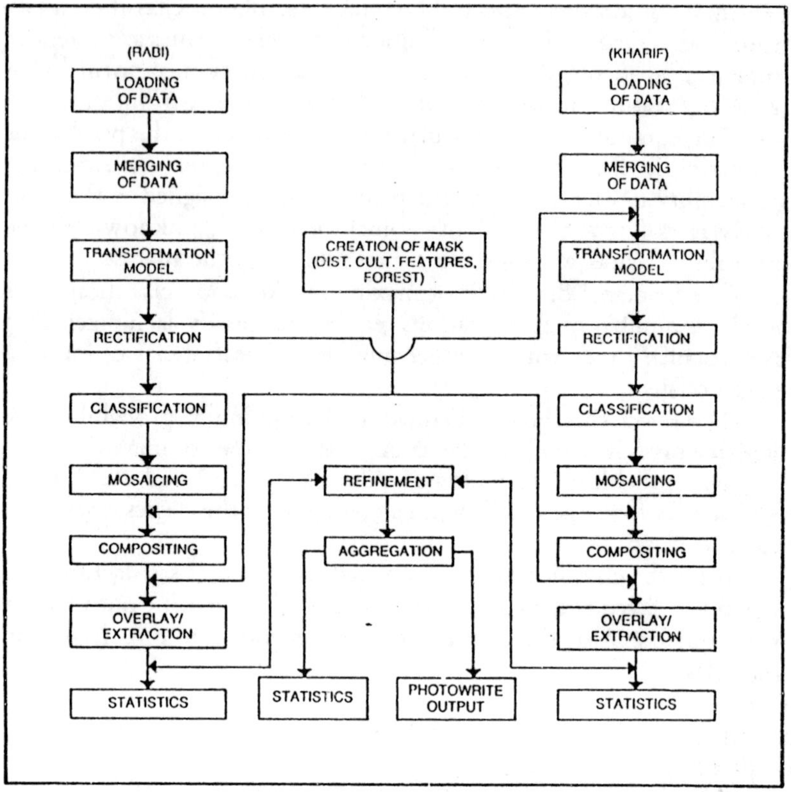

5. Refinement.
6. Aggregation of rabi and kharif classification.
7. Statistics and final output.

Supervized classification is carried out in stratified manner for both rabi and kharif seasons with maximum likelihood classifier. Stratification is effected by digitization of forest boundary from Survey of India (SOI) topographical maps (also other sources) and creation of mask files. The classification proceeds through selection of the training sets, calculation of the statistics of the training sets and the decision boundary of maximum probability based on mean vector, variance, covariance and correlation matrix of the pixels.

Normalized Difference Vegetation Index (NDVI) is adopted for classification of forest areas. Gaussian post-normalization is used in bringing the NDVI in the range of 0-255. Look-up table (LUT) is prepared for output grey values for each project area based on limited ground truth.

The methodology allows human logic and intuition through a specifically developed program REFINE, for correcting and modifying discrepant classification arising out of spectral similarity of two or more classes in a non-forest stratum. In referential refinement, classification of a pixel in one cropping season is evaluated and, if necessary, corrected with reference to its classification in the other season.

Rabi and kharif seasons classified scenes are reformatted to a single output through the process of pixel to pixel aggregation. Finally the land use statistics and the photo-write compatible tape of the aggregated classified output are generated for the project area.

This methodology has been successfully followed in generating district-wise land use/land cover maps of 168 districts.

Land use/land cover mapping using IRS-1A LISS-I data has been a unique exercise for three major reasons. First, it has served to highlight the special merits of IRS data for land use mapping under Indian conditions. Secondly, it has been synergistic in developing operational methodologies, both for visual interpretation and digital analysis. And finally, completion of mapping in 442 districts in record time of one year (effectively operational) has enthused a particular sense of accomplishment and rendered a high degree of confidence to tackle similar projects of national importance. Overall, it can be concluded that IRS-1A data has come of age in India in providing a viable, authentic and cost effective means of obtaining land use resource inventory, operationally.

Chapter 11

Principles and Methods for Terrain Analysis: A Pilot Study of Kerala

Srikumar Chattopadhyay and Mahamaya Chattopadhyay

Introduction

Increasing population pressure and indiscriminate use of capital resources like land and water and consequent environmental problems warrant a fresh look at the ensuing development processes and resource management. It is now well known that for development to be sustainable, it has to depend on judicious management of renewable resources like land and water, the prime movers of the economy. A prudent management plan can be worked out provided sufficient analytical information of resources is available. This has become all the more important due to alarming land degradation in the form of soil erosion, landslides and loss of soil productivity. Inappropriate use of land has also aggravated problems like deforestation recurrence of flood, coastal erosion, non-perenniality of rivers, drying up of springs in the highlands and such others.

In this context, terrain analyses have assumed significant importance due to their wide ranging use as the basis for planning and development, particularly for land and water use. Multiple usability of land poses a serious challenge to the decision makers for devising appropriate use. An apparently appropriate use may turn to be counter-productive in the long-term perspective. It is thus important to have a complete evaluation of land resources. Terrain analysis forms the basis of such an evaluation. Once terrain character is analyzed, detailed evaluation for programme implementation can be taken up. In this paper, the various aspects of terrain analyses—principles, approach, classification system etc.—have been dealt with to provide a comprehensive idea about the subject of terrain analysis with specific examples from Kerala, India.

Principles of Terrain Analysis

The term terrain refers to a complex of surface and near surface attributes significant to man. The abiotic attributes such as relief, geological/geomorphological processes, lithology, soil and hydrological conditions complemented by vegetation/land cover types characterize the terrain (Van Zuidam, 1985). A terrain unit, thus, groups the aspects of geomorphologic origin, physiography, lithology, morphometry, soil geography and to some extent land cover (Meijerink, 1988). The term terrain has been used with the aim to minimize conceptual problems, often encountered in the literature of land evaluation. A terrain unit is integrated in nature and is the resultant of inter-relationships among landform, lithology and soil. It is distinctly differentiable from the surroundings, hence, boundaries are real and not imaginary.

Terrain analysis is indeed a process to classify the earth's surface into units/sub-units, so that, a complex system can be simplified, ordered hierarchically and understood to help in proper assessment or appraisal. However, terrain classification itself is inherently difficult in terms of complexity, extent, association and state (Mitchell 1973, Mabbutt 1968). It is necessary to take into account all these four aspects while advocating a satisfactory classification system. Again, as Mabbutt (1968) has pointed out, the character of land cannot be fully understood in terms of local controls acting in isolation but is in part determined by relationships with adjoining areas with which it interacts with sediment transport and water movement. A parcel of land is thus an open system rather than closed system and this adds further to the complexity in classification process.

The various approaches followed for terrain classification can be categorized into three, namely, (i) the genetic approach; (ii) the landscape approach; and (iii) the parametric approach.

The landscape or terrain approach is preferable as it takes into account a number of factors ranging from geomorphic processes to soil geography. Moreover, landscape units are readily recognizable in field, topomap, airphoto and image. Another advantage of this approach is that the units can be grouped into higher order or can be sub-divided

FIGURE 1

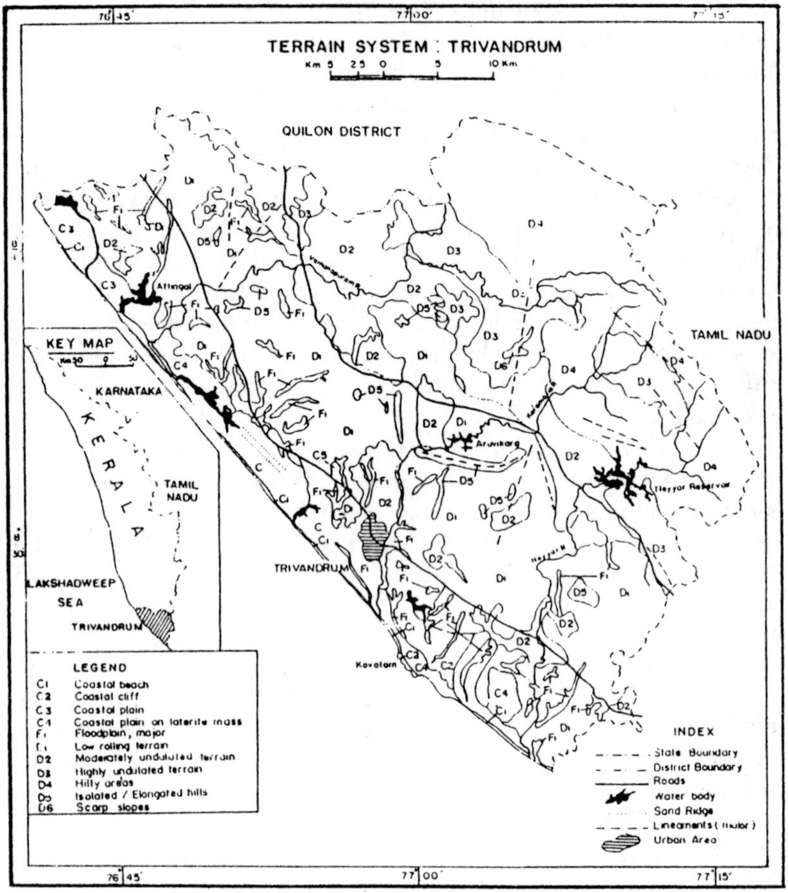
TERRAIN SYSTEM : TRIVANDRUM
QUILON DISTRICT
TAMIL NADU
KEY MAP
KARNATAKA
KERALA
LAKSHADWEEP SEA
TRIVANDRUM
Attingal
Aruvikara
Neyyar Reservoir
Kovalam
LEGEND
C1 Coastal beach
C2 Coastal cliff
C3 Coastal plain
C4 Coastal plain on laterite mass
F1 Floodplain, major
D1 Low rolling terrain
D2 Moderately undulated terrain
D3 Highly undulated terrain
D4 Hilly areas
D5 Isolated / Elongated hills
D6 Scarp slopes
INDEX
State Boundary
District Boundary
Roads
Water body
Sand Ridge
Lineaments (major)
Urban Area
76°45′
77°00′
77°15′

into lower order depending upon the number of variables considered. In this context, genetic approach is basically similar to this approach only in a higher order. In fact, Mitchell (1973) has considered genetic approach for large scale landscape units and landscape approach for small scale land units, while considering both the approaches as part of same system of classification.

The prevalent approaches may also be classified as analytic and synthetic. While the analytic approach is mono-disciplinary and includes data on morphogenesis/morphochronology morphostructure, the synthetic approach investigates the relationship of landform/geomorphic layout of land on one hand and environmental parameters—geology, hydrology, soils, landuse, morphometry—on the other. Synthetic approach and landscape approach are thus similar presenting a holistic picture of the earth's surface and therefore considered to be significant for application purposes.

However, it must be made clear here that incorporation of details essentially depends upon the level of mapping, i.e., scale of the map. When the number of variables increase, the number of units or subdivisions also increase. To depict these units properly, maps should be in large scale. Accordingly, it is possible to establish hierarchical classification system for terrain analysis by involving more and more parameters at different levels. Initiating the classification process with geomorphologic origin followed by specific origin, lithology, morphometry (relief, valley density, slope form) and finally incorporating slope/catena information, sequence can be established. Morphometric and slope/catena information can be for representative/sample location for each terrain unit.

Classification System

It is indicated in the foregoing section that a hierarchical classification system for terrain analysis will be useful to incorporate generalized, as well as detailed data at different levels. The main advantage of this approach is that different users can imply different values to a hierarchy. Moreover, the capacity to incorporate data at different levels makes this classification system simple and useful. It also reduces the chance of redundancy of a classification system when new data and or detailed data are generated as these can be fitted within the classification system. It is always possible for identification or addition of sub-units at any level.

Table 1 is compiled to show the hierarchical classification system followed in various countries/institutions. What emerges from the Ta-

Table 1

Hierarchical Classification System

Level	*Scale*	*CSTRO Australia*	*Biophysical (Canada)*	*Oxford*	*Physiographic*	*ITC (Netherlands)*	*Germany*	*Soviet*
I	1:250000	Terrain Province/complex land system	Eco area/ecoregion	Land region	Physiographic province	Terrain Province	Macrochore	Landscape (mestnest)
II	1:250000	Terrain pattern/land system	Eco zone eco-district	Land system	Main physiographic unit	Terrain system (pattern)	Mesochore	Urochische
III	1:50000	Terrain unit/land unit	Eco section	Land facet	Detailed physio graphic unit	Terrain Unit	Microchore	Urochischa
IV	1:10000	Terrain component/site	Ecosite	Land element	Physiographic element	Terrain component	Ecotope/ complex	Facies

ble 1 is that there lies a certain amount of similarity of thought among various countries about the occurrence of identifiable units of landscape, which can be arranged into a hierarchical order. In the lower rung of this order lies, which Mitchel (1973) termed a "small basic indivisible unit of terrain". This concept of identifying the smallest indivisible basic terrain unit is fundamental to all the terrain classification systems prevalent in the world. This is very significant in systematizing the classification system. It has been pointed out by Linto (1951) that the ultimate units of relief could be regarded as flats and slopes, which are easily detectable in the field and are not susceptible to further subdivision on the basis of form. This lowest level unit is variously referred to as site, element, facies, ecotype, complex or terrain component. The catena concept, intended to depict linkage between morphogenesis and pedogenesis, finds its application at this lowest level.

In the next higher level, the same details could not be depicted and certain generalizations are necessary to prepare terrain maps. The same holds true for the next higher level and so on.

The main characteristics and unit determinants for each level of classification are discussed here.

Level I: Terrain provinces/physiographic provinces/eco-region: The largest unit. Basically uniform in broad genetic, relief, climatic or lithologic characteristics. Highly generalized. Units represent zones of potential primary productivity. Useful at the regional level for provisional decision making. Scale is normally smaller than 1:250,000. In 1:1,000,000 scale maps are available.

Level II: Terrain system/main physiographic unit/land system/or eco-district: This refers to landscape units of characteristic relief development in a certain ecologic environment, frequently determined by genesis, lithology and climatic sub-classes. Moderately generalized. The unit demarcates the area of recurring pattern of relief. The determinants for unit identification are origin (process)/specific origin, lithology and morphometry (internal relief, slope, etc.). Useful for district planning, prioritization, etc. Scale of the map is normally 1:250,000.

Level III: Terrain units/detailed physiographic unit/land unit/eco-section: These units are single landform units or association of homogeneous landforms. Due to internal homogeneity, the unit boundaries are sharp/clear-cut. No or minor generalization for areal classes. The unit determinants are relief, lithology and genesis. As a sub-unit of the previous level, specific origin and landform associations are important demarcating criteria. It includes geomorphic/hydrologic process data and their local expression. Used for developmental planning at the district level, block level, soil erosion potential mapping, prioritization etc. Scale of the map is 1:50,000.

Level IV: Terrain components/physiographic element/land element/ecosite: This is the lowest level or base level of terrain classification. No generalization in data presentation, the units are uniform. They can be identified based on relief criteria, landforms dominated by specific processes, hazards and even selected properties can be the basis of unit demarcation. Catenas and slope properties (crest, slope, valley) are considered for unit demarcation. The unit boundaries are objective and easily identifiable. Data are related to slope processes. Used mainly for microlevel planning, special planning, etc.

In the framework of this conceptual background the present paper advocates a method of terrain analysis with examples from Kerala.

Data Source

IRS 1A image, TM data product and topomaps of 1:250,000 and 1:50,000 scale have provided the basic data used for this study. Field investigation has been conducted in sample areas to develop image interpretation key at the first instance and subsequently to verify terrain maps.

Geological and other relevant data are obtained from published literatures and maps.

Terrain Determinants in Kerala

Kerala, covering an area of 38,860 km^2 lies in the south-western part of peninsular India. It extends over a distance of 560 km along the coast. The Western ghat crestline reaching to a maximum altitude of 2695 m at Anamudi lies within a short distance from the coast. The Western ghats being the plateau scarp of the south Indian shield has a pronounced effect on the terrain character of Kerala. Relief distribution in terms of area-altitude ratio is asymmetric. Around 62 per cent of the total geographical area lies below 100m. Widespread lateritization is another important aspect of Kerala's terrain. Kerala is endowed with heavy rainfall (350m annually). Seasonal variation in temperature is low. Influence of sea and orography is well pronounced in climatic condition.

The principal terrain determining factors are listed below. Terrain forming processes act in conjunction with these factors, resultant of which is the present day terrain condition.

Geological Formations (GSI 1976, Soman 1980)

(a) Crystalline rocks of precambrian-charnockite khondalite gneisses, granites, dykes, etc.
(b) Sedimentary rocks of tertiary-quilon formations, sand-stone, pebble beds, etc.
(c) Recent and sub-recent formation—sediments forming the low lying areas and river valleys.

Lineaments (Sinha Roy and Mathai, 1979)

Three prominent sets: NW-SE, WNW-ESE, NNW-SSE N-S and NE-SW.

Plantation Surfaces (King 1950, Vaidyanathan 1967, Sinha Roy 1979 among others)

Number of planation surfaces identified. Apart from the coastal plain prominent surfaces are at 20m-50m 75m-100m, 150m-220m, 300m-360m, 600m, 900m and 1800m. As morphostratigraphic units, these surfaces are resultant of the peneplanation/pediplanation processes and contribute to the shaping up of the terrain condition.

Lateritization (GSI 1981, Subramanian 1978, Mallikarjuna et al 1981, Rajendran and Narayanswamy 1987).

Three spells of lateritization pre-tertiary, post-tertiary and post-pleistocene.

Laterites marked as mesa (duricrust), mounds, interfluves and also slopes. Covers 60 per cent of total geographical area. Hard crust facilitates pediplanation/parallel slope retreate.

Drainage

Major rivers 44, of which three rivers are east flowing. Major slope towards west. Structurally controlled rivers characterized by two major knick points at the altitudinal range of 90m-150m (midland-upland junction) and 300m-540m (upland-highland junction) Abrupt fall in gradient.

Physiographic Setting

Broad physiographic units five, namely, western ghats (600m) in two patches separated by the Palghat gap. Foothill region (300-600m), upland region (100-300m), midland (20-100m) and coastal strip. Raised beaches, sand bars, back waters, kayals estuaries etc. significant in coastal strip.

In micro scale, sheet, rill, gully erosion, landslide and mass wasting, etc. play important role in terrain formation. Domination of lateritization processes in terrain formation is overwhelming in Kerala. Due to this, the processes of pediplanation is dominant resulting in flat bottomed valleys flanked by steep side slopes. Due to concentration of heavy rainfall within a span of 6 to 7 days, excessive loose materials are produced and get accumulated in the valleys. This also contributes to the flatness of the valley bottom.

Classification Method

The determinants of terrain system and the classification process described in the foregoing section indicate that the morphogenesis/ geomorphological processes should form the basis over which lithologic, morphometric and other environmental data need to be incorporated. Thus the classification process must begin with the 'main origin'—the dominant process currently operative. All terrain units or landforms can be related to the exogenous or endogenous processes responsible for their development. As far as Kerala is concerned, the present terrain forming processes are mostly exogenous. Although the formation of the Western ghats and certain coastal features can be directly related to faulting and hence structurally controlled, their present outlay is predominantly the result of the ongoing exogenous processes. Chemical weathering widely manifested through lateritization do have a significant role in terrain development. However, it acts more as a control mechanism on denudational processes.

The following main and specific origins are identified in the case of Kerala.

Marine:
- Erosional
- Accretional
- Complex

Fluvio-marine/estuarine:
- Forms associated with brackish water.

Fluvial:
- Accumulational
- Transitional
- Erosional
- Complexes

Denudational/accumulational:
- Terrain of half orange relief

Denudational:
- Units associated with plantation,
- Mesa dominated areas.
- Hills and slopes

Under each of these processes, a number of units have been identified. A brief description of these units is provided here so that the classification scheme advocated in this study may be understood clearly.

Units Under Marine Origin

Erosional forms: Coastal cliff, abrasion platforms and lateritic coastal plains are included in this category. Coastal process with high energy environment has given rise to these types of terrain units.

Accretional forms: Beach, coastal plain (clayey/marshy, sandy) tidal flats, mud flats, etc. constitute this category. These units occur under low energy environment.

Kerala coast is significant for sand bar/barrier beach formations, which is partially responsible for development of backwater systems parallel to the coast. Coastal dunes, landform of aeolian origin are not separately marked.

Complex: Plains with paleo-strand lines, i.e., older coastal plain with beach ridges, etc., can be categorized as complexes.

Units of Fluvio-marine/estuarine Origin

Under this system, the units are mostly depositional. Estuaries and tidal water bodies commonly known as back waters are demarcated. Islands which are mostly braided bars are also marked under this unit.

Units of Fluvial Origin

Accumulation forms: Units developed under fluvial origin are mainly accumulational or depositional. Flood plains, valley fills, etc., are marked as individual units without any complexity. Terraces adjoining the main river, levees, back swamps and alluvial fans are considered in this category.

Transitional forms: Interior plain away from the main rivers, adjoining the undulating topography or foot slopes has been categorized in this group. Alluvial/colluvial deposits alternated by slopes and low rolling hills also characterized this unit.

Erosional forms: High level fluvial terraces are generally erosional terraces.

Complex units: Younger deltaic plains and older deltaic plains are the two complex units under fluvial origin. Delta landscapes are conjugation of individual units, like active flood plain, terraces, levees splays, etc. Demarcation of these individual units are not possible given the scale and the method of analysis. In the deltaic environment these features can be separated only in case of a detailed survey and having substantial unit-wise areal spread.

Units Under Denudational/accumulational Origin

Hummocky terrain or units of half orange relief: In a hilly undulated topography like Kerala, large areas exhibit hummocky land forms. Small mounds surrounded by near stabilized slopes are separated by flat-bottomed small valleys. Separation of these valleys from the slopes is possible while mapping is done in a large scale, i.e., at the component level only. These features are marked together as part of a terrain unit in this scale.

Denudational Including Structural Units

Denudational landforms are the result of denudational processes (weathering, erosion, etc.) acting upon the lithology. Weathering includes chemical and physical processes. Erosion refers to the rills, sheet, gully, mass movement, river erosion, etc.

Therefore, the denudational units will be associated with weathering phenomenon like lateritization in a larger magnitude and in a local scale, slope formation, mass wasting, landslide, soil erosion, etc., will contribute.

Apart from these, variations of denudational units depend upon lithological variations, presence of relict landforms, structural adjustment of topography and finally altitudinal variations.

The denudational units are ordered principally on the basis of plantation, slope condition and hilliness. Isolated hills are mostly lithological/structural. Scarp slopes bordering the plateaux and mountains are morphostructural features. The denudational units are arranged as:

Units associated with plantation surface, lateritic mesa: About 60 per cent of Kerala's land is covered by laterite or lateritic materials. Lateritic mesas are conspicuous features in the state. Widespread mesa formations are evident in the northern districts. Mesa tops/crests are separated. Slopes around the mesa are steep and mostly denudational. Here also valley and side slope of a mesa are not separable in this scale.

Units associated with lithology, slope/relief: Based on the degree of undulation, various units are marked from low rolling terrain to highly undulating terrain and hilly areas. Lithological effect is pronounced in the case of isolated hills and scarp slopes. Table 2 summarizes the discussion on systems of terrain classification followed in Kerala.

Once units have been identified based on this procedure, the detailed characteristic features covering relative relief, slope, drainage,

Table 2

Systems of Terrain Classification

Origin	*Specific processes*	*Terrain system*	*Remark*
Marine	Accretional	Beach	Includes sandbar
		Coastal plain	Sandy, clayey/Marshy other than rocky
		Tidal flats/mud flats	Usually flooded during high tide.
			Also includes reclaimed portions of tidal flats and mud flats.
	Erosional	Coastal cliff coastal plain lateritic	
	Complexes	Plain with paleostrand lines	
Fluviomarine/estuarine	Units associated with brackish water	Estuaries/backwater	Alternate fresh and tide water surge
		Islands	Braided bars
Fluvial	Accumulational	Floodplains, valley fills	Includes levees, back swamps
	Erosional	High level fluvial terraces	Erosional terraces adjacent to main channel
	Transitional transitional/interior plain	Transitional between undulating terrain and flat, sandy, clay area	
Fluvial	Comolexes	Older deltaic plain	Include saucer shaped basins, cross channel defunct

Contd...

Contd...

Fluvial	Complexes	Younger deltaic plain	Includes levees, back swamps, cross channel active
Denudational cum accu-mulational	Association of both	Hummocky terrain (terrain of half orange relief	Patches of flood plain included. Association of valley fills with near stabilized slope.
Denudational	Unit associated with planation/lateritic mesa formation	Mesa surface	Top surface/crest of the lateritic mesa, including 'Soup Plates'.
		Mesa bounding slope	Include terraces and narrow flood plain along the river
	Units associated with relief/slope and lithology	Low rolling terrain	Gently undulating low relief area.
		Moderately undulating terrain	Moderate relief areas
		Highly undulating terrain	Area of strong relief.
		Hilly areas and mountains	Includes western ghats mountains.
		Isolated hills	Structurally controlled hills are included
		Scarp slope	Steep plateau bounding slopes, morpho structural features.

soil and landuse of each of these units can be computed.

Results and Discussion

Terrain system mapping of the state of Kerala has been attempted following this procedure. Results for the district of Tiruvananthapuram is presented here as a sample.

The district of Tiruvananthapuram covers an areas of 2186 sq. km. It extends from the coast to the Western ghats. Therefore, the main processes operative for the Kerala region are prevalent in this district also. Altogether, 11 terrain system units have been identified excluding waterbodies, man-made reservoirs (Neyyar, Aruvikara and Peppara) and backwaters, both are present in this district.

Landform controlled by fluvio-marine/estuarine processes covers little over 7 per cent of the total geographical area. Coastal plain exhibits evidences of paleo-sand ridges/strand lines. The Kovalam cliff on crystalline rocks is a notable feature. Low lateritic cliff is marked towards south of Vizhinjam. Between Kovalam and Vizhinjam, pocket beaches are well developed. Varkkailai cliff on tertiary laterite is a type locality for lateritic studies.

Tiruvananthapuram district is drained by three major rivers, namely, the Neyyar, the Karamana and the Vamanapuram. It is notable that flood plains could not be marked in continuous stretches along these rivers. Field investigation indicates that the rivers are incising—cutting down its own flood plain. Like other rivers these three rivers also join the sea through a parallel running backwater system. It is important to note that the outfall of the Neyyar river indicates a oscillatory course. Emergence of marine terraces can also be marked in close examination of this area. Meanders in midland and highland region are structurally controlled.

Terrain system under denudational origin covers around 90 per cent of total area. Low rolling terrain covers maximum area (Table 3). Alternate valleys/basins and hills characterize this unit. Altitudinally, this unit lies below 100 m contour. Although this unit has been grouped under denudational processes, it exhibits accumulational features also. In fact rolling nature is due to alternate accumulational valleys and denudational low hills.

The units of D3 and D4 form parts of the hilly Western ghats. The Ponmudi and Agasthamalai are the two important peaks in this district. Scarp slopes are actually fault/fault line scarp characterized by bare rocks. Parts of D3 and D4, provenance zone, are highly susceptible to erosion. Isolated hills represented as D5 are structurally

Table 3

Terrain Units and Their Characteristics, Tiruvananthapuram District

Origin/ Specific origin	*Unit name*	*Map symbol*	*Area (%)*	*General characteristics*				*Land use*	*Remarks*
				Relative relief (metre)	*Slope (%)*	*Drainage density (m/km^2)*	*Broad soil character*		
MARINE									
Accre-tional	Beach	C1	0.7	5	—	—	Sand	Bare sand	Narrow between high and low water mark
	Coastal plain	C3	5.6	15	4.5	0.5	Sandy	Settlement cultivable land, coconut	Wide in places with paleo ridges
Erosional	Coastal cliff	C2	0.1	30	15.0	1.6	Shallow Soil, lateritic	Settlement tree crops, coconut	Kovalam-Vizhinjam, Varkala area
	Coastal plain lateritic	C4	1.2	30	5.0	0.5	Lateritic	Settlement with trees, coconut	Mostly adjoining cliffs
FLU-VIAL/									
Accumula-tional	Flood plains/valley fills	F1	2.1	15	7.0	1.5	Alluvium, colluvic in valley fills	Seasonal crops some coconut	Marked in patches some places, reclaimed, include lower terraces also

Contd...

Contd...

DENUDATIONAL									
Associated with relief/slope and lithology	Low rolling terrain	D1	42.8	20	10.0	1.0	Alluvium/laterities	Cultivable land, settlement with trees	Covers wider area
	Moderately undulating terrain	D2	13.5	60	20	s2.0	Lateritic	Tree crops, rubber plantation, settlements with trees	Extensive around Vamanapuram river
	Highly undulating terrain	D3	10.0	95	35	2.0	Lateritic	Mixed tree crops, scrubs, sparse settlement	Foothills of western ghats
	hilly area	D4	19.9	150	30	4.0	Forest loam, shallow soil	Forest plantation, tribal settlement	Western ghats, dissected
	Isolated hills	D5	1.1	60	30	2.6	Lateritic, and residual soil	Mixed trees, rubber plantation, rocky	Structurally controlled
	Scarp slopes	D6	0.1	495	55	5.3	Bare rock, shallow soil	Rocky Scrubs	Erosional scarps
	Water bodies		3.0						

controlled. The trend of the Nedumangad hills is well marked in IRS image. Table 3 provides terrain system and their characteristics.

Conclusion

This paper covers the methodology developed for the ongoing project on "Terrain Analysis in Kerala through Remote Sensing".

There exists a close correspondence between terrain character and landuse. A longitudinal zonation is marked in both the cases. Table 3 brings this out quite explicitly.

It emerges that the method of classification followed here, is quite appropriate. Linking of terrain maps of large scale with small scale perhaps is possible only by introducing a classification system, which is open ended and capable of integrating data at different levels. The hierarchical system advocated in this study serves the purpose. In this scheme, subsequent works become complementary and a step forward to assimilate data of further details. In this connection, the approach adopted here has far reaching consequences. It can successfully form the base for natural resource data management system (NRDMS).

References

Geological Survey of India (GSI), (1976: *Geology and Mineral Resources of the States of India*, Part IX Kerala, Misc. Pub. 30.

Geological Survey of India (GSI) 1981: *Lateritization Process*, Oxford and IBH Pub. Co., New Delhi.

King L.C. 1950: The study of world's plainlands: A new approach in geomorphology. *Quart J Geol. Soc.* V. 106, pp. 101-127, London.

Mabbutt J.A., (1951), Review of concepts of land classification, In G.A. Stewart ed. *Land Evaluation*, Macmillan of Australia.

Mitchel C.W., (1973), *Terrain Evaluation*, Longman, London.

McFarlane M.J., (1976), *Laterite and Landscape*, Academic Press, London.

Mallikrjuna C., Vidyadharan K.T., Power S.D. Senthiappan M. and Francis P.G. (1981): Geological geochemical and geotechnical aspects of the laterites in Kerala, In *Lateritization Process*, GSI, Oxford and IBH, New Delhi.

Meijerink A.M.J., (1988), Data acquisition and data capture through terrain mapping units. *ITC Journal*, 1 pp. 23-44.

Rajendra C.P. and Narayanswamy 1987: A note on lateritization cycles associated with sedimentaries, Kasaragod district, Kerala, *J Geol Soc. Ind.* V. 30, pp. 309-314.

Subramanian K.S., (1978), How old are laterites in the Indian peninsula? A suggestion, *J. Geol. Soc. Ind.* v. 19, pp. 269-272.

Sinha Roy S, and Mathai T., (1979), Development of western continental margin of India and plateau uplift as related to geology and tectonics of Kerala. Professional paper No. 5, Centre for Earth Science Studies (CESS), Tiruvananthapuram.

Sinha Roy S., (1979), Fluvial and landform morphology of the Karamana drainage basin. Professional Paper No. 2, CESS, Tiruvananthapuram.

Soman K., (1980), Geology of Kerala, Professional paper No. 8, CESS Tiruvananthapuram.

Vaidyanadhan R., (1967), An outline of the geomorphic history of India, south of north latitude 18, Seminar vol. *Geomorphologial Studies in India*, Univ. of Sagar, pp. 121-130.

Van Zuidam R.A., (1985), *Aerial Photo Interpretation in Terrain Analysis and Geomorphological Mapping*, Smit Pub., The Hague.

Chapter 12

Remote Sensing in Erosion Surveys: An Approach to Regional Disparity Measure through Land Resource Assessment

S.P. Mishra

The disparity in socio-economic conditions of people in any area is largely related to the quality of land and its nature of utilization. This is quite true in those areas where agricultural practices are predominant in economic activities. The quality of land is decreasing regularly by the process of erosion as the eroded soil contains a certain amount of nutrients and their removal results in a loss of fertility. Williams and Evans (1977) estimated a replacement cost each year of $24 per acre for three nutrients, N, P, K from a 5 t/acre (11 m.t./ha) soil loss, although in long run. The problem of erosion and its control has now become a very important aspect of environmental planning and land resource management. Its first component is the development of gully and dissection of land which create unsuitable land for cultivation. The second component is the re-deposition of eroded materials on down slope either on fertile flood plain or more seriously in reservoirs. In both the situations, it creates a great problem and has become a challenge to the planners and scientists. It has attracted the attention of not only the scholars of related disciplines like agricultural engineering, pedology, geomorphology, geology, etc. but also of social workers, administrators and planners. In general, there are two areas where we need more information: (i) evaluation of erosion, damage cost in terms of production, pollution and loss of water storage and (ii) erosion control measures (Moldenhaur, 1980).

Remote sensing can provide a very powerful source of information (Rao, 1991) with a clear synoptic view of the distribution of factors which influence the erosion hazard. It allows a constant evaluation of the problem by providing repetitive coverage of the area. This may help to adopt proper land management and conservation measures and to develop a mutually satisfactory planning approach for farming practices. Remote sensing technique provides a reliable data source, relatively cheaper than any other source of information. It has increased the potentiality of surveys and minimized the cost by saving time and manpower. The unique contribution of the technique lies in its role for survey of those areas which were beyond the range of traditional methods of survey (Mishra, 1991). The present research paper is also an attempt to analyze the applicability of remote sensing technique in erosion surveys, accounting the factors involved, process and mechanics of erosion. The evaluation of the facts has also been supported through a case study of Hissar district from Haryana, India.

Mechanics of Erosion and Controlling Factors

The process of erosion may be grouped in three phases, i.e., (i) detachment of individual particles from the soil mass, (ii) their transport by geomorphic agents (running water, wind, etc.) and (iii) deposition of eroded materials which is effected by the availability of sufficient energy to transport the materials. The severity of erosion depends upon the quantity of materials supplied by detachment and the capacity of eroding agents to transport it (Morgan, 1979). The energy available for erosion is of two forms: (i) potential and (ii) kinetic (Norman, 1979). Potential energy (PE) results from the height differences between two bodies. It can be stated as a product of mass (m), height difference (h) and acceleration due to gravity (g), i.e., PE = m h g (in units of kg, m and ms^{-2} respectively, yields a value in joules). PE for the erosion is converted into kinetic energy (KE), the energy of motion. This is related to the mass (m) and velocity of the eroding agent, in the expression: $K = 1/2\ m\ v^2$ (in units of kg, and $(ms^{-1})^2$ also gives value in joules). The details of these attributes can be seen in Norman (1979).

The terrain parameters to erosion susceptibility have been emphasized by geomorphologists (Rao, 1975; Williams and Morgan, 1976; Verstappen, 1970, 1983). The study and mapping of various kinds of geomorphological processes may be very useful to attain a full understanding of the present situation of erosion including its development in the past and in the future (Verstappen, 1983: p. 370). In this context, the geoscientific approaches account two factors as more important for soil erosion survey. These are: (i) slope characteristics and processes involved and (ii) rock and soil types.

Morphological characteristics and nature of slope play a very crucial role in the process of soil erosion by water. The morphological characteristics of slope are considered as gradient, length, micro-relief, configuration in plain and foreland (Stokking, 1972). These aspects along with different forms of slope (concave, convex, rectilinear, cliff, etc.) largely affect the overland flow and infiltration. The erodibility is increased on a steep slope which permits higher velocity of flow and lower infiltration rate than the gentler slope with same lithologic materials. Such situations are common in mountainous areas where the eroded materials are carried out by rivers and deposited in the foot hill zones. Owing to this, a series of piedmont fans have been developed in the foot-hill zones of Lesser Himalayas and can be seen as best example of erosional activities due to gradient differences.

Lithology of the eroding slopes is also a major factor which governs the distributional pattern of erosion by water (Verstappen, 1983: p. 371). Knowledge of the underlying materials can largely help to study the susceptibility of the various processes of erosional works on slopes. Therefore, the identification and mapping of different lithomorphological units would be of prime importance in the assessment of erosion. Likewise, certain characteristics of soil profiles have a great effect on matters such as permeability, infiltration rate and storage capacity (Bernett et al., 1971). Other matters related to soil, i.e., texture, organic content, permeability of sub-soil, drainage condition, etc. should also be given emphasis while the erosion studies are being conducted.

Remote Sensing in Erosion Survey and Mapping

There are as much as 16 methods of soil erosion assessment applied in various studies as listed by Zachar (1982) but among them, the remote sensing is the most recent one. Both the airborne and space-borne data are being used for this purpose, but the former is more applicable for large scale survey. To obtain a global and synthetic view of a region, remote sensing techniques particularly satellite imagery is very useful. The major weakness of satellite imagery is the necessity of ground truth collection with the background knowledge of the area. Although erosion is not directly visible on small scale imagery except for a synoptic view and some very strong geological erosion, the relationship between geographical areas can be observed with greater clarity. Definite boundaries of some geological phenomena which had not previously been identified even in well documented countries like USA, have now been made easier with this technique (Keech, 1978).

Aerial photography has considerable advantages in the preparatory stages of terrain studies and mapping of erosion-prone areas. The chief advantage of this method lies in its ability to measure the very small formations on soil surface and their changes by taking repeated photographs. Research work based on aerial photographs requires little field work and evaluation is quick and reliable (Zacher, 1982). This technique has largely been used in investigation of erosion and its control measures by Gorrie (1935), Cooper (1942), Margruder (1949), Pronicheva (1955), Semenova (1959), Stubner (1955), Ramusson (1962), etc. Among these, the work of Stubner can be especially mentioned who has widely used photogrammetrical method in his research on soil erosion and control measures. Recently, the launching of different satellites equipped with developed scanning systems in various range of spectral resolution have brought about a drastic change in the remote sensing techniques but application of aerial photography for large scale analysis is still valuable.

Erosion survey can be grouped in three categories based on the aim and scale of survey (Verstappen, 1983). These are:

(i) detailed survey based on large scale aerial photographs (1:1,000-1:5,000) and extensive field observation,
(ii) medium scale survey covering one or more complete drainage basin (scale 1:20,000-1:25,000), and
(iii) small scale survey taking entire country or region for nation-wide inventory based on small scale air photos, aerial mosaics (e.g. 1:50,000-1:70,000) and satellite imagery or enlarged photographs upto scale 1:200,000 or 1:250,000.

A model study for forecasting large-scale patterns of soil erosion in semi-arid Australia has been presented by Pickup and Chewings (1988) by using Landsat MSS data. Alams and Haris (1987) have studied the soil erosion and reflectance in Moorland (N. England) and observe that the prevailing ecosystem has lost its balance between the process of erosion and the natural surface cover. The study has focussed on the relationship between spectral reflectance and ground variables pertaining to erosion.

In assessing the value of remote sensing in planning erosion control and survey, it is necessary to identify the factors that influence it and then define the extent to which these factors can be recognized on remotely sensed data. These important factors are: (a) erosivity of rainfall, (b) slope, (c) cover, (d) erodibility of soil, and (e) human influence

(Keech, 1978). United States Department of Agriculture has presented a Universal Soil-Loss Equation (USLE) (USDA, ARS, Agricultural Handbook, 282, 1965) as given below, which expresses the factors involved in soil erosion:

$$A = R \times K \times L \times S \times C \times P$$

where,

A = soil loss in short tones/area
R = rainfall erosivity index.
K = soil erodibility factor—soil type
L = length of slope factor
S = slope factor
C = crop management factor (cultivated bare-fallow)
P = conservation practice factor.

The application of above USL equation has widely been done in numerous studies especially in USA (Wischmeier, 1976; Wischmeier et al., 1971; Wischmeier and Smith, 1978). Qualitatively the principle of soil erosion can be expressed as function of erosivity and erodibility [erosion = f (erosivity) (erodibility)]. Erosivity is related to the energy, i.e., rainfall, while erodibility indicates the physical characteristics (soil) and management (land and crop) system. Soil erosion in arid/semi-arid regions is mainly caused by wind action and other related process somewhat different from those of the humid regions. Therefore a different equation has been developed for arid/semi-arid conditions (Chepil, 1963):

$$E = f(I, C, K, L, V)$$

where,

E = soil loss by wind erosion
I = erodibility that is vulnerability to wind erosion
C = factor representing the local wind condition
K = soil surface roughness
L = width of the field in prevailing wind direction and
V = measure of the vegetative cover.

The erosivity of rainfall and other climatic data cannot be derived directly from remote sensing. This can be done through the analysis of drainage basin morphometry, drainage network, vegetation growth and existing landforms which are well recognizable on remote sensing data. Secondly, reliable base map by using band five of Landsat (Scale 1:250,000) or IRS-IA (Scale 1:250,000 or 1:50,000) can be prepared to superimpose the climatic data. The synoptic view of terrain conditions is easily perceived on imagery and it can provide a balance idea pertaining to most dominant erosion agent of the region (may be water or wind). This would lead the observer to adopt an appropriate methodology of erosion assessment.

Slope, the second factor of erosion can be measured more precisely through vertical aerial photographs by using parallax bar under mirror stereoscope. Since, the scale varies away from the nadir/principal points (both are same on vertical air photographs), so it is difficult to compute the angle of slope quickly for a larger area. However, it can be done at sample sites to study the sheet and rill erosion, development of rill into gullies and creation of ravines and valleys. Repeated photographs at a certain lag of time provide a better knowledge pertaining to these aspects of erosion. A comprehensive application of large-scale aerial photographs for slope estimation using different stereo-techniques has been presented by Turner (1977). As regards the satellite imagery, it is not particularly good as information source for slope measurement. Identification of subtle changes in grey tone in Landsat imagery which arise as a result of the varying angles of incidence of light onto the reflecting surfaces and texture of the images can give an idea of the slope intensity (Keech, 1980). With the help of drainage networks recognized on imagery, the degree of dissection which is indirectly related to slope can frequently be marked.

The third factor of erosion, i.e., land cover is the factor most easily recognized on Landsat imagery and the subtle changes of grey tone are of great importance in this respect (Keech, 1978). With the help of the colour additive viewer, the combination of B5 and B7 of Landsat (red and green colour) gives a false colour simulation which can be used for the study of vegetation cover. As such, the imagery of the critical season can provide a sound information by demarcating the risk areas through the analysis of cover data. As regards the pan-chromatic B and W aerial photographs, the stereoscopic image provides a very detail information of terrain by which different types of vegetal cover can be identified confidently. Soil erodibility data, the fourth factor of erosion can be extracted from both satellite imagery and aerial photographs. The Landsat data or IRS-IA product (B and W or FCC or enhanced form) can be used as a reliable source of information by developing reconnaissance maps of soils. Aerial photography is an aid to soil mapping but it may not be used as a substitute of ground field work. The human influence on land can easily be identified on imagery and aerial photographs. The erosion processes can more actively be involved along lines of weakness caused due to human interference like road and other development activities, cultivation etc.

Case Study

The case study pertains to the district of Hissar in western Haryana (India) which is characterized by semi-arid climatic conditions and wind is the main geomorphic agent of erosion. At present, there is only one seasonal river, i.e., river Ghaggar, flowing in the northern part of the district. Relict rivers Saraswati and Chautang (Dhrisdawati) used to flow through the district in the past and now palaeo-channel traces remain. Both panchromatic black and white aerial photographs (Scale 1:50,000) and satellite imagery (IRS-IA product scale 1:250,000 and Landsat TM 1;50,000) were used in the analysis of factors of erosion. Different units of terrain were identified and mapped on the basis of intensity of erosion and the results were transferred on base map (1:250,000). Verification of the facts was done during selective field checks (October-November 1989) and incorporating the corrections, a final map showing different units of erosion was prepared (Fig. 1, Table 1).

It is felt necessary to present a brief description of palaeoclimatic/geomorphologic conditions prevailing in the area during the past to evaluate the existing terrain and erosion activities. The archaeological evidences in Hissar district provide ample means of evaluating existing terrain, dating of geomorphological features like abandoned river beds and the climatic conditions. The remnants of the ancient settlement sites found at places in the district especially in the villages of Siswal, Bonawali and Rakhigarhi indicate the favourable physicoclimatic conditions for human inhabitation since the dawn of Indus civilization, say about 5,000-4,500 B.C. A humanized development of such kinds may not be possible in unsuitable conditions. However, Oldham and Stein claim that a riverine culture like the one along the Ghaggar-Saraswati does not necessarily mean greater humidity to the adjacent areas (Verstappen, 1970).

Hissar district has locationaly a bowl-like shape where rivers originating from Himalayas in the north and north-east direction, and from Aravali in the southern direction used to flow. The rivers flowing through the district (Saraswati and Chautang) were governed to a great extent by their upper catchment in the Himalayas Mountain system. It is also believed that the diversion in the flow direction of the river system into river Yamuna, now flowing towards river Ganga may also be the cause of the dryness of Saraswati (Ghaggar) river due to the consequent drying out of Chautang river system rather than cli-

FIGURE 1

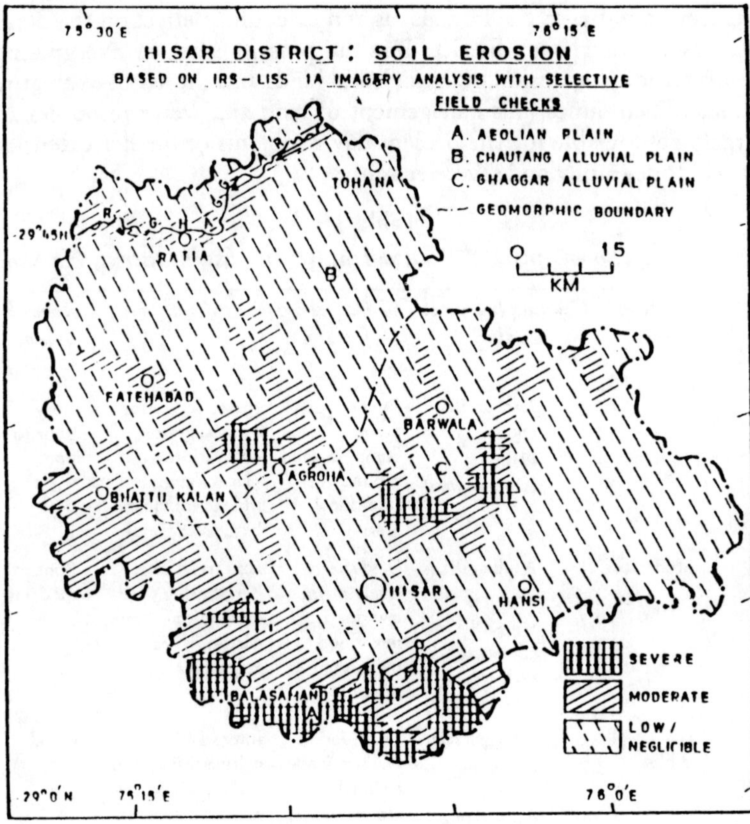

matic change. But this view is not so convincing in Verstappan's opinion (1970) who has investigated a deteriorating climate by the ample evidences of dry river beds found in various parts of Thar desert. Such fluctuations in climatic conditions may also be assumed with reference to Hissar district and surrounding dry regions. It is evident from the relict courses observed in southern, south-western parts of the district (near Chaudhariwas, Burak, Rohillan Kalan villages) which may have been the tributaries of the Chautang (Dhrisdavati) river and that these originated in Aravali areas and dried up later due to low rainfall and choking of stream beds by aeolian sands (Mishra and Mohammad, 1989; Mishra, 1991). It can be stated in a nutshell that the expansion and creation of desert/semi-desert topographic conditions in south, south-west and other parts of the district may have occurred due to climatic fluctuation, choking of stream beds by aeolian sands and past tectonic activities in the Himalayas and its counter effect on the drainage system in Hissar district. But the present state of overgrazing, deforestation, expansion of agricultural lands and the act of excavating on stabilized dunes, mismanagement of land and water resources are largely responsible for the present day problems of further extension in arid-topography and severe erosion.

Table 1

Different Erosion Units and Related Features in Hissar District, Haryana

	Erosion units		*Geomorphological units*	*Topographic features*	*Vegetation*	*Remarks (land quality)*
1.	Severe	1:1 1.2	Aeolian Plain Chautang Plain (Dhrisdawati)	Sand dunes, dune, complex, sand mounds, Interdunal areas	sparse vegetation, bushes, grasses, cultivation at places, (gram, millets etc.) jhar bari, trees (jand)	Very poor to poor
2.	Moderate	2.1 2.2 2.3	Aeolian Plain Ghaggar Plain Chautang Plain (Dhrisdawati)	Sand sheet, sandy plain, riverine areas, new flood plain, sand mounds	jand trees, jhar, beri, bushes, cultivation—gram, cotton, wheat, vegetables	Poor to moderate
3.	Low/negl igible	3.1 3.2	Ghaggar Plain Chautang Plain (Dhrisdawati)	Old flood plain, palaeo-channels, sandy patches	Intensive cultivation cotton, paddy, wheat; plantation-garden and groves etc.	Good

Source: Imagery interpretation and selective field checks.

In order to carry out an erosion survey efficiently, a systematic approach has been followed by geomorphologists (Rao, 1975; Verstappen, 1983). Geographers are more interested in finding the spatial distribution of erosion (location, expansion, etc.), processes acting there upon and its impact on socio-economic conditions of the people. In present study of erosion activities in Hissar district, a systematic approach has been followed by covering the following aspects:

— lithology
— geomorphological unit
— slope classes (in dunal plain)
— process of erosion and slope instability
— soil and cover types
— structural data, topography
— hydrographic data
— man-made features
— erosional features and progress
— sub-division of terrain into erosion units.
— proposed conservation measures.

After analyzing these factors the terrain has been divided into three erosional units: (i) severe, (ii) moderate, and (iii) low/negligible. Severe erosion process is the characteristic mainly of aeolian plains lying in southern and south-western parts of the district. The direction of wind during field investigation (October-November 1989) was observed from west to east and from north west to south east. The nature of sand dunes is largely unstable, although some stable dunes covered with bushes may also be seen. The stabilized dunes are now being disturbed due to human activities like cultivation and digging for landfilling purposes in urban areas (e.g. sand dunes in Mayar areas along Hissar-Hansi road and Hissar-Chaudhariwas road). These human interferences have activated the erosional processes by disturbing the natural landscapes. The unstablised dunes are the major areas of severe erosion. The nature of complex dunes shows the variability in wind direction and its due impact on erosion. The dunes near Chaudhariwas, Balasamand, Burak villages are of such type. The erosion and migration of sand particles are causing a big hurdle to human activities not only in these areas but also in surrounding regions. Some of the severe erosional patches can be observed in Chautang alluvial plain (Fig. 1), which are also of dunal nature. Severe erosion processes are more common in dry seasons especially summer when the vegetative covers are negligible and the dry sands are lifted easily by the eroding agent, i.e., wind. The topographic features, vegetative covers and quality of land under different units can be observed from Table 1.

Moderate erosion process is largely occurring in Chautang alluvial plain and aeolian plain. The working geomorphic agent in these areas are wind while in Ghaggar alluvial plain, the river Ghaggar is the eroding agent. The occasional flood in this river in the rainy season creates the problem of erosion along river sides in northern part of the district. The main topographic features of moderate erosion unit are sandy plain, sand sheets, sand mounds, sand dunes, new flood plain etc. The cultivation of wheat, paddy, cotton and gram is being practised in those areas where the facilities of irrigation is available. The third unit of erosion is low/negligible areas of erosion confined mainly in alluvial plains of Ghaggar and Chautang. These areas are characterized with old flood plains, palaeo-channels and small sand mounds, etc., with better quality of land. Intensive cultivation of cotton, wheat, paddy is being practised here. Gardens of guava, orange, grape can be seen in these areas. The problem of these areas are the drifted/lifted sands from nearby dunal areas that being deposited on fertile surfaces every year and increasing impact of salinity in soil and underground water.

Conclusion

It is clear from the above discussion that remote sensing is a very powerful technique in erosion survey as it provides (i) reliable data source, (ii) increasing economy of time and survey efficiency, (iii) erosion incidence forecasting, (iv) strategic plan to control erosion, and (v) applicability in remote areas. The assessment of terrain under different erosion units carried out in Hissar district shows that the IRS-LISS-1A and Landsat TM imagery are very useful for such investigations. The rate and trend of dunal extension, although not analyzed because of non-availability of relevant data (i.e. imagery/aerial photos of past years) were collected through local enquiry during field investigations. The process of severe erosion can create a challenging pressure on human life in the concerned areas where it is occurring and also in surrounding regions where the lifted sands are being deposited. Past climatic fluctuations, tectonic activities in Himalayas and its counter effect on river systems of Hissar district, and choking of stream beds by aeolian sands may be held responsible for arid/semi-arid nature of terrain, but overgrazing, deforestation and human interference on stabilized dunes are the factors responsible for the present day extension of erosion activities. The checking of human interference on established sand dunes, plantation in inter-dunal areas, proper management of land and water resources can be adopted as precautionary measures of erosion control. If proper attention towards this alarming problem is not paid, the degradation in land quality may create a greater havoc in regional socio-economic condition. This may change the scenario of the district from "grain-bowl" of Haryana state to the unproductive desert land with saline areas in near future.

References

Alam, Molis and Haris, Ray (1987), Moorland soil erosion and spectral reflectance, *Int. J. Remote Sensing*, 8(4); 593-608.

Bernett, A.P., et al., (1971), Erodibility of tropical soils, *Trans. Amer. Sci. Agri. Eng.*, 14; pp. 496-499.

Chepil, W.S. and Woodruff, N.P., (1963), Physics of wind erosion and its control, *Advances in Agronomy*, 15; pp. 211-302.

Cooper, W.E., (1942), First site determination by soil and erosion classification, *J. of Forestry*, 40; pp. 709-713.

Gorrie, R.M., (1935), The use and misuse of land, *Oxford Forestry Memories*, 37-47, pp. 66-74.

Keech, A., (1978), Remote sensing in planning the control of erosion; in (Eds), M. De: Boodt and D. Gabriels, *Assessment of Erosion*, John Wiley and Sons, pp. 419-425.

Magruder, E.W., (1949), Aerial photographs and soil conservation service, *Photogrammetric Eng.*, 4; pp. 517-527.

Mishra, S.P., (1991), Remote sensing for hydrogeomorphological investigations in part of western Haryana, in P.R. Sharma and S.P., Mishra (eds), *Applied Geomorphology in the Tropics*, Rishi Publications, Varanasi.

Mishra, S.P. and Mohammad, N. (1989), *Hydromorphogeological Investigations in Hissar District, Haryana: Based on Remote Sensing techniques and Selective Field Checks*, Unpublished project report submitted to Indian Institute of Remote Sensing (NRSA), Deptt. of Space, Government of India, Dehradun.

Moldenhaur, W.C., (1980), Soil erosion: A global problem, *Assessment of Erosion*, in M. De. Boodt and D. Gabriels (eds), John Wiley and Sons, 419-425.

Morgan, R.P.C., (1979), *Soil Erosion*, Longman, 5.

Norman, H., (1979), *Soil Conservation*, B.T. Batsford Ltd.

Pronicheva, M.V., (1955), About growth velocity of gullies in Middle Russian Upland (in Russium), *Trudy Inst. Geogr.*, 65.

Rao, D.P., (1975), Applied geomorphological mapping for erosion surveys: the example of the Oliva Basin, Calabria, *ITC Journal*, 3; 341-350.

Rao, U.R. (1991), Remote sensing for sustainable development, *Photonirvachak, Jl. of Indian Soc. of Remote Sensing*, Vol. 19(4), 217-235.

Rasmusson, G., (1962), Sandstorm effects on areable land as seen on Air Photos: A study of wind eroded area in Vomb Valley, Scania, Sweden, *Lund Series in Geography Ser. C, 3.*

Pickup, G. and Chewings, V.H. (1988), Forecasting patterns of soil erosion in arid lands from Landsat MSS data, *International J. of Remote Sensing*, 9(1); pp. 69-84.

Semenova, N.N., (1959), *Investigation of Soil Erosion Using Air Photographs* (in Russian) Poehvovedenie 6.

Stokking, M.A., (1972), Relief analysis and soil erosion in Rhodesia Republic, *Stud. Geom. Carpatho-Balcanica*, 9: pp. 159-167.

Stubner, K., (1955), *Luftbild and Boden Erosion*, Verlag Teehnik, Berlin.

Turner, H., (1977), A comparison of some methods of slope management from large scale air photographs, *Photogrammetria*, 32; 209-237.

Verstappen, H. Th. (1970): Introduction to the ITC system of geomorphological survey, *KNAG Geografisch*, Tijdsehrift, 4(1); pp. 85-91.

Verstappen, H. Th. (1983), *Applied Geomorphology*, Elsevier, New York.

Williams, A.R., and Morgan, R.P.C., (1976), Geomorphological mapping applied to soil erosion evaluation, *J. Soil and Water Conservation*, 31; pp. 164-168.

Williams, W.O. and Evans, C.E., (1977), Our soil is valuable, editorial, *J. Soil and Water Conservation*, 32, 258-259.

Wischmeier, W.H., (1976), Use and misuse of Universal Soil Loss Equation, *J. Soil and Water Conservation*, 31 (2).

Wischmeier, W.H., et.al. (1971), A soil erodibility nomograph for farmland and construction sites, *J. of Soil and Water Conservation*, 26, 189-198.

Wischmeier, W.H. and Smith, D.D., (1978), Predicting rainfall erosion losses: A guide to conservation planning, *U.S. Deptt. Agric. Handbook*, 537.

Zachar, D. (1982), *Soil Erosion*, Elsevier New York.

Chapter 13

Geographic Information Systems: An Overview of Concepts, Components and Capabilities

R. Nagaraja

Background

In the past 20 years, a host of professions have been in the process of developing automated tools for efficient storage, analysis, and presentation of geographic data. These efforts have apparently been the result of increasing demands by users for data and information of a spatial nature. This rapidly evolving technology has come to be known as "Geographic Information Systems". The uses of this technology are vast and cuts across virtually all professions. This is well illustrated in Figure 1 which is a matrix diagram indicating the relationship between a series of selected responsibilities which normally involve the use of geographic data and general tasks functions supported by geographic information systems (i.e. maintenance of geographic records, graphics display, statistical reporting, planning, management, and policy making). The responsibilities listed from top to bottom of the chart correspond loosely to the overlapping stages of activity involved in development of a region, state or nation.

Graphics and more specifically maps, have historically been a structure for most disciplines concerned with spatial analysis. For the past 4,000 years various cultures have used graphic symbols to represent spatially distributed phenomena. Graphics in the form of maps have historically provided us with the useful medium for record keeping, conceiving of ideas, analyzing concepts, predicting the future, developing decisions about geography, and finally, communicating spatial concepts to others.

Today, geographic information systems and computer graphics are providing a similar framework for conducting spatial analysis. However, there exists a tremendous gap between the levels of technology that are available for geographic and graphics analysis and the various individuals and organizations who need to use it. It is felt that in order to advance this technology into the application environment, it is necessary to develop clear and concise information for GIS systems, the spatial data entities which they contain, and the various manipulation techniques which are possible from such systems.

In developing this information, it is useful to refer and keep in mind the historical methods of manual mapping as a benchmark and context for developing a common spatial information language.

Automated Systems

Proponent of the automated geographic system technology point out a whole series of advantages which are enumerated in the literature. They include the following:

* Data are maintained in a physically compact format (i.e., the magnetic file).
* Data can be maintained and extracted at a lower cost per unit of data handled.
* Data can be retrieved with much greater speed.
* Various computerized tools allow for a variety of types of manipulation including map measurements, map overlay, transformations, graphic design, and data base manipulations.
* Graphic and non graphic (i.e., attribute information) can be merged and manipulated simultaneously in a related manner.
* Rapid and repeated analytic testing of conceptual models about geography can be performed (i.e., land suitability/capability). This facilitates the evaluation of both scientific and policy criteria over large areas in short periods of time.
* Change analysis can be efficiently performed for two or more different time periods.
* Interactive graphic design and automated drafting tools can be applied to cartographic design and production
* Certain forms of analysis can be performed cost effectively that simply could not be done efficiently if performed manually (i.e., digital terrain analysis, calculations such as slope aspect, sun inten-

Figure 1

Selected Relationship Between Responsibilities and GIS Applications

Responsibilities	*Examples of data*	*General task functions supported by GEO, INFO*					
		Maintenance of geographic records (i.e., operational and inventory data	*Graphic display (drafting)*	*Statistical reporting*	*Planning*	*Manage-ment*	*Policy making*
Territorial control	Boundary survey	0	0				
Natural resource exploitation	Geophysical, topo, geology, vegetation, soils	0	+		0		
Taxation and ownership monitoring	Cadastral surveys and tax records	0	0	+			
Land use/infrastructure planning	Opportunities and constraint data				0		
Land use zoning	Zoning records	0	+		0		
Land use/infrastrucute design/construction	Enginnering surveys/data		0		+		
Construction facility record keeping and management	As built drawings of utilities, buildings, etc.	0	0		+		
Development measurement	Land use survey	+	+	0	+	0	0
Census of statistics	Population, housing, health and economic data		+	0	0		0
Event monitoring	Police/fire statistics		+	+	+	0	0
Natural resource management	Ongoing forest record keeping	0	0		0	0	
Monitoring of environment	Wildlife, vegetation, air, soil, water, etc.	0	+	0	0		0

0 – Major + – Minor

sity, watershed, overlay analysis of multiple sets of complex polygon map sheets, etc.)

* There is a resultant tendency to integrate data collections, spatial analysis, and decision making processed into a common Information flow context. This has great advantages in terms of efficiency and accountability,

Along with all of these advantages there are also a series of disadvantages that must be evaluated carefully before the user invests in the development or acquisition of such a system. They include the following:

* High cost of initial acquisition of systems;
* The cost and associated technical problems of converting existing geographic records into an automated file (i.e., digitizing, scanning, or related data conversion);
* The large amount of technical as well as financial overhead which is required to maintain automated files (i.e., computer, skilled technicians, software maintenance, etc.)
* Marginal cost benefits in certain application areas.

Hardware

The basic component of a simple GIS system is shown in Figure 1A. It comprises of a standalone PC/Workstation and connected to necessary accessories like Digitizer, tape drive/CD ROM drive (for input of data) and thermal laser printer, plotter, film recorder (for output of data). Figure 1B shows the layout of a distributed GIS system. In the recent years, the hardware environment has undergone sea changes as the GIS technology developed. As a result today the key word is distributed processing.

Distributed Systems, distributed commuting and data management resources reduce front end costs, allow phased growth and easy upgrading/modification. High power, high resolution graphics can be provided to each user. Flexible growth is possible with localized power but database is shared over the network. The database maintenance is localized but access is shared over the network. Heterogeneous networks are possible with Open Systems Standards.

Architecture: Several architectures are possible depending on the scale of operations. Systems can be grown from simple installations to extensive ones as the need arises. Some of the more popular architectures are:

* Low cost, single user station: PC

* High performance single user station: Workstation
* Low cost multi-user system, PC terminals networked to a workstation
* Low cost multi-user system with diskless nodes, file server for OS, GIS and data
* High performance Distributed system,
* Dataless Nodes have disks with copy of OS and GIS but data is on server
* Datafull, Data is also on nodes with master copy on server
* Remote Users: connection over PSPDNs
* High Transaction Data Entry System, Mini/Server with alpha-numeric terminals for attribute data entry

Software

The major aspects related to software are the operating system, the GIS toolkit and the DBMS. The trend today is away from proprietary operating systems and towards open systems. The preferred operating system today is UNIX. However, UNIX takes getting used to and users miss the comfortable familiarity of proprietary systems like VMS. The advantage of UNIX is that it allows a heterogeneity of systems. The user does not have to relearn the operating system as they migrate from platform to platform. The choice of the DBMS is always relational. This offers the best features for storage of both feature and attribute data. Data updating and modification can be handled easily. Most GIS give bridges to all popular relational DBMS. Thus older data can be used with GIS with minimum of disturbance.

An important feature of the software is customization. Often used procedures can be written up as macros which are hardware independent and hence can be used over a network. The software also provides library calls which can be embedded in user programmes.

Current Type of Systems

Within the past ten years, GIS systems have begun to surface which have real and practical benefit to a variety of geographic problems. These systems are just beginning to be adapted to actual information flows and processes within governmental and private organizations. At this point, it is a very delicate technology in the sense that there has been considerable investment of various resources, and there is only beginning to emerge evidence of successful applications which make a difference.

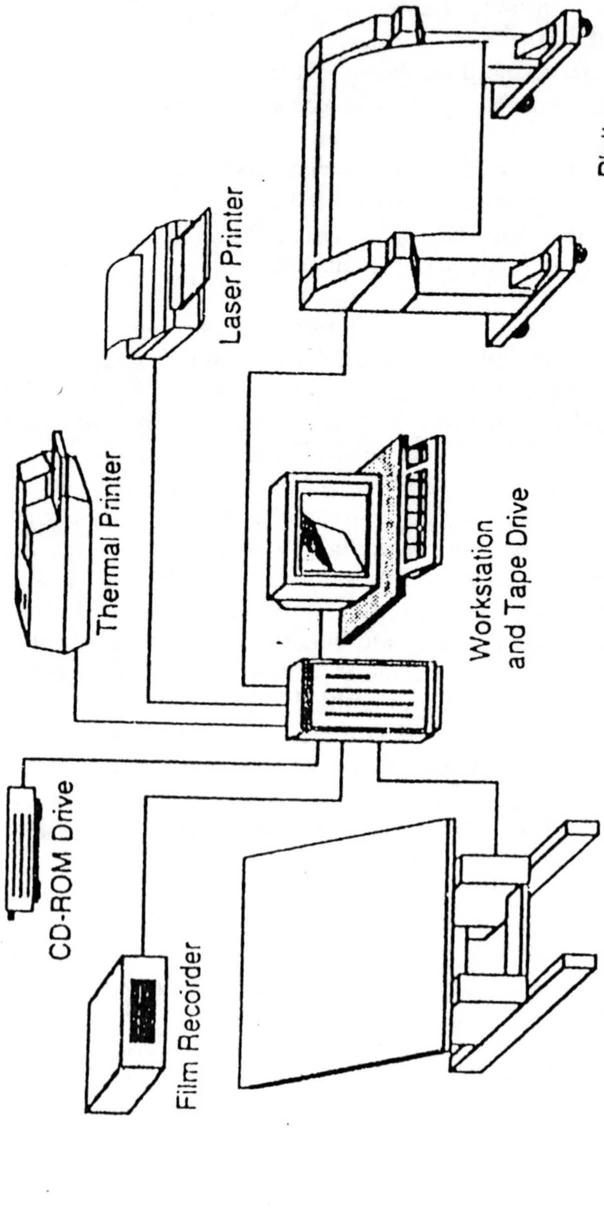

Figure 1A A Simple GIS System

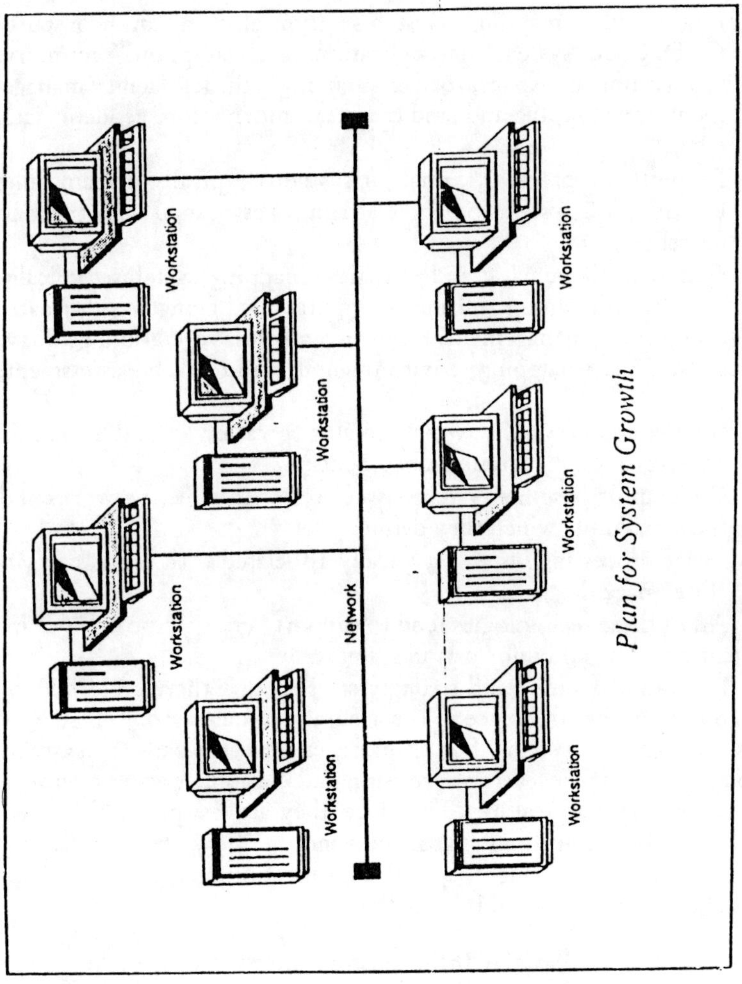

Figure 1B A Distributed GIS System

At present, there are several categories of information technology which tend to be associated with vendor or government developed hardware/software systems. They generally fall into the following categories:

* Engineering mapping systems (typically a minicomputer CAD/CAM system for applications such as photogrammetry, topographic basemaps, road engineering, utilities, facility management, tax mapping and land cadastral information, geodetic data, etc.);
* Property or parcel information systems (typically a mainframe based DBMS system to handle attributes associated with the land parcel);
* Generalized thematic and statistical mapping systems (typically on both mini-and mainframe computers and being used for natural resource management, forest inventories, vegetation, geology, soils, census mapping, environmental planning and assessment, etc.);
* Bibliographic systems which catalog a variety of bibliographic data sets about geographic documents;
* Geographic base file systems associated with street networks and the aerial units which they define;
* Image processing systems (typically associated with processing satellite image data).

All of these technologies tend to support very specific types of information flows and information systems.

It should be noted and strongly stressed that there are orders of magnitude in the difference in the accuracy of dale among these various information systems. For example, engineering basemap systems typically use higher levels of precision and consume greater overhead for describing map features. Therefore, they are less practical for certain types of applications. Also, the vendors of systems use varying types of data management, spatial identification techniques, and approaches to the display of information.

Spatial Information Concepts

This section presents a series of concepts useful to generic definition of GIS components.

Basic characteristics of spatial data and its management: Geographic Information is most commonly thought of as having two basic characteristics; (a) the actual phenomenon or characteristic, such as the variable, its classification, value, name, etc.; and (b) its spatial location (i.e., that location within geographic space where it resides). However, a third characteristic which is particularly relevant to GIS systems is that of time.

Figure 2 is a conceptual diagram of the relationship of these three elements (i.e., locational data, nonlocational data (attributes), and time). From this diagram, one can observe that management of spatial data can become quite complex because locational data and attribute data often change independent of one another with respect to time.

Therefore, effective spatial data management requires that location data and nonlocation data be variable independent of one another. That is, attributes can change character but retain the same spatial location, or vice versa.

In conceiving of the overall structure of a data base for geographic information processing, it is useful to realize that data management must occur on both location data, as well as on nonlocation data. Different software and system designs have called for handling these two types of phenomena differently. In some cases, location data is considered as an additional attribute associated with the geographic characteristic. In other systems, the geographic location of a characteristic is kept separately from the actual attribute phenomena associated with that. The latter approach allows for more flexibility, with respect to handling data change—specifically, change associated with time.

Types of geographic data and its spatial representation within GIS systems: In general, there are three basic notations used for representing the spatial location of geographic phenomena—points, lines and polygons.

Figure 3 presents a breakdown of seven types of geographic data techniques for spatial representation, as mentioned above. They are (a) feature data; (b) aerial unit information; (c) network topological data; (d) sampling data; (e) surface information; (f) lable text information; and (g) graphic symbol data. Graphics in the chart indicate how these seven data types are most commonly portrayed using point, line and polygon locational identifiers.

Points, lines, and polygons are most commonly defined on maps using x,y cartesian coordinates such as longitude/latitude based on principles of Euclidean geometry. This cartesian coordinate system is the most commonly used tool for measuring spatial location and analyzing various properties of spatial location, inducing measurement, etc. Figure 4 shows conceptually how a typical map with poinᵗ, line,

Figure 2

Three Conceptual Components of a Geographic Based Information System

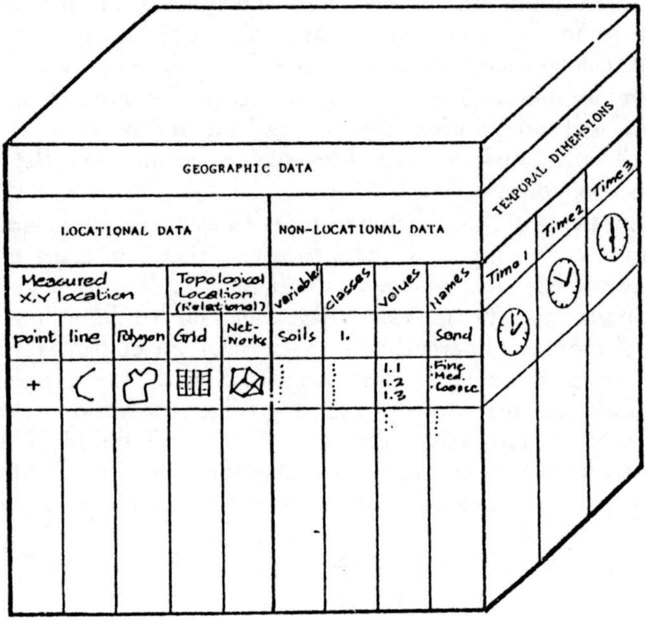

Figure 3

Breakdown of Geographic Data Types and Methods of Representation

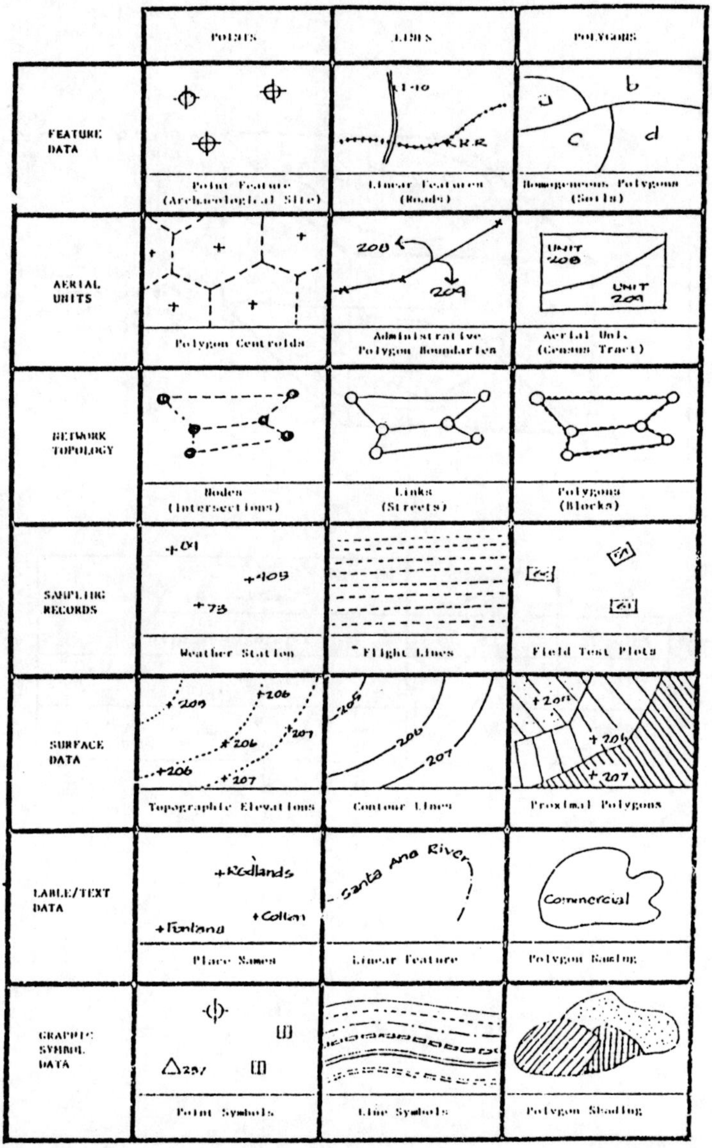

Figure 4

X, Y Coordinate File

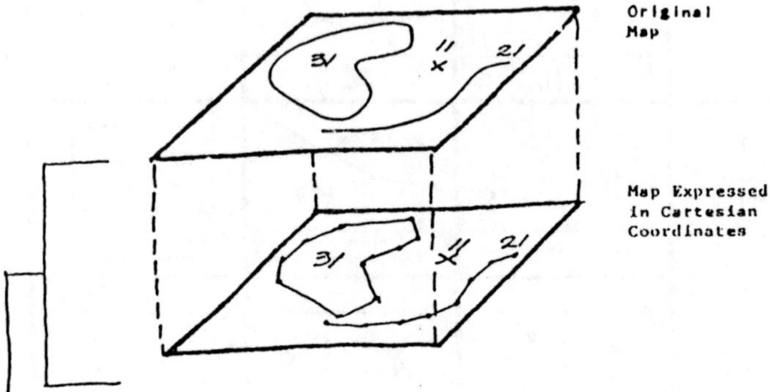

	Feature Number	Location
Point	11	X,Y (Single Point)
Line	21	$X_1Y_1, X_2Y_2, \ldots\ldots X_nY_n$ (string)
Polygon	31	$X_1Y_1, X_2Y_2, \ldots\ldots X_1Y_1$ (closed loop)

Figure 5

X, Y Coordinate Node File

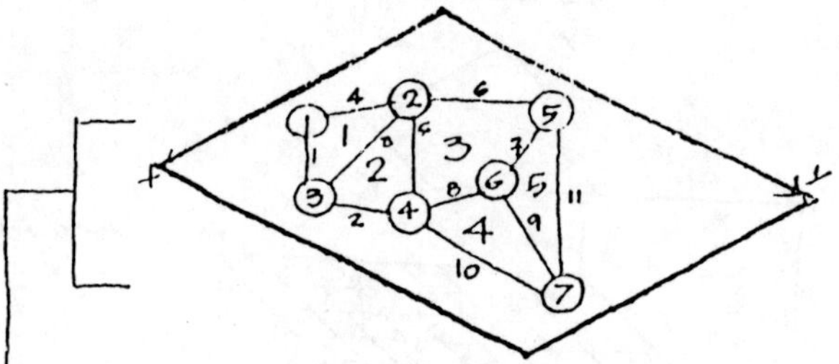

Coded Network Map

Link #	Right Polygon	Left Polygon	Node 1	Node 2
1	1	0	3	1
2	2	0	4	3
3	2	1	3	2
4	1	0	1	2
5	3	2	4	2
6	3	0	2	5
7	3	3	5	6
8	4	3	6	4
9	5	4	7	6
10	4	0	7	4
11	5	0	5	7

Topologically Coded Network & Polygon File

Node #	X Coordinate	Y Coordinate
1	23	8
2	17	17
3	29	15
4	26	21
5	8	26
6	22	30
7	24	38

X,Y Coordinate Node File

Figure 6
Grid File

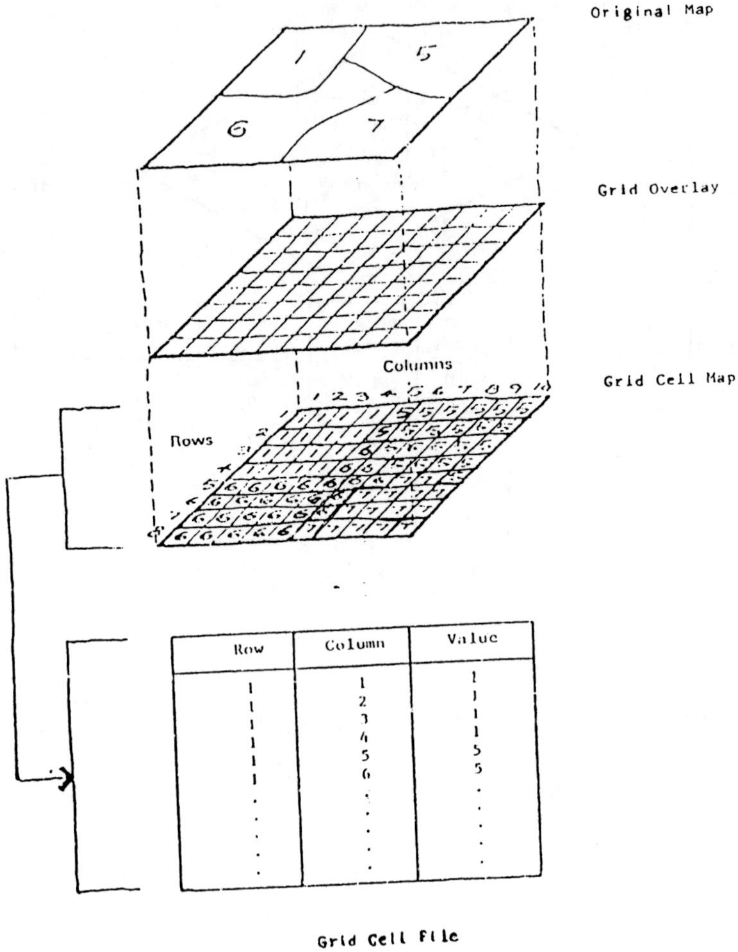

and polygon elements is expressed in cartesian coordinates and subsequently transferred to a x,y coordinate GIS file.

In addition to expression of geographic phenomena using cartesian coordinates, one can also use principles of graph theory involving topological relationships to express the relative location of various map elements. Perhaps the first and most commonly used GIS system applying graph theory to maps is called Dual Independent Map Encoding (DIME) and was developed by the US Bureau of the Census. DIME is actually a combined x,y coordinate and topological encoding system. The DIME system involves topologically structuring the graph elements of a map (i.e., nodes, line segments, and polygons). DIME also allows for inclusion of x,y coordinates associated with the node points or intersections connecting the line segments bounding polygon areas. Figure 5 shows how a typical polygon/network map can be abstracted into seven nodes, 11 links or line segment, bounding five basic polygons. By numbering these links and associating them with nodes as well as polygons on the right and left, a basic map notation system can be derived. By adding x,y coordinate encoding at each of the nodes, one has a dual system for spatially identifying all elements of a map. This facilitates not only analysis using x,y coordinates but also use of mathematics associated with graph theory involving network, spatial aggregation, dropline, etc.

Topological quoting defines a location of geographic phenomena relative to other phenomena, but does not require the use of the concept of distance in defining these relationships. Therefore, it is totally possible to have a spatially defined map without coordinates entirely.

A second technique which also applies certain relationship principles, involves the use of a grid mesh to define a regular but arbitrary polygon framework for holding geographic data. The grid technique inherently involves association with a coordinate system, but it does not necessarily require precise association. Grid uses an ij matrix for representing variations of geography to the computer. Figure 6 illustrates how an original polygon map overlaid on a grid can be abstracted into row/column values expressing geographic variation.

In summary, there are basically two methods for spatially identifying this information. The first is to use actual measurements in the form of x,y coordinates. The second involves defining geographic phenomena by way of point and line relationships, networks, polygon adjacencies, and cell contigulties. These are graphically portrayed in figure 2.

Automation Techniques for Locational Data

There are seven basic techniques used for spatial identification of geographic data. They include the following:

* Encoding of geographic data to cells;
* Topological coding of nodes, line segments, and polygons (DIME system);
* Input of survey documents;
* Manual entry of points, lines, and polygons using manual digitizer,
* Automatic entry at time of data capture;
* Automatic line following techniques; and
* Optical scanning

These techniques are described below:

1 *Cell encoding*: Manual encoding of cellular data involves a process wherein each point within an overall grid is encoded by observing the dominant feature within a given cell, writing it onto a coding form, and subsequently key entering the coding form into an automated file using a keypunching technique (see figure 7).

2 *Topological coding of map features*: This effort again involves manual coding from the map of the relationship of each point, line and polygon to each of its adjacent neighbours. For example, each line (link) is assigned two nodes which are its end points. Also each link is assigned the polygon which is at its right and left sides. In this manner, all graphic entities are fully documented, key entered, and edited for final corrections.

3 *Input of survey documents*: Input of survey documents is typically done through the manual key entry of key x,y reference points, bearings, and distances relative to specific features desired for encoding. This technique is often used for entry of ownership boundaries, roads, buildings, etc. The process involves the use of coordinate geometry techniques which have been developed especially for entry of the survey documents and generation automatically of associated cartesian coordinates.

4 *Manual digitization using a digitizer*: Manual digitizing technique involves the use of an electromagnetic, electrostatic device called a digitizer. The digitizer converts movements of a cursor or point locator into electrical identified locations which are read directly into the computer. Digitizers are usually designed to be very accurate and can be programmed with a minicomputer to capture data in varying formats of points, lines, and polygons. The digitizer

Figure 7 and 8

Manual Cell Encoding and Manual Digitizer

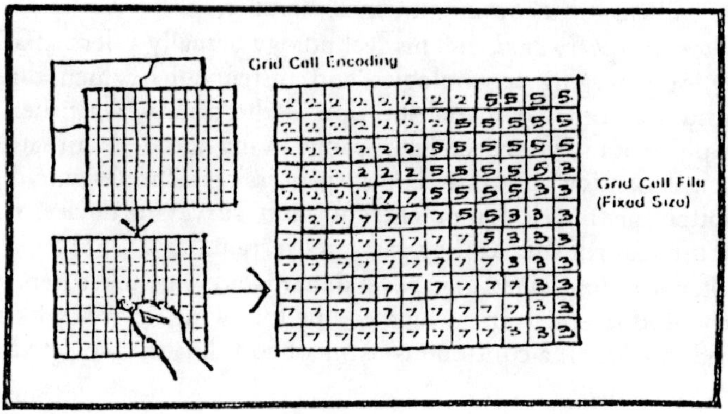

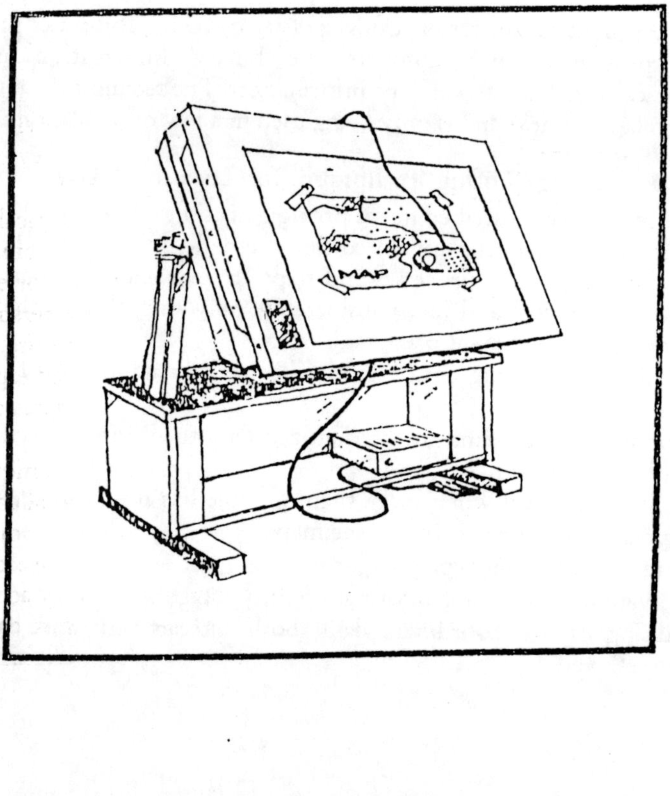

can record the position of each point, line, or polygon in either a point by point mode or by a continuous mode incrementing by time or by distance moved of the cursor on the digilizer table. Figure 8 illustrates a common manual digitizer.

5 *Automatic entry devices*: This technology actually refers to a variety of emerging technologies and instruments which directly capture automated spatial location al the time when other geographic data is recorded. These range in magnitude from satellites such as Landsat and related image processing technology to digital plotters, geometric equipment, and "auto surveying devices which capture coordinates as they pass over terrain.(E.g., GPS).

6 *Automatic line following*: Several hardware manufacturers have produced laser driven automated line following devices which are used to scan off a continuous string of coordinates associated with lines on a map.

7 *Scanning*: Automated scanner technology typically operates in the form of raster scan measuring binary (on/off) positions representing the points, lines, polygons, and textual data appearing on a map.

Subsequent to this raster scan is a raster-to-vector computer processing program which converts the binary information into topologically correct vector type information. The technology in this area is relatively new and is only being used in a few organizations.

Processing/Editing Techniques for Locational Data

All the techniques described in the previous section involve a substantial amount of processing and/or editing subsequent to the initial data capture. Because these processes and steps are extremely system and technique dependent and vary considerably, only an outline of the basic steps of the processes is presented:

* Plotting or printing out of digitized or coded data for visual editing;
* Topological checking of the digitized data to insure correctness within the data set;
* Splinter removal when more than one line has been captured to represent the same vector on the map;
* Handling of donut type polygons;
* Polygonization of area information into polygons;
* Editing of x,y coordinate data (both interactively and batch modes); and

* Edge match analysis.

In the case where arc data is entered, the editing and processing activity may include things such as creation of topologically correct data structures including automatic left and right labelling of arcs based on codes assigned to centred data associated with a polygon file. In addition to the inaccuracies in the source document, a number of data errors arise from the digitizing process. It is, therefore, essential to correct these errors before the digitized data is used for further analysis. The main error types are shown in Figure 8A.

Manipulation Techniques

This section describes the various analytic functions and data processing functions that can be performed on spatially automated data. Within this section, the actual function is described in a narrative outline and referenced to a pictorial representation of conceptually how each function is performed. No attempt is made to describe these functions in detail as different software system approach the solution using alternative types of algorithms. Alternatively, emphasis is placed on defining the actual function which is being performed. It should be mentioned that these descriptions are meant to be representative and there will be examples left out.

Data Retrieval

This series of techniques involves the basic extraction, query, and Boolean manipulation of informatiõn contained In an organized geographic information system. Figure 9 describes the following data retrieval functions:

(a) *Browsing*: This task would consist of browsing through the graphic and nongraphic data files associated with various maps and groupings of maps.

(b) *Windowing*: This function calls for the ability to allow the user to specify windows (either by x,y coordinate or textual informal ion). Spatial data base management typically calls for the organization of map sheets into some form of modular relational structure allowing thereby the illusion to the user of a continuous map being contained within the computer.

(c) *Query window generation*: This function involves the ability to generate points, irregular shaped polygons, squares, circles, and corridors for interactively overlaying with data planes contained within the geographic file. These windows are typically used to perform spatial (coordinate) retrieval of points, lines, and poly-

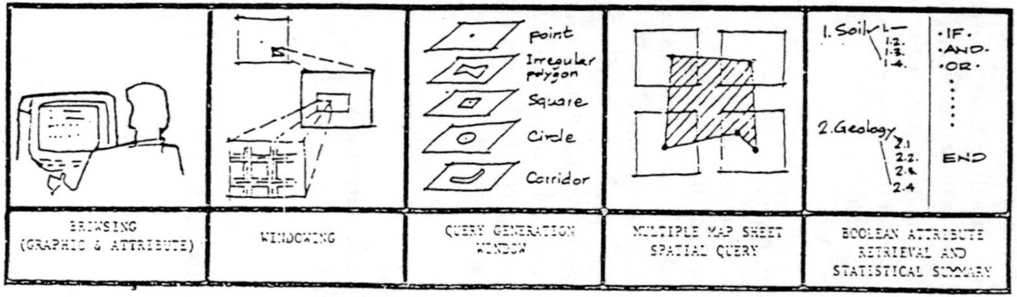

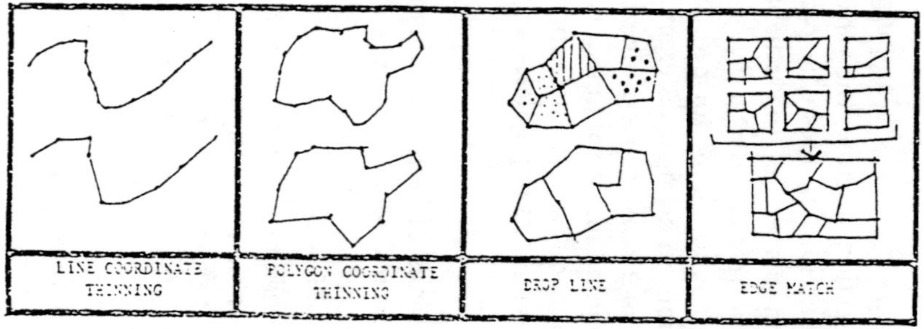

Figure 9 and 10 Data Retrieval and Map Generalization

gons from various map layers which coincide in space with these generated query windows. Three techniques are used in extracting information from layers associated with these generated query windows. They are:

* Adjacency analysis (i.e., selection of specific points relative to a given point);
* Point and polygon retrieval (i.e., the selection of all points, lines, or polygons falling entirely within or partially within the query window); and
* Polygon overlay (i.e., selection of only those portions of geographic entities which fall within the boundaries of the query window polygon). In this case, all lines as well as parts of polygons which fall outside of the query window are snipped off using the polygon overlay routine.

These query windows are typically used in asking questions such as—Give me all polygons of the harvestable timber falling within the query window A (a user specified polygon).

(d) *Multiple map sheet spatial query*: Frequently the spatial query which is being conducted (i.e. described above) is being done over multiple map sheets. Therefore the data retrieval software must have within it the ability to create a polygon which stands across map sheet boundaries extracts those portions of the map sheet which are relevant to their query window and organizes the map element data into a continuous window automatically. This is typically done in one or more steps on the current software modules which are available.

(e) *Boolean attribute retrieval and statistical summary*: This function involves the ability to specify various Boolean type criteria for extraction of information based on nongraphic attribute data. An example of this would be—Give me all of the polygons of a certain type of soil which have an area of greater than 50 acres and also produce a statistical summary of the polygon acreages perimeters and their total. It should be noted that most users who have this retrieval type capability become most excited when they are able to conduct the query type retrievals using both the locational window as well as the attribute query. An example of this would be "Give me all of the polygons which fall in a certain window which are of a certain vegetation type and over a certain size". Typically the output of such a search is displayed graphically on a screen printed out in alpha numeric form on a hard copy unit and if desired plotted out on a plotter.

Map Generalization

Figure 10 refers to four basic types of map generalization. This series of generalization tools is most frequently used when map scales are changed. They are described below:

(a) *Line coordinate thinning*: This is a technique for reducing the number of coordinates defining a given line.

(b) *Dropline*: This is a technique wherein a polygon boundary separating two polygons of similar characteristics can be dropped and the remaining line segments making up the two previously separate polygons can be rejoined together to form a new polygon unit comprising the area of the two previously separate polygons. This is often a technique used in Integrated Terrain Unit Mapping (ITUM) where multiple attributes are assigned each polygon and when single maps are desired for extraction form the data base. To accomplish this function a check is made of the characteristic on the right and left side of each polygon line segment to determine which line segments should be dropped.

(c) *Edge matching*: Edge matching consists of a series of procedures of bringing together a large number of map sheets and compositing them into one continuous map. Problems which must be resolved are—joining lines and polygons from adjacent maps matchings of the boundaries between the maps and dropping the lines which separate polygons having the same characteristics. It should be kept in mind that although automated techniques are useful in this exercise basic errors made on the cartographic manuscripts input into the systems are often the source of great problems in making clean edge matching occur.

(d) *Polygon thinning*: This is a similar exercise to item "2a" above, except that the problem is somewhat more complex because when doing polygon thinning vertices thinned for one polygon must be consistent with vertice thinning on adjacent polygons; otherwise lines which are shared in common will have sliver errors gaps and overlaps due to indiscriminate selection of the vertices which can be dropped. Thinning of polygon arcs instead of complete polygon entities can resolve this problem.

Map Abstraction

Map abstraction is closely associated with map generalization but involves five different forms of technology. These are graphically presented in Figure 11 and described below:

(a) Calculation of centroids;

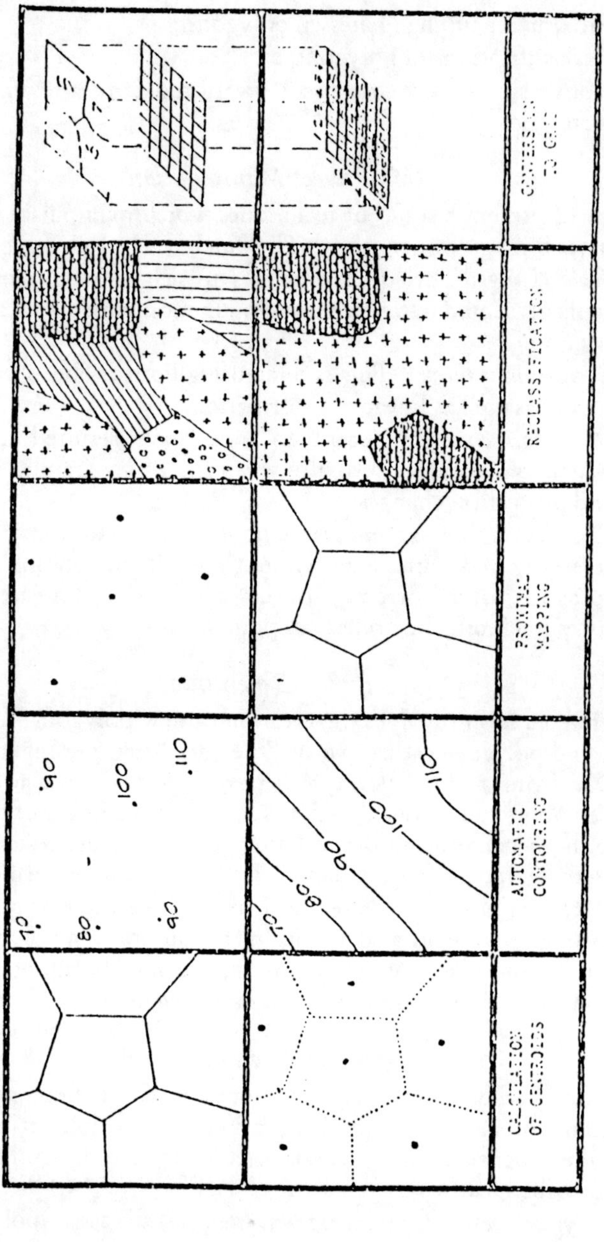

Figure 11 Map Abstraction

(b) Automatic contouring from randomly spaced data;
(c) Proximal mapping (Thiessen polygons);
(d) Reclassifications of polygons; and
(e) Conversion of x y coordinate location data to a regular and uniform grid.

Map Sheet Manipulation

Figure 12 present a series of techniques which manipulate the x,y coordinates for a given map sheet. They include the following:

(a) *Scale change*: This often involves us age of map generalization tools presented in figure 10 in conjunction with actual scale modification.
(b) *Distortion removal*: This is done using both rubber-sheeting techniques as well as linear transformation.
(c) *Projection changes*: Recent advances have resulted in software which can conduct virtually any type of geographic coordinate and protection changes.
(d) *Coordinate rotation and translation*: This function involves the alteration of coordinate sets either though their rotation or shifting so as to match correctly overlapping or sets of adjacent coordinates (including key reference points).

Buffer Generation

Buffer generation involves the creation of new polygons from points, lines, and polygon features within the data bank (see Figure 13). specifically from a given point or series of points, circular as well as square buffers can be calculated. Likewise, from a string of points (i.e., a line) both narrow and broad buffers can be calculated and, in cases where these line buffers overlap, new polygons can be formed.

Polygons can be generated both around the exterior perimeter of an existing polygon as well as within the interior of a polygon, resulting in a dual set of polygons measuring horizontal distance relationships relative to a given geographic element.

Polygon Overlay and Dissolve

Polygon overlay and dissolve techniques involve the compositing (integrating) or extracting (dis-integration) of multiple maps (two or more) in order to create a new data set. These are shown in Figure 14 and described below:

(a) *Polygon overlay for creating new files*: In the case of polygon over-

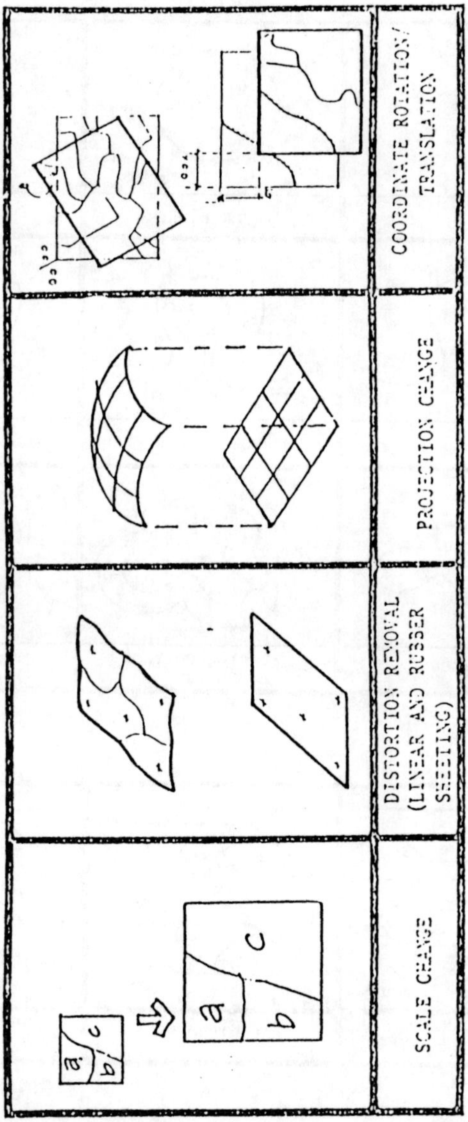

Figure 12 Map Sheet Manipulation

Figure 13 and 14

Buffer Generation and Polygon Overlay/Dissolve

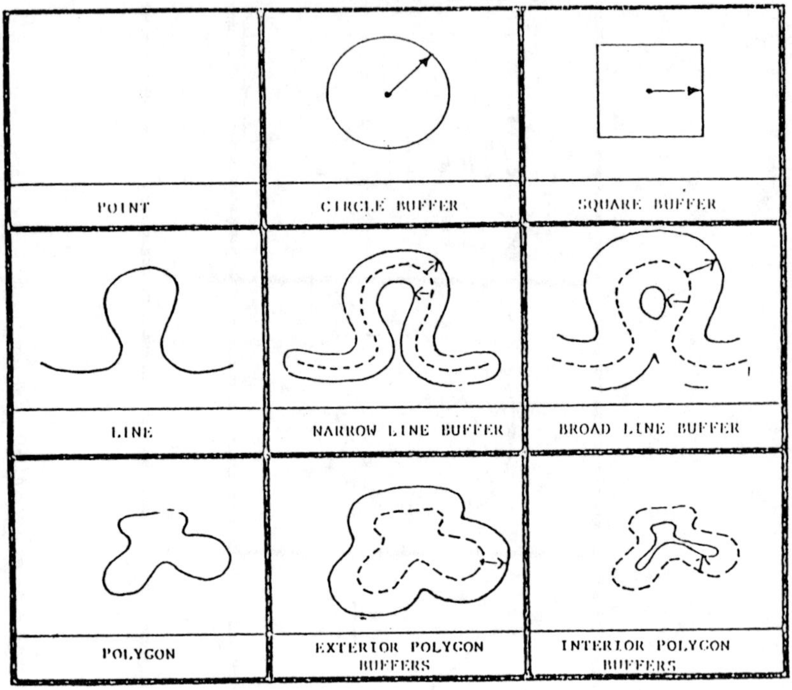

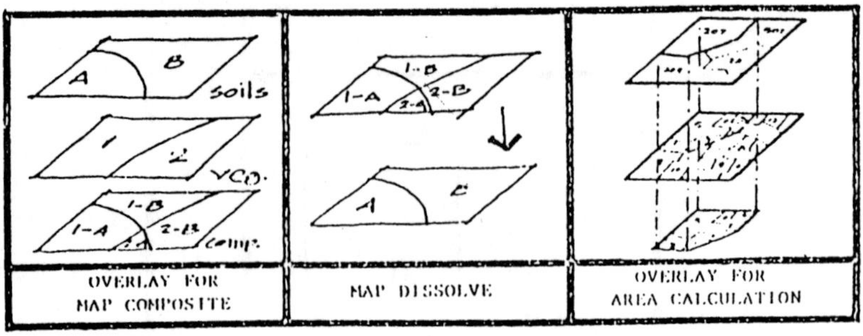

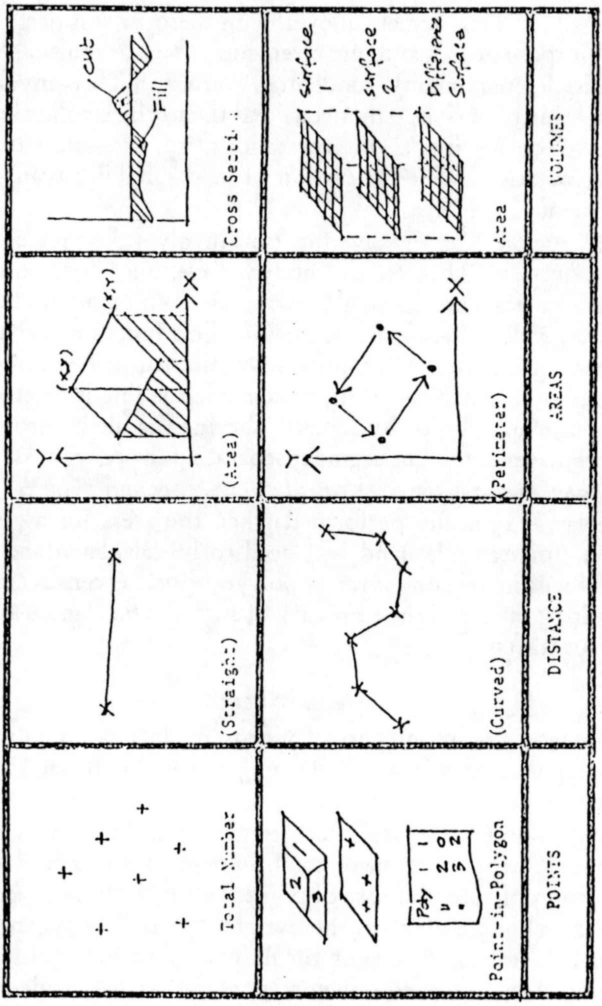

Figure 15 Measurement

lay, a new data set is created, containing new polygons created from the intersection of the boundaries of the two or more sets of separable polygon layers. In addition to creating new polygons based on the overlay of the multiple layers, these polygons are assigned multiple attributes (i.e., the attributes which were attributed to each separate overlay before the composition occurred). The mathematical overlay of these maps is performed for the purpose of area and measurement, as well as multiple attribute (multiple parameter) modeling exercises. This involves the weighting of various parameters and their sub-classifications in order to create model interpretations; an example of such an interpretation is the generation of land suitability/capability assessments.

(b) *Map dissolve*: Map dissolve function involves the inverse of polygon overlay. That is, the ability to extract from a multiple attribute polygon file single attributes, both by attribute description as well as locational definition. This function is the same as shown on Figure 10-'Dropline'. Dropline or map dissolve can be done both "graphically" (in which case the line is deleted on the output map only) or by actually altering the file by dropping the coordinates of the line segment separating the polygons.

(c) *Polygon overlays for area calculation*: A second type of polygon overlay is typically performed when the areas for a given data layer (for example, land use) need to be calculated and summarized within a second layer of polygons such as census tracts. The resulting output is the summary of statistics (i.e. land use areas by census tracts).

Measurement

The four most common types of measurement tasks involve points, lines, polygons and volumes. They are presented in figure 15 and outlined below:

(a) *Points*: The two typical measurement activities associated with points are enumeration of total number of points and also enumeration of total number of points falling within polygons. The latter technique involves the use of a "point-in-polygon" routine which effectively counts up the number of various types of points falling within selected polygon types (i.e., crime incidents within police patrol districts).

(b) *Line measurement*: Two basic forms of line measurement are point to point and measurement along a curvilinear line.

(c) *Measurement of areas*: The two basic types of area measurement are—the area of a polygon and the perimeter of a polygon area.
(d) The fourth category of measurement involves volumetric measurement which is performed either through a cross-section technique or through overlays of multiple surfaces (i.e. before grading, after grading, and difference computation).

Grid Cell Analysis

Figure 16 illustrates five examples of basic analytic activities that are performed using grid cell data. These techniques are similar to the types of map analysis that are performed in x,y coordinate data structure but have more generalized spatial resolution. It should be pointed out that the grid cell technique for map manipulation is typically much more efficient both in data storage as well as in the operation of the analytic tasks. The five are described in the following pages:

(a) *Grid cell overlay*: This involves the development of Boolean type map overlays in order to create composite maps. Typically, this involves the weighing of seceded classifications for multiple map layers, resulting in a numeric surface of composite data, expressing the users Interpretation. This surface is then typically displayed using computer graphics.
(b) *Area calculation overlay*: This is a similar type of polygon overlay as was shown in figure 14, except that it uses a gridded technique, rather than a polygon technique.
(c) *Search radius aggregation*: This is a technique for moving a circle with a specified radius across a grid cell by cell searching out from each cell. This routine counts up the number of events, activities or related geographic phenomena that fall within the circle relative to each grid cell and stores that enumerated value In a new grid array. The output from such a computation is a frequency/accessibility array surface.
(d) *Distance calculation*: This is a routine similar to the previous one, in that, each cell examined relative to its adjacency to other phenomena in surrounding cells. In this case, however, the computation applied is a distance calculation to the nearest event or geographic characteristic which Is defined by the user. A typical application is calculation of the distance from each cell to a stream network, road network, etc. The output from the analysis Is the gene ration of a file of accessibility.
(e) *Optimal corridor selection*: This analysis involves the computation of a least cost between two points. Specifically, a friction surface is

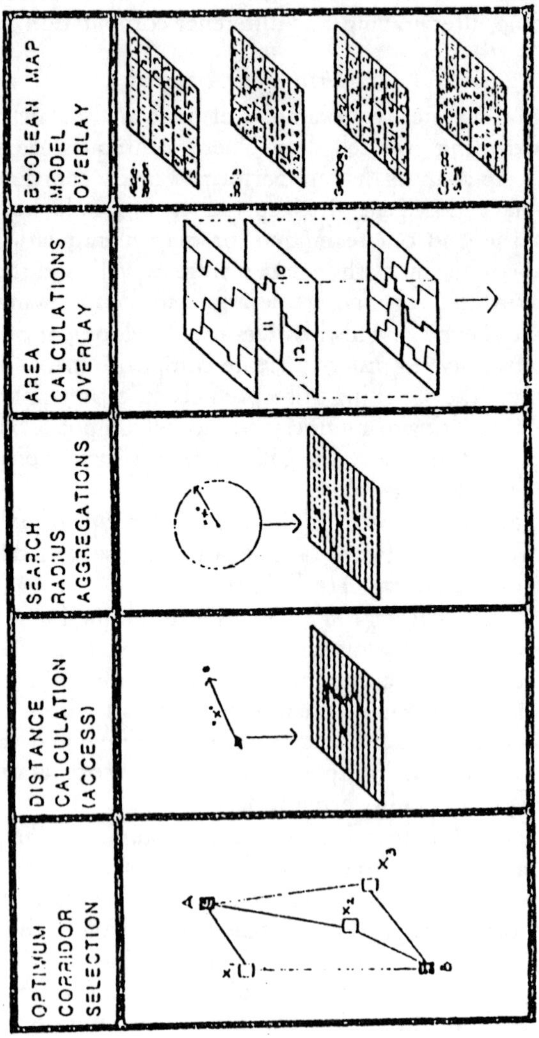

Figure 16 Grid Cell Technique

computed away from the origin and also away from the destination. These friction surfaces are numerical summaries of cost based on an original input grid of costs computed using the grid weighted overlay technique described above. This original map (actually surface of grid data) expresses for each cell the cost to move across it. These costs can be economic costs, environmental costs, social costs, etc., and are summarized based on multiple parameter overlay. After computing the two friction maps (origin and destination), they are overlaid and the resulting surface is an optimum route selection with gradients computations of increased costs away from the optimum.

Digital Terrain Analysis

Digital terrain analysis involves the computation of a variety of outputs from a digital elevation model (see Figure 17). There are various forms of digital elevation models and therefore different forms of actual analysis that can be performed. The following is a description of the most common of these analyses:

(a) *Visual display*: These consist primarily of cross-sections and three-dimensional views.

(b) *Interpolation/contouring*: Typically, this involves the ability to take random or regularly spaced data, generate a grid or other structured model framework on which automated contouring can occur. Based on this interpolated model, a contourings program actually computes and subsequently draws out the contour lines.

(c) *Slope/aspect/sun intensity*: This primarily involves the calculation of slope aspect and in some cases, the relationship of this slope aspect to solar radiation in the form of sun intensity.

(d) *Watershed computation*: This involves the computation of the watershed boundaries, drainages, topographic pits and peaks and, in some cases, this data is used to compute surface flow.

(e) *Visibility*: This analysis is primarily used in conjunction with determining what can be seen and not seen from a given x,y and z coordinate. Output is in the form of a grid of values indicating seen and non-seen area values.

Output Techniques

Figure 18 illustrates the basic four output formats from a GIS system. They are as follows:

(a) Hard copy maps;

(b) Statistical tabulations;

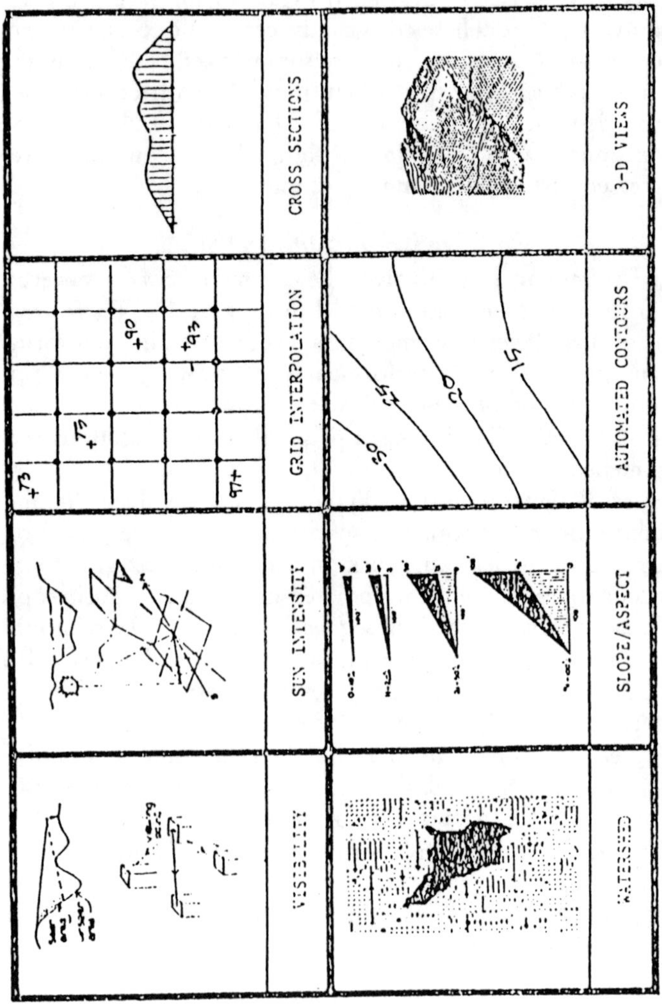

Figure 17 Digital Terrain Analysis

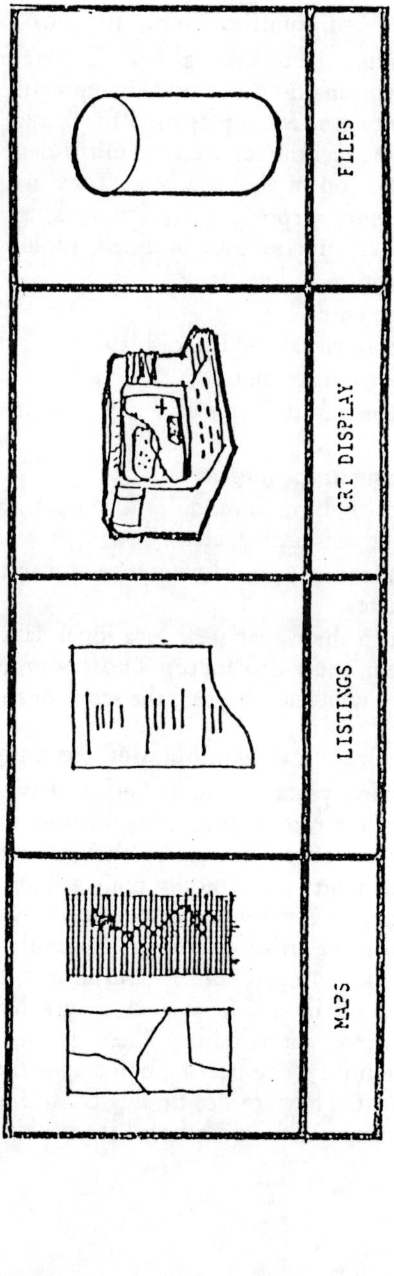

Figure 18 Output Format

(c) CRT interactive displays (both graphics and attributes); and
(d) Computed data files resulting from various manipulations generated on the data.

Data Base Manipulation Techniques for Location Data

This section outlines the technologies which are commonly used in association with the maintenance and manipulation of the data base. Many of the software techniques used for spatial data base management are the same techniques used for initial data automation and in analytic manipulation of the data base. They are simply used differently for different purposes (i.e., for making routine data base adjustments). These functions are outlined as follows:

* Basic file creation and update
* File managements
* Basic search, retrieval and list/display
* Query of selected attributes
* Query of selected attributes by geographic area 6. Widowing manipulations
* Edge-matching of the files
* Grouping of multi-map modules for larger area continuous map measurement and display, etc.
* Conversion from x,y coordinates into grid and also from grid into x,y coordinates.

In addition to these spatial or locational data management functions, GIS systems must also address a host of typical attribute related DBMS functions which are beyond the scope of these notes.

Graphical Manipulation Techniques

Within the past five years, substantial efforts have been made to adapt the CAD/CAM interactive graphic capabilities to automated cartography. These types of technologies, although working with many of the same data elements, are typically not classified in the same context as the more analytic Geographic Information Systems. They are primarily focused on the creation, storage, manipulation and display of a variety of graphic map symbolisms and in fact, treat the geographic elements contained in a GIS system as graphic files, rather than topologically correct analytic files. These systems have great use, particularity in the utility/engineering basemap and related tax/cadastral map environment. They are also finding considerably high acceptance In the photogrammetric field where stereo plotters are being interfaced in support of basic mapping activities.

Figure 19 indicates the typical labels and text, as well as graphic symbolism vocabulary, which is operable on virtually all of these interactive graphic systems. Functions include:

* *Text label data*: These systems have multiple fonts with various sizes, scales, and a variety of capabilities including multiple font selection sizing, slanting, scaling, rotating, and in some cases, skewing along a curvilinear line.
* Creation of a symbol library from a digitizer and association of symbols to an interactive menu.
* Storage of symbol menus for interactive recall and display on maps and graphs. These symbols are typically associated with points, but they also involve symbols along lines and shading within polygon areas.
* Some of the basic interactive functions are:
  (a) Windowing, enlarging, and graphic symbol manipulation;
  (b) Editing of cartographic elements (i.e., rotation, enlargement, transformation, and deletion);
  (c) Graphical compositing of multiple graphic overlay files; and
  (d) Overlay of a graphic reference grid.
* Entry interactively (typically from CRT or digitizer) of points, lines, arcs, curvilinear lines, and polygons for various forms of graphical display.

Modelling

In a GIS environment, a set of tools are normally made available in the software to simulate a process or predict an outcome of the process using a combination of logical expressions, analytical procedures and criteria on a data set. This kind of approach for a problem solving is referred to as modeling. This aspect is shown in Figure 20.

Common Applications

Although automated geographic information systems are really just beginning to have practical benefits, they have been adapted to many application areas. The following is a summarized list of some of these:

* Engineering mapping
* Automated photogrammetry
* Subdivision design (cut/fill, street layout, parcel layout)
* Tax mapping (cadastral mapping)
* Highway mapping

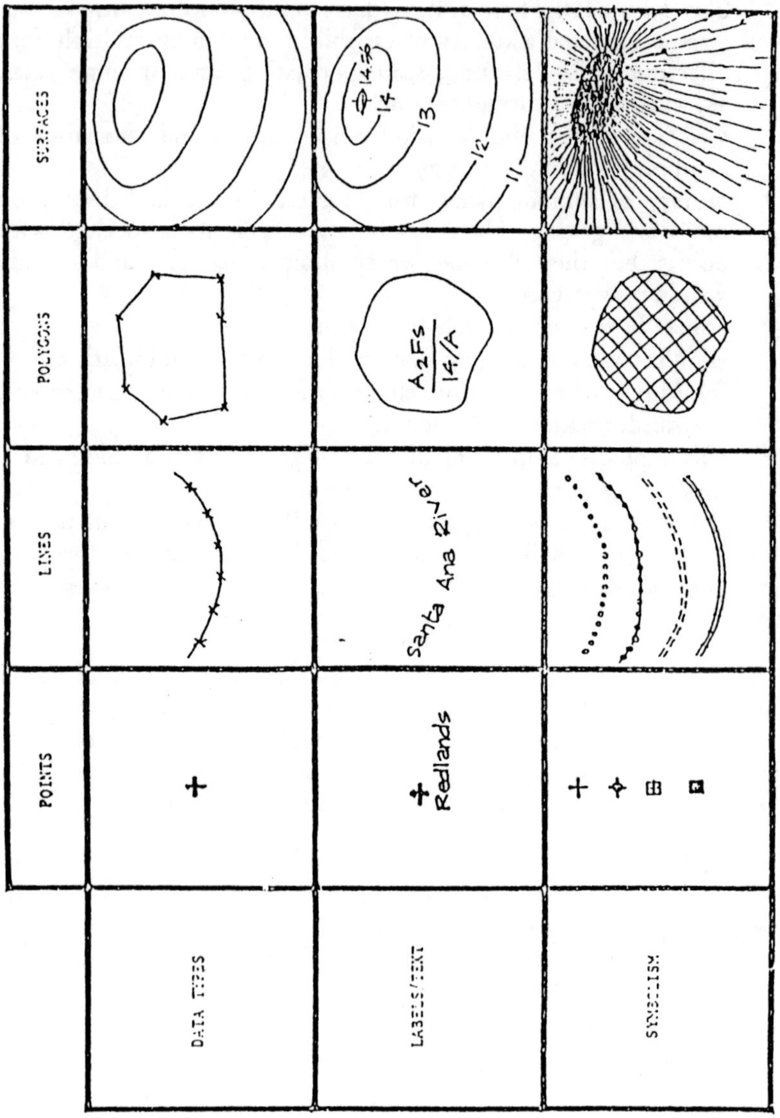

Figure 19 Map Symbolism

Figure 20
Developing a Model

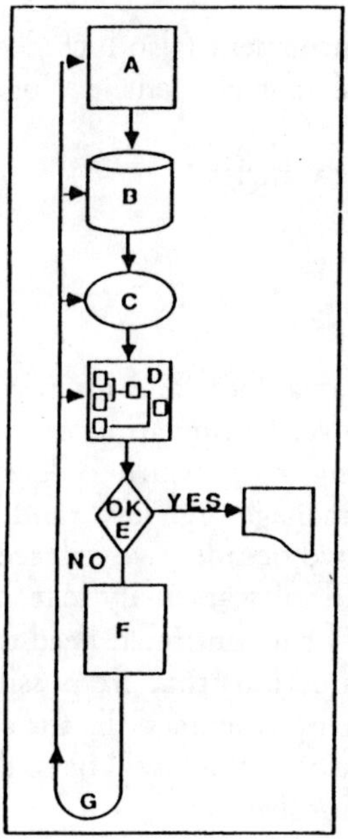

A - Define Specific Objectives

* Purpose of Model
* Results Expected

B - Identify Specific Data Required

* Determining Factors
* Relationships Among Factors

C - Define Logical Criteria / Decision Rules, Weighting Schedule, Analytical Procedures

D - Implement Criteria / Rules, Analytical Procedures

E - Evaluate Results

* Compare with Objectives

F - Revise Model, if Necessary

* Objectives
* Data
* Criteria / Rules, Weights, Analytical Procedures

G - Repeat Implementation

* Utility facility mapping and management
* Geodetic mapping
* Event mapping (accidents, crime, fire, facility breakage, etc.)
* Census and related statistical mapping
* Managements of well log data
* Land use planning and management
* Environmental impact studies
* Natural resource mapping and management (also included would be forest management, agricultural management, ecological and biological studies)
* Routing of buses and similar service vehicles
* Urban and regional planning
* Route selection of highways/pipelines.

Summary

It is apparent that there is increasing awareness and interest in geographic phenomena (i.e., natural resources, population distribution, land uses, etc.). This interest is increasing the pressure to develop better ways to record, store, analyze, manage, retrieve, and display geographic information. In the future two decades, we will see a revolution in the integration of hardware and software analytic techniques.

As this trend continues, there will be a continued need to better understand and define these analytic functions that are possible and, even more importantly, a need to develop human skills for adapting this technology to very specific applications which will be so demanding of the knowledge GIS systems will inspire.

APPENDIX 1

Structuring of Data Layers

As computers are not organized like human minds the data have to be structured in an efficient way and then stored on magnetic devices. Although it is not essential for the user of GIS to understand in detail how the data can be organized inside the computer a little knowledge of data structuring methods will help him to understand working of the systems their limitations and advantages. The most important features of a data storage system are data accessibility and its quick retrieval. The three main types of database structure are hierarchical network and relational.

In a GIS kind of study relational data base structure is more relevant than the other two types of database structures. So exclusive efforts are made to explain about relational database structure in the following paragraphs.

In relational database structure, the data are stored in simple records known as TUPLES containing an ordered set of attribute values that are grouped together in two dimensional tables known as relations. Data are extracted from the relational database through a procedure in which the user defines the relation that is appropriate for the query. This relation is not necessarily already present in the existing data flies. The controlling program uses the methods of relational algebra to construct new tables.

Relational databases have the advantage of flexible structure meeting the demands of all queries that can be formulated using the rules of BOOLEAN logic and of mathematical operations. Addition or removal of data is very easy.

The disadvantages of relational database is that many of the operations involve sequential searches through the files to find the right data. This is to satisfy the specified relations. This procedure delays the analysis in the case of large databases.

Computer Representation of Geographical Data

Essentially there are two contrasting but complementary ways of representing spatial data in the computer. They are referred to as explicit and implicit ways of describing spatial entities. Explicit representation means that the form of an object is built from a set of points on a grid or RASTER. The implicit representation makes use of a set of lines defined by staring and end points and some form of connectivity and is referred to as VECTOR representation.

Raster Data Structure

The simplest raster data structures consist of an array of grid cells and each grid cell contains a number representing the type or value of the attribute being mapped. Each coordinate space of an object is quantized for the entire object.

Vector Data Structure

The vector representation of an object is an attempt to represent the object as exactly as possible. The coordinate space unlike in the case of raster space is continuous one. All the positions lengths and dimensions of the object are defined very precisely.

The two dimensional data in these two structures are encoded in several methods within a computer for optimizing computational speed and data storage space. Some of them are quadtree runlength etc.

Database Design in a Geographical Information System

The design of the data base in a GIS must cater to the needs of the application problem to be tackled. It should allow the user to view the database in its entirety so that the massing linkages between the data elements can be identified and corrected. Updation must be possible for incorporating new data in the database. There are three design aspects to be considered while creating a database. They are concept design, logical design and physical design.

Conceptual design basically deals with the usefulness of the database in resolving the application requirements.

The logical design of the database is concerned with its logical structure that meets the requirements of the GIS software package.

The physical design deals entirely with the hardware and software requirements such as memory, disk space, access, speed etc.

APPENDIX 2

Definitions and Concept of Coordinate System

A coordinate system is a frame of reference in which geometrical positions of point objects can be uniquely defined. The frame of reference is chosen according to the convenience (mainly computational and storage related) for the given set of problems. Thus definition of a coordinate system requires:

* a reference point known as the origin
* a number of (linearly or functionally) independent directions
* scale definition in each direction.

Though this definition of coordinate system is not the most general in strict mathematical sense it is sufficient to cater to most of the problems in GIS. Moreover, usually the number of linearly independent directions is restricted to two or three.

Importance of Coordinate System in GIS

The importance of precise knowledge of coordinate systems involved in GIS comes from the very definition of GIS as science technology and art of generating and manipulating various spatial data structures.

They held in numerical representation of position of various objects. Working out precise transformations between coordinate systems helps in relating data sets collected by different methods or at different times.

Geographic Coordinate Systems

The issue of defining position of a point on the earth's surface in a natural manner and computation of various metric quantities like length and area using a earth based coordinate system are described below.

Earth's Frame of Reference

The physical shape of earth is too irregular to be used directly for computational purposes. Therefore various fictitious mathematical surfaces have been defined to approximate the shape to various degrees of precision. Best approximation to the real earths surface is described by the geoid an equipotential surface for gravitational field at mean sea level. It is an undulating surface smooth and continuous fictitiously expending under the continental surface at the same level. By definition it is perpendicular to the direction of gravity at any point. This makes it a convenient reference for measurement of height of points. Height above mean sea level is the most popular way of describing altitude of a point on or near the earth's surface.

A severe disadvantage of geoid is the complexity of its mathematical description. Another disadvantage is that the geoid is not completely known everywhere. This leads to the necessity of next level of approximation to the earth's surface by a best fit ellipsoid called reference datum. A number of best fit ellipsoids have been determined in different parts of the world. Everest datum is used for all survey work in India. An ellipsoid is fully described by the position of its center semi-major axis and eccentricity or minor axis. The position of center is determined in astronomical coordinate system. For Everest datum semi-major axis is 6377276 m resulting in a compression ratio of 1:300.8. Coordinate systems for geo-referencing are defined with one of datum ellipsoids as reference.

Coordinate Transformations

Coordinate transformations are required when two sets of coordinates for objects in the same area are existing. This situation arises either at the time of preparation of a GIS layer when input is available from more than one source or while attempting to overlay two GIS layers.

In this section parameters of some simple transformations are described. In practice these parameters have to be determined from known data which is usually in the form of common points.

Affine Transformation

Affine transformations are defined as the class of transformations which keep parallel lines parallel. These are essentially linear transformations which carry out the following elementary transformations:

* translation, i.e., shift of origin without rotation of axes,
* scaling: scale along one or both axes can be changed,
* rotation without shift of origin,
* reflection, i.e., orientation of one or both coordinate axes gets reversed.

Map Projections

The basic problem of map projections is representation of curved surface In a plane. For the representation of earth's surface i.e., part of an ellipsold or sphere on a paper map various map protections have been devised. It has been shown that there is no perfect solution to this problem. All the same, it is much more convenient to handle data on a plane rather than on an ellipsoid or sphere (even in the age of electronic computers). The basic projection surfaces are shown in Figure 21.

Concept of Map Projection

Though the aim of map projection is to represent the curved surface (ellipsoid or sphere) on to a plane this is usually carried out through an intermediate surface which is developable into a plane without any further distortion. Examples of developable surfaces are cylinder and cone. Sphere is an example of non-developable surface. A projection from the datum surface could be direct i.e. directly transforming points to projection surface or it can be double i.e., involving a transformation first from datum to a sphere and then on to the projection surface.

The transformation from datum surface to projection surface could be geometrical, semi-geometrical or mathematical in nature. Though the most natural projection seems to be the perspective protection in practice very few transformations are truly perspective in the geometrical sense.

As such it is convenient to define map projection as a systematic arrangement of intersecting lines on a plane, that represent and have a one to one correspondence with the meridians and parallels on the datum surface.

The arrangement follows some consistent principle in order to fulfill certain specified conditions. Thus there exist in principle an infinite number of map projections depending on the conditions.

For defining a map projection completely, following three elements should be considered:
* the datum surface,
* the projection surface, and
* the projection process per se.

The datum surface can be either sphere or ellipsoid.

Importance of Map Projections in GIS

Traditionally the map projection concept was considered of prime importance to the surveyor and mapper and used for the purpose of computation of positions, distances and angles between discrete points lying in a limited area of interest. Graphical representations of earth's surface for various purposes was and is of prime importance to mapmakers.

Some of these functions need to be performed by scientists and engineers involved in GIS preparation or usage. Accordingly the importance of knowledge of map projections is necessary. Also in a GIS environment the concept and usage of map protection is necessary for following other reasons:-
* maps are a common source of data for a GIS. Often input maps are in different projections thereby requiring transformation one or all maps to make their coordinate systems compatible.
* when GIS projects are of global or regional scale it becomes necessary to consider effect of earth's curvature. A suitable selection of map projection is very helpful in minimizing computations while retaining reasonable geometrical accuracies.
* monitor screens are flat and to get a proper feel of distances and areas on the ground suitable map projection needs to be used.

The two projection systems known commonly are explained below:

Polyconic Projection

In terms of the classification scheme a polyconic projection shown in Figure 22 can be classified as having following properties:
* It is conical i.e. the projection surface to which a given point on

Figure 21
Basic Projection Surfaces

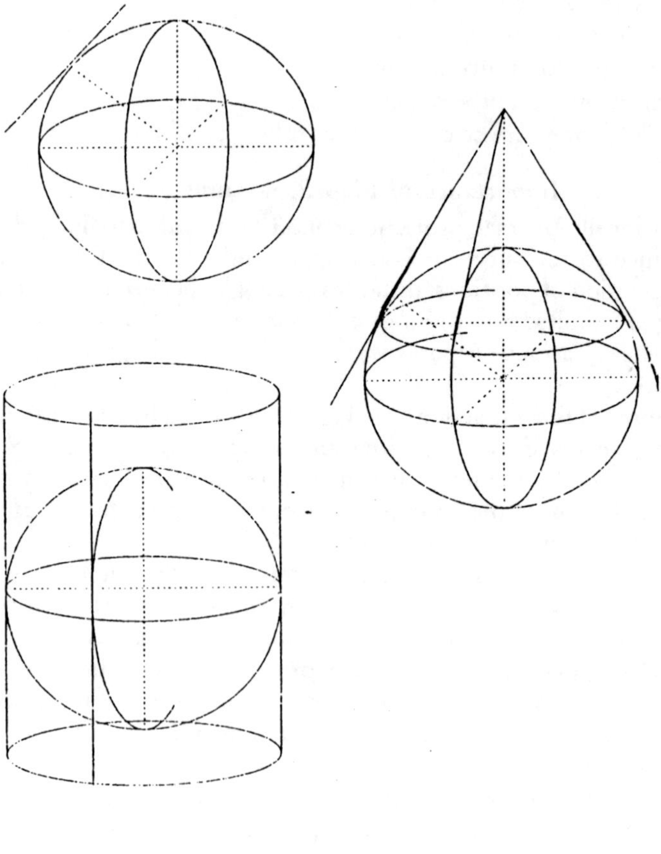

Figure 22

Multiline Contact for Polyconic Projection

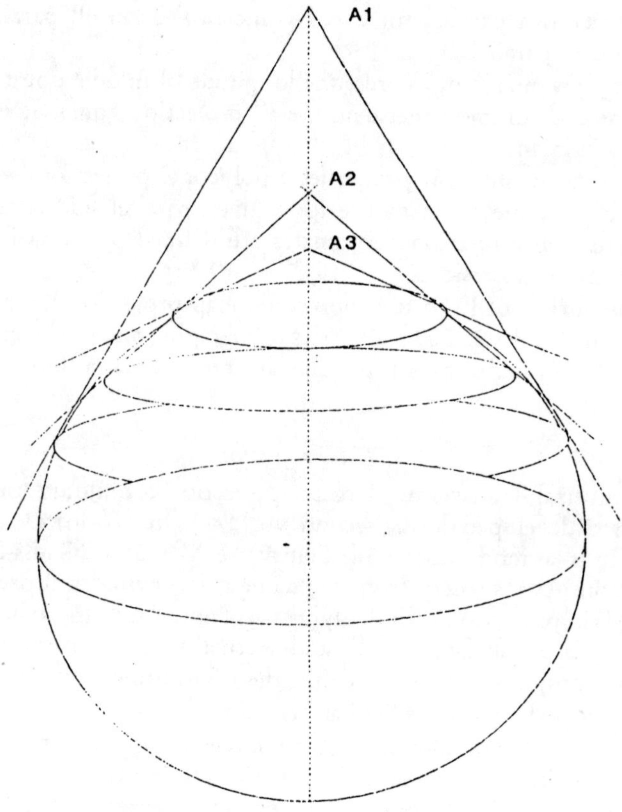

datum surface is transferred is a cone.

* In terms of contact or coincidence it is polyconical. A different cone is used for transferring points having different latitudes to the final projection surface which is a plane. The line of contact is a circle.
* The cones are assumed to be in normal position. As the line of contact is a parallel for a polyconic projection all parallels are standard parallels.

For a given area of interest the longitude of middle point is used to define the common meridian for all projection cones. It is called central meridian.

In terms of intrinsic properties a polyconic projection is equivalent and is geometric in nature for a given parallel. However for a given area the projection coordinates are defined by using involved mathematical expressions.

The Survey of India uses polyconic map projection for its 1:250 000 1:50 000 and 1:25 000 scale series topographic maps. The grid lines provided on gridded SOI topomaps are however in a different map projection.

UTM Projection

The Universal Transversal Mercator projection commonly known as UTM was developed during second world war for worldwide applications. It is a modification of Transverse Mercator (Gauss-Kruger) projection. As is evident from the name it is a cylindrical projection with axis of projection cylinder lying perpendicular to the axis of symmetry of datum surface i.e. ellipsoid. Actually a number of transverse Mercator projections together define the UTM projection.

The basic features of UTM are as follows:

* The world is divided into 60 zones each expending through six deg of longitude. Zones are numbered consecutively from one to 60 beginning with the zone between 180 degrees west and 174 degrees west and continuing eastwards. In the geometrical sense the transverse cylinder is tangent along the central meridian of each zone.
* A scale distortion of 0.9996 is applied along the central meridian of each zone. This results in the transverse cylinder becoming secant to the datum and the scale distortions getting more favourably distributed over the zone. The choice of scale factor 0.9996 was made so as to limit the scale error to 1:2500 within the zone.

* A plane rectangular metric grid is superimposed on each zone, assigning a 500,000 m false Easting to the central meridian, a 0 to Northing to equator for the northern hemisphere and a false northing of 10,000,000 m to the equator for the southern hemisphere. This arrangements is made to eliminate occurrence of negative values.
* The UTM system is used between latitudes of 84 degrees N to 84 degrees S. The polar regions are covered by Universal Polar Stereographic (UPS) projection.
* A grid overlap of approximately 40 km on either side of the zone boundary kept.

Precise mathematical formulation for conversion of geographic coordinates to UTM and vice versa can be found in literature.

References

1. Jeffrey Star and John Estes, Geographic Information System, Prentice Hall, 1990.
2. P.A. Burroughs, "Principles of Geographical Information Systems for Land Resources Assessment", Clarendon Press, 1986.
3. D.J. Maguire, M. Goodchild and D.W. Rhind, "Geographical Information Systems, Principles and Applications", Longman Scientific and Technical Publications, 1990.
4. K.C. Clarke, "Recent Trends in Geographic Information Systems Research, Geo-Processing, Vol.3, pp 1-15, 1986.
5. Andrew D. Frank, Max J. Egenhofer and Werner Kuhn, "A perspective on GIS technology in the nineties", PE&RS, Vol. 57, No. 11, pp. 1431-1436.
6. David M. Mark and Michael D. Gould, "Interacting with geographic information: A commentary", PE&RS, Vol. 57 No. 11, pp 1427-1430.
7. David R. Maidment and Thomas A. Evans, Expert GIS: Linking ARC/INFO to the NEXPERT OBJECT expert system shell, ARC News, Vol.13, No. 4, pp 3-4.
8. Jean-Christophe Hadom, "Mac turns up trumps", Space Technology International 1992, Cornhill Publications, pp 65-66.

9. Stephen Colwell, "GIS and GPS: A New Partnership" , Space Technology International 1992, Cornhill Publications, pp. 73-75.
10. Anon, "Integrating CAD and GIS, ARC News, Vol. 14, No.1, pp. 2-3.
11. M.J. Jackson and D.C. Mason, The development of integrated Geo-Information Systems, IJRS, Vol. 7, No. 6, pp. 723- 743.
12. Michael F. Goodchild, "Geographical Information Science, IJGIS, Vol. 6, No. 1, pp. 31-45.

Chapter 14

Application of Geographical Information Systems Technology for Environmental Monitoring and Forecasting in India

R.B. Singh

Introduction

The environmental problems emerging from economic development and anthropogenic transformation of space constitute some of the major challenges facing the globe today. In developing countries, the population explosion combined with poverty has put increasing pressure on land leading to the depletion of natural resources and imbalances in the ecosystems. The tropical mountain ecosystems have been particularly affected adversely through this process. At any stage interaction of man and his environment is depicted through socio-economic and technological development. One of the functions of geography is to analyze the consequences of man-nature interaction in various regional mosaics by considering spatio-temporal framework of several interactive systems, i.e., man-biome interactive systems, water and land interactive systems and highland-lowland interactive systems.

The understanding of environmental change requires reconstruction of earlier landscape processes, modelling of the dynamics of existing landscapes, analysis of causes and consequences of anthropogenic changes in specified regions, appraisal of social responses to change and enhanced Geographic Information Systems (GIS), supported by detailed site studies (Kotlyakov et al., 1988). An important task of geographical monitoring is to observe the state of land-use changes in both natural and anthropogenically modified geosystems at regional and local levels for improvement, development and amelioration of human habitat. This includes considerations of the following dimensions:

(i) Historical development of the natural geosystems and their environmental history.

(ii) The current state of the environment including its resource base.

(iii) The channels of human activities influencing the environment and the feedback of the main and side effects of human activities.

(iv) Socio-economic needs of the region in the context of future development.

(v) Forecasting environmental transformation due to development in the future.

Environmental monitoring as well as developmental planning for diverse geographical environments in developing countries have recently become information-intensive. The combined use of geographical information systems, digital image processing and simulation models provides new possibilities for better environmental monitoring and forecasting. Later, use of GIS in spatio-temporal perspective may lead to the development of a viable forecasting model for achieving the goals of public policy in future.

GIS is an integrated data-base, containing spatial information about different levels of observation. This is emerging as a powerful tool for integrating earth-based data of diverse types in the field of environmental studies and natural resource management. The task of GIS is to harmonize the available information from various sources, i.e., field work, aerial photographs and satellite imageries with existing data sets as well as maps so that the resultant synthesis becomes compatible with the National/Global Data-Base Management Systems. The emphasis of remote sensing and GIS technology should be based on the specific needs of operational programmes and not only as an academic exercise. This type of study will help in the selection, planning, implementation and evaluation of various projects. Thus, GIS should become an integral part of decision support system in national developmental planning (Raza and Singh, 1988).

The Research Problem: Emerging Scenario

The recent ecological changes affecting the Himalayan environment are the result of a combination of natural and anthropogenic factors. The human impact mainly takes the form of over-cultivation, over-grazing, over-clearing of woodland and, in fact, in the over-use of all mountain resources. The anthropogenic aspects are technogenic in nature, and include forestry, mining, transport, industry, urbanization and tourism, etc. In this way, development of anthropogenesis has taken place with increasing pace of sociogenesis and technogenesis (Singh, 1987). In the Himalayan geosystem, there is evidence of constant change, both spatially and temporally. Thus, the structure and functions of geosystems need continuous monitoring as a part of geographical investigation.

There is a general lack of knowledge pertaining to the complex environmental conditions prevailing in man-environment interactive systems of mountainous terrains. The rate and scale of change in these systems is so large that it is not possible to make a correct assessment of the consequences of the changes. Also, there is general uncertainity regarding the actual impacts of anthropogenic activities upon mountain environment (Ives and Messerli, 1988). Despite the prevalent uncertainty, both mismanagement and ill-planning in anthropogenic activities have resulted in land instability through soil erosion and land degradation hazards that adversely affect socio-economic conditions of inhabitants, which, often result in decline in the quality of life. While there is increasing awareness among the people about the impending disaster and the concerned governments too are taking remedial measures, the complexity of the various ecosystems, particularly the interaction between the highland and lowland geosystems need to be understood more clearly for formulating and implementing public policies.

With increase in altitude in mountainous terrains, the capacity to absorb ecological disturbances decreases. This aspect renders highland environments ecologically fragile in nature. The underlying geology and climate is partly responsible for the high degree of vulnerability of the system to soil erosion and its hydrologic and geomorphic degradation. It is necessary to derive new data from the existing data sets by using several types of models to estimate the risk of soil erosion and flood hazards. In this context, a satisfactory answer has to be provided to the following pertinent points:

(i) Identification of the characteristics of the components and indicators of various geosystems at national and regional levels, and assessing their viability for geographical information collection and their suitability for the control and forecasting the state of geosphere.

(ii) Appraisal of the causes and modes of modification, degradation and destruction of natural environment with regard to anthropogenic impact.

(iii) Assessment of the extent and zones of environmental hazards subsequent to anthropogenic activities at various elevations and under varying vegetal cover.
(iv) The question of appropriate siting of monitoring stations for development of micro-level geographical database.
(v) Preparation of an ecologically compatible land-use programme and the mode of its implementation in the region.

One of the important objectives of the National Agricultural Policy of the Government of India is to monitor national soil and land resources which will detect significant changes in soil characteristics. This directly or indirectly affects the quality of the land and its ability to produce basic needs, i.e., food, fibre and timber. An integrated assessment of the status and risk of soil degradation will provide one of the essential data sets for such a national understanding (Singh, 1989). The objectives to prepare soil degradation map is to strengthen the awareness of policy makers on the dangers resulting from inappropriate land and soil management to the national well being and to improve the capability in regional and national institutions to deliver accurate information for agricultural planning purposes.

Aims and Objectives

Landscape perception and evaluation has two main functions, namely (a) hazard avoidance, and (b) guidance on suitability for major land use type. The systematic and comprehensive evaluation of landscape is an important aspect in any research work related to environmental issues and concerns in any region because of its potentiality for resource inventory, carrying capacity decisions and environmental assessments. The present research programme intends to enhance the existing information system in the mountainous region of Chakrata tehsil for a systematic analysis of the geosystem and forecasting anthropogenic stress on the state of the biosphere. Its main objectives are as follows:

1. To apply environmental remote sensing, digital image processing and GIS technologies for environmental monitoring and forecasting.
2. To diaganose the extent and intensity of ecological degradation through monitoring changing land-use patterns, particularly forest cover with increase of anthropogenic activities.
3. To forecast environmental impacts through soil erosion hazard.
4. To present a model of sustainable land use on the basis of land suitability for agriculture.

The Study Region

The study area—Chakrata tehsil (Dehradun District, Uttar Pradesh) is a rugged mountainous tract, marking the divide of the upper Yamuna valley in the extreme north-west of the Garhwal Himalaya. The region measures about 1002 km^2, and is located between 30°31'N to 31°3'N and 77°42'E to 78°7'E. Administratively, the region includes two development blocks, i.e., Chakrata and Kalsi and has one town—Chakrata, 357 villages and six forest ranges. It is bordered by the districts of Tehri Garhwal in the east, Uttarkashi in the north and the north-east, tehsil of Dehradun in the south (all in Uttar Pradesh) and Mahasu district of Himachal Pradesh in the west. Its potential for research is immense due to the good quality of forest reserves, integrated network of rivers and valleys and its distinct culture and human resources.

The present micro-level study in a part of the Himalayas will provide an opportunity to understand the existing land use changes in microcosm and its ecological implications in varying intensities. The impact of severe soil erosion is particularly significant in this area. An attempt will also be made to promote the understanding of the highland and lowland land-use processes and interactive systems.

Materials, Methodology and Analysis

Computer Configuration

Hardware:

- IBM-PC/AT Computer: 512 Kbytes memory; 1.2 Mbytes floppy-disk drive; 80 Mbytes hard disk; IBM monitor/printer adaptor; IBM Monochrome display; DOS 3.1.
- Compaq-DESKPRO 386 computer.
- IMB-PS System.
- VAX system with ARC/INFO and ELAS software.
- CIPHER Tape Drive; Density 1600 BPI; 3200 BPI.
- TEKTRONIX 4695 Ink-Jet Printer.
- WANG Line Printer.
- IBM PROPRINTER XL 24.
- GTCO DIGI-PAD.

Software:

- ERDAS (Earth Resources Data Analysis System), version 7.2; Raster based.
- ARC/INFO, version 4.0; Vector based.

Basic Data Sources:

1. *Satellite Image*: LANDSAT-MSS 3, four bands, CCT Interleaving Format: BSQ, CCT density: 6250 BPI, Data Tape Generated: May 12, 1980; Atmospheric Corrected; MSS Index Path-D157/Row 39; Source: USGS EROS Data Centre.
2. *Maps and Statistics*:
   - — Survey of India Topo Sheet, Scale: 1:250,000, 1976.
   - — Survey of India Topo Sheet, Scale: 1:253,440, 1946.
   - — Map of Chakrata tehsil with village administrative units, Census of India, 1981.
   - — Forest Cover Map, NRSA, 1980.
   - — Population Statistics, District Census Handbook-1981, Dehradun District, A: Primary Census Abstract, B: Village Directory.
   - — Maps and Statistics, Chakrata Forest Division Working Plan, 1986.
   - — Maps and Publications, Forest and Soil Survey Department.

Database Digitization and Compilation

Different computer softwares were used to compile, analyze, display and print the basic database. The software processes geographically referenced data from satellite image and various other sources. Data digitization from maps and tables could be processed and merged for multi-grid integration and analysis. In this study, the requirements were successfully met by providing a highly integrated raster/vector processing. The initial task in the application of GIS technology was to identify specific factors influencing the research problem, i.e., deforestation, soil erosion and subsequent land suitability analysis. In this context various basic factors like physiography, forest cover for two periods, soil and vegetation characteristics, climate, drainage systems and population pressure were identified for monitoring and modelling. Map digitization was performed in vector form using the VAX computer with ARC/INFO system. Data digitized in vector mode were further transformed into raster format so that this should be compatible for processing on ERDAS.

Image Classification

Before registration and geometric correction through rectifying the image, the general land cover classification was performed on ERDAS system using IP module. This was done to ensure that classification errors contributed by the resampling process were avoided. Two well-known supervised and unsupervised classification techniques were used to compare the result. The procedures were used to classify image into few general classes of interest. Under unsupervised classification, clustering was a technique for pattern classification in terms of groups of pattern or clusters that possess strong internal similarities (Moik, 1980). The cluster labelling procedure was utilized three times to classify raw image into 27, 15 and 10 clusters. Finally, the result of 10 clusters were considered satisfactory to have a land cover classification.

A supervised classification method was also applied on raw image and transformed spectral data as input to MAXCLAS programme of ERDAS. The various geometric algorithm was performed to identify different general land use category. For the supervised classification, training samples for each of generally known classes were identified. The land cover map having above mentioned four basic class types were prepared at 1:219900 scale. Subsequently for monitoring forest change, only forest and non- forest classes were taken into consideration. Finally, all classified images were geo-referenced using earlier coefficient matrix.

Monitoring, Modelling and Discussion

Elevation Model

The elevation model was prepared on ARC/INFO surface modelling sub-system called TIN (Triangular Irregular Network). TIN is a structure in which a surface is represented as a series of non-overlapping contiguous triangular facets, of irregular size and shape (Chen and Guerara, 1987). It should also be noted that elevation data were very generalized matching with 1:250,000 scale and small scale of the DEM, which allows for the modelling of a large area but not detail information. However it reduced the time required to develop a probability model. Subsequently other important terrain informations, i.e., slope and aspect were derived on ERDAS using TOPO module. The slope and aspect of each point was calculated by overlaying polygon coverages created from the TIN through SLOPE programme of TOPO module. The programme created about more than 34 per cent slope under 32 per cent of the study area. This was further merged under five categories: less than 1, 1-5, 6-15, 16-33, and more than 34 per cent for analyzing potential soil erosion.

Monitoring Forest Change

The land use provides an important input in the analysis of rural and regional development of any region. The general land cover classification may be usually adaptable for monitoring past changes in land use in general and forest change in particular. Deforestation is the focal ecological problem in the Himalayan degradation as forest satisfies basic needs, i.e., fuel, fodder and shelter of the local people.

For monitoring forest change, MATRIX analysis (GIS module) was performed taking two GIS files, i.e., forest map of 1920 and forest map of 1980 prepared by NRSA based on LANDSAT imagery with limited ground truth (Table 1 and Fig. 1). The result indicates that about 33 per cent areas deforested but 11 per cent areas also regenerated under this long time span. With increase of population, the growing demand for more agricultural land has forced people to destroy the forest to cultivate marginal land. There are also positive relationships between deforested zone and densely populated area. The study reveals that satellite remote sensing can be effectively used for land use mapping and for monitoring forest degradation process in the country. Due to rapid change, the information collected by conventional methods becomes outdated.

Table 1

Monitoring forest change
MATRIX analysis on ERDAS system (area in per cent)

1980	*1920*	
	Forest	*Non-Forest*
Forest	1 Unchanged 17.10	2 Afforested 10.73
Non-forest	3 Deforested 32.69	4 Unchanged 39.49

The estimation of soil erosion potential and its effects on soil productivity are essential for agricultural development and regional environmental planning. The hazards of soil erosion need to be carefully examined in Indian Himalaya where intensive agriculture with subsistence economy is predominant. A large proportion of agricultural land is already suffering from serious erosion problem. This study was done on small scale map. Therefore it is difficult to give detailed explanations. However, it gives trend and magnitude of the

FIGURE 1

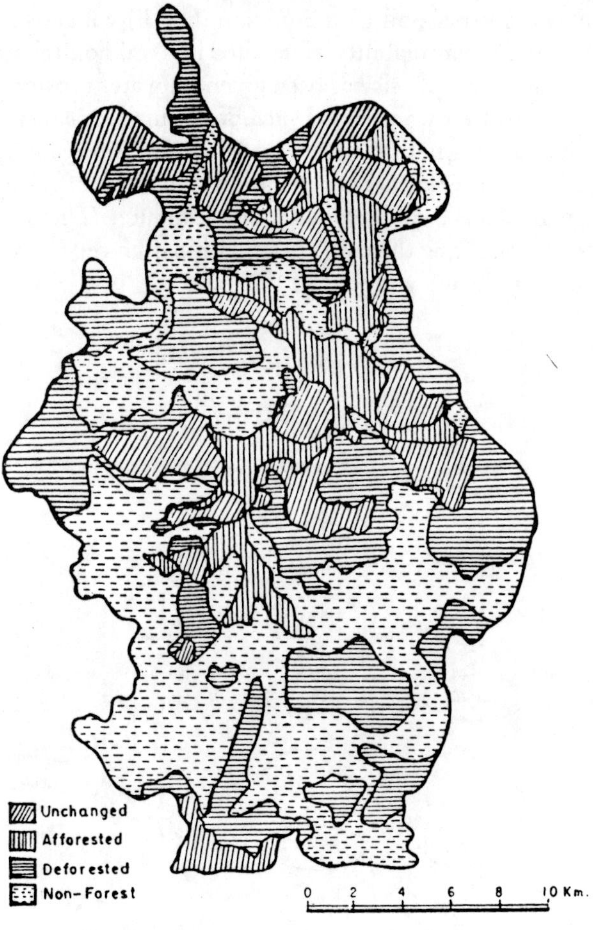

Fig. 1. Forest change monitoring of Chakrota Tehsil (Dehradun Dist., Uttar Pradesh) intergrating two forest files of 1920 and 1980 by applying MATRIX analysis on ERDAS GIS software.

problem. The potential problematic areas can be examined further. Slope and climate are the most important natural factors contributing to the soil erosion. It is also assumed that where there is more dense spatial distribution of population, there is more intensive use of land, resulting into land degradation and soil erosion.

There is no generally accepted model for soil erosion in developing countries largely due to limited availability of data. FAO/UNEP methodology is largely adopted in the project. It is considered simplification of Universal Soil Loss Equation (USLE) which is not possible to apply due to unavailability of detailed information relating to natural phenomena. Emphasis has been given on water erosion. Data used for locating soil erosion hazard includes rainfall-erosivity, slope, soil erodibility, and vegetation cover (model 1). The job of interpreting applicable characteristics (slope, erodibility and run off potential from the original data is a simple one for the computer. The overlay analysis consists evaluating the data values within each cell in the combined grid matrix (Lillesand and Kiefer, 1979).

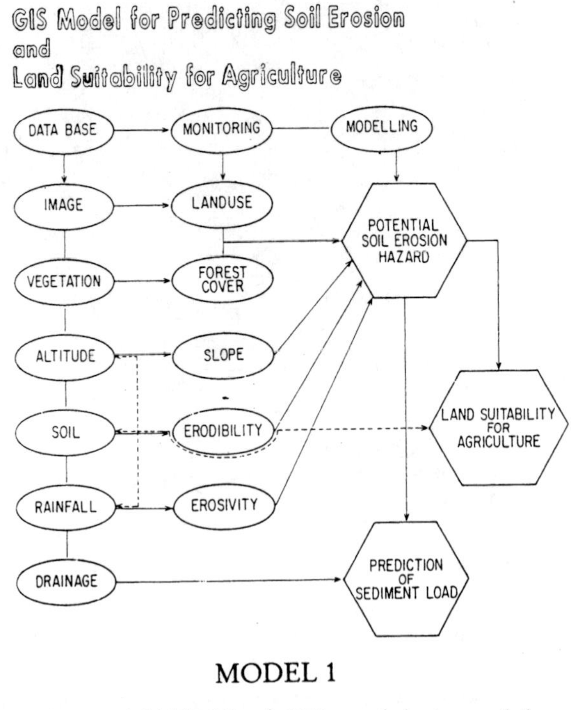

MODEL 1

The programme MATRIX of GIS module is used for analysis, performing a coincidence analysis for combination of two files giving precise distribution of various features. The analysis has been performed by merging three sets of derived information by overlay method. Firstly, two critical factors, i.e., slope and rainfall are merged together (Table 2). In second set, soil erodibility and vegetation cover

FIGURE 2

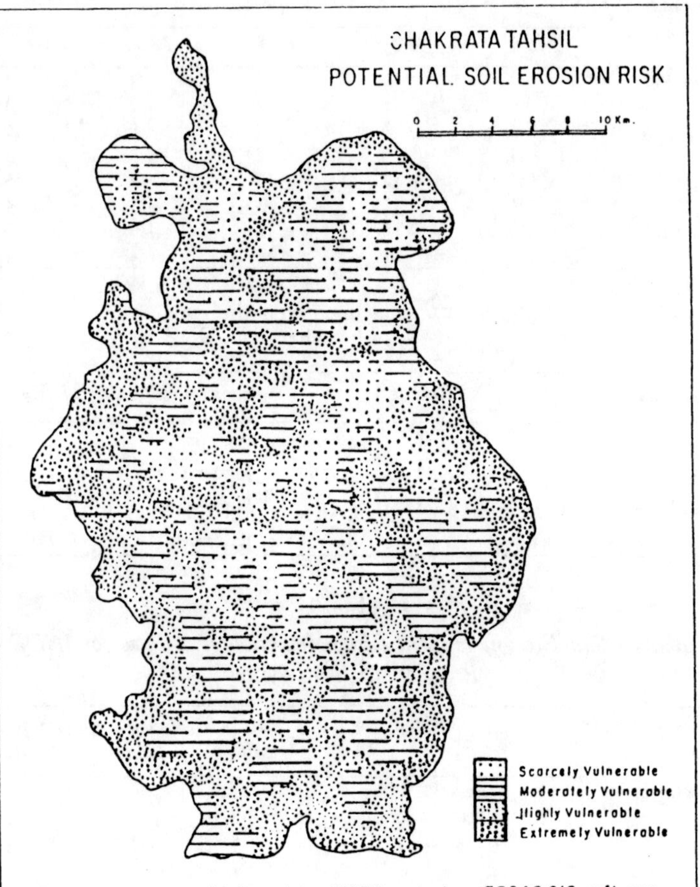

Forecasting erosion risk by applying INDEX analysis on ERDAS GIS software

are merged. After combining these two sets of combination, the potential soil erosion risk map is prepared (Fig. 2). The high soil erosion risk indicates steep slopes, highly erodable soil, high rainfall-erosivity and lack of forest cover. The following results were obtained after final aggregations of composite values for potential soil erosion risk:

Table 2

Potential Soil Erosion Hazard Risk Matrix Analysis

Rainfall (cm)	*Slope %*				
	Below 1	*1-5*	*6-15*	*16-33*	*Above 34*
Below 140	1	2	3	4	5
	1	1	2	2	3
140-160	6	7	8	9	10
	1	1	2	3	3
160-200	11	12	13	14	15
	1	2	3	3	4
Above 200	16	17	18	19	20
	1	3	4	4	4

Matrix Class Value → $\frac{20}{4}$ ← Score given the class value after RECODE

Class Value	*Recode*	*Erosion risk vulnerability*
1,2,6,7,11,16	1	Scarcely
3,4,8,12	2	Moderately
5,9,10,13,14,17	3	High
15,18,19,20	4	Extremely

Table 3

Potential Soil Erosion Hazard Risk, Methodological Plan for INDEX Prog. on ERDAS System

Erosion Factor	*Major types*	*Rating value*	*Weighting factor*	*Composite score*
Slope factor	1. Below 1%	1		5
	2. 1-5%	2		10
	3. 6-15$	3	5	15
	4. 16-33%	4		20
	5. Above 34%	5		25
Vegetation cover	1. Forest	1	4	14
	2. Non-forest	4		16
Soil erodibility	1. Brown forest soil	2		6
	2. Clay and sandy loam of hill	3	3	9
	3. Sandy loam of valley	4		12
Rainfall erosivity	1. Below 140 cm.	1		2
	2. 140-160 cm.	2	2	4
	3. 160-200 cm.	3		6
	4. Above 200 cm.	4		8

Final aggregation after INDEX analysis

S.No.	*Characteristics*	*Score value*	*Area (%)*
1.	Scarcely vulnerable	Below 27	13.15
2.	Moderately vulnerable	28-38	33.93
3.	Highly vulnerable	39.50	26.36
4.	Extremely vulnerable	Above 51	26.55

INDEX (GIS module) which performs a weighted-sum analysis of multiple input files, was also used for predicting soil erosion risk (Table 3). This is further compared with population density of the region using summary criteria. The analysis shows close relationship between soil erosion risk and population density (Table 4). The spatial distribution of potential soil erosion zone will give direction to planners and decision makers who are dealing with soil productivity. Soil suitability and ecological suitability for specific land use and crop types may be prepared. This will four rational management efforts and practical solution of the problem.

Table 4

Comparison of Two Methods for Forecasting Potential Soil Erosion Risk Vulnerability (area in per cent)

Overlay Method	*Index method*			
	Scarcely	*Moderately*	*Highly*	*Extremely*
Scarcely	43.56	52.40	4.04	
Moderately	6.34	44.68	32.46	16.52
Highly	1.91	17.32	41.93	38.85
Extremely	—	4.16	15.26	80.58

(Based on Summary Prog. on ERDAS System).

Comparison of Potential Soil Erosion Risk and Population Density (area in per cent) (persons per ha.)

	Population Density			
Erosion	*Below 1*	*1-5*	*6-10*	*Above 10*
Scarcely vulnerable	35.05	60.78	3.95	0.21
Moderately vulnerable	24.58	71.76	3.52	0.15
Highly vulnerable	21.56	73.08	4.76	0.60
Extremely vulnerable	15.59	76.19	5.48	2.74

(Based on Summary Prog. on ERDAS System).

Land Suitability for Agriculture

Land suitability requires all the relevant data on the site characteristics and environmental factors which enable the user to decide the proper land use for optimum production without risk of soil erosion. The important inherent characteristics of the land suitability for agriculture are water availability, nutrient contents, altitude and zone of potential soil erosion risk (Model 1). The terrain information and topographic characteristics are considered most important indicators for the land suitability. Terrace cultivation has been practiced on slope steeper than 33 per cent, the present deadline for arable farming. It causes problem of soil erosion. After taking into consideration the above factors, a composite index is developed, identifying areas suitable/not suitable for agriculture.

Table 5

Land Suitability for Agriculture Methodological Plan for INDEX Prog. on ERDAS System

Suitability factor		*Major types*	*Rating value*	*Weighting factor*	*Composite Score*
Potential Soil Erosion Risk	1.	Scarcely	4		20
	2.	Moderately	3	5	15
	3.	Highly	2		10
	4.	Extremely	1		5
Water Availability (rainfall in cm.)	1.	Below 140	1		4
	2.	140-160	2	4	8
	3.	160-200	3		12
	4.	Above 200	4		16
Nutrient Content	1.	Brown forest soil	2		6
	2.	Clay and sandy loam of Hill	3	3	9
	3.	Sandy loam of valley	4		8
Altitude	1.	Below 2000'	4		8
	2.	2000-4000'	4		8
	3.	4000-6000'	3	2	6
	4.	6000-8000'	2		4
	5.	Above 8000'	1		2

Final Aggregation After INDEX and OVERLAY Analysis

S.No.	*Characteristics*	*Score Value*	*Area (%)*
1.	Highly suitable	Above 47	2.41
2.	Moderately suitable	38-46	26.13
3.	Low suitable	29-37	35.48
4.	Very low suitable	Below 28	1.84
5.	Forest	—	25.43
6.	Water bodies	—	8.71

INDEX (GIS module) was used for classifying agricultural suitability. INDEX performs a weighted-sum analysis of multiple input files. The programme also gave ideas about the major capabilities of GIS technology for data manipulation and analysis. The factors like rainfall pattern, soil quality, altitude and zone of soil erosion risk were recorded according to their contribution for soil erosion along with weighting the factors, creating a composite index for the whole region (Table 5). Subsequently, forest and water bodies were overlayed on the map. The following classes were obtained after final aggregation of all factors:

— highly suitable (2.41%).
— moderately suitable (26.13%).
— low suitable (35.48%).
— very low suitable (1.84%).
— forest (25.43%), and
— water bodies (8.71%).

Table 6 shows close relationship between agricultural suitability and potential soil erosion risk.

Table 6

Comparison of Agricultural Suitability and Potential Soil Erosion Risk (area in per cent)

	Erosion Risk			
Suitability	*Scarcely vulnerable*	*Moderately vulnerable*	*Highly vulnerable*	*Extremely vulnerable*
High suitable	100.00	—	—	—
Moderately suitable	32.48	50.22	17.12	0.18
Low suitable	3.40	30.45	42.03	24.12
Very low suitable	—	—	47.22	52.78

(Based on Summary Prog. on ERDAS System).

Concluding Remarks

Human beings can not survive without the natural resources, and no rise in living standards is possible without increasing the rational use of natural resources. The achievement of sustained development and the rational use of environmental resources are simply inseparable. Land and soil are the most valuable basic resources of the study area. Out of the total area in the region, about 50 per cent require soil conservation measures at the top priority level. To have a sustainable and continuous use of environment, there is a need for local and regional

FIGURE 3

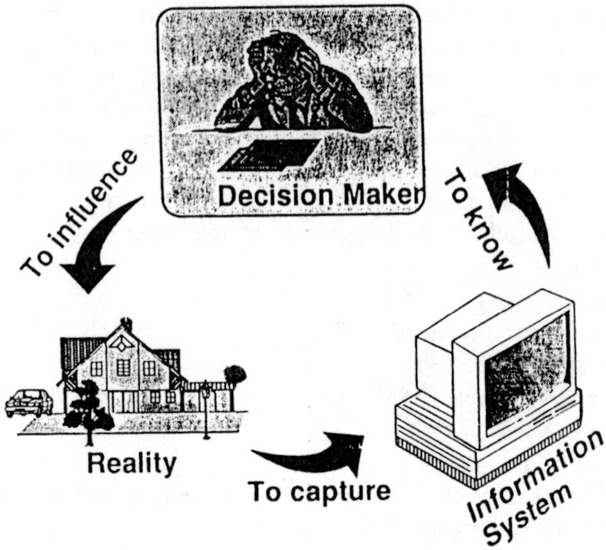

Reality-Information-Decision

level studies of landscape evaluation, soil conservation and regulation of land use. The landscape evaluation has potentiality to improve resource inventory, carrying capacity decisions and environmental impact assessment. In an increasing competition between various uses of land, there is a great need to classify landscape in order to develop a land-use pattern according to their best capability and discourage wasteful land-use.

A GIS approach could be considered useful for qualifying the sensibility of land to erode, and consequently to better implement land and water management programmes. It is easily possible to prepare a thematic map showing susceptibility of a specific region to erosion based on consideration of the various attributes of topography, rainfall, soil and land-cover aspects and population pressure. Identification of specific locations and quantification of critical trouble spots have been also made. It will help local planners, resource managers and environmental management experts to assign priority to future land and water conservation efforts. Finally, this will provide ground to suggest appropriate land uses in order to achieve sustainable regional development. The false colour composite maps could be easily understood by policy makers and planners and even ordinary people in the field of GIS technology (Fig. 3).

References

Chen, Zi-Tan and Guevara, J. Armando, (1987), "Systematic selection of very important points (VIP) from digital terrain model for construction triangular irregular networks", in *Autocarto-8 Proceedings*, Eight Int. Symp. on Computer Assisted Cartography.

Ives, J.D. and Messerli, B., (1989), *The Himalayan Dilemma* UNU Pub., London: Routledge.

Kotlyakov, V.M. et.al., (1988), "Global Change: Geographical Approaches (A Review)" *Ecology*, Proc. Natal. Acad. Sci. U.S.A., Vol. 85, pp. 5986-91.

Lillesand, T. and Kiefer, R., (1979), *Remote Sensing and Image Interpretation*, Wiley, pp. 170-87.

Moik, J.G., (1980), *Digital Processing of Remotely Sensed Images*, NASA Pub., NASA SP-431.

Raza, M. and Singh, R.B., (1989), "Network of Research Stations for Geographical Monitoring and Forecasting: The Indian Scenario" *Geographical Monitoring and Forecasting*, Eds. N. Wace and S.A. Evteev, Canberra: ANU.

Singh, R.B., (1987), "Some Thoughts for Research Strategy in Himalayan Region" paper presented before *JNU Workshop on Research Strategy in Himalayan Region*, ICIMOD, Kathmandu (Unpublished).

Singh, R.B., (1989), "Application of Digital Remote Sensing and GIS Technology for Monitoring FOrest Change, Forecasting Soil Erosion Hazards and Planning Sustainable Land use in Indian Himalaya: A Case Study" Preliminary Report submitted to GRID-UNEP, Geneva during UNEP/UNITAR Training Programme in GIS Technology in the Field of Environment (Unpublished).

Singh, R.B., (1989), "Emerging Frontiers in Environmental Geography: An Introduction' in Contributions to Indian Geography, Vol. 11-*Environmental Geography*, ed. R.B. Singh, New Delhi: Heritage Pub.

Singh, R.B., (1995), Global Environmental Change-Perspectives of Remote Sensing and GIS, New Delhi; Oxford & IBH Pub.

Chapter 15

Gaming Simulations and Systems Analysis: Two Factions of the Truth

G.P. Chapman

Introduction

The structure of two gaming simulations, the Green Revolution Game and Exaction, is outlined, and an example of a game run of each of them is discussed. The characteristics of such simulations are discussed, and in particular their value in increasing understanding, despite the fact that they are not predictive, is stressed. The purposes of gaming simulation are summarized. Part II of the paper considers a typology of disciplines and subject matter, from hard and a historical science, to soft and historical social sciences, and shows how the applicability of computer simulations is necessarily limited to one part of this domain, and that therefore gaming simulations are qualitatively different, and necessary to explore the other half of the domain.

Part I

Two Gaming Simulations

The Green Revolution Game

The game is played with between 12 and 24 participants, arranged in pairs, each pair managing one farm in the 'village'. A game Manager runs the game and effectively remains outside it, working with packs

---

Reproduced from *Journal of Applied Systems Analysis*, Volume 14, 1987.

of cards (or optionally a micro-computer) to generate the environmental circumstances the participants face. A Banker and a Trader on the other hand are very much key figures in the game, and their relations with the farmers and their policies can have a significant effect on what happens.

Each pair manages one family and its farm. Family and farm size are dealt out randomly at the beginning of the game, and are not necessarily in balance, so that farm sizes vary and so do the man-land ratios.

The farmers go through annual cycles of growing crops of rice which they use to feed their families, and, if a surplus is generated, to sell to provide income for investment. Farmers can invest in technical innovations to increase yields (fertilizer and high-yielding seed varieties) or to counteract negative effects of the environment (wells to protect against drought and pesticides to combat pests). They may have to hire in labour, or more likely seek employment on other farms for their surplus labour. The technological investments are all risky—their success being contingent on many circumstances.

The farmers are responsible for feeding their families, and if in any year they have a food deficit, they try to cover this by any possible means—including begging, borrowing, and stealing; or death will strike some member of the family.

This core structure contains the motivation for the strong social interaction that usually develops. Relationships of debt, patronage, outright exploitation, and benign cooperation may emerge. A key point here is that there are no rules governing the village—the game is played with model people and model acres of land and tokens for rice and fertilizer. So the constraints on the village are the actual amounts of physical resources, which will be used and shared as a result of the economy and society that develops.

At the end of the game there is a long debriefing period during which participants discuss the broader significance and implications of what happened. This debriefing may continue spontaneously for days afterwards. On many issues participants may never agree on the relative importance of certain factors.

This game is summarized in Table 1.

An Example Played in New Delhi

Only one farm was in labour deficit at the beginning, so he had a powerful bargaining place in the labour market. Mishra contemplated forming a union, but realized that with six unemployed persons

Table 1

Green Revolution Game

New Delhi	*Rice sold (Mds)*	*Total Deficits (Mds)*
RRR	210	-56
RRD	409	-26
RRD	415	-16
RRD	475	-155
RRD	411	-79
RRD	355	-139

	Start Fam.	*End Fam.*	*B/D*	*Start Acre*	*End Acre*	*%W*	*NP*	*NP/SA*	*ML*	*Residual*
Mishra	10	11	+1	4	4	25	757	189	2.5	508
Sadhu	5	7	+2	3	2	100	-97	-26	1.7	-394
Patel*	6	8	+2	9	14	90	11031	1225	0.7	157
Ghosh	6	9	+3	4	6	100	2725	681	1.5	230
Raos	9	12	+3	4	3	25	-1248	-312	2.3	-147
Thakur	8	10	+2	3	2	7	-233	-74	2.7	399
Raji	10	12	+2	6	6	66	3774	629	1.7	332
Mukerjee	9	10	+1	3	0		-3849	-1283	3.0	-578
Sunehri	6	8	+2	4	4	50	1415	353	1.5	-98
Singh	8	10	+2	5	2	50	-1305	-261	1.6	-635
Mahar	7	7		3	2	50	328	109	2.3	274

* Farm in labour deficit at start.
Correlation between NP/SA and ML is r - 27
Threshold for breakeven is 2.1 persons per acre.
Population increase is 3.6% compound.
Total Def. is the total of deficits from all farms in deficit (in maunds).
Total supl. is the total surplus of all farms in surplus (in maunds).
Agg. Surplus is the difference between the previous two, and shows how much would still be available for export from the village after all persons had been fed.
R is Rain.
D is Drought.
Consumption is food requirement of the family.
Deficits (Surpluses) is Production minus Consumption.
Start Fam. is size of family at start.
End Fam. is size of family at end.
Start Acre is size of farm at start.
End Acre is size of farm at end.
%W is percentage of farm with irrigation in last season.
NP is net profit.
NP/SA is net profit per starting acre.
ML is starting family divided by starting acres.
Residual is NP/SA less predicted NP/SA from regression between NP/SA and ML.

chasing every job it would not succeed. Mukherjee was clearly going to have trouble and ended landless. Patel not only grew, but became an aggressive capitalist. Mukherjee, in debt to Patel and ultimately landless, was taken on by Patel to be farm manager, to help with the complexities of Patel's business. In this position Mukherjee was constantly able to defraud Patel, and therefore was loyal in his post. Mishra had one of the highest positive residuals ever seen, as a result of clever labour bargains, and also as a result of continual petty pilfering. Singh took a loan from the bank, but did not understand the repayment conditions, and the bank foreclosed on his land (this was a very angry moment).

The Bank operated too complex a set of schemes, and became a log-jam in the transactions. Villagers assisted Patel to get to the bank first each year, to that he could complete his great transactions, on which so many other side deals depended (he became the source of liquidity in the village). By the end the well-meaning banker was a disliked bureaucrat, whereas Patel could have been elected headman. The marketed surpluses declined again at the end, as Patel responded to social pressure to disburse more in the village.

Exaction

Exaction is an extension and elaboration of the Green Revolution Game, designed to a requirement of the World Bank. It incorporates a town with industrialists and urban labour, international trade in dollars, and, most importantly, a role for government. It is run with the help of a second manager. The government, headed by a President, can have a considerable impact on what happens.

This game is summarized in Table 2a and Table 2b:

An Example Played in Washington

Table 2a

Exaction 9 farms: exaction MK II Washington D.C. 3.10.83

Year	*1*	*2*	*3*	*4*	*5*	*6*
Weather	*RRR*	*DRR*	*RRR*	*RRD*	*RRR*	*RRD*
PRODN	927	849	1027	727	1220	956
ACRES	39	39	39	39	39	39
A.V. YIELD	23.7	21.7	26.3	18.6	31.00	24.5
TOTAL DEF	-15	0	-8	-98	-36	-70
TOTAL SURPL	436	309	468	198	368	351

Contd...

Contd...

AGGREG. SURPL	421	309	460	100	332	281
PRICE	13	14	14	14	14	14
VALUE	5473	4326	6440	1400	4648	3920
NAT. CONS	621	664	696	770	791	817
NAT. SURPL	306	185	228	-43	429	139
RURAL B/D	+4	+4	+6	+1	+3	
URBAN B/D	+1	+1	+2	+1	+1	
MONEY SUPPLY	4600	9600	19800	19800	19800	19800
EXCHANGE RT	8	8	8	8	8	8
I$RICE		140		934	36	
I$AGRI. INPUT		127	270	233	372	
I$RAW. MAT	212	125	183	344		
I$FACT		75	300		275	
E$AGRIC	518	672	1180	1250	752	
E$MFG		285	270	400	578	
EX	518	957	1450	1650	1330	
IM	0	554	695	1350	1027	
BALANCE	+518	+403	+755	+300	+303	
GNP	15978	12636	18978	11528	21780	19554
%AGRI	81	93	75	76	78	68
%INDUST	19	7	25	24	22	22
RURAL TRD%	34	34	34	1	21	20

Price is government proclaimed price, which may or may not be enforced.
Value is aggregate surplus multiplied by Price.
Nat. Cons. is total national food requirement.
Nat. Surplus is national production minus nat. consumption.
Rural B/D is rural births and deaths.
Urban B/D is urban births and deaths.
Money Supply is initial stock of rupees in economy plus the amount of rupees taken from Game Manager by Government.
If the Government takes more than it releases, this figure is overstated
Exchange rate is official exchange rate.
I$ RICE is dollar value of rice imports.
I$ AG. INPUT is dollar value of agricultural input imports, e.g., fertilizer.
I$ MAT is dollar value of imports of industrial raw materials.
I$ FACTOR is dollar value of imported factories.
E$ MFG is dollar value of manufactured exports (bicycles, pumpsets, godowns, agro-chems).
E$ AGRI. is value of raw and processed agricultural exports (rice and sugar).
EX is total dollar exports.
IM is total dollar imports.
BALANCE is dollar balance of trade.
GNP is value of agricultural production at official price, plus value of industrial output at actual received price.
%A is % of GNP from agriculture.
%I is % of GNP from industry.
RURAL TRADE is value of aggregate rural surplus as % GNP.

Table 2b

Exaction

Name	SA	SF	M/L	EA	EF	Birth/deaths					Consumption Req						Surplus/deficit						NP	NP/SA
						1	2	3	4	5	1	2	3	4	5	6	1	2	3	4	5	6		
Singh	4	7	1.75	4	11	+1	+1	+1		+1	51	60	69	78	78	87	81	28	91	26	36	37	2670	667
Ali	6	5	0.83	6	8	+1	+1			+1	35	42	51	51	51	60	163	110	18	56	162	156	6582	1097
Maharaja	3	6	2.0	3	7		+1				42	42	51	51	51	51	-3	24	57	15	-6	42	1297	423
Young	3	7	2.3	3	10	+1		+1	+1		51	60	60	69	78	87	-12	6	-5	-3	-30	-42	150	50
Tue	4	7	1.75	4	8			+1			51	51	51	60	60	60	1	1	1	-8	72	9	684	171
Das	4	9	2.25	4	11	+1	+1				69	78	87	87	87	87	63	19	45	-35	9	47		
Thim	3	8	2.66	3	10			+1		+1	60	60	60	69	69	78	39	6	-3	-29	21	-17	1395	126
Tran	4	9	2.25	4	10			+1			69	69	78	78	78	78	63	19	63	-23	52	-2		
Kamu	8	10	1.25	8	11			+1			78	78	78	87	87	87	26	98	193	101	116	51	6666	833

This game was remarkable for the extremely favourable weather conditions—three of the six monsoons being, in terms of rain at least, perfect.

The game started with a large national food surplus. The Buyer was initially refused a licence to trade abroad, and faced bankruptcy as a result. He had a stand-up row with the President, which he won by sheer aggression, and as a result of which he traded on the foreign market thereafter more or less without supervision or interruption. The Foreign Trade Minister was inclined to control all foreign trade where possible, and the commonest expression heard near the 'ports' in the first round was 'pro forma invoice'. The industrialists failed to get their raw materials as a result, and had to close down for a year. The Seller seemed uninterested in satisfying the demands of the farmers, and it was obvious that this channel would become a log-jam. (The Government knew there was a problem for the farmers in getting their inputs, but never actually identified where it was).

In the second year there was still a dearth of inputs: the Government misunderstood the farmers' low levels of investment, and arranged for the bank to give cheap loans. The farmers re-lent these loans to industry at higher charges. Industry became politically acceptable to Government for a while, and was rehabilitated, at the same time as urban labour set up its own factories with government help. In the first and second seasons the government announced a minimum price for rice of Rs. 14/- a maund, and subsequently did not change it.

By season three it was obvious that there were serious problems in the village in response to which the Government hired more civil servants, and set up a court. The Government also announced maximum prices for pumpset, (Rs. 600/-) but did not check on its enforcement. (Some were sold as high as Rs. 900/-). The Buyer was loaded with dollars. Rural labour began to drift to town.

In season four the country overall went into food deficit, and the export of food was banned. Industry had arguments with labour about the priorities of importing raw materials rather than food, while the government literally sat on a pile of dollars. The rupee money supply was being rapidly increased.

Urban unemployment reached 46 per cent. The industrialists complained about lack of information about rural demand.

By the end of the game, rural investment rates had stayed low, industry was collapsing, and was having its cost structure examined by a government commission for the third time, the extension agent in the village had been asked to report on villagers who were illegally holding foreign exchange, and another agent was solemnly publishing a notice saying: 'the Government is seriously considering the establishment of an agro-chemical complex'. When asked if he believed it, the agent said 'I am paid to put it up'.

In this game the extraordinarily favourable circumstances were squandered. All the way through the country ran a favourable balance of trade, but failed to free industry sufficiently to produce the goods for rural areas, and failed to allow the alternative of direct importation of at least some of the commodities. The penetration of dollars into the rural economy was the inevitable consequence.

At some stages rice was being imported into the urban area, while exported from the rural areas.

The rural areas stayed near subsistence level. At the official price, agriculture was still contributing nearly 70 per cent of GNP at the end, though at the world prices it would have been even higher. Yet the value of rural surpluses traded in the money economy fluctuated much more wildly, and was declining towards the end to as little as 20 per cent.

In debriefing, an assessor concentrated on what he described as the 'psychic energy factor'. Any government has a limit to its psychic energy, and cannot hope to control everything, unless by control it simply means total prohibition. It was apparent that the Government tried to attend to too many things, and therefore in each field was operating with inadequate information and often in consequence framed and pursued inappropriate policies. It would have been far better to concentrate on a few problems and solve them properly. Throughout the game government had been unaware that the proclaimed minimum price for rice was way below world levels; and that the Buyer had made massive profits in consequence, which represented the surplus in the economy that was never properly invested. The effect of the minimum price had been in fact to depress farmers' incomes. The assessor stressed the need for the fact finding missions to get relevant information, not to go on a trawl which would produce too much of everything. A further point was that policy disagreement at the highest levels in government had lead to vacillations in policy, which had clearly had adverse effects on industry and employment.

The Characteristics of Simulation Games

These games have the following characteristics, none of which is reproducible on a computer.

1. The components are creative autonomous devices (the players)

with differential memory, diplomatic and negotiating skills etc.

2. The players' attitude towards problems is often radically changed by these games because they have experienced a situation rather than merely being informed of a situation.
3. The combination of components and their emergent properties is unpredictable: they form cooperatives, exploit each other, defraud, corrupt, assist, sympathize, antagonize etc.
4. It is impossible to re-run exactly the same set of circumstances: even with the same players in the same situations with the same external shocks, they will not forget their earlier experience. Even if they could, it is clear that identical circumstances would have different results because of the creative imaginative inspiration which is a characteristic of being human.
5. The result is demonstrably unreal in that all participants will willingly suggest additional components that could be added (for 'more reality').
6. The results are palpably believable.
7. The results are unpredictable—and such unpredictability adds credibility to the model (it does have true information in it).
8. The degree of understanding generated has nothing to do with the (lack of) value of the models as predictors.
9. No participant has other than a minor and fragmentary view of the 'total information' (whatever that is) that was potentially available, and no participant can state what was the 'whole picture'.
10. Although in economic text books possession of money capital can be equated with possession of capital goods of equal value (e.g. pumpsets, storage silos) there is a 'hassle' factor in converting from one to the other, which can cause damaging delays.

Before I have run these simulations I have often been challenged by computer enthusiasts that they could put it all on a computer, and use random numbers to simulate the probability or a revolution etc. No one has ever, after participation, taken up the challenge. To do so they would have to model the following: anger, envy, responsibility, irresponsibility, foolishness, hassle, theft, misunderstanding and so on.

The Purpose of Gaming Simulation

It is clear that these games are rarely used for prediction. They are used to enhance understanding, sometimes to generate hypotheses, and certainly to increase empathy or sensitivity to the human subjects of policy decisions.

I am often asked what I expect participants in the Green Revolution Game to learn. My answer can only be to unlearn everything they knew before. And if they play it a second time, to unlearn everything they learnt the first time! The answers to what happened in the village are always contingent. One man may be ruined because in his haste to get a loan from the bank he does not understand the repayment conditions. Another may succeed because he pledges labour to a large farmer who in return underwrites a loan. A large farmer may become a popular source of credit because he is easily accessible, and he may prevent a potential revolution by wise use of his patronage. A farmer may succeed with new varieties without protection because he is lucky, another may fail because at a critical moment food supplies are inadequate, and in addition a debt goes bad.

Specifically the game is used with the following target groups:

1. Specialists who need to put their own particular expertise in a broader social and economic context;
2. Students of development studies who need to experience the problems of small farmers so that they can read the literature critically;
3. Professionals and volunteers who are going to work in development projects, to enhance understanding of small farmers and the constraints under which they operate, and to expose the participants' own value systems and preconceptions;
4. Managers of development projects, to demonstrate the effects of macro-scale policy at the level of the individual farmers;
5. Policy-makers who wish to generate research hypotheses and undertake sensitivity analyses of policy implementation;
6. Extension agent training managers, and extension agents themselves.

Part II

The Relevance of Gaming Simulations: The Limits to Systems Analysis

Gaming simulation is not 'just a different animal' from systems simulation on a computer. The differences between the two can be traced to fundamental philosophical problems in the social sciences, which show why systems simulation by computer will always be limited in its applicability.

A Typology of Systems

I start with a schematic diagram of subject matter and a few related disciplines (Figure 1). This diagram has no objective value, it is merely a personal view which should be treated as more or less useful, but neither right nor wrong. This will lead me eventually to an example of a typical system problem which simultaneously spans many apparently separate modes of conceptualization and analysis.

A distinction is drawn, following Popper and Eccles[1] quoted in Hagerstrand[2] between Three Worlds: these are the world of real physical objects—World 1—the world of thought within any one individual's head—World 2—and the collectivity of human thought (more than just the sum of all the Worlds 2)—which is World 3. But my knowledge of all these three worlds rests in my own World 2—hence Figure 1 contains itself, and hence World 2 is written both outside the biggest box, and also inside it where I conceive it to be. It is like the painting of an inn, whose inn-sign depicts a painting of the inn, whose inn-sign depicts a painting of the inn...

The majority of the detail in Figure 1 is in the three left hand columns, which cover the domain of World 1, the world of physical things. It is about this world that science has made most 'progress'. But if I were to redraw Figure 1 to discuss the intellectual history of mankind including all art, music and literature, World 3 would be greatly expanded.

The divisions between the four columns are important. On the left we stay firmly within the domain of physics and chemistry, and the realm of reductionist explanation. This is true even to the extreme, where at the largest scale astrophysics is tied intimatedly to the smallest scale, of particle physics. The next column is the world of artifice—the machines of mankind that obey the laws of physics and chemistry, but which have not been observed to occur spontaneously. Although all these machines and buildings perform, in so far as they do, according to non-teleological explanation, their existence is understood in teleological and ecological terms—they are invented and built by man for man's own purposes. They are therefore split from the other 'natural' world of the inanimate by the 'purpose' divide.

The divisions between the inanimate world and the world of biology can be made on several grounds. The most immediate one is self-reproduction—perhaps one definition of life.

The next division is accordingly between the 'real' world of physical existence—World 1—and the worlds of conscious and reflexive thought—Worlds 2 and 3. Note that the brain therefore simultane-

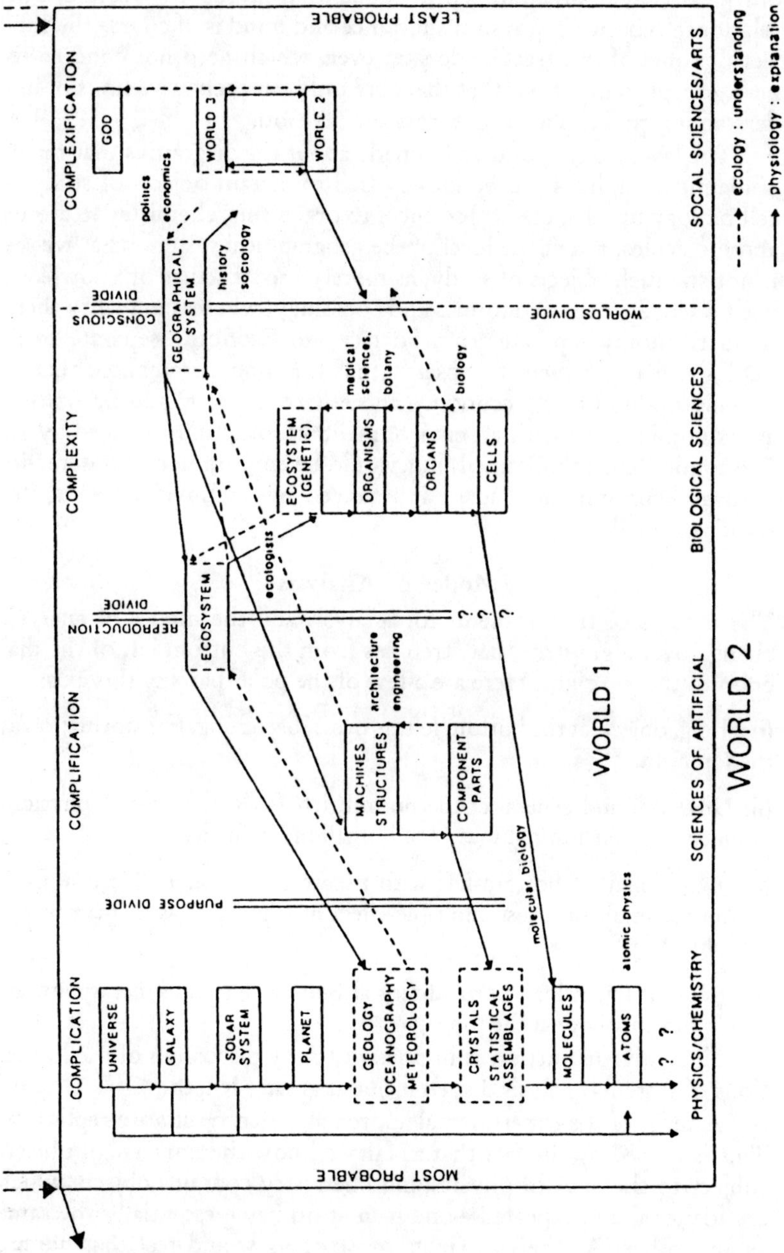

FIGURE 1: A view of subject matter and disciplines.

ously exists as an organ in World 1, and as 'thinking' in World 2. The relationship between physical substance and mind is of course the subject of some of the greatest debates ever, which need not concern us here, except to point out that there are only very tentative links of understanding and explanation across the division.

The last general point to be made about the diagram is that many academic disciplines can be loosely tied to certain objects of study—cell biology to cells, medical sciences to organisms, chemistry to atoms and molecules. But at the level of the geographical system what we see is not so much objects of study, as merely the structure of knowledge itself. Hence we see Economics and Sociology, whereas in reality there is no Economy separate from Society, no Economy separate from Ecology. It is pertinent to observe that J. Maini[3] commented that in Canada studies linking economy and environment would be written as economic tracts with an environmental footnote if financed by an Economic Research Council, but would be environmental statements with an economic appendage if financed by an Environmental Research Council.

Modes of Analysis

The natures of the problems for analysis and the modes of analysis change over a gradient that stretches from the bottom left of the diagram to the top right. Here are a few of the polar pairs of this axis:

(i) Thing, object, at the bottom left: process, becoming, transformation at the top right.

(ii) Universal and general at the bottom left (as in the laws of physics): uniqueness at the top right (as with human individuality).

(iii) Experiment at bottom left with isolated causes and effects: non-experimental multiple-cause multiple-effect at top right (as in man in the biosphere).

(iv) Replication, risk and probability at bottom left: idiosyncrasy, uncertainty and creativity at the top right.

Since this distinction is important to my discussion of the limitations of systems analysis, I spell it out at greater length.

A tenet of the experimental approach is that results are replicable. This is helped by the fact that as far we know the universe of objects subject to the laws of physics and chemistry contains objects which are identical and repeated—one iron atom being essentially the same as any other. At the top right, most of us would feel that we are unique and unrepeatable, idiosyncratic to the very core.

If I have repeatable objects and events, then it becomes useful to talk in terms of probability and risk. Roulette is a game of risk: that is, the set of possible outcomes and their probabilities are known, and the game itself is repeatable. If all events are unique, historical, and tomorrow's set of possible outcomes contains new outcomes, but only one will be realized, then probability does not apply, nor does the notion of Shannonian information as surprise. In Shackle's words[4] the experiment is non-divisible, and no average expectation can be given. In short, we have uncertainty, which thus defined is a very different animal from risk.

There is a neat illustration of the way in which a shift in our thinking can alter the rules which apply. To each of us, our lives are important and unrepeatable. For me to be told I have a ten per cent chance of dying tomorrow is useless. Either I do or I don't, and there is no way I can average out the occasions when I do die with those when I don't. The quotation of a risk is based on mistaken generality. But to an army commander, his men are objectified: he can attack the enemy and expect losses of 10 per cent. (The English euphemism is so quaint: how can a commander be so careless as to lose a few men?) But the dead are not 10 per cent dead, nor the living 90 per cent alive.

(v) Externality: reflexivity

This also needs some elaboration. At the bottom left, we observe phenomena (subject ultimately to Heisenberg's Uncertainty Principle) as if the observation did not affect the phenomena, and as if the 'facts' were independent of theory and in some sense can pre-exist theory. Philosophers of science of course adopt a variety of postures around this problem. "In extreme versions of deductivism, the theory-observation dichotomy is taken to imply... that truth and falsity are properties only of observation statements, while theories are not prepositional and do not purport to describe the real, but are only instruments for correlation and prediction of observation".[5]

Others adopt less extreme views, and consider observation and theory to be part of an iterative process, and consider that though the 'facts' are 'out there', which facts we observe and the manner in which we measure them are very much based on the evolution of conjectual theory. Measurement can also be seen to be both measurement of an immanent property of a thing (no matter whether we weight something by a fulcrum balance or by a spring scale, it is supposed to weigh the same) or as a process of interaction between observer and observed. Any social scientist who has used a questionnaire would understand that view.

What happens when we get to Worlds Two and Three? If we observe ourselves, then we observe ourselves observing ourselves. Human contemplation of the realm of the human changes it.

In these circumstances the notion of objectivity becomes problematical, and so in particular does the notion of prediction. Imagine that in the UK all people are involved in activities A through Y, but the government does not know which, yet needs to know for effective and responsible policy making. Let us suppose that activity Z is to type into a computer console what one is doing at a certain time. In the extreme event all persons could spend their time in activity Z, abandon A through Y, and the act of observation would have changed the society completely. Hesse does not necessarily think that objectivity will break down in social sciences, but does recognize this information constraint as most important. She notes that science has been peculiarly 'successful' as a learning machine, where observation and theory have gone through iterative processes. "However, it is the characteristics of prediction, test, and subsequent modification of theory that may be missing in the social sciences. On the assumption that there is a 'social world' to act as environment of the learning machine in the way the 'natural world' does for the natural sciences, there are at least three ways in which the learning process may be conceived to break down.

1. The process of data collection may so interfere with the antecedent external state of the world that empirical input ceases to represent its state independent of that process. Input becomes an artifact of learning...
2. Prediction may become impossible because manipulable amounts of data may not sufficiently represent the fine structure of the external world, so that errors and loss of information in receiving and coding data may cumulatively diverge, leading to extreme under-determination or undue instability of 'best theories' with respect to changing data. Where natural science has been successful, we must assume that the structure of the world is sufficiently simple relative to the structure of the learning process to permit learning. The social world may not, of course, be so simple as to be similarly learnable.
3. In the case of both natural and social science, the very operation of the learning process may change its own goals".

(vi) Computer: brains

Both computers and brains as organs belong to World 1, but to different hierarchies, one in the inanimate, the other the animate. More importantly, the thoughts of the brain are World 2. This distinction between the left and right of my diagram could have been made in the section above, but there are some important issues which need stressing, hence I have put this in a section of its own.

Any output of any program of any computer can always be explained by reductionist argument—back to the binary operations that generated it. These were completely determined by the external instructions fed in by human agency, no matter at what remove, no matter how indirectly. When particular combinations of parameters occur in the execution of a program, no emergent effects can be spontaneously 'created'. A 'pseudo' emergent effect may be programmed in, but that is all. Neither do computers create their own self-intervention, unless programmed to do so, in which case it is not self-intervention.

No program no matter how many random numbers are used, can redefine the constraints laid down before its execution. (There are some advances in languages such as ADA[6] which help the experimenter to step back further in his own mind than he would otherwise do, but the fundamental truth remains.) To this extent all the dynamics are reducible and are what I call pseudo-dynamics.

(vii) The four faces of complexity:

Much of the above can be summarized for the four columns of Figure 1, in terms of the different meanings that I attribute to 'complexity'.

Complication is a quantitative escalation of that which is theoretically reducible. We may observe phenomena at particular scales (planets, continents, estuaries) as a short hand, but all are explicable in terms of their component molecules and attendant physical and chemical laws. This does not preclude cooperative phenomena, where particles in proximity to each other in close assemblies influence each other's state.

Complification. In this category it remains true that explanation is still reductionist, and that therefore complexity is still merely a quantitative escalation. But I make it a separate category because this is the world of the artificial, the artifact, that we make for a purpose which is usually attained only with all parts working simultaneously and in cooperation. This is true for a watch, for a car, for the Space

Shuttle. In other words, whereas the outcome of complication is just an outcome (an estuary, a beach, a planet) the outcome of complification is a higher hierarchical goal to which the behaviour of the parts is subordinated. (The fact that the outcome of complification can be self-reinforcing does not break the distinction; e.g. the fact that a river erodes its bed and initiates an increase in basin area, that reinforces the river, does not mean that there was ever a 'purpose' to the river in the first place to which the parts are subordinated).

Complexity is that stage where we find that we are no longer sure that reductionist explanation by physics or chemistry will suffice. Living organisms describe themselves and reproduce themselves, as totalities. If we remove some part of an organism and see how it behaves, we have no proof that that is how it behaves when not removed. But although we may be dealing with holistic properties, these are not reflesive. (For a rejection of all kinds of holism, see Phillips[7]). It is at this stage that concepts of multiple cause and effect first become prominent.

Complexification I reserve for those phenomena which are not reducible, which are consciously reflexive, which have an autonomous force (creative will), which can change purposefully their own state. This is the world of individual men and of society. This is the world where we contemplate the 'meaning of meaning'. It is also the level of which Hesse says we may well be facing limits of our ability to know, to generate relevant data fast enough.

An Example of a Systems Problem

I have my own example of a complex technical, economic, political and environmental system, namely large-scale irrigation schemes in India which continually perform below expectations[8]. Such schemes are things: concrete channels. They are also processes of flowing water, of agricultural change, defining and reinforcing their own structures, which are ultimately in any complete sense, unknowable. Such irrigation schemes exhibit complication: the number of channels and distributaries, sluices and valves, is very large: but in principle the mechanics of the physical apparatus and flowing water are explicable by classical reductionist methods. The schemes also exhibit complification, in that the design of any part is related to the aggregate water availability and aggregate demand, so that the design purpose of each is subordinate. The schemes exhibit complexity, in the way in which crop output is a synergistic response to soil, water, weather, chemicals, farming practice, and that in turn to the expanding sets of multiple causes, of education, farming extension, etc. The schemes exhibit complexification: the actors within the command areas, farmers and politicians, can redefine the scheme towards their own ends, and re-schedule dry land (land zoned for crops with low water requirement) to wet land (zoned for crops which are water intensive, but usually more profitable).

The usual analysis of and response to these kinds of problems limits itself to more investment in channels and sluices. But World 1 analysis and solution does not dictate to Worlds 2 and 3.

The Limitations of Systems Analysis

Systems 'analysis' is in many ways a misnomer. Algebraic analytical statements about system behaviour have to be limited to examples of only a few components, and then on the unwarranted assumption of a trend towards some equilibrium point.[9,10] With more than a few components, the equilibrium point (if any can be found at all), becomes dependent on the numerical value of coefficients, and not on the algebraic relations.

As an alternative to true analysis, systems modelling has been developed. Modelling exercises have undoubtedly contributed enormously to our appreciation of the possible behaviour of many-part dynamic systems with leads and lags, and feedback. The patterns of oscillating variables and multiple quasi-equilibria, between which the system may flip, are enormously seductive. But we have to ask ourselves, on what technology are these simulations based? The answer is of course, in 99 per cent of the cases, the technology of the digital computer.

This technology as it is currently used imposes severe limits on our capacity to model. The computer belongs to the world of complification, and therefore none of the properties of the worlds of complexity and complexification can be reproduced by it. Everything is built in by the programmer from the bottom up, and the whole program is subordinated to his purposes and his goals. Everything is the result of his act of definition, and in one very real way the 'results' contain no information at all, in that they are the inevitable consequence, a mere transformation, of what has been put in.

The computer cannot evolve mutant sub-routines, as mosquitoes acquire resistance to DDT, it can only be programmed to follow preselected alternatives. The computer has no consciousness of its involvement with society, although any device of intelligence would realize that, as well as observing society, it was a part of it that it should recursively include a model of itself.

Computers exist in the world of 'complification'. Any simulation by a computer is unable to model the qualities of complexity and complexification.

I was struck by a remark made at a conference by Senator M. Kirby[11] of Canada—that he, a policy maker, will listen to systems analysts (simulators) because to have 50 per cent of the truth is better than having 0 per cent. This implies that the worlds of complication and complification are the basic components of systems, and that complexity and complexification are mere additions to it.

I cannot agree with the assumption and its implications. Any economic model of the UK at the moment which excludes the personality of the miners' leader Arthur Scargill will not predict the outcome of a miners' strike. Does this mean that we have a model which would be 100 per cent right if Scargill did not exist, or is there any sense in which we can say that because he does exist the model is only 40 per cent right? Do we then enact 40 per cent of its policy conclusions?

By contrast, gaming simulations are embedded in the world of complexification.

Conclusions

1. Systems which involve human beings are characterized by emergent effects, holistic dynamics (resting on combinatorial preconditions), and unrepeatable idiosyncratic performance.
2. The systems are reflexive, acting on component decision makers, who through their own actions and perceptions, act on the system.
3. These perceptions are by definition partial and imperfect.
4. Since any computer can do no more than use established criteria to select between computable alternatives, we cannot expect computer-based simulations to devise truly new (i.e., new information content) criteria nor imaginatively create truly new alternatives.
5. We have no means of generating imperfect information in a computer (imperfect information includes both not knowing what is knowable and also not knowing what is not knowable. In a computer, restricting information available to a component only simulates the former).
6. The only simulations which can include self-transformation and reflexive thought are those which use biological and human com-

ponents (Gaming Simulations).

7. The purpose of gaming simulation is to achieve understanding not to achieve prediction.

ADDENDUM

Commissioned Work on Gaming Simulation[12, 13, 14]

The initial work undertaken on the Green Revolution Game was not funded by an outside agency. The impetus for its development came from a real teaching need. The success of this game has attracted many users, one of whom, the World Bank, specifically commissioned the development of Exaction. The felt need in this case was to demonstrate that government did have the power to intervene in agricultural pricing policies, and that it mattered that it did so. In fact it has probably shown that although intervention is possible, it is very difficult, and even more difficult to do well: the biggest obstacle is the generation and timely use of good data on what is happening. A computer simulation would assume that the effects of price changes on farmers' behaviour were known, and it would assume that the government would intervene, otherwise there would be nothing for the 'president' to test. Although it might be possible to simulate the effects of missing and incorrect data being handed to the policy maker, true lack of information and misleading information cannot be generated by such a simulation.

Subsequently I have been commissioned by the Ford Foundation in India to study the feasibility of gaming simulations in Irrigation Systems (Chapman, 1983). Some of the proposals in that report suggest hybrid systems: part (the main canals) could be modelled by a conventional system simulation, and part (the recipient village community), by a gaming simulation. In this way the complification and complexification of irrigation systems would both be mirrored. The aim of these simulations is to sensitize Irrigation Managers to the impact that unreliable water supplies have on farmers, and to highlight all the ways in which historical legacies (evolving social and political structures) and current creative imagination can frustrate the intentions of the system designers.

Notes

1. Popper, K.R. and Eccles, J., *The Self and its Brain: An Argument for Interactionism*, Springer International, 1977.
2. Hagerstrand, T., 'Time Geography. Focus on the Corporeality of Man, Society and Environment' (Mimeo). UNU, Montpellier, 1984.
3. Maini, J., Personal Communication, 1984.
4. Shackle, G.L.S. *Decision, Order and Time in Human Affairs*, 2nd Edition, Cambridge University Press, 1969.
5. Hesse, M., 'Models versus Paradigms in the Natural Sciences' in Collins L. (Ed.), *The Use of Models in the Social Sciences*, Tavistock, 1976.
6. Healey, R.J., 'ADA and the Simulation of Evolving Regional Economic Systems' Mimeo, ADA UK, 3rd Annual Conference, University of York. (Also Mimeo, Department of Geography, University of Edinburgh), 1984.
7. Phillips, D.C., *Holistic Thought in social Sciences*, Macmillan, 1976.
8. Chapman, G.P., 'Underperformance in Indian Irrigation Systems: The Problems of Diagnosis and Prescription', *Geoforum*, 14, 1983.
9. Williams, R.B., 'Steadystate equilibrium in simple nonlinear food webs'. In Patten, B.C. (Ed.), *Systems Analysis and Simulation in Ecology*, Vol. II, 213-40, Academic Press, 1972.
10. Chapman, G.P. *Human and Environmental Systems: A Geographer's Appraisal*, Academic Press, 167-74, 1977.
11. Kirby, Senator Michael, 'Thoughts on Coping with Complexity from the Perspective of a Politician', Mimeo, Montpellier, UNU Conference, 1984.
12. Chapman, G.P. and Dowler, E.A., *The Green Revolution Game*, Marginal Context Ltd., Cambridge, 1982.
13. Chapman, G.P., 'The Evolution and Impact of the Green Revolution Game and Exaction', Mimeo, World Bank, Washington and Department of Geography, Cambridge, 1983.
14. Chapman, G.P., 'Gaming Simulations of Immigration Systems: Prospects for Management Training', Ford Foundation, *Working Papers*, New Delhi, 1983.

Chapter 16

Methodological Inquiry into Social Mobility with Examples from India

Bam Dev Sharda

Interest in social mobility goes back to Marx and Weber, yet the prevailing conceptualization of social mobility may be largely traced to Sorokin's pioneering work. Sorokin (1927) defined the phenomenon of social mobility, an account of main factors responsible for it, and a classification of various forms of mobility. Social mobility has become one of the major subjects in sociology. Basic theory of social mobility has been elaborated in different ways, and methodologies of studying mobility have been developed accordingly.

Social mobility is defined as movement of individuals or groups between social positions. The unit of analysis may be individuals, the family or some other social group such as the caste in India.

Mobility can also be classified according to the direction of the move. A movement involving a change on a stratification criterion (such as prestige) is denoted as vertical mobility; the movement within the same social class is referred as horizontal mobility. Furthermore, total amount of mobility can be broken into two basic components: structural mobility and exchange mobility.

Among these different types of social mobility, sociological research usually concentrates on intergenerational mobility, vertical mobility and exchange mobility. Historically, the analysis of mobility started from simple cross-tabulations between fathers and sons status and the measurements of association, between the two. However, these approaches were found to be inadequate due to sampling difficulties and other methodological concerns (see e.g., Duncan 1966) and a variety of models of mobility have been developed to deal with these concerns. These methods can be classified into two basic approaches: status attainment approach and mobility table approach. The present paper examines these approaches with examples from India.

Status Attainment Approach

Before the mid-1960s, empirical investigation into social stratification and mobility focused primarily on tabular analysis of occupational distributions. Social mobility was generally represented by the cross-tabulation of father's and son's occupational positions, which had been classified into gross categories of manual vs. non-manual, occasionally with the third category of farm occupations. With the appearance of Blau and Duncan's (1967) influential work, *The American Occupational Structure*, social mobility research in the US turned in a dramatically new direction: the status attainment process. Instead of simply examining the extent to which one's origin, denoted by fathers occupational category, differed from one's destination, denoted by sons (respondents) occupational category, status attainment models further explored the way origins affect destinations, and introduce factors that mediate the relationship between origins and destinations. Blau and Duncan's basic model is the most representative of this approach. We examine this approach and its success after we describe the simple cross-tabulation approaches which seem to be frequent in empirical studies of mobility in India even today.

Comparisons of Distributions: A Model of Cross-tabulation

Status attainment models describe factors that determine a persons' social status. The most simplistic way to look at this relationship is through a cross-classification table. Matras (1975) illustrated this approach by considering ways of studying relationships between three variables:

— place of birth: urban (u) or rural (r),
— educational attainment: high school (h) or college (c),
— social position: white collar (w) or blue collar (b).

Suppose one hypothesizes that the urban-born people have higher social position than the rural born. We can simply cross classify these two variables as in Table 1.

Table 1

Place of birth by social position: percentage distribution

Social position %	*Place of birth %*		
	U	*R*	*Total*
Total	100	100	100
W	Uw	Rw	Tw
B	Ub	Rb	Tb

Notes: U - Urban born, R - Rural born, W - white collar B - Black collar, T - Total

If Uw > Rw, or Ub < Rb, it indicates that white collar positions are positively associated with urban born confirming our hypothesis. However, it is argued that this association is spurious due to educational differences of the two categories of people.

Now the issue is to separate the effects of both the place of birth and educational achievement's influence on social position. We can set up "first order table"—a sub-table containing covariation between two variables, given a third control variable, educational attainment in this case. These associations are displayed in Table 2.

Table 2

Percentage Distribution by Social Position by Place of Birth and Educational Attainment

Social position	*Place of birth and educational attainment*								
	Total			*Urban-born*			*Rural-born*		
	Total	*H*	*C*	*Total*	*H*	*C*	*Total*	*H*	*C*
Total	100	100	100	100	100	100	100	100	100
W	Tw	Hw	Cw	Uw	UHw	UCw	Rw	RHw	RCw
B	Tb	Hb	Cb	Ub	UHb	UCb	Rb	RHb	RCb

Note: For W, B, U and R, see Table 1.
H - Education up to higher school
C - Some colleges or college

If the percentage of people in white-collar positions is greater among the urban-born category regardless of educational achievement (i.e., UHw > RHw, and UCw > RCw), we may assert that the relationship between the urban-born and white-collar categories holds independent of the effect of educational achievement. If, on the other hand, the percentage of urban-born college graduates in white-collar positions is about the same or less than the percentage of rural-born college graduates in white-collar position, or the percentage of urban-born high school graduates in white-collar position does not exceed that of rural percentage e.g., $\underline{UC_w}$ $\underline{RC_w}$, or $\underline{UH_w}$ $\underline{RH_w}$), then we may conclude that the empirical relationship initially noted between urban birth and white collar position was spurious and was caused by the third variable: educational achievement. That is:

This elementary model presents the relationship between social

Figure 1

Place of Birth ⟶ Educational Achievement ⟶ Social Position

status, place of birth and educational achievement in a relatively straight forward way. However, as additional variables are introduced into the model the cross-classifications become too cumbersome. In addition, cross table approach is useful only with simple categorical measures of variables; e.g., social position measured as high and low; educational achievements up to high school and college (post high school) etc.

From Cross Tabulation to Multiple Regression Models

Regression technique can be used to account for variations in status as a function of independent and control variables. This approach can be seen as an extension of cross-table approach. For one, the model assumes that the variables are measured at the interval level. This is especially true of the dependent variable (e.g., social position).

$$\underline{Y} = \underline{a} + \underline{b}_1 X_1 + \underline{b}_2 X_2 \ldots + \underline{b}_n X_n \qquad \ldots\ldots (1)$$

Where the partial regression coefficient $\underline{b}_i$ represents an amount of change in $\underline{Y}$ resulting from one unit change in X_i when holding the other $\underline{X}$s constant. By using this equation, we can predict one's social position $\underline{Y}$ in terms of his birth place (X_1) and educational achievement (X_2).

This equation demonstrates the very basic idea of regression approach on assessing status attainment. We estimate this model on data from rural India (see Sharda, 1977) where current occupation (OCC) is regressed on SES background (JATI, caste rank; LAND, amount of land owned by father; and FOCC, father's occupation), achievement (EDU, educational achievement of the respondents) and other life cycle contingencies (1JOB, status of first job of respondent), the

FIGURE 2

Basic Status Attainment Model

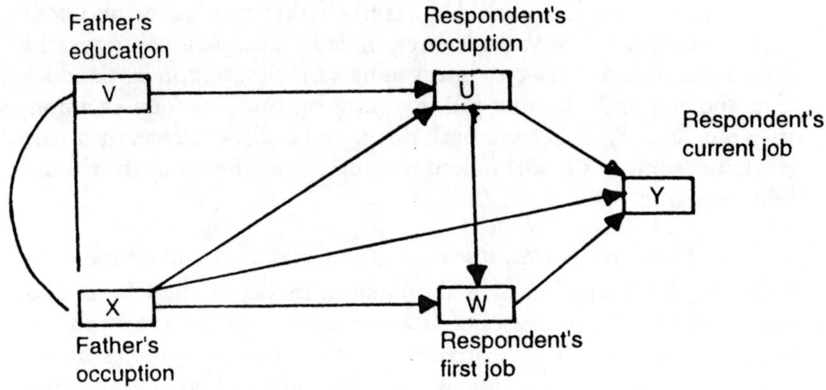

equation is:

OCC = SES background (JATI, LAND, FOCC) + Achievement (EDU) + Contingency (1JOB) .

The unstandardized regression estimates of the model are:

OCC = 8.22 + JATI (.006) + LAND (-.247) + FOCC (.397)* + EDU (-1.247) + 1JOB (.489)*

The estimates point out that only two variables, FOCC and 1JOB, (with *s) are significant. $\underset{\sim}{R}^2$ for the model was .62 indicating that 62 per cent of variation in OCC can be accounted for by family background variables, EDU and 1JOB jointly. One problem with this model is that we only estimate the direct effects of background variables on OCC. However, these variables can also have indirect effects on OCC via EDU and 1JOB. This will be described later.

Sorensen (1975) elaborates regression model where occupational achievement is a function of two main sets of factors: characteristics of individuals and structural characteristics of society.

Causal Models

The cross-tabulation model simply indicates whether or not there is a relationship between social position and the other factors. The regression model can measure the strength of this relationship. Causal models not only assess the degree of the association among variables, but also relate variables into a causal sequence. A well known causal model for occupational status attainment is Blau-Duncan's path model.

Besides antecedent variable (origin)—father's education and occupation, and dependent variable—respondents' occupational status, this model also included the two intervening variables: respondent's education and respondent's first job. By showing causal sequences among variables, and by indicating both direct and indirect effects of origins on destination, this model indeed revolutionized the occupational mobility research.

A Patterns of Attainment in Rural India: An Example

I (Sharda, 1977) applied Blau and Duncan model to rural India data, and compared the processes of attainment of rural India with that of the rural United States (Sharda, 1981), the rural sub-samples having origins in agriculture and non-agriculture, and to different age cohorts of the rural sample (Sharda 1984). This comparative model was "modified" by excluding father's education as an origin variable because data on this variable was not available. However, no causal model of occupational status attainment is complete without assessing the role of *Jati* (caste) hierarchy on occupational attainment (the destination) in India. Similarly, no causal model of a rural occupational attainment can be complete without reviewing the role of land ownership. We, therefore, estimated an "extended model" (see Figure 3).

The findings presented confirm some portions of conventional theory about Indians stratification, but also raises serious doubts about other portions of this theory. For example, it is clear that *Jati* has more to do with who gets more education and who gets less or none at all. Net of father's occupational status, and his land holdings, the higher one's *Jati* ranking, the higher his chances of having more schooling. Interestingly, both the father's high occupational status and land ownership negatively affect educational attainment. This may look odd to an outsider but not to a scholar of rural stratification. Higher occupational status is accorded to larger and small land owners, the owner cultivators of rural India (Sharda 1979), who are also the major segments of rural population. Similarly, brahmins, banias and other high castes are more likely to send their sons to school (and keep them in school longer) than the land owning *Jatis*. Thus, the

FIGURE 3

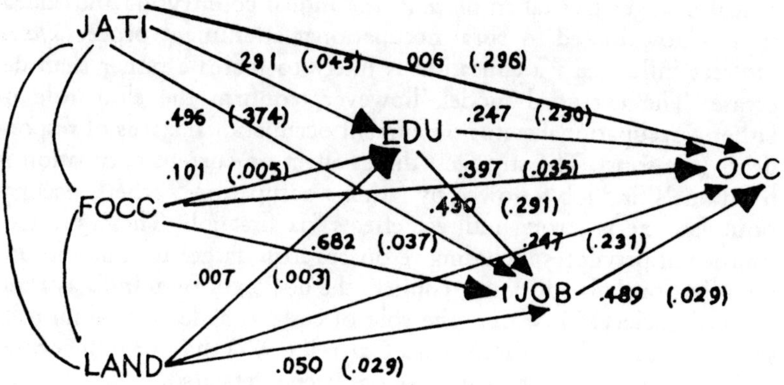

Note: (1) The figures outside the ( ) s are unstandardized regression coefficients whereas those within the ( )s are their standard errors.

(2) Curved lines represent bivariate correlations, straight lines with arrows at the end represents regression net of other variables in the equations, and thick lines with the causal directions are statistically significant whereas thin lines represent statistically non-significant effects.

positive role of Jati rank and negative role of father's occupation and father's land ownership on educational attainment becomes clear.

The direct effects of land ownership on both the first job and the current occupation are statistically non-significant. It may be argued that whatever effects fathers land ownership have for their sons are passed indirectly through son's own occupation (either straight forwardly or via first job of the respondents). Contrary to the conventional theories of "caste mobility", We were surprised to find that one's *Jati* status (origin) exercises very little influence on current occupational achievement or on the first job. Whatever, bivariate correlations existed between *Jati* and first job (r = .303) and current occupation (r = .310) were washed out in the extended causal model. *Jati* had the major influence on educational achievement but (in the 1960s) was not directly linked to the occupational achievement of rural India as observed in the extended path model. The implication is that if changes had taken place in the Indian countryside and education is now linked to rural occupational attainment process, *Jati's* indirect influence via education is likely to increase rather than decrease. The extended model, however, confirm the clear role of father's occupational status on current occupational status of respondents (the sons). The strongest direct effect on current occupation is from one's first job followed by father's occupation. Father's occupation also exerts strong indirect effects via first job. These stronger transfer of privileges including resources from father to son, without modifications, via education, confirm the notion of rural India as a traditional society. However, the role of caste is at least minimum in such a description. We agree with Gartrell (1977) that the influence of caste on Indian social stratification has been overstated.

Blau-Duncan's basic model was elaborated by adding some social psychological variables in the popularly known Wisconsin model. This approach has been improved further by using "loglinear structural equation" (LISREL) model. To our knowledge LISREL has not been used in the study of Indian stratification so far.

Mobility Table Approach on Studying Social Mobility

The first approach—status attainment approach—calls for identifiable social position, analyzing the ways in which each is attained and factors mediating such attainment, and classifying or measuring these factors. The second approach—analysis of mobility table, in contrast, examines the patterns of movement, or mobility among the positions. Simply speaking, for mobility table, "our problem, therefore, is to measure the relationship between achieved status and origin status" (Duncan, 1968).

What justifies an extended treatment of the bivariate mobility table when multivariate structural equation models (refined status attainment approach) have been proved useful in elaborating process of social mobility? Hauser (1978) stated that although interval measurement of status attainment variables provides greater parsimony and greater statistical power than nominal or ordinal measurement in mobility tables, the latter have their own advantages. They permit a more detailed examination of rate and patterns of movement between occupations than do scaler measurement of association. Likewise, the categoric measurement of occupations makes possible a more detailed representation of the occupational structure—the origin and destination distributions of the mobility classification than does measure on numeric scales. Finally, the mobility table may be used to study the interaction among several dimensions of occupational classification. In short, mobility tables are useful because they encourage a direct and detailed examination of movements in the stratification system.

Regarding the mobility table, there have been numerous models designed by many researchers. (Bishop, 1975; Boudon, 1975; Clogg, 1981, 1983; Duncan, 1961, 1979, 1966; Fienberg, 1980; Goldthorpe, 1971; Goodman, 1979, 1972, 1969, 1968, 1965; Haberman, 1974; Hauser, 1981, 1978; Hout, 1983; Logon, 1983. etc.) It is impossible for this paper to go over all of these models. However, we can present the basic ideas of a mobility table by selectively examining several models. Before doing so, let us go through some basic components of a mobility table.

Basic Components of Mobility Table

Occupational mobility tables cross-classify persons according to their occupations at two points in time. The early point is referred to as the origin; the latter point the destination.

After selecting origin and destination variables, occupational categories must be defined and coded. Criteria for selecting an appropriate number of occupational categories vary, most researchers just mix theoretical and pragmatic concerns. Another consideration is the comparability with the coding procedures of past studies (Hout, 1983). Let us use three occupational categories—professional (P), other white collar (W) and blue collar (B) to construct the mobility table.

Table 3

Father's occupation (origin) by son's occupation (destination)

Father's occupation (a)	*Son's occupation (b)*			
	Total	*Prof.*	*White collar*	*Blue collar*
Total (N)	N	EP	EW	EB
Professional (P)	EP	PP	PW	PB
Other white-collar (W)	EW	WP	WW	WB
Blue collar(B)	EB	BP	BW	BB

Mobility and immobility: In Table 3, the chance of stay (or immobility) could be measured by the diagonal cells (PP WW BB0 since subjects' present position (i.e., destination) coincide with their positions of origin; while the probability of move is measured by off-diagonal cells since the subjects' present occupational positions reflect the departures from their positions of origin.

Upward mobility and downward mobility: If we take the "professional", "other white collar", and "blue collar" positions to imply a scale or hierarchy, then cells below diagonal (WP BP BW) measure upward mobility since the subjects' occupational position are all higher than that of their origin; while cells above the diagonal (PW PB WB) measure the downward mobility since subjects' current positions are lower than their origin.

Structural mobility and exchange mobility: A net change in the occupational distributions of the fathers and their sons is sometimes referred to as "structural mobility". A conventional way of measuring such a difference is by Index of Dissimilarity, which is computed as one half the sum of the absolute values of the differences of percentage of fathers, $\underline{A}_i$, and of sons, $\underline{D}_i$ in each of the respective occupational categories, $\underline{i}$., as follows:

$$\text{Index of Dissimilarity} = \Delta = \frac{\Sigma \mid \underline{A}_i - \underline{D}_i \mid}{2}$$

The structural mobility is also called "minimum mobility". It refers to the minimum proportion of a group which must change category in order for the two distributions to be alike. The difference between the total mobile and "structural mobility" (index of dissimilarity) is called "exchange" mobility since it refers to the turn over of individuals between origin and destination positions not of the creation of new positions ("structural mobility"). However, this needs to be explored further.

Social Mobility in India: An Example

In this example, we analyze the occupational mobility table and various components of it. Occupations are classified in to five major categories: (i) upper non-manual, (ii) lower non-manual, (iii) upper manual, (iv) lower manual and (v) farmer. Some 4065 respondents reported in Cantril (1965) represents a national sample. These data are cross-classified by their father's and their own occupational categories (e.g., stratum) in Table 4.

Table 4

Occupational Mobility in India (Cantril Data)

Son's Stratum (D)
Father's (O)

Stratum	*UNM*	*LNM*	*UM*	*LM*	*FARM*	*TOTAL (%)*
1. UNM	143	207	32	15	38	435 (10.7)
2. LNM	95	242	70	34	56	297 (12.2)
3. UM	14	53	158	33	57	315 (7.7)
4. LM	8	26	51	227	23	335 (8.2)
5. FARM	72	226	290	180	1,715	2,484 (61.0)
Total	332	754	601	489	1,889	4,065 (100.0)
(%)	(8.1)	(18.5)	(14.7)	(12.0)	(46.4)	(100.0)

About 2,485 or 61.0 per cent of the respondents are in the OD diagonal cells indicating *immobility*. About 1015 or 25 per cent are below the diagonal indicating *upward mobility* whereas 565 or 14 per cent are above the diagonals indicating downward mobility. Index of similarity is calculated for Table 5 with equation (2).

Table 5

Index of Dissimilarity, India Marginals (Cantril Data)

	% Fathers (a)	*% sons (b)*	*% difference*
1. UNM	10.7	8.1	2.6
2. LNM	12.2	18.5	6.3
3. UM	7.7	14.7	7.0
4. LM	8.2	12.0	3.8
5. FARM	61.0	46.4	14.6
			E = 34.2

Index of Dissimilarity = 34.2/2 = 17.1

Exchange Mobility = 39.0 -17.1 -21.9 per cent.

From this data, one infers that 17.1 per cent of the sample must change their categories in order for the two distributions to be alike. Although 39 per cent of the sons have different stratum from their fathers, 17.1 per cent was attributed to the "structural" differences of the two samples and the rest 21.9 per cent is "exchange or pure" mobility.

Elementary Operations for Mobility Table

The elementary procedures used to analyze any cross-classification are useful starting points in the analysis of mobility tables.

Outflow and inflow analyses: The most elementary operation for cross-classifications of origins and destinations are outflow and inflow tables—the calculation of percentage distribution within rows and columns. The row percentages are named outflow and record the distribution of destinations for each category of origin. The inflow percentages record the distribution of origins for each destination outflow and inflow rates for Cantril data are provided in Table 6.

Table 6

Example of Outflow and Inflow Table (India 1962, Cantril Data)

		Outflow					
Father's Stratum		*Son's Stratum*					
		1	*2*	*3*	*4*	*5*	*Total*
1.	Upper non-manual	32.8%	47.5%	7.3%	3.4%	8.7%	100% (435)
2.	Lower non-manual	19.1%	48.7%	14.0%	6.8%	11.2%	100% (497)
3.	Upper manual	4.4%	16.8%	50.1%	10.4%	18.0%	100% (315)
4.	Lower manual	2.3%	7.7%	15.2%	67.7%	6.8%	100% (335)
5.	Farm	2.8%	9.1%	11.6%	7.2%	69.1%	100% (2483)
	Total	332 (8.1%)	754 (18.5%)	601 (14.7%)	489 (12.0%)	1889 (46.4%)	4065 (100%)
	Inflow						
1.	Upper non-manual	43.0%	27.4%	3.0%	2.0%	(10.7%)	(435)
2.	Lower non-manual	28.6%	32.0%	11.6%	5.9%	3.0%	(12.2%) (497)
3.	Upper manual	4.2%	7.0%	26.2%	6.9%	3.0%	(7.7%) (315)
4.	Lower manual	2.4%	3.4%	8.4%	46.4%	1.2%	(8.2%) (335)
5.	Farm	21.6%	29.9%	48.2%	36.9%	90.7%	(61.0) (2483)
	Total	332 (100%)	754 (100%)	601 (100%)	489 (100%)	1889 (100%)	4065 (100%)

In general, the outflow and inflow tables tend to verify our beliefs in the Indian occupational mobility regime but also show considerable mobility, more upward than downward. In examining patterns of *occupational inheritance* we look at the diagonals of inflow and outflow tables. The outflow diagonals indicate that whereas only about one-third (32.8%) of upper-manual fathers could pass on that status to their sons over two-thirds (69.0%) of farmer fathers did. In fact there seems to be a linear association between stratum rank of fathers and their passing on status to their sons—the higher the stratum rank of fathers, the lower their ability to pass on their stratum rank to their sons, and vice versa. There is, however, no simple linear association of this kind in the inflow table. Whereas 90.7 per cent of farmers are themselves sons of farmers, this tendency is cut almost in half (46.4%) for son's of lower manual workers. The tendency of self recruitment is the least for son's of upper-manual workers (26.2%) increases to nearly one-third (32.0%) for sons of lower non-manual workers and increasing to 43 per cent (almost close to the sons of lower manual workers) for upper non-manual workers. The self recruitment of farmers is understandable but is an extreme "outlier" in otherwise curvilinear tendency of self recruitment of sons in their fathers stratum rank.

In examining the trends of occupational stratum *mobility* we notice that nearly half (47.5%) of the lower non-manual fathers were successful in supplying their sons to upper non-manual positions—the most dominant trends of upward mobility in the entire table, especially the outflow section. Secondly, both the upward and down supply of sons has been to the closest stratum indicating that most of the father to son mobility has been short distance. The dominant trend of self-recruitment (different from fathers) as evidenced in the inflow section of the table has been to farming. It is interesting to note that this trend should be stronger even among sons whose fathers have been in non-manual occupations that over one-fifth (21.6%) of all sons who had upper-manual fathers and nearly one-third (29.9%) sons who had lower-manual fathers end up in farming. In traditional scales of measurements, as I have also implied here, these moves will be labelled "downward". However, elsewhere I (Sharda (1979) have shown that farming occupations in India enjoy a very high prestige. The other interesting feature of this table is that 28.6 per cent of the sons who are upper non-manual are the sons of lower non-manual workers. This upward mobility trend is supported by our analysis of the outflow table.

In summary, then we say that: (1) dominant upward mobility has been from lower non-manual to upper non-manual stratum; (2) most of the self recruitment mobility has been to farming; (3) short distance mobility, both upward and downward is a more common feature of Indian society than long distance mobility.

Perfect Mobility and the Mobility Ratio Index

In order to go beyond the descriptive analyses of "structural" and "exchange" mobility scholars (Glass, 1954; Rogoff, 1953) popularized the concept of mobility ratio index or index of association. This index is a measure of deviation from the hypothetical "perfect" mobility regime. The concept of perfect mobility implies that destinations are completely independent of origins. This is stated as a null hypothesis.

For example, under "perfect mobility" model, all categories of row one of Table 4 would be 10.7 per cent as other categories of other rows would be identical to their marginals. In such a situation the index of dissimilarity would be zero and circulation mobility 100 per cent, an unlikely occurrence in any society. The x^2 test is applied to judge whether deviations from perfect-mobility in a table be attributed to sampling errors.

Destination distributions of an actual mobility table are compared with the hypothetical perfect-mobility regime. Mobility ratio index or index of association is a ratio of the actual percentage in a diagonal cell to the expected percentage in the same cell under "perfect-mobility'. Mobility ratios are calculated by the following equation:

$$R_{ij} = f_{ij}/E_{ij}$$

Table 7

Mobility ratio index (India)

1.	Upper non-manual	$\frac{32.8}{8.1}$	-	4.0
2.	Lower non-manual	$\frac{48.7}{18.5}$	-	2.1
3.	Upper manual	$\frac{50.1}{14.7}$	-	3.4
4.	Lower manual	$\frac{67.7}{12.0}$	-	5.6
5.	Farm	$\frac{69.0}{46.4}$	-	1.5

Source: Table 6 (outflow).

Table 7 indicates that the index ratios are high for sums of lower manual workers, followed by sons of upper non-manual workers and sons of upper manual workers. Whereas, they are lowest for the sons of farmers and lower non-manual workers. These findings, however, are suspect because as Featherman and Hauser (1978: 142) suggest "Conceptually the model . . . is appealing, but . . . the interpretation of the mobility ratio as a parameter is a fundamental error." Unfortunately $\underset{\sim}{R}_{ij}$ does not measure the strength of the association which it claims to measure. "Often the mobility ratio gives imperfect clues to the association in the table...worse, it is often misleading." (Hout, 1983: 18).

Quasi-Perfect-Mobility Table: As discussed above perfect-mobility model does not describe the mobility data adequately. In addition to the diagonal cells of a mobility table, barriers to mobility also exist elsewhere in the table. The concept of "quasi-perfect-mobility" describes a situation in which the observed pattern of mobility is due to two different processes. One part allocates stayers (non-movers) to destinations from their origins (in the diagonal cells). For the second part, some movers end up in destinations of their origins, despite their moves. Goodman (1965) blanked out-the diagonal cells to construct the quasi-perfect mobility table. Although other models of quasi-perfect mobility exist, I prefer Goodman's model because of its internal consistency. I now turn to the analyses of mobility table.

Log-Linear Models of Mobility

Log-linear analysis is in many respects similar to well established statistical procedures such as analysis of variance and regression analysis. The goal of this analysis is a model that accounts for variation in cell probabilities. More specifically, log-linear model is a statement of the expected cell frequencies of a cross-tabulation ($\underset{\sim}{F}_{ij}$) as functions of parameters representing characteristics of the categorical variables and their relationships with each other.

Different researchers use different notations to denote the models (e.g., Hout, 1983; Knoke, 1976; Reynolds, 1977). We will use Reynolds' notation to present these models.

Saturated log-linear model: General log-linear model for a two-way classification such as of a mobility table is:

$$\log (\underset{\sim}{E}_{ij} = \underset{\sim}{U} + \underset{\sim}{U}^{y}{}_{i} + \underset{\sim}{U}^{x}{}_{j} + \underset{\sim}{U}^{y}{}_{i}{}^{x}{}_{j} \,. \qquad \ldots . (4)$$

Where log ($\underset{\sim}{E}_{ij}$) is natural logarithm of expected cell frequency, and

$\underset{\sim}{U}$ is the grand mean

$U^y{}_i$ and $U^y{}_j$ are the row and column effects respectively.
They are defined as departure from the grand mean
$U^y{}_i x_j$ is the interaction effect.
These parameters are subject to the constraints:

$$\sum_{i}^{I} UU_i^y = \sum_{j}^{I} U_j^x = \sum_{i}^{I} U_{ij}^{yx} = \sum_{j}^{I} U^{y_i x_j} = 0 \quad \ldots\ldots (5)$$

This property, similar to the behaviour of treatment in the analysis of variance, results from their being deviations from means.

Saturated model has no parsimony since it represents C cells with exactly C effects. The expected frequencies from such model always perfectly match the observed frequencies.

In analyzing mobility table, the saturated model usually needs to be modified.

Independent log-linear model: If we set interaction effect $U^{y_i x_j} = 0$ for saturated model. The equation will become:

$$\log (E_{ij} = U + U^y{}_i + U^x{}_j \quad \ldots\ldots (6)$$

This is called an independent model or perfect mobility model since row (e.g., father's status) and column (e.g., son's status) have no association, the son's status are independent from father's status.

Quasi-mobility log-linear model: Quasi-mobility model is the combination of saturated model and independent model. The former is applied to off-diagonal cells and the latter is applied to diagonal cells. The log-linear equation for quasi-mobility are:

$$\log (E_{ij} = U + U^y{}_i + U^x{}_j + U^{yx}{}_{ij} \text{ for } i = j$$

$$\log (E_{ij} = U + U^y{}_i + U^x{}_j \text{ for } ij \quad \ldots\ldots (7)$$

The $U^{yx}{}_{ij}$ are the immobility effects. They are the only interaction parameters in the model. They measure the deviation of the diagonal cells from the pattern of perfect mobility. The equation for cells in which $i=j$ are identical to equations for the model of perfect mobility, except for the condition that i must not equal j.

The log-linear models presented above may also be written as

$$F_{ij} = \mu \; r_i^y \; r_i^m \; r_{ij}^{ym} \quad \ldots\ldots (8)$$

Parameters of log-linear and multilicative models are linked by the simple relationships: However, constraints implied by equation 5 now become

$$\pi_i r_i^y = \pi_j r_j^m = \pi_i r_{ij}^{ym} = \pi_j r_{ij}^{ym} = 1 \quad \ldots\ldots (9)$$

To test whether or not these log-linear models fit data, an appropriate statistics is a modified chi square test which compares expected and observed frequencies. If expected frequencies estimated by the models are not far from observed frequencies, the model is acceptable; if the discrepancy between the two frequencies is significant, the model should not be accepted.

Occupational Stratum Mobility in India and the United States: Comparison with Log-linear Models

As an example I compare the occupational stratum mobility regimes of India and the United States. I have already described some features of Indian mobility regimes in Tables 4 to 6 by analyzing Cantril's (1965) data. This data pertains to 1962. Also analyzed here is 1962 US data, for year comparability, gathered by Current Population Survey of the US Census and designed by Peter M. Blau and Otis D. Duncan (1967). This data file is known by the project title: Occupational Changes in a Generation or OCG. This, however, is a large data set outnumbering the India data by nearly 10 to 1. In order to make the sample size close to each other the OCG data is multiplied by 1/10.

The raw frequencies of the father-son mobility table are presented in Table 8 for both India and the United States:

Table 8

Frequency distribution of origins by distributions in USA and India

Country (C)	*Son's occupation (D)*	*Father's occupation (Q)*				
		UNM	*LNM*	*UM*	*LM*	*FARM*
	UNM	216	59	41	45	5
	LNM	197	105	64	73	7
U.S.A.	UM	159	105	184	172	7
	LM	168	136	208	378	17
	FARM	111	132	207	371	226
	UNM	143	207	32	15	38
	LNM	95	242	70	34	56
India	UM	14	53	158	33	57
	LM	8	26	51	227	23
	FARM	72	226	290	180	1715

The total frequency is 7458

Source: India, see Cantril (1965); U.S.A., See Blau and Duncan (1967).

Log-linear models are estimated from the data provided in Table 8. Father's occupation is denoted as O (origin), sons occupation by D (Destination) and country as C. Models are presented hierarchically in Table 9.

Table 9

Log-linear models for India and the United States, 1962

	Model	G^2	PEARSON	DF	∝	Δ	G^2_n/G^2_t
I	(O) (D) (C)	6045	6895	40	.000	38.23	100
II	(OC) (DC)	3307	3943	32	.000	25.75	54.7
III	(OD) (DC)	1429	1384	20	.000	17.81	23.6
IV	(OD) (OC)	542	517	20	.000	8.12	9.0
V	(OD) (OC) (DC)	285	282	16	.000	6.37	4.7

Notes: G^2 - Likelihood ratio statistics for maximum likelihood estimates of F_{ijk}.
Δ - % cases misclassified by the model.
G^2_n/G^2_t - Likelihood statistic ratio as a proportion of the likelihood of the base model.

The first model (I) is estimated by equation (6). As was pointed out, this is known as perfect mobility model where all the three variables O, D and C are independent of each other. The model has a G^2 of 6045 with 40 degrees of freedom. The model is statistically independent at .000 level but misclassifies (Δ) 38.23 per cent of the cases and is, therefore, not acceptable. We, however, use this model as our baseline model with which we compare models II-V.

The next model (II) hypothesizes that the country (C) interacts with both the origins (O) and destinations (D) to produce unique mobility experiences in the two countries and O and D are conditionally independent of each other. This (and models III-V) are quasi-independent models and are estimated by equation (7). We have obtained a G^2 of 3306 with 32 degrees of freedom. This model is also statistically significant at the α = .000 level. However, this model still misclassifies (Δ 25.75% of the cases and is not acceptable. We, therefore, cannot conclude that the mobility experiences of India and US samples are due mainly to their societal characteristics (level of development, organization, etc.).

In model III we hypothesize that the destinations (D) interact with both the origins (O) and countries (C) whereas the O and C are conditionally independent. This model is an improvement over the baseline model I (G^2_n/G^2_t = 23.6) and is better than model II. This model obtained a G^2 of 1429 with 20 degrees of freedom but still leaves 17.81 per cent of the cases misclassified and hence not acceptable.

Model IV hypothesizes that social origins (O) interact with both the destinations (D) and countries (C) whereas D and C are conditionally independent. This model is a considerable improvement over the baseline model (G^2_n/G^2_t = 9.0) and is better than models II and III with G^2 of only 542 with 20 degrees of freedom. The model remains statistically significant and misclassify 8.12 per cent of the cases. This means that father's occupation (O) is an influential variable in explaining the differences in patterns of mobility in the two countries as it (O) interacts with D. Is there a room for further improvement?

Model V posits all two way interactions between O, D and C, but not a three way interaction (ODC). This model shows still more improvement (G^2_n/G^2_t = 4.7) with G^2 = 285, reducing degrees of freedom to 16. However, it still misclassifies 6.37 per cent of the cases. It seems only the saturated model (estimated by equation (4)) in which three way interaction , ODC, is added could classify all the cases. However, as we have suggested earlier; "saturated model... has no parsimony since it represents C cells with exactly C effects." We, therefore, suggest that model V provides a useful explanation by correctly classifying 93.63 per cent of the cases in the mobility table. We reject the hypothesis of independence hypothesized in model I for both India and the US We also do not believe, as is suggested in model II, that mobility differences of India and the US are due to some structural differences of the two countries. Son's (D) chances of being in different countries and being born to certain parents explains some cases but the better explanation is found in models IV and V. It seems that for both India and the US (C), fathers status (O) provides opportunities to their sons (D) either by providing inheritance or chances of upward mobility (model IV). I, therefore, prefer model IV which seems to me to be parsimonious despite its shortcomings that it still misclassifies 8.12 per cent of the cases.

Summary and Discussion

With the growing interest in social mobility research, the methodologies on studying social mobility have been developed correspondingly. The earliest methods on research mainly focused on certain elementary techniques such as comparison on crosstabulation and index of association. Today, many rather sophisticated procedures and models have been created and applied. Looking back at the methodological development on social mobility, the many methods employed so far can be roughly divided into two main categories: status attainment approach and social mobility table approach.

The status attainment approach emphasizes social origin and other background characteristics as factors in achievement, while the mobility table approach focuses on the comparison of origin and destination status in order to characterize patterns of occupational inheritance and mobility. But, two approaches are inseparable since they both measure the same thing (see e.g., Duncan 1979).

Despite many improvements and refinement on mobility research methods, they still have many limitations. Mobility tables analysis, for example, just focus on two major variables; and number of categories which can be put into the table are quite limited. Also different mobility tables are seldom comparable due to differences in time intervals and number of categories. This is one reason for using the 1962 data in our examples. Further improvement in methodology for social mobility research is the pre-occupation of some of the best minds in sociology.

References

Bishop, Y.M.M. ed., (1975), *Discrete Multivariant Analysis: Theory and Practice*, Cambridge, MA: MIT Press.

Blau, P.M. and O.D. Duncan, (1967), *The American Occupational Structure*, New York: John Wiley.

Boudon, R., (1975), *Mathematical Structures of Social Mobility*, New York: Elsevier.

Cantril, H., (1965), *The Pattern of Human Concerns*, New Brunswick, New Jersey: Rutgers University Press.

Clogg, C.C., (1983), *Introduction to Structure Models for Qualitative Data*, New York: Academic.

—, (1981) "Latent structure models for mobility tables," *American Journal of Sociology*, 86: 836-852.

Duncan, O.D., (1979), "How destination depends on origin in the occupational mobility table." *American Journal of Sociology*, 84: 793-803.

—, (1966), "Methodological issues in the analysis of social mobility', pp.

51-97 in N.J. Smelser and S.M. Lipset (eds.) *Social Structure and Economic Development*, Chicago: Aldine.

— (1965), Patterns of occupational mobility among Negro men, *Demography*, 5: 11-22.

—, (1968), "Social stratification and mobility problems on the measurement of trends, *Indicators of Social Change*, Eds. E.B. Sheldon, New York: Russell Sage Foundation.

—, (1978), *Sex Typing and Social Roles, and Research Report*, New York: Academic Press.

Featherman, D.L. and R.M. Hauser (1978), *Opportunity and Change*, New York: Academic Press.

Gartrell, J.W., (1977), "Status, inequality, and innovation: The green revolution in Andhra Pradesh, India," *American Sociological Review*, 42: 318-337.

Glass, D.V., (1954), *Social Mobility in Britain*, London: Routledge and Kegan Paul.

Goodman, L., (1979a), "Simple models for the analysis of association in cross-classifications having ordered categories.", *Journal of American Statistical Association*, 74: 1179-1259.

—, (1979b), "Multiplicative models of the analyses of mobility tables and other kinds of cross-classification tables," *American Journal of Sociology* 84: 804-819.

—, (1972), "Some multiplicative models for the analysis of cross-classified data." pp. 649-696 in J. Neymann (ed) *Proceedings of the Sixth Nerleley Symposium on Mathematical Statistics and Probability*, Berkeley: University of California Press.

—, (1969), "How to rasack social mobility tables and other kinds of cross-classification tables." *American Journal of Sociology*, 75: 1-39.

—, (1968), "The analysis of cross-classified data: independence, quasi-independence, and interaction in contingency table with or without missing entries," *Journal of American Statistical Association*, 56: 841-868.

—, (1965), "On the statistical analysis of mobility tables" *American Journal of Sociology*, 70: 564-585.

Haberman, S.J., (1974), "Log-linear models for frequency tables with ordered classifications," *Biometrics*, 30: 589-600.

Hauser, R.M., (1981), "Hope for mobility ratio", *Social Forces*, 60: 572-584.

—, (1978), "A structural model of the mobility table," *Social Forces*, 56: 919-953.

Hout, M., (1983), *Mobility Tables*, Sage Publications: Beverly Hill.

Knoke, D., (1976), *Log-linear Models, Sage University Paper Series on Quantitative Application in the Social Science*, Beverly Hill. CA: Sage.

Logon, J.A., (1983), "A multivariate model for the mobility table," *American Journal of Sociology*, 87.

Matras, J., (1975), *Social Inequality, Stratification and Mobility*, New Jersey.

Pullum, T., (1975), *Measuring Occupational Inheritance*, New York Elsevier.

Rogoff, N., (1953), *Recent Trend in Occupational Mobility*, Glencoe, IL: Free Press.

Reynolds, H.T., (1977, 1984), *Analysis of Nominal Data*, Sage Publications.

Sharda, B.D., (1977), *Status Attainment in Rural India*, Delhi: Ajanta Books International.

---, (1979), "Occupational prestige in rural India," *Rural Sociology* (44(4): 705-718.

---, (1981), "Convergence and divergence in stratification processes: Comparison between the rural sectors of India and the United States", *Rural Sociology*, 46(I): 20-41.

---, (1984), "Return mobility and the process of stratification in rural India", *Journal of Asian and African Studies*, XIX (1-2): 64-72.

Sorokin, P.A., (1927), *Social and Cultural Mobility*, New York: Free Press.

Sorensen, A.B., (1975), "Models of social mobility", *Social Science Research*, 4, 65-92.

Yasuda, S., (1964), "A methodological inquiry into social mobility", *American Journal of Sociology*, 29; 16-23.

Chapter 17

The Building Blocks of Participation: Testing Bottom-up Planning

Michael M. Cernea

Rhetoric or Method

No matter how intense or loud, the advocacy for people's participation in development programmes it remains empty rhetoric if it is not translated into a "how to" social methodology for making popular participation real.

People's participation in government-sponsored development programmes cannot be achieved just by emotional exhortations. Nor can it be brought about only by intellectual arguments about its usefulness. In the last instance, participation depends on social arrangements and political relations. It also depends on economic incentives and on administrative approaches. Economic benefits must give people reasons to participate. Administrative arrangements must link the decisions of state bureaucracies to the will of local communities. In sum, for popular participation in government programmes to occur, it must be socially organized. Actually doing this social organizational work is more difficult by far than waxing romantically or sloganeering rhetorically about the blessings of people's participation.

The Need for Method

India has been one of the major developing countries which several decades ago has put community development and community participation as goals on its development agenda. Other countries have followed suit. Today, interest in participation is often reaffirmed. But actual progress in many countries has been slow. Programme after government programme, donor-assisted project after project, inscribe participation on their frontispiece. Yet evaluation report after evaluation report usually show that these projects were as short on accomplishments as they were long on intentions.

Exceptions do exist. Here and there a project demonstrates that popular participation is alive and very effective. But there is wide agreement that popular participation in public programmes is insufficient. Thus, the need to analyze positive experiences wherever they are available. Exploring the social mechanisms that have led to successful participation is an effective way to develop new approaches for overcoming non-participatory routines and bureaucracies.

Despite the ubiquitous presence of the topic of participation in the current development literature, the "participation problem" is not a general problem common to every single kind of development. It rather is a problem limited essentially to one kind of development, namely government-induced development. Historically, the issue of participation is intrinsic to public programmes. This issue does not arise in spontaneous development that is initiated, financed, and done by the producers, so to say by the "people themselves" through their regular activities, since this development happens precisely because the people *accomplish* it. They initiate it and carry it out, without having to be called "to participate".[1] Overall development is the composite result of myriad such self-started activities and of the interactions, clashes, and linkages of their social actors.

The situation becomes different, however, in development programmes that are initiated and managed by the state. The fact that one or another government agency designs a plan intended to benefit a certain category of the citizenry (or the public at large) does not automatically bring the public into the fold of that program. The "need for participation", or the "non-participation" as a problem, occur therefore in public sector programmes. Since governments have a large potential to generate programmes often divorced from the genuine interests or immediate needs of their publics, and/or since even good government programmes tend to be costlier and less effective if not supported by the public, participation becomes a matter of extraordinary importance for programmes that are launched, financed and implemented under the aegis of the state.

The recognition that a partnership between public public programme and people must be ensured through "popular" participation has been propelled by at least three key circumstances:

(a) the enormously expanding role of the public sector in launching such programme in developing countries, without a commensurate improvement of the mechanisms for the public's involvement;

(b) the growth of international aid which amplifies the financial resources, scope and number of government programmes, while increasing the distance between the programmes' "centre" and "periphery"; and

(c) the traceability of recurrent failure in public programme to alienation from their own intended beneficiaries.

Participatory approaches within the public sector's development programmes are hampered by a lack of adequate methodologies for organizing such participation. Introducing the concept of "social methodology" in this context may bring additional light to the subject.[2] New approaches to designing and administering public programmes require well thought-out sequences of steps for eliciting the desired forms of convergent actions by individuals and groups. But because the diffuse know-how for accomplishing this task has not been codified, such social methodologies are still to be crafted systematically, one after the other.

Generally, such social methodologies should include the following elements:

— identification of the social actors who will carry out the programme;

— conceptualization of the programme goals and participatory principles, in line with the socioeconomic interests of the social actors;

— establishment of adequate linkage systems and forms of cooperation between government agencies and the social actors;

— establishment of information and communication patterns;

— procedures for joint decision making, particularly to allocate financial resources to selected priorities;

— and mobilization through the structures endogenous to the group of social actors themselves.

Combining these elements into a unified social methodology, tailored for one or another major activity, is not easy; moreover, participatory structures and methods cannot be blueprinted for all programmes, because they vary with the nature of the task at hand and with the characteristics of the social groups (urban or rural, small farmers or landless people, etc.) Therefore, generating such methodologies must become an integral part of organizing the participatory process itself.

PIDER and the Decentralization Project

This paper examines a participatory strategy for allocating investments at the community level that has been embodied in a sequence of rural development programme and projects financed by the World Bank in Mexico over the past two decades. The most recent project in this sequence is the Decentralization and Regional Development Project for the Disadvantaged States started in 1991 (World Bank 1991). It followed the large-scale PIDER programme (*Programme Integral para el Desarollo Rural*—Integrated Programme for Rural Development), which began in the early 1970s as a multisectoral program to alleviate poverty by investing in a score of local projects in the "poverty pockets" of the country. At the Mexican government's request the World Bank made a series of loans for three PIDER projects (PIDER I, PIDER II, and PIDER III) between 1975 and 1988 (World Bank 1975; 1977; 1981). These projects were part of the overall PIDER programme, which benefited from the Bank financial, conceptual, and technical assistance. This strategy of investment in local projects has been resumed and continues in the 1990s through Mexico's recent decentralization project.

The methodology for planning and implementing community investments formulated and tested in Mexico is relevant to the quest of many social researchers for replacing the woolly rhetoric around participation with a pragmatic and codified approach.[3] And this concern lies at the heart of current efforts in India for learning from the community development approach and improve upon its past achievements.

As India has gained historical merits in asserting the need for popular participation in public programme, and in influencing the course taken in many other countries in pursuing this objective, it may be of interest to examine some of the more advanced experiences from other countries and their transferability. The specific case discussed in the present essay falls in this category. Many elements of the Mexican experience, particularly the action research and the administrative reforms, may be transferable, with adjustment, to other countries. Among projects assisted by the World Bank, PIDER stands out as one of the most systematically concerned with participation,[4] and within Mexico itself it also compares favourably with other large scale development programmes.

This essay has the benefit of hindsight, as the period it covers is rather long. The design and testing of PIDER's methodology for community participation started in early to mid-1970s and continued throughout the 1980s, including some major ups and downs in Mexico's economy.

Between 1950 and the mid-1970s Mexico enjoyed a period of high growth, with low inflation and moderate external debt. Real growth averaged 6.4 per cent per annum, while the poverty rate (percentage of households below the poverty threshold) declined by 15 to 20 percentage points. In this economic context, important public investments were made including those in the PIDER programme. The total of these investments in 139 PIDER microregions, with about 9,000 communities, approached two billion US dollars.

In 1982, however, the situation in Mexico changed dramatically, as falling oil prices and rising world interest rates put an end to the country's expansionary policies. A severe economic crisis started. Structural adjustments cut public investments from 10 per cent of the gross domestic product in 1982 to only 4.4 per cent in 1988. Government programmes and agencies shrank, and real minimum wages fell by one-half.

As a result, many projects like PIDER were severely curtailed. The PIDER III project lost its poverty focus; its much reduced resources for investment had to be spread thinly during the crisis. The participatory approaches painstakingly promoted by PIDER over the previous decade were largely pushed aside by a return to excessive centralization.

This turmoil ridden period, however, makes the retrospective analysis even more interesting. It allows us to seek answers about the effects of participation in public programmes and the resilience (or pershability) of participatory planning under the hammer of economic crisis, structural adjustments and austerity reforms.

According to a wise adage, the way to the truth is as important as the truth itself. Sociologists agree when they assert, albeit in a less colourful way, that the process is as important as the end product. In this spirit, the present paper examines the experimentation process that created PIDER's methodology for getting the beneficiaries to participate in the actual planning of state investments for local projects. This methodology is a product of applied social research. The focus in the paper is on the type of social craftsmanship that was mobilized within PIDER in order to design and test out the methods of participatory, bottom-up planning; the final product itself will be also summarized, with more details available in the bibliography.[5] Mobilizing similar skills in other projects or contexts, and developing comparable tools and processes, will produce better results than mechanically copying the methodology that worked in Mexico's context.

Field research carried out in 1988 and 1989, some half-dozen years after the onset of the economic crisis, has generated data about the actual contribution of participating beneficiaries to local development projects and about the survival of participatory approaches during Mexico's economic crisis. These data, along with the new developments under the ongoing decentralization project in four of Mexico's disadvantaged states, are examined in the last sections of this paper.

Developing Methodologies for Participation

The pragmatic questions that must be addressed by the managers of each public programme intended to be participatory are as follows:

* What can stimulate people's interest in participation?
* What specific actions should project managers take to organize participation?
* Who can prepare the tool-kit of concepts, methods and examples on how to proceed in practice?

To begin with the first question, it is clear that no administrative decree can automatically induce farmers to participate in the execution of investment programmes if they don't recognize their own interests in such programmes. No participatory approach can evolve in a sanitized executive office away from the communities for which it is destined, and then be imposed from on high. No design of participatory procedures can be perfect and workable on first attempt. Although these truths would seem self-evident, the designs of many rural development programmes testify to the contrary. They simply proclaim participation as a goal and assume that once proclaimed it will happen by fiat. When little actually happens, the programmes fail lamentably.

Why doesn't participation just "happen" and why do good intentions about encouraging participation fail? Very often, the reason is that such programmes have not taken the organizational steps to translate the desirable participation into practice, or did not provide economic gains to the people expected to participate.

In the case described in this paper, a team of social researchers was created under Mexico's PIDER in order to prepare the methodology for participation. They focused on remodelling the process of selecting and planning local investments and on modifying the work pattern of state agencies that decide upon investments and carry them out. By analyzing this team's activities—with both its strengths and weaknesses—we may peer into what commonly remains a black box in projects, namely, how to create a system of bottom-up planning and promote various patterns of participation in its implementation.

Although tested methods are available for building the "hardware" components of development projects, very few similarly tested methods are available for building the "software"—the institutional and other sociocultural components of these projects. Such methodologies are needed in conceptual and operational forms, but governments seldom call on social scientists to help produce such social methodologies.[6] Government agencies too often prefer the spurious comfort of what I call econoratic or technocratic approaches to planned development (Cernea, 1991a). Social scientists associated with the bilateral development agencies of several donor countries (Archetti 1991; Kievelitz 1991; Olsson 1991) have recently offered significant supporting testimony for this view and have proposed revisions of current routines.

The lack of social methodologies also reflects the relative youth, and weaknesses, of development sociology and anthropology. Social scientists share some of the responsibility, because they have talked about the need for participation more than they have worked to perfect the social techniques for achieving it. Individual social analysts may make valuable contributions to development projects, but their contributions remain piecemeal and particularistic if they are the occasional products of talented individuals rather than the translation of a sociological methodology (Cernea 1991 b). Often development agencies must rely excessively on a social scientists' personal flair in the field, rather than on a codified disciplinary approach. The intuition and ad hoc judgment of the individual sociologist are indisputedly important, but in the long term it is essential to replace ad-hoc-ism with a systematic body of sociological know-how that is readily transferable operationally. It is therefore essential to aim deliberately toward working out such social methodologies as valid products of applied social research.

I turn now to a presentation and discussion of the Mexican projects in which social methodologies of this nature were meticulously, step-by-small-step, developed.

Reversing Conventional Planning

Mexico is a federation of 32 states with some 3,000 municipalities and a population of about 88 million. One-fourth of its people, about 21 million, have incomes below the poverty threshold, and about two-thirds of the poor inhabit the rural areas. Almost all of Mexico's indigenous population lives below the poverty line.

Three Types of Local Projects

PIDER was a programme for rural development targeted primarily to the poorest municipalities of the country, including areas inhabited by indigenous groups. PIDER's enormous financial resources were allocated not for a few large, very costly infrastructural investments, but for thousands and thousands of small projects to meet the needs of small villages or subgroups within these communities. Administratively located within Mexico's Federal Secretariat of Programming and Budgeting (SSP), PIDER did not dispense these investments itself but used technical or line agencies to channel funds to specific small rural projects.

In carrying out these local projects PIDER sought to develop a model not only for consulting the farmers about these investments but, even more important, for getting communities involved in initiating, selecting, planning, and executing the most needed local projects. This institution-building goal, and the creative and imaginative work by which it was accomplished, yielded some of PIDER's most worthwhile lessons.

The vast array of small local projects eligible for PIDER's investments can be loosely grouped into three clusters:

(a) *Productive projects* such as small-scale irrigation schemes, fruit-tree plantation, agroindustry units, and livestock units;
(b) *Economic support* projects, such as construction of stores and warehouses in rural areas, construction of rural roads, rural electrification and development of local markets; and
(c) *Social infrastructure* projects, such as construction of schools, health centres, community halls and recreation areas, establishment of water supply and sewerage systems.

The Search for a Bottom-up Planning Approach

The problem that emerged at the outset was how to select the projects that most deserved financing from among the multiple and simultaneous needs of the poorest communities? Past practice in Mexico was hardly a guide for locally sensitive planning. The conventional planning system was unambiguously top-down: investment agencies and administrative/planning authorities first decided which local projects would be started and only afterwards, if at all, notified the communities.

Early in PIDER's beginnings it became obvious that the planning system shouldn't continue the same way. It was clear that government planners lacked the requisite knowledge of local conditions to choose widely among the multiple projects that could be undertaken. The local elite and various politicians exploited the planners' lack of information and contact with the grass-roots to capture public investments for projects that primarily benefited them, disregarding the acute needs of the poorest strata. Without proper knowledge of local needs and potentials, even well-intended planners could do no better than choose to make the investments they themselves assumed were needed.[7] The process proved largely unresponsive to the needs of the poverty groups and often represented a siphoning of public resources to the private pockets of small local elite.

The involvement of local beneficiaries in initiating projects and making local investment choices appeared, therefore, as the only alternative. PIDER began getting people involved not solely for the purpose of "democratizing the development process" (Clark 1991)—even though the political and educational justifications for participation are worthy goals in themselves, and democratizing the process of public investment is a key to capacity building. PIDER pursued participation also for explicit reasons of economic efficiency and technical soundness.

In 1974, PIDER's management resolved that new procedures were necessary to identify priority needs and optimal investments at the community level. Planning of the public financing for local projects was to be based not just on "consulting" the peasants about projects proposed by the bureaucracy, but on getting the peasants to become the social actors of planning by initiating the projects needed with priority. Thus, planning was to take into account the peasants' knowledge of available resources and their definition of needs, and to get them involved in carrying out the planned projects.

PIDER asked the Research Centre for Rural Development (CIDER—*Centro de Investigation para el Desarollo Rural*) to prepare, design and test out empirically a set of procedures that would eventually become an overall methodology to replace the top-down imposition of investment decisions with a system of planning from the bottom-up. CIDER's contribution was expected to be a large scale action-research exercise, rather than a desk-bound report. The ultimate objective was to make beneficiaries, planners, and line agencies jointly contribute to planning and implementing local projects.

Building Capacity in Projects

PIDER's aim—to organize the participation of the local population in investment planning—embodied a courageous political orientation. It confronted the lack of prior experience, the political opposition of vested interest groups, and the stifling routines of entrenched bureaucracies.

Both PIDER and CIDER realized that introducing community participation in investment planning was a formidable task. It not only required getting large numbers of expected beneficiaries into becoming actors in activities they had not done before; it also required changing the situation in which state bureaucracies were accustomed to be the only actors, but now have to share their role with the local people. New procedures for planning had to be invented, new institutional arrangements had to be made, and legal provisions about resource allocation had to be changed. In short, the entire machinery of the public sector involved in PIDER had to become capable to work (specifically, to select, design, and carry out local investments) in a new, participatory manner. Such a capability could be developed only gradually. Therefore, staff and resources had to be assigned to the special effort for building a new capacity.

To prepare PIDER for participatory activities, CIDER created a special working group of professional researchers[8] with a multidisciplinary skill mix (sociology, economics, social anthropology, agronomy). PIDER management gave this group the authority to design new methods of mobilizing local communities and to subject the proposed procedures to repeated experiments during the actual planning for investments in PIDER microregions. Formulating a social methodology for community participation in local investments was to be the heart of the entire capacity-building process, and the primary task of the working group. Further in this paper I shall refer to this group as PIDER's "capacity-building" group.

The first important lesson to be learned by other projects from PIDER's experience is precisely the creation of such a special group to actually do the job of casting the framework for participation. There IS such a job to be done in virtually every programme, and it requires time, brainpower, and leg work. Surprisingly, countless development projects that are intended to include community participation do not even provide a budget for this job to be done as a distinct activity. They decree participation in a "thou shalt..." manner and do not realize that a purposive effort is a prerequisite. Thus, the first answer to the question what specific action project managers should take to organize participation? Is the creating in each programme the capacity for organizing participation must be an integral, yet a clearly distinct, part of the programme.

Components of the Capacity-building Process

Capacity building is not a one-shot affair: It requires long-term commitment and staying power. Creating the working group was only the beginning of the road. The central CIDER-PIDER capacity-building group helped to establish in the states several local multidisciplinary teams (consisting of sociologists, economists, planners, and technical experts) that carried out similar work in the microregions—consulting beneficiaries, examining planning procedures, and the like. The researchers were thus linked to an actual development programme and its agencies at the central and local levels; they could "work from within" learn from observation of the process and to obtain a multiplier effect by constantly interacting with the personal of the line agencies.

In hindsight, the six main components of PIDER's capacity-building process through which the participatory approach was introduced in practice, were:

(i) Creation of a multidisciplinary group responsible for promoting participation,
(ii) Elaboration of a conceptual framework to define the participation strategy,
(iii) Sociological understanding of the population affected,
(iv) Action research and experiments, with frequent returns to the drawing board,
(v) Training, and
(vi) Institutionalization of the participatory planning methodology.

Although the capacity-building group spearheaded the effort, PIDER and CIDER management constantly backed up the work and "products" of the group with its political and managerial weight. PIDER's leaders negotiated with other entities of the state apparatus to obtain "the room" for experimenting and doing action research. Bringing a vast programme like PIDER on a participatory track required the sustained support of the top leaders throughout the long process of testing, revising, and enacting new norms.

The components of this capacity-building effort will be examined further.

The Conceptual Framework for Participatory Planning

The search for a participatory planning methodology was guided by a conceptual framework gradually developed by CIDER's capacity-building group and with PIDER managers. This conceptual framework consisted of several main ideas and principles, and it was informed by the sociological understanding of Mexico's rural population—its stratification, culture, and structures—which CIDER's various studies provided.

First, community development was to result from combining the efforts of the communities themselves, and their locally available resources, with the work and resources of government agencies at all levels—municipal, state, and federal. The participation process had to aim at mobilizing latent local resources, and do this more effectively than is done (if at all) by bureaucratic planning. It also aimed at avoiding the kind of unilateral decisions (and errors) usually made by the government agencies' technical staff who neglect to consult community members or local authorities. Of course, it was also recognized that mobilizing local resources would stretch public funds and benefit more people.

Second, the "self-definition of interests" by the beneficiary peasants was proposed as the keystone for the local plan. Because recognizing peasants' own definition of their interests and "felt needs" is crucial for securing their participation, investments in each regional programme must support proposals initiated by the peasants themselves. PIDER emphasized that although expert technical knowledge is indispensable for identifying development potential, officials and experts do not automatically have a better perspective on peasants' problems than the peasants themselves have; nor are officials and experts necessarily the best exponents of peasants' interests.[9] The experts and officials fulfill their role as agents of change when they help the peasants become more aware of what the technical options suitable to their own interests and development are.

Third, community diagnosis was proposed as the key to understanding local social stratification and socioeconomic structures neither the peasant communities nor the "peasants' perspective" is monolithic. Therefore, community diagnosis must ensure that village social stratification is identified, and that the economic priorities of various subgroups (e.g., farmers who irrigate and farmers who don't within the same community, landless peasants, youth, and women) are reflected as much as possible in the scheduling of priority investments.

Fourth, local priorities should be reconciled with, and integrated into, the broader regional social and ecological systems. Local participation is not a recipe for autarchy. To achieve overall balanced development, and to enable each locality to contribute to the progress of its surrounding area, the local plans must be integrated and reinforced by the regional plan.

Fifth, to determine the best mix of investments to meet the needs of various peasant groups, CIDER/PIDER proposed "iterative planning" which ultimately consisted of three phases: field assessment, preliminary programming, and final programming. (These are discussed in the next section).

This conceptual framework was continuously enriched over the years as the new bottom-up planning approach was tested and improved. One significant enrichment (through a "support programme for rural community participation" adopted in 1982[10]) was the recognition of the importance of disseminating information for fostering grass-roots participation. Special guidelines were developed for PIDER staff to use in systematically informing rural communities about PIDER's objectives, strategies, resources, and interventions. Furthermore, it was decided to inform local communities of contractors' timetables and public resource allocation. This information dissemination strategy tended "to increase the beneficiary population's bargaining position with the [government] agencies and entities taking part in the programme" (see SSP 1982c).

Guided by this conceptual framework, CIDER's capacity-building team then spent several years conducting social experiments in which the intermediate "products" (the methods for community diagnosis, the guidelines for consultation procedures, the planning methods, etc.) were subjected to one real-life test after another. The same team both designed and tested the new procedures. This enabled them to avoid the trappings of a purist academic approach, detached from the trade-offs present in real life: instead, they learned from field difficulties and continuously enhanced the practicality of the proposed methodology.

The Three Phases of Participatory Local Planning

This section summarizes the three-phase model for local planning devised by PIDER and its capacity-building team (field assessment, preliminary programming, and final programming), with particular emphasis on the first phase. (Of course, this model, which is presented here in its final version, was arrived at gradually. The research from which it evolved is discussed in the next section).

The sequence of three phases recommended in PIDER's methodology is:

(a) Phase one: field assessment
(b) Phase two: preliminary programming
(c) Phase three: final programming.

The roles of both actors—agencies and peasant groups—are carefully defined in each phase. The procedures for each phase cover both the sociological and the technical elements of investment planning. They define what the local community must do not what kind of technical-economic feasibility analysis the specialized agencies should undertake. The three phase planning processes results in a medium term programme (for a duration of three to four years); at the beginning of each year, the annual slice of the medium-term programme is rechecked and specified through a simpler exercise colloquially called "reprogramming".

The norms incorporated in PIDER's programming methodology are binding for the technical (or line) agencies that execute PIDER investments. However, because these norms require the staff of these agencies to do more field work in remote communities than other programme require, there has been constant pressure to simplify the phases of the participatory methodology. Flexibility in adapting the programming procedures to local circumstances was, of course, encouraged, but the primary responsibility of PIDER staff was to enforce the participatory procedures and avoid a too soft interpretation of their flexibility. The call for flexibility is sometimes used as an excuse for unwarranted sidestepping of participatory procedures. The risk involved in an excessively flexible interpretation at local levels is precisely that it might circumvent some of the innovative, albeit more difficult, steps of the new methodology.

Community Diagnosis

In the first phase, the main method for understanding the farmers' perspective is the community diagnosis.* In the conceptual framework of the CIDER team, field assessment is a comprehensive term under which several activities have to be carried out: data on the existing population, infrastructure, and resources in the microregion must be

* See for more detailed PIDER guidelines and manuals listed in the Reference List.

collected; past programme must be assessed; communities eligible for the programme must be selected and the needs of each selected locality diagnosed; and planners must meet with local groups to select investment proposals and prepare a report on the proposed strategy.

Chart 1

Patterns for field teamwork

Activity	*Purposes*	*Carried out by*
1. General information meeting	(a) To announce the purpose of the programme preparation to the village population at large (b) To talk with small groups or individuals and to find best informants. (c) To identify natural leaders in the different community strata. (d) To ask the authorities for census data (on 2.c below).	Field team, in cooperation with population
2. Locality study	To ascertain, in general terms: (a) The status of the existing general infrastructure and technical packages being used) (b) The available potential resources and those to be rehabilitated. (c) The existing social groups and their salient features (first approximation). (d) The village power structure.	Part of the field team (division of work)
3. General programming meeting	To ascertain: (a) The estimated production targets. (b) The approximate credit, input, and other needs. (c) The investment proposals and the social group making them. (d) The ranking of the investment proposals.	Part of the field team
4. Follow-up of the locality study	(a) To check the technical feasibility of the proposals in the field (b) To check the social acceptability of proposals through talks with individuals or groups	Part of the field team

The challenge for PIDER was to get planners who were unaccustomed to consulting people (and who simply did not know how to do it) to go into those communities, elicit people's views, and understand their needs and priorities. The consultation mechanisms developed by PIDER may be particularly useful today for organizing the consultation of project area populations as required by environmental impact assessment (EIA) and social impact assessment (SIA) procedures.

The types and sequence of activities to be performed by a team in the field in carrying out the PIDER pattern of community diagnosis are graphically represented in Chart 1.

Before the field work began, however, the planners collected all available background data on the microregion and its municipalities (with respect to population, ecology, natural resources, land tenure, productive activities, employment, etc.) needed for identifying the area's growth potential and constraints. Then several field teams (each with two to three members) were created, consisting of staff from PIDER and from technical agencies. Each team was assigned a number of localities in which to carry out the village diagnosis. Before going out to the villages, the teams attended a two to three-day seminar at which the objectives and procedures were explained, routes were assigned, and material support organized.

The field diagnosis of each village took about two days and included meeting and surveying the village, holding meetings with various sub-groups, identifying needs, and defining development priorities.

The teams used the trip through the village to become acquainted with the social groups and the physical environment in which activities are to be carried out, and to inform the residents of the objectives of the study. The teams then conducted a survey using selected informants who always included the authorities (*ejido* leaders, security committee (*consejo de vigilancia*), municipal delegate), the local school teacher, medical personnel (if any), and the leaders of other local organizations (parents' association, credit groups).

The teams recorded the data collected[11] through this kind of inquiry on a survey form that, although the content remains broadly similar, was adapted to the specific conditions in each region. At first the teams found that use of the form helped them manage the discussions, but as teams became more experienced, they were able to use the survey form only for recording answers, while giving free rein to the discussions to cover any subject of interest to the group.

The teams then held meetings with the community in one of two ways: discussing selected issues with certain groups separately or discussing matters of common interest with a large, integrated group. The second method was found to be preferable except where irreconcilable internal community differences exist, because it allowed for a comparison of views and provided more reliable background information. The composition of these meetings also varied according to the time available, the social characteristics of the village, or the particular topic discussed. In some cases, men, women, and young persons met together; in others, separate meetings were held with each group. In certain cases of sharply polarized communities, positive results were achieved by holding meetings with different strata (rural dwellers with land and without land; with cattle and without cattle; etc.). In Oriente de Morelos, for instance, three different groups were established for a regular programming exercise: peasants with irrigated land who emphasized the need for technical assistance and marketing; those with rain-fed land, who gave priority to irrigation; and those with wage earnings, who proposed investments that did not involve landownership, such as agroindustry and hog farms.

In some cases when the field terms—and particularly CIDRE researchers—had plenty of time and resources to work for programming, they carried out surveys with individual questionnaires among a sample of peasants at different socioeconomic levels. However, because the cost in time and human resources ruled out widespread application of this procedure, this detailed information gathering was not included in the final methodology.

The participatory methodology contains no formal recipe for organizing the discussions between the expert team and rural dwellers at these meetings, but recommends possible procedures for reaching agreement on investment proposals and for assigning priorities to them.[12] It is important, though, for the diagnostic team to strive to get the "farmers' perspective" on each proposed investment and record it on the report form.

In sum, the individual discussions and group/village meetings brought the planners and the communities together to share information, to identify needs, and to define the development approaches and priorities. The planners explicitly expected both to learn from the local population and to inform the population about their technical assessments of the local opportunities for development investments; often, the people do not have the information on which to base judgments on using all the local potential. Community readiness to contribute to the investments for various projects (through labour, cash, or other contributions) also was assessed during the village diagnosis.

It is not surprising that the investment requests made by the peasants during this public analysis are often different from the solutions proposed by the experts. For instance, in the microregion Baja California Sur, the livestock experts responded to the farmers' requests for breeding cattle by recommending the purchase of Swiss cattle, which, they argued, would be an excellent solution for meat and dairy needs if crossed with the local Chinampo cattle. The villagers, however, insisted on Zebu cattle, and the discussion ended only after one determined farmer described his own experience: on the recommendation of the experts, he had purchased two Swiss breeders out of his own funds, but one cow died during the first dry season and he had had to keep the other in his home because of its poor physical condition. Looking into the causes, the farmer observed that during the dry season the animals had to be able to eat the top leaves off the bushes and to walk enormous distances to find water, even drinking sea water at times. The Swiss cattle, which had short legs, could not get food and water in this way, but the Zebu, which had long legs, were able to reach the highest branches and could travel to the most distant watering points. This ended the discussion.

Technical and Economic Analysis

Following consultations and community diagnosis, agency staff make their professional contributions in the following two planning phases, particularly through their professional expertise for technical and economic analysis.

In the second phase, preliminary programming, the sectoral online agencies must prepare integrated investment plans for microregions. This work takes one to two months. These agencies, and PIDER experts, analyze the investment proposals put forward during phase one using the following criteria:

— good quality of the detailed preparation studies
— complementarity between projects
— relatively low investment per beneficiary
— comparatively lower investment per man employed, and
— estimated benefits and relatively greater impact per unit of investment (per family, per hectare).

The preliminary investment programme has to establish which of the proposed local projects can be approved for inclusion in the final current programme, which one will be included for study in the next annual programme and which one will not be included in the programme at all.

In the last phase, final programming, the specific microregional project plans are completed and consolidated into the regional PIDER programme once their overall technical and economic feasibility have been determined.

At the end of this three-phase process, it is recommended that the final investment programme be made known to the beneficiaries who requested the projects in the first place. The community must have a thorough knowledge of the investments that have been approved, of the implementation schedule, and of the resources provided by the government or to be contributed by the beneficiaries if the programme is to be effectively implemented and locally monitored.

Experimenting: Back to the Drawing Board

As already mentioned, the process through which the participation model was painstakingly developed stretched over several years. Chart 2 shows the main stages and events of this process in a chronological manner. It conveys a crucial message about what capacity building for organizing participation actually means.

What Can a Chronology Indicate

To highlight this message, I would like, at this point, to invite the reader to pause for a minute, hāve a long look at Chart 2, and ponder the lessons embedded in it. Indeed, only a line by line examination of the chronology can convey the volume of work, the patience, and the commitment that were involved in preparing the participatory methodology, and in refining it, step-by-small-step. Reviewing these stages, one gets the image of an incessant "dialogue" between work at the drawing board, field testing, and actual application. In fact, this back-and-forth process, from design to field testing and then to redesign and training of staff to apply the new design on a larger scale, was more complex than the chart can suggest. And while this back-and-forth process continued creatively, the diffusion of participatory procedures into actual operations gradually gained more ground. This is why I feel that this simple chronology embodies and conveys the essence of this paper's argument.

As the chart shows, the design of the participatory methodology started in 1975. Its testing in practice began in the Mazahua microregion of Mexico State. The process involved meetings at the community level, village diagnostic assessments, and other procedures.

Chart 2

Chronology of the Preparation, Testing, Application, Revision, and Retesting of the Guidelines for Participatory Programming

	Period	*Stage of work*	*Who did the work*	*Areas of testing or application*
1975	August-September	Design (preparation of first methodology)	CIDER/PIDER staff	
1975	October-December	Field testing	CIDER/PIDER staff	Mazahua (Edo. de Mexico)
1976	January-March	Field testing	CIDER staff	Tejupilco (Edo. de Mexico; Ensenada (Baja California Norte) and other microregions (for annual reprogramming)
1976	April	Revision and training seminars (for PIDER's technicians) on programming	CIDER staff CIDER, PIDER, and state staff	Headquarters; Baja California sur; Sur de Yucatan; Hecelchacan (Camp); Sur de Nuevo Loan
1976	October-December	Revision and document preparation (PIDER's programming methodology)	CIDER/PIDER	Headquarters
1977	February-June	Application and training seminars (in different regions for PIDER and agency technicians)	CIDER/PIDER and state staff	Oriente de Morelos Poniente de Morelos
1977	July-October	Revisions and document preparation (new document of programming)	CIDER/PIDER	Headquarters
1978	February-April	Application	CIDER/PIDER	Sur de Yucatan
1978	June-October	Partial application (of CIDER's methodology on PRODERITH/SARH Regions)	CIDER	Ostuta (Oaxaca) Huixtla (Chiapas) Tixcancal (Yucatan)
1979	February-December	Application (including the entire plan for Zacatecas)	CIDER/PIDER and state staff	Chatina (Oaxaca); Valparaiso, Norte Sombrerete, Pinos, Fresnillo, Jalpa (Zacatecas)
1980	January-February	Revision and document preparation (new manual)[a]	CIDER/PIDER and coordinator	Headquarters

Contd...

Contd...

1980	March-April	Application (for full-scale programming)	SSP and agencies' staff—federal and state	Full-scale programming in eight microregions as basis for appraisal of PIDER III Project: Norte and Mocorito (Sinaloa), Atoyac and Costa Chica (guerrero), Tlaltenango and Valpariso (Zacatecas), Sur and Litoral Norte (Yucatan)
1981		Application (for full-scale programming)	SPP and agencies' staff	Additional 9 microregions financed under the PIDER III Project
1981	April	National seminar on PIDER	SPP federal and state staff	Reviewed national experience with PIDER, including participatory methodology for transfer of certain responsibilities to state level.
1982	March	Issuance of Guidelines of the Support Programme for Rural Community Participation (PAPCO) (focused on information and motivation)	SPP/CIDER	Application in several microregions
1982	May	Issuance of two manuals (on the socioeconomic analysis of rural communities and on the formulation of productive project)	SPP/PIDER	
1982	June	Issuance of manual on PAPCO (revision of March 1982 guidelines)	SPP/PIDER	
1982	July	Issuance of manual (on procedures for programming- budgeting in PIDER)	SPP/PIDER	
1982	August-September	Issuance of two manuals (on project implementation monitoring and evaluation)	SPP/PIDER	

a "Manual de procedimientos para la programmacion de invesrsiones publicas para el desarollo rural (Mexico, D.F.: SPP and CIDER, January 1980).

With some corrections, at initial programming design continued to be tested during the first quarter of 1976 in a larger area consisting of eight microregions: Tejupilco (Mexico State), East Morelos (Morelos State), Ensenada (Northern Baja California), and Chol, Cintapala, Zoque, Lacandona, and Bellavista (Chiapas). These tests were carried out either as an initial programming of investments for a given microregion, or as part of the annual exercise for reprogramming allocations made previously.

As a result of these experiments the first guidelines were drastically modified and a more down-to-earth document was prepared. At that point, and at PIDER's request, CIDER also organized a training programme to educate PIDER staff in the principles and procedures of the emerging methodology.

It is not my purpose here to reconstruct and describe each one of these initial or intermediate methodologies, which were provisional when they were drafted, and were improved or partly discarded under a succession of revisions. Rather, the intent is to emphasize the process of working out a methodology through trial and error, through iterative approximations and refinements.

As can be seen from the chronology, two more rounds of testing and adjustments followed in 1976 and 1977 (the first in South Yucatan, Hecelchacan, and other microregions, and the second in the Western and Eastern Morelos microregions). These resulted in new recommendations that were applied in early 1978 through actual planning in limited areas.

The difference between simply "testing" and "applying" was that the latter was done as part of the regular annual programming exercise. Its results were incorporated into the investment plan. Staff from CIDER/PIDER and from several technical agencies were involved, so that the methodology emerging from these rounds was not just the brainchild of a few imaginative minds in the CIDER capacity-building team, but the result of dialing with real planning dilemmas.

The social experiments were difficult, at times puzzling. The lessons derived from microregions with various socioeconomic structures and institutions differed. The field tests often yielded contradictory and unclear results, so that new tests were necessary. Successfully tested principles had to be solidified in clear prescriptions, and areas of uncertainty had to be gradually narrowed. Firmness, through normative prescriptions, had to be built in, combined with overall flexibility, so as to allow room for local differences in applying the guidelines. The entire sequence was a long learning process.

During the designing, testing, and refining of these procedures, PIDER and CIDER continuously stressed the linkage between the sociological and the technical sides of the planning process. Participatory planning was intended to mean more than collecting a "shopping bag" of community proposals and accepting them without sound review. Understanding the sociology of the given community, its power and economic structures, was important but not enough. The social engineers of the participatory approach soon learned that a careful technical-economic scrutiny and justification of each proposal was also required. Social engineering had to go hand in hand with, and not substitute for, the technical engineering and analysis of financial soundness.

Because the proposals emerging from communities often contained no backup technical information and economic justification, the research team had to produce analytical instruments to assess the technical and economic soundness of local investment proposals.[13] Therefore, PIDER issued instruments and standard forms for the technical and economic justifications of projects proposed at the local level, standard checklists for investment analysis, and identification guidelines for assessing the engineering requirements of projects. The use of these instruments enhanced the quality of microprojects, particularly their economic and technical preparation.

Another mid-term correction of PIDER's overall approach was the result of a belated recognition of the need for community participation not only in initiating and planning the investments, but also in implementing and monitoring them. This modification was triggered by the mid-term evaluation of the PIDER project, which uncovered many cases of serious waste of resources (Cernea 1979). Such waste, it was felt, could have been prevented or mitigated if the beneficiaries had been more closely involved in the execution of the local projects and in the monitoring of private contractors' work.

Extension of the New Approach

A further phase in testing the participatory programming methodology was its application in 1979, for the first time, to an entire state—Zacatecas.

The challenge of preparing the statewide investment plan (see CIDER 1979; Plan Estatal 1979) and the staff resources required were much larger than those in any earlier testing. Nearly 200 staff from different agencies carried out diagnostic work in some 1,050 village communities in Zacatecas. The survey work itself had two foci—locality studies and sectoral studies. For the former, 60 field teams using a total of 120 technical experts carried out the diagnostic work; in the sectoral studies eight groups including some 100 technicians were involved.

The survey results were impressive: it was estimated that about 80 per cent of the total population of the Zacatecas state was contacted; a total of over 4000 investment proposals were received from communities and an additional 2200 were made by government departments. Fruitful interaction between local communities and government planners was achieved in each of the three phases of planning.

Weaknesses of PIDER's Participatory Approach

The chronology in Chart 2 also reflects some of the weaknesses and discontinuities that sometimes disrupted the process of producing and testing the new methodology. In 1980, the relationship between PIDER's management and CIDER became somewhat tense, partly because of personality clashes, partly as a result of their subordination to different ministers and partly for reasons related to political events in Mexico. In 1981, CIDER ceased to be institutionally involved in the further refinement or application of the participatory methodology, and this development proved to be detrimental to both CIDER and PIDER, particularly the latter. The subsequent repeated reorganizations of PIDER also had disruptive effects on the implementation of the participatory approach, a matter that is discussed later in this paper.

Furthermore, a weakness of the PIDER/CIDER approach was its relative neglect of other forms of building participation, beyond the concern for developing bottom-up planning. Indeed, PIDER didn't put sufficient effort into assisting the creation, or the strengthening, of grassroot organizations of farmers, which would themselves mobilize and sustain the active involvement of peasant groups in development activities. Helping such stable forms of peasant self-organization to emerge is essential, because it creates enduring structures critical for generating the synergy from individuals' efforts and effective in building long-term sustainability (Cernea 1987, 1983).

The community meetings organized by the planning teams with various population segments were an useful, but somehow a short lived, transitional form of group action. The interaction between planners and local communities could not be maintained and sustained on a regular basis after the field teams departed from the village. When village grass-root organizations exist, or when they can be encouraged and established, they tend to be more effective in carrying out development activities. Even the most dynamic individuals are limited in their effectiveness if they are scattered and isolated, and if their efforts are not reinforced through group structures and group action. In hindsight, the availability of PIDER's sensitive change agents, who learned to know and respect local communities, could have been used far beyond involving villages in bottom-up planning, specifically as organizers and catalysts for creating stable group structures, various associations, etc. Such organizations are apt to have more lasting effects in building participation than securing the "atomized" participation of individuals from those communities.

Institutionalization Through Formal Norms

By early 1980s the process of designing, testing, and revising the methodology was virtually completed. The essential lessons had been learned and the methodology for participatory investment programming had become reliable enough for widespread application. The time had come to move ahead from experimenting to institutionalizing, from testing approaches to prescribing procedures for mandatory application in PIDER.

Thus, in 1980, SSP issued its Manual for Programming containing the strategy and the detailed procedures that had emerged from the previous several years of testing (SSP 1980). This Manual became the norm for programming PIDER III areas. Numerous training seminars were organized for staff at various levels and in different regions to familiarize them with the manual. The four states (Sinaloa, Guerrero, Zacatecas, and Yucatan) that were to receive financing under the World Bank-assisted PIDER III project were required to use the methodology prescribed in the manual. Investments in the first eight microregions were programmed according to this methodology in 1980 and in early 1981.

Conflicts: The path towards this "final" methodology was not free of conflicts. Besides the difficulties inherent in the mechanics of testing, there were institutional and political obstacles to overcome. Various conflicts emerged between PIDER and line agencies at work in the same areas, either on substantive or on procedural matters—for instance, over the kind of compensation to be provided for labour on community projects, as it happened in Quintana Roo (Koch-Weser, 1979). The bureaucracy in one or another agency sometimes opposed the new approach openly and at other times paid it lip service while sidestepping it. Even within PIDER, staff and managers only gradually, and not monolithically, accepted the methodology. In fact, at every stage that a new, revised methodology was readied, it had to clear significant resistance before it could be formally applied. Such open resistance was not a surprise: in fact, it is to be expected in every government programme attempting to promote participation.

Whereas the capacity-building group responsible for testing and refining the methodology acted basically as a team of applied social researchers, those who had to approve and enforce its implementation were managers, politicians, and administrators—and the views and interests of these groups often clashed. The managers often felt pressed by time and execution deadlines; they were concerned that the application of the participatory model might lengthen the planning process or entail excessive costs and staff resources. Bureaucratic administrators felt that their power was diminished.

Various management teams that succeeded each other at the helm of PIDER over the years were not equally committed to ensuring participation. Some were not convinced that the improvements resulting from the participatory procedure would justify the greater efforts involved in planning. In turn, some line agencies at the local level did not apply the proposed procedures in earnest.

The social researchers involved in refining the new methodology derived strength during this process from their increasing immersion in the practicalities of investment identification and planning, as well as from the ultimate support given by SPP/PIDER's senior management. This support was instrumental in keeping the social experiment going and in triggering some reorientation within the line agencies as well.

Preparing Staff to Implement the New Methodology

The capacity-building process is not complete without some adjustments in organizational arrangements and in the training of staff.

Cultural constraints to promoting broader participation, and specifically bottom-up planning, are often overlooked, but they are nonetheless a major slowing down factor. The promotion of participation confronts not only political constraints and vested interests, fearsome as these are, but bureaucratic and cultural impediments as well. A specific expression of such cultural constraints are the value systems of the army of technicians, planners, bureaucrats, etc., who, in PIDER's case, were called upon to embrace a new style of planning and interact with new (for them) clients. Overcoming such constraints requires organizations changes, training and related measures, with their share of efforts and costs.

There are indeed significant transaction costs involved in shifting from an old to a new administrative approach. The new approach cannot be simply superimposed over existing bureaucratic structures. Some reorganization is required: staff resources must be reallocated, functions and responsibilities redefined, existing staff must be trained and retrained, learning-from-doing mechanisms must be incorporated, and linkages between administrative units must be rearranged to improved work patterns. Korten and phoff (1982) defined such processes as a "bureaucratic reorientation". Without such reorganization a new participatory methodology would remain an utopian notion, and business as usual would continue.

Particularly relevant to facilitating participation was the decentralization of certain administrative functions started in Mexico in 1981, when some prerogatives were transferred from the federal government to state governments. The maintenance of right central control over each microregions was not consonant with progress in vesting rights in the local communities. Subregional Rural Development Committees were established for each of the PIDER microregions. Additional staff were assigned to act as "support groups" (Grupos de Apoyo) to inform communities about PIDER and to make socioeconomic analyses and diagnostic assessments of project communities by working directly with their populations.

Concomitant with the devolution of important functions from the centre to the local settings, SPP considered it necessary to set up four support programme within SPP headquarters. These were programme to:

(a) assist the participation of rural communities;
(b) perform socioeconomic analysis of rural communities;
(c) help formulate productive projects; and
(d) monitor, control, and evaluate project implementation. These four central programme also had the task of issuing guidelines and manuals about their activities for general application in all states.

The institutionalization of these methodological activities in SPP/PIDER headquarters provided additional structure and focus. In a short time, a flurry of "*Lineamentos Metodologicos*" (methodological guidelines) and "*Manuales*" were issued. Of particular interest is the "Manual for the Support Programme for Rural Community Participation" (PAPCO) which sets forth the strategy for "information and motivation" in other words, the approach to explaining to communities the goals and means of PIDER (see SPP 1982c). At about the same time two other manuals were prepared and published on the socioeconomic analysis of communities and on the formulation of productive projects for local communities (SPP 1982a, 1982b). In July 1982 a revised manual was issued on procedures for programming and budgeting in PIDER, summarizing both the justification of the participatory approach and the procedures for carrying it out. Two other manuals on project monitoring and control of execution followed (SPP 1982d, SPP 1982e, SPP 1982f). Each one specified ways in which communities should be involved not just in initiating and selecting investments but also in implementing and monitoring projects.

To sum up, the process of capacity building led to the establishment of organizational tools and staffing patterns that supported the participatory approach. Errors were corrected through built-in learning mechanisms. The institutional memory of PIDER has been captured in printed guidelines and manuals, even though some of this experience was lost because of the high turnover in staff and managers. New managers often were not equally committed to the guidelines they inherited, and the orientation towards participation was at times weakened.

The economic crisis that hit Mexico in the early 1980s, as is shown in the next section, curtailed many development programmes, including poverty alleviation programme and their participatory approaches. Yet Mexico's new Decentralization Project (World Bank 1991), which started as the economic crisis was ending, builds directly on some of PIDER's key accomplishments. The continuing orientation towards decentralized decision making is a vindication of the essence of PIDER's participatory strategy in the new circumstances of the 1990s.

Decentralization Facilitates Participation

Given the complexity and vastness of PIDER and the unevenness of its results in different places, it is not surprising that PIDER's accomplishments over almost two decades have been both heartily praised and severely criticized. From calls for emulation to labeling the programme's results as "unsatisfactory", the spectrum of the conflicting judgments is broad.[14] Moreover, the economic crisis in Mexico after 1982-83 reduced PIDER's financial and institutional resources to such an extent that many of its results were deemed unsatisfactory when compared with goals and expectations.

Can Participation Survive an Economic Crisis

Despite its various shortcomings PIDER had accomplished, among other gains, one remarkable breakthrough: it shook up Mexico's entrenched bureaucratic planning systems and promoted substantial consultation and participation of local communities in the allocation of resources for local development. The decentralization to the microregional level was an important social innovation that has had a profound influence.

Although the austerity measures introduced in the mid-1980s reversed some of this progress and undercut the decentralization trends, these setbacks could not wipe out all the progress regarding participation introduced by PIDER. Nor did these austerity measures and structural adjustments substitute more effective alternatives for getting people involved in public sector programmes. Some of the institutional gains achieved in PIDER proved enduring, and the new decentralization project (World Bank 1991) attempts to continue and expand them.

During the preparation of the decentralization project, the Government of Mexico and the World Bank carefully reviewed the experience of prior programmes. Mexico's National Institute of Statistics, Geography, and Information (INEGI) surveyed PIDER III subprojects and derived conclusions for an overall strategy report (see World Bank 1989). INEGI found that direct participation by beneficiaries had contributed significantly to the construction of a large number of local projects and that beneficiaries expressed high rate of satisfaction with most local projects: about 65 per cent of the sub-projects were judged successful by the beneficiaries, and the social infrastructure and economic support projects rated above 70 per cent. The productive projects received a lower rating.

The beneficiaries contributed substantially to the cost of certain types of local projects, as shown on Chart 3: 23 to 64 per cent of labour costs and 40 to 47 per cent of the cost of land for setting up agroindustry units, small scale irrigation systems, fruit-tree plantations, and livestock units. Beneficiaries were actively involved in identifying projects. They reduced costs and improved the quality of maintenance by getting directly involved in maintenance, along with the employed technicians or the executing agency.

Decentralization and Popular Participation

Under the decentralization project that started in 1991, the World Bank is supporting the Mexican Government's efforts to resume the

Chart 3

Structure of Community Participation by Type of Activity

Activity	*Small-scale Irrigation (%)*	*Fruit Trees (%)*	*Livestock (%)*	*Agro-Industry (%)*	*Stores (%)*	*Ware-houses (%)*	*Roads (%)*	*Electricity (%)*	*Water Supply (%)*	*Sewerage (%)*	*Education (%)*	*Health (%)*
Beneficiaries' Contributions to Costs												
Land	40.9	43.8	41.2	n/a	n/a	42.3	0.0	6.1	6.3	22.2	15.8	
Machinery and equipment	4.5	6.3	—	—	n/a	n/a	3.8	—	—	—	—	—
Financial	9.1	3.1	17.6	11,8	n/a	n/a	11.5	75.0	33.3	43.8	33.3	15.8
Materials	9.1	0.0	14.7	17.6	n/a	n/a	11.5	0.0	6.1	6.3	19.4	5.3
Labor	31.8	46.9	26.5	23.5	n/a	n/a	30.8	25.0	42.4	37.5	25.0	31.6
Other	4.5	0.0	0.0	0.0	n/a	n/a	—	0.0	12.0	6.3	6.0	31.6
All projects	100.0	100.0	100.0	100.0	n/a	n/a	100.0	100.0	100.0	100.0	100.0	100.0
Participants' Shares in Project Identification												
Beneficiaries	63.2	68.4	58.8	—	—	—	—	—	—	—	—	—
Community	26.3	21.1	29.4	41.7	54.2	25.0	50.0	54.5	38.5	41.2	40.7	30.0
Ejido	—	—	—	58.3	20.8	12.5	—	36.4	15.4	11.8	11.1	0.0
Municipality	—	—	—	0.0	4.2	25.0	25.0	9.1	26.9	11.8	11.1	30.0
Inst./authority	10.5	5.3	11.8	0.0	20.8	0.0	20.0	—	15.4	23.5	37.0	40.0
Individual	0.0	0.0	—	—	—	—	—	—	—	—	—	—

Contd...

Contd...

Other	0.0	5.3	0.0	0.0	0.0	37.5	5.0	0.0	3.8	11.8	0.0	0.0
All projects	100.0	100.0	100.0	100.0	100.0	100.0	100.0	100.0	100.0	100.0	100.0	100.0
Participants' Shares of Maintenance												
Beneficiaries	18.8	n/a	21.4	35.7	n/a	n/a	16.7	0.0	35.0	20.0	65.2	25.0
Municipality	—	n/a.	—	—	n/a	n/a	16.7	—	—	—	8.7	—
Technicians	56.3	n/a	78.6	64.3	n/a	n/a	44.4	5.9	60.0	70.0	—	56.3
Executing agency	18.8	n/a	—	—	n/a	n/a	—	94.1	—	—	21.7	—
Other	6.3	n/a	0.0	0.0	n/a	n/a	22.2	0.0	5.0	10.0	4.3	18.8
All projects	100.0	n/a	100.0	100.0	n/a	n/a	100.0	100.0	100.0	100.0	100.0	100.0

Source: INEGI surveys.
n/a = not available.

Note: The percentage represents the breakdown of participation by different groups or institutions for each type of activity.

countrywide decentralization and foster stronger population participation.

The principal objective of the decentralization project is to increase the access of poor and indigenous populations in the four poorest states of the country—Chiapas, Guerrero, Hidalgo, and Oaxaca—to basic infrastructure, social services, agricultural technology, and larger markets. To achieve this broad objective, one of the specific goals of the project is

> "to strengthen the decentralized municipal institutions to identify, prepare, build, operate and maintain the investments in a more participatory manner" (World Bank Staff Appraisal Report, 1991, p. 19).

The process of selecting and prioritizing small scale local investments under the decentralization project will follow closely, and improve upon the participatory planning model previously developed under PIDER (see Chart 4). The planning process is to start at the community levels, where the projects should be identified and prepared. Communities are to be informed, when their proposed projects are not approved at the subsequent stages, about the reasons for rejection. Thus, the earlier approaches and solutions PIDER arrived at, despite having been temporarily pushed back, or apparently discarded, have returned on today's agenda for careful reconsideration and use. This is a case akin to what Hirschman called the "principle of conservation and mutation of social energy" (Hirschman 1984).

The "heritage" of PIDER is visible at every stage of the current planning process and the new guidelines are seen as the "grandchildren" of PIDER, while some of the leaders are described as "PIDER-veterans". Indeed, the resumption of the PIDER approach was definitely helped by the fact that some of the key Mexican officials involved in the preparation of the decentralization programme, and now in its implementation, have been associated during earlier years with PIDER or CIDER and have been formed in the spirit of PIDER's "school of thinking".

Summarizing the main elements that currently embody both the continuity and the changes in planning methods for local projects, the World Bank's task manager for the ongoing decentralized project wrote;

> 1. The regional planning mechanism started under PIDER is being institutionalized and embedded in the federal structure of the Mexican administration. Specifically, the manuals for operational controls

Chart 4

Decentralization and Regional Development Project for the Disadvantaged States
Project Selection: Institutions, Functions, Processing Steps, and Products

	Institutions		Functions and Processing Steps		Products
1.	Community committee	*	Identifies/prepares project (preparation can be contracted)	*	Project proposals
		*	Submits proposals to municipality on a standard form		
2.	Municipality	*	Reviews proposals in light of exclusion criteria[1]	*	First selection of projects
		*	Returns rejected proposals to community	*	Rejection of project, with explanation
		*	Reviews remaining proposals according to criteria, filling out a score sheet on each project; projects receiving less than 25 points are returned to communities for modification	*	Second selection of projects, with respective score sheets
		*	Ranks projects in priority order by scores and submits selected projects, score sheets, and list to state planning and SPP/Delegation	*	First list of priority projects
3.	State planning	*	Reviews proposals according to exclusion criteria	*	Third selection of projects
		*	Returns rejected projects to municipality	*	Rejection of project, with explanation
		*	Reviews remaining proposals to nesure that selected projects meet expected standards	*	Fourth selection of projects
		*	Returns projects not in compliance to municipalities for modification[2]	*	Explanation of reasons for rejecting projects
		*	Recorders list of projects by priority and submits new list with funding for each group of projects to COPLADE[3]	*	Second list of priority projects

Contd...

Contd...

4.	COPLADE	*	Decides on package of proposals and priority list; returns package to state planning, and submits new package of projects/priorities to SPP/Delegation	* Third list of priority projects
5.	SPP/Delegation	*	Ensures that proposals are not in exclusion criteria	* Rejection of project, with explanation
		*	Returns rejected projects to state planning	
		*	Reviews remaining proposals to ensure that criteria were adequately applied on each project.	
		*	Returns improperly selected projects to state planning for modification and deletes them from funding request to SPP/Mexico	* Explains reasons for rejecting projects
		*	Reviews rankings of projects according to scores assigned and submits state program package without basic project forms or score sheets to SPP/Mexico	* Fourth list of priority projects.
6.	SPP/Mexico	*	Reviews state submissions and decides on programme financing	* Issurance of project funding authorization

Notes: 1. Any municipality not able to carry out this screening can request assistance from a state planning or regional SPP office.
2. Such proposals, if modified, may be resubmitted for consideration in the current or next fiscal year.
3. State Coordinating Planning Committee.

used presently are the grandchildren of the manuals developed by PIDER.

2. The planning mechanism has evolved and further improved, so that nowadays the state COPLADES (state coordinating planning committees) are the primary body responsible for regional planning. In these committees are represented all sectoral federal and state agencies. They elaborate the annual operational plan that is then revised and approved by the federal planning ministry. The need to extend the planning system to the whole country and establish a regular federal structure was the factor that required such a change.

3. PIDER's microregion planning concentrated resources on particular microregions. Nowadays planning is conducted at several levels: municipal and state so it can become comprehensive and integrate all the microregions in a state. One of the criticisms of the microregion approach was that it created islands, without coordinating planning and the required institutional support with the other microregions that were not covered by PIDER. Currently, all microregions are covered. And the basic concept of the microregion, which was the unit introduced through PIDER, still permeates regional planning today.

4. The present challenge in Mexico is to extend the public administration structures down to municipalities. A large number of them exist only on paper, so special emphasis is given to creating local structures that are participatory. In this process, institutionalized throughout the Municipal Solidarity Fund, we have certainly used a lot of the ideas of the PIDER experiences (Mateus 1992).

The decentralization project contains two special institutional arrangements for channeling resources to the most deprived local communities: (a) the Municipal Solidarity Funds: (b) and the Development Funds for Indigenous Populations. These funds are accounts created at the municipal and community levels to provide budget financing for small community projects. They will simulate and strengthen communities' social demands; emphasize the consultation, participation, and direct contribution of beneficiaries; and introduce competition among the providers of services to those communities. Thus, the contradiction that weakened PIDER—keeping project financing overly centralized while democratizing project planning—was overcome under the new Mexican programme, which gives municipalities control over funding many local projects.

Early reports from the field about the first year of project implementation confirm that activities under these two funds have indeed attracted substantial participation of local groups from the outset (Davis 1992; Mateus 1992). Another field report (Binswanger 1992) notes that "the pace and manner in which the municipal funds have been taking off are exceeding any expectations we could have had during the design and the preparation of the decentralization project." The same report indicated that in all the local projects visited, the communities provide local materials and contribute unskilled labour, leading to beneficiary shares in capital cost from 10 to 70 per cent, depending on the labour intensity of projects. About 14,000 microprojects have been completed in the first year of the project. Local microprojects include construction of schools or classrooms, road segments, additions to water supply and electrification, health facilities and drainage systems. The unit costs of projects are similar to those of line agencies, or cheaper. Community input further reduces the cost, while the ceiling on project size and cost prevents concentration of projects in municipal headquarters and favours projects in smaller settlements.

Perhaps the best summing up conclusion about the developmental value of the strategy discussed in this paper is an excerpt from a field supervision report written by an experienced project officer about the mechanisms and impact of the project's approach. The excerpt has the earmarks of the rapid and sparse style of a routine back-to-office report, yet it insightfully captures the essential strategic lessons:

> "The theory underlying the decentralization project seems to have worked well so far in this component of the project: change the destination of the resources from the line agencies to the municipalities; give them control over the resources within a transparent and internally consistent project appraisal and selection system; put the burden of sub-project coordination on them and give them the money to do so; involve all elected officials in the municipality and the settlements jointly with the beneficiaries in the project selection; clearly spell out the conditions under which a project can receive financing; require community labour input and thereby eliminate all projects for which no one is willing to volunteer labour. Then rely on the executive capacity dormant in the thousands of villages and slum areas... This programme appears to be a victory of municipalities over the line agencies in the competition for government resources..." (Binswanger 1992).

Lessons on Generating a Social Methodology

This paper has not attempted to give a full description of the methodology for organizing popular participation, as it is formulated in various manuals (see the bibliography and, for a more detailed description of the participatory planning methodology and the decentralization measures, Cernea, 1983; World Bank 1991). Nor does it try to demonstrate all the benefits achieved by applying this methodology to the selection and realization of local investments. Rather, the purpose here was to determine how the capacity-building path that CIDER/PIDER followed has also resulted in an usable model and a kit of practical tools for identifying, selecting, and carrying out investments with people's participation. The lessons for social researchers and development practitioners interested in replicating similar efforts in other countries can be summarized as follows:

The set of circumstances crucial for setting the climate and working out a participatory methodology include:

— Agency awareness of failure (meaning the candid recognition of the ineffectiveness of prior programming procedures) and consensus on the need for change;
— Establishment of a multidisciplinary (basically social science) capacity-building group, with a shared conceptual framework, to design the new approach;
— Support from the top echelons of the government agency;
— Willingness to experiment in the field, to take risks, and to learn from mistakes; and
— Recognition that innovative social engineering takes some time before it can be implemented on a large scale, but once ready it requires formal institutionalization and staff rearrangements.

The core component of this capacity-building process was a sustained action-research effort. The researchers were concerned with modelling the social process of local investment planning and implementation for applied purposes. All three principal functions for which action research can be applied were exercised: action research was used as a social research tool, a training tool, and a management tool (Lenton 1981). The duration of this action-research, however, was perhaps too long, and at times the process became cumbersome. Further similar action-research can be shortened by building on the already existing experiences and on prior tested approaches.

When action research and social diagnoses are accompanied by recommendations for problem solving, policy makers and practitioners are more likely to respect and apply them. Such recommendations should offer more than a solemn pronouncement: "thou shalt...": to facilitate application, recommended solutions should be developed and articulated as step-by-step methodologies for social action. Methodologies of this nature show how to achieve a certain development. Rather than rehashing endlessly what the policy objectives should be, they spell out in detail how to take action for translating objectives into reality.

The operational maturity of social researchers in recommending participatory development policies and approaches to governments is measured not just by their advocacy effort but by their capability to offer guiding models for action. Development practitioners are entitled to expect that sociologists and anthropologists who theorize about participation are able to transform their ideology into an applicable social engineering of participation.

Introducing bottom-up planning is not an operation free of incremental costs. It requires more staff time for the diagnosis phase than conventional top-down planning, and costlier logistical means. If people's involvement in public programmes is to be expanded, these specific costs must be recognized and assumed, otherwise the approach will be vulnerable to real or claimed staff constraints, to short-sighted cost-benefit arguments, or to expediency counter-arguments.

While there are indeed incremental costs for organizing participation, the cost-benefit argument against assuming the extra effort is valid. True, the economic benefits of participation and the participation-induced increase in the effectiveness of public programme do not always lend themselves to easy measurements. Many benefits will remain "invisible", but they nevertheless are real: we will never know the number of unsuitable projects which have not been included and financed due to the peasants' participation, and the amount of money thus saved. In PIDER, many inadequate investments were screened out early by the farmers' sense of feasibility and priority. The lesson is that the opportunity costs of not involving the peasants as participating actors in public programme is unaffordable, since the alternative is likely to be repeated failure or diminished effectiveness of the financial resources committed.

Furthermore, several conclusions about the innovative social engineering needed for organizing participation can also be derived from this experience. Although none of them is necessarily a novelty to applied researchers, or to development practitioners and project managers, the approaches involved are far from being unanimously accepted and applied in projects. In this light, the Mexican experience strongly supports the following conclusions:

— The elaboration of a social methodology requires the joint effort and integrated skills of professional researchers and development practitioners; they must together design for "software".
— Education alone is not sufficient for organizing participation: sound and innovative social engineering, in the sense of gradual creation of new institutionalized arrangements, is necessary. This can be done through experiments, as opposed to the desk-bound concoction of schemes. The model for participation of beneficiaries in development projects is not an abstract prescription, but a pattern of social organization for joint action. To establish such a pattern, researchers must patiently observe their experiments, learn from errors, and repeatedly return to the drawing board.
— Training is critical for good social engineering because even partial, results have to be communicated to, and learned by, the client audience; ongoing training builds up the receptivity for the products of innovative approaches.
— Sustained political commitment to the innovative social engineering approach is necessary for fighting off entrenched bureaucratic opposition and vested interest obstacles.
— Normative institutionalization of participation has to follow immediately after the experimental period.
— Organizational and staffing adjustments are integral to the capacity-building process. No new methodology can be effective or sustainable without the necessary organizational and administrative resources.

The process described above, impressive as it is in terms of continuity and the quality of its outcomes, nevertheless should not be seen as the only way to produce a methodology for a certain type of social action. Moreover, this process should not be idealized, because it had its own weaknesses, some of which were pointed out here. Yet, this is one of the relatively few cases in which a team of applied social researchers worked with continuity over a period of several years to produce a methodology for community participation in bottom-up planning that was professionally designed on the basis of social analysis and field trials, rather than improvised hastily with more enthusiasm than meticulousness.

If theories and methods for purposive development activities are to be improved, and if organized community participation in publicly financed programme is to become more widespread, the action-research experience described here needs to be replicated by other applied researchers, with adjustment to their contexts.

Notes

* This essay is based on my field work in Mexico carried out over several years during the preparation, appraisal, implementation, and monitoring of the PIDER program (*Programa Integral para el Desarollo Rural*). In recent years my other colleagues in the World Bank who have been involved in the latest evaluation of the PIDER projects and in the appraisal and implementation of the recent Decentralization and Regional Development Project in Mexico have assisted me with new data and with their insights. For this, I owe a debt of thanks particularly to Abel Mateus, who led the preparation and appraisal of the decentralization project, and to Hans Binswanger, Hubertus von Pogrell and Ingrid Buxell.

A summary version of this paper was presented in the World Bank's International Workshop on Participatory Development (February 26-28, 1992) in Washington, DC. I express my grateful thanks to V. Rajagopalan, who encouraged and steadily supported my work on social participation in public sector development programmes. My appreciation goes also to Alexander Shakow, who started the "lesson learning exercise" on participation, and to A. Williams, D. Beckmann, B. Bhatnagar and the other colleagues in the World Bank's core team on popular participation, whose comments helped finalize this paper.

During my field work in Mexico, many individuals have contributed to my knowledge and understanding of the country's development needs and programmes. Among my colleagues in Mexico, I would like to thank in particular Marcos Arellanos, Victor Chagoya, Jorge Echenique, Jaime Mariscal, Antonio Monzon, Rudolfo Stavenhagen, and Arturo Warman.

Thanks are also given to Gracie Ochieng, who skillfully processed this manuscript more than once.

1. For instance, farmers acting as economic agents—or any other entre-

preneurs—do not just "participate" in development: they simply do it. They carry out productive activities according to their own goal, plans, designs, and resources. They are the actors and managers of their own economic growth, survival, and change "programmes".

2. Methodologies for social action are a specific product of applied social science (Cernea 1991b). These methodologies codify existing social experiences, sociological theoretical knowledge, and empirical findings into sets of procedures for organizing human activities in order to achieve defined goals. Such methodologies should be regarded as social technologies and are part of what is often called (under parallel but overlapping conceptualizations) either "human engineering", or "sociotechniques", or "social engineering" (Barnes 1980; Firth 1981; Rossi and Whyte 1983). They represent codified knowhow suitable for guiding the actions of human groups and institutions. Professionally crafted social methodologies—and not just happenstance and casual procedures—are indispensable for building up the "software" of development programs.
3. Anders Rudqvist, for instance, describes the research programme initiated by SIDA (Swedish International Development Agency) as just such a quest: "the main objectives of the program are to identify preconditions, problems and possibilities for the promotion of popular participation in rural development projects... The activities include desk studies..., field studies and trial operations..." (Rudqvist 1990).
4. William Nagle and Sanjoy Ghose provide a broad overview of community participation in World Bank supported projects (Nagle and Ghose 1990).
5. The actual "product"—namely, the set of principles, approaches, and procedures that together represent a methodology for community participation in local investments in Mexico—is described in detail in a number of manuals and guidelines (see bibliography). See also Michael M. Cernea, *A Social Methodology for Community Participation in Local Investments: The Experience of Mexico's PIDER Programme*, World Bank Staff Working Paper No. 598, and the *World Bank Staff Appraisal Report---Mexico: Decentralization and Regional Development Project for the Disadvantaged States*, March 1991, on which this paper draws.
6. The scarcity of social methodologies for developing the software of development interventions is doubly counterproductive: it leaves the operational questions unanswered, and the vacuum is filled by amateurism and incompetence. A vicious circle results: first, many decision makers and politicians abet such incompetence and deny their support for developing the methodologies for participatory social action. Then,

in a surprising volte-face—which Alan Dershowitz would see as a fitting illustration of the chutzpah concept (Dershowitz 1991)—the same decision makers invoke this scarcity as an excuse for low performance in the social components of projects. The net result is more failures in development interventions.

7. Jorge Echenique, (1979), who played a key role in designing PIDER's participatory approach to local planning, characterized this situation in Mexico in the following way: There is a tendency for rural development programs, PIDER included, to proclaim farmer participation, organization, and self-management... But these goals are never actually defined or explained in detail... As a result, this approach often goes no further than the pronouncement stage, and is not reflected or put into practice during the course of the programme. The official agencies, whose inertia is evident, mostly act along their old hidebound traditional lines, defining what is to be done, how it is to be done, and who is to benefit, without having any specific knowledge of the real social and cultural context in which they are operating. Limited to a superficial view of the natural environment and resources, they entertain the naive conviction that the aspirations and needs of the rural population match their own institutional priorities, and continue to dwell in the blissful certainty that the peasants know nothing of technology, projects, and serious things of that kind.
8. The core members of this team were Jorge Echenique, Marcos Arellanos, Victor Chagoya, Antonio Monzon, and Alfonso Cano.
9. One of the local investment projects examined by the CIDER/PIDER team vividly illustrates how peasants' perspective and definition of their own needs may reflect aspects that the experts may not perceive. During a conventional investment planning exercise, the technical planning staff of a line agency mockingly rejected a "crazy" written request from a village where the farmers proposed that a dance hall be constructed. The CIDER team then decided to visit the *ejido* that had proposed that unsuitable expenditure. It found that many of the peasants in the village were musicians and that their reputation was so good that on Sundays and holidays inhabitants of surrounding areas came to dance on improvised, open-air grounds. Most of the *ejido* members thought a dance hall would be the best means of attracting much more visitors, selling more local products, getting added revenue, and generating employment. In terms of rural development, as the CIDER capacity building group commented afterwards, "we wondered whether the request for a dance hall was not more justifiable than many of the 'white elephants' included by the experts in PIDER program-

ming."

10. *Programa de Apoyo a la Participation de la Communidad Rural* (PAPCO).
11. The kind of data gathered in this part of the field work for community diagnosis should point up land tenure systems and agrarian problems; total and active population and seasonal migration; the land resources, quality, and distribution; production activities, and their relative importance; agricultural output, productivity, and markets; ownership of cattle; production technology; other production resources and the degree to which they are used; the condition of the social and economic infrastructure (water supply, road, marketing, telecommunications and postal services, electrification, health, education, and drinking water); credit and technical assistance; internal social organization of the village; institutional activities and works undertaken; investment needs and priorities.
12. The recommended procedures for conducting such consulative village meetings were described by Jorge Echenique, the head of the capacity building group, as follows:

    The data obtained by the field team from various informants should be summarized and presented at the village meeting (especially with regards to potential resources and their use, agricultural production and related problems, employment and migration). A review of the production support services (credit and technical assistance) and social services (education, health, drinking water, electricity, communications, etc.) should be part of this presentation. In making this presentation, the field team members should instigate the meeting to express views on proposals collected during the village survey by asking direct questions about them. For example, if the team is told that in one *ejido* a large part of the irrigated land is sown once each year, the question can be asked: why not twice? This question starts off the discussion, which must not be allowed to end until the opinions of all present have been made known, however contradictory these may be. Subsequently, possible solutions to the problems can be discussed, as well as the extent to which PIDER can provide the answer. In the preceding case, for instance, the main reason for a single sowing may have been the lack of water, the possible solution being to expand the storage reservoir and to build canals. In such a situation, the meeting would probably tend to apply for such a PIDER investment.
13. The simultaneity in preparing both types of "instruments"—social and technico-economic—was in fact an adequate response to two fallacies often present in the arguments for or against participation—the "popu-

list" fallacy and the "paternalistic" fallacy. As has been correctly argued, the populist fallacy which contends that the rural majority always "knows better" than the technical personnel and has sufficient skills is as erroneous as the paternalistic fallacy which pretends that the bureaucracy knows best and can do alone all that is needed for development (Uphoff and Esman 1974).

14. Some of these evaluations simply misjudged the significance of PIDER's experience in participation: an example is the paper "Integrated Rural Development in Latin America" by R.L.J. Lacroix, World bank Staft Working Paper No. 716, 1985, which reports interesting empirical facts about the practice of participation yet evaluates them, in my view, inadequately.

References

Archetti, Eduardo P., (1991), The Role of Social Scientists in Development: The Norwegian Experience, in vol. *The Sociocultural Dimension in Development: The Contribution of Sociologists and Social Anthropologists to the World of Development Agencies*, Sonderpublication der GTZ, No. 249, Working Group on Development Anthropology (AGEE), Frankfurt.

Barnes, J.A., (1980), *Who Should Know? Social Science, Privacy and Ethics*, New Work: Cambridge University Press.

Binswanger, Hans, (1992), *The Municipal Funds*, memo, processed, January.

Cernea, Michael M., (1979), *Measuring Project Impact: Monitoring and Evaluation in the PIDER Rural Development Project----Mexico*, World Bank Staff Working Paper No. 332, Washington, DC.

Cernea, Michael M., (1983), *A Social Methodology for Community Participation in Local Investments: The Experience of Mexico's PIDER Programme*. World Bank Staff Working Paper No. 332, Washington, DC.

Cernea, Michael M., (1984), Can Local Participation Help Development? *Finance and Development*, December.

Cernea, Michael M., (1987), *Farmer Organizations and institution Building for Sustainable Development*, World Bank Reprint Series Number

414, Washington, DC.

Cernea, Michael M., (1991a), "Sociologists in a Development Agency: Observations from the World Bank." In *The Sociocultural Dimension in Development: The Contribution of Sociologists and Social Anthropologists to the Work of Development Agencies*, Sonderpublication der GTZ, No. 249, Frankfurt.

Cernea, Michael M., (ed), (1991b), *Putting People First: Sociological Variables in Rural Development*, second edition, revised and enlarged. New York: Oxford University Press.

CIDER, (1979), "Notes on the preparation of the Zacatecas State Rural Development Plan," Mexico, DF Mimeo.

Clark, John, (1991), *Democratizing Development. The Role of Voluntary Organizations*, London, England: Earthcan Publications Ltd.

Davis, Shelton, (1992), *Decentralization/Regional Development Project, Cultural Patrimony and Indigenous Development Fund*, January, memo, processed.

Dershowitz, Alan M., (1991), *Chutzpah*, Boston: Little, Brown and Co.

Echenique, Jorge, (1979), *Notes on Peasant Participation in Rural Development Planning*, paper prepared for the Sociological Workshop on Participation, The World Bank, Washington, DC, mimeo.

Firth, Raymong, (1981) "*Engagement and Detachment: Reflections on Applying Social Anthropology to Social Affairs*", *Human Organizations* 40(3).

Hirschman, Albert O., (1984), *Getting Ahead Collectively. Grassroots Experiences in Latin America*, New York: Pergamon Press.

Kievelitz, Uwe, (1991), "Two Steps Forward, One Step Back? A Critical Self-Reflection of Social Science Involvement in GTZ Over the Last 10 Years. *The Sociocultural Dimensions in Development: The Contribution of Sociologists and Social Anthropologists to the Work of Development Agencies*, Sonderpublication der GTZ, No. 249, Frankfurt.

Koch-Weser, Maritta, (1979), *Beneficiary Participation in PIDER Microregions in Yucatan, Quintana Roo, and Campeche*, Rural Development Divisions, mimeo.

Korten, David C. and Norman Uphoff, (1982), *Bureaucratic Reorientation for Participatory Rural Development*, NASPAA Working Paper Number 1, Washington National Association of Schools of Public Affairs and Administration.

Lenton, Roberto, (1981), "*A Note on the Relationships Between Action Research and Other Forms of Engineering Research*", In ODI Agricultural Administration, Network Paper, February.

Mateus, Abel., (1992), *Comments on Participation*, memo, February.

Nagle, William and Sanjoy Ghose, (1990), *Community Participation in World Bank Supported Projects*, Processed.

Olsson, Gunilla, (1991), "The Social Anthropological Contribution to Swedish Development Cooperation." In *The Sociocultural Dimension in Development: The Contribution of Sociologists and Social Anthropologists to the Works of Development Agencies*, Sonderpublication der GTZ, No. 249, Frankfurt.

Plan Estatal de Desarollo del Estado de Zacatecas (State Development Plan for the State of Zacatecas), 1979, November.

Rossi, Peter H. and William F. Whyte. (1983), "The Applied Side of Sociology", in Freeman, Dynes, Rossi and Whyte (eds.) *Applied Sociology: Roles and Activities of Sociologists in Diverse Settings*, San Francisco and London: Jossey-Bass Publishers.

Rudqvist, Anders, (1990), "Fieldwork Methods for Consultations and Population Participation". Working Paper No. 9, Development Studies Unit, Department of Social Anthropology, Stockholm University.

SSP (Secretaria de Programacion Y Presupuesto), (1980), "Manual de Procedimentos para la Programacion de Inversións Publicas para el Desarollo Rural" (Manual for the Programming of Public Investments for Rural Development). Mexico, D.F.: SPP, Direccion General de Desarollo Rural Integral, and CIDER.

—, (1982a), "Manual del Programa de Analisis Socioeconomico de la Comunidad Rural" (Manual for the Programme of Socioeconomic Analysis of the Rural Community). Volumes 1 and 2. Mexico, D.F.: SPP, Direction General de Desarollo Rural Integral, and CIDER.

—, (1982b), "Manual del Programa de Apoyo a la Formulation de Proyectos Productivos" (Manual for the Support Programme for Formulating Productive Projects), Mexico, D.F., SPP, Direction General de Desarollo Rural Integral, and CIDER.

—, (1982c), "Manual del Programa de Apoyo a la Participation de la Comunidad Rural" (Manual for the Support Programme for Rural Community Participation), Mexico, D.F.: SPP, Direction General de Desarollo Rural Integral.

—, (1982d), "Manual de Procedimientos para el Control de la Ejecucion" (Manual of Procedures for Monitoring project Execution), Mexico, D.F.: SPP, Direction General de Desarollo Rural Integral.

—, (1982e), "Manual de Procedimientos para el Seguimiento de la Operacion" (Manual of Procedures for Monitoring Project Operations), Mexico, D.F.: SPP, Direction General de Desarollo Rural Integral.

----, (1982f), "Lineamientos para la Evaluation en el PIDER" (Guidelines for PIDER Evaluation), Mexico, D.F.: Direction General de Desarollo Rural Integral.

Uphoff, Norman, (1986), *Local Institutional Development: An Analytical Sourcebook with Cases*, West Hartford: Kumarian Press.

Uphoff, Norman, (1991), "Fitting Projects to People", In Michael M. Cernea, ed., *Putting People First: Sociological Variables in Rural Development*, New York: Oxford University Press, 2nd edition.

Uphoff, Norman, and Milton Esman, (1974), *Local Organization for Rural Development: Analysis of Asian Experience*, Ithaca, New York: Cornell University, Rural Development Committee.

World Bank, (1975), "Staff Appraisal Report: Mexico Integrated Rural Development (PIDER I)", Washington, DC.

----, (1977), "Staff Appraisal Report: Mexico Integrated Rural Development (PIDER II)." Washington, DC.

----, (1981), "Staff Appraisal Report: Mexico Integrated Rural Development (PIDER III)," Washington, DC.

----, (1989), "Mexico's Strategy Proposal for Regional/Rural Development in the Disadvantaged States-2 vols. Washington, DC, May 26.

----, (1990), "Project Completion Report: Mexico Integrated Rural Development (PIDER III)", Washington, DC.

----, (1991), "Staff Appraisal Report: Mexico Decentralization and Regional Development Project for the Disadvantaged States", March

Chapter 18

Participatory Rural Appraisal: A Methodology for Participatory Development

Neela Mukherjee

Some Realizations from the Top

In recent years, indigenous knowledge system constitutes an alternative model for sustainable development. It is the sum total of experience and knowledge of a given group that forms the basis for decision-making in the face of familiar and unfamiliar problems and challenges (Warren and Cashman: 1988). It is being gradually appreciated by policy makers, planners, administrators and donor agencies that until and unless the rural people can participate in rural development programmes, such programmes administered by outside agencies remain 'exogenous' to the rural community and can adversely affect the results of these programmes.

One way to narrow the gap is by getting closer to rural people and learning from them. By 'getting closer' is meant establishing better rapport and channels of communications. For this purpose, the attitudes have to be friendly and the conventional methods for knowing them would have to undergo significant changes with the objective of empowering the rural people in their pursuit of a better quality of life.

The Search for Reality: Emergence of Field-Oriented Methods

As a result of the disillusionment from the conventional models some efforts were being made in different quarters towards realistic methods, models and approaches. As a result, a multitude of field-oriented methods emerged on the scene. The necessity of disaggregating economic and social data by people and geographical areas was realized so as to highlight the relatively depressed areas and people. New approaches and methods such as Farming Systems Research, Exploratory Survey, Rapid Rural Appraisal and others, whether through observation or through participation, attempted to understand the problems of resource-poor farmers and improve the quality of information collected on them by overcoming the deficiencies of the conventional survey method. These approaches incorporated flexibility of methods and elements of people's participation in different measures in order to reflect field-level realities. As we shall see many of them combined elements of both quantitative and qualitative methods in different proportions.

It is of utmost importance to understand the intricacies of socio-economic and ecological environment within which resource-poor farmers operate and to resolve their problems by collaborating with them according to their needs and priorities. It was to deal with this issue that the Farming Systems Research (FSR) was evolved in the 60s whose objective was to further research in the area of farming systems, analyze problems and plan research and extension activities. The form of evolution of FSR was different in agricultural institutions located in different countries. However, the common theme in the evolution was a field-oriented and comprehensive approach of a multi-disciplinary team through repeated farm trials with some degree of farmers' participation. FSR, used many traditional methods while innovating new methods to yield quick and realistic results.

A host of field-oriented methods evolved over time. They were efficient enough to yield the same volume of information or even more, in a short period of time, as compared to the survey method which was time-consuming and involved a lengthy procedure for collection and analysis of data. Such methods from various sources were put together with a different label known as Rapid Rural Appraisal (RRA).

Rapid Rural Appraisal or RRA developed as a methodology in the 1970s, influenced by FSR and other methods. Some of the early path-breakers of such methodology were Robert Chambers, Peter Hildebrand, Robert Rhoades and Michael Collinson who along with others met in Conferences at the Institute of Development Studies in October 1978 and December 1979. Through the literature, the concept of RRA spread in different parts of the world and in the mid-eighties there was a wide array of experience from the applications of RRA in different field situations.

As a methodology for agricultural development RRA was developed for quick field-oriented results with objectives as follows.
(i) appraising agricultural and other needs of rural community,
(ii) prioritizing areas of research tailored to such needs,
(iii) assessing feasibility of developmental needs and action plans, and
(iv) implementing action plans, monitoring and evaluating them.

RRA is a way of organizing people for collecting and analyzing information within a short time span. It can be defined as any systematic process of rural investigation to acquire new information in order to draw and validate inferences, hypotheses, observations and conclusions in a limited period of time. It has flexibility to adjust to situations because it does not imply or recommend a standard set of methods to be applied in each case. The methods very from situation to situation and are determined by local conditions, local problems and objectives at hand.

The Transition of Participation

RRA and similar methods remain 'extractive' i.e., researchers observing, writing and analyzing. The field-oriented methods have much scope for inducing greater element of participation. The requirement of the shifting paradigm of development was not only a relatively quicker method of data collection but also one which would help local people to perform their own analysis. Hence, certain elements were required to be incorporated in RRA and other field-oriented methods to make them participatory and more broad-based in terms of their applications. It was a shift of emphasis from 'rapid' or 'quick' to 'participatory' and 'empowering' which fitted well with a participatory approach to rural development and became the starting point of Participatory Rural Appraisal (PRA). The origin of PRA as a methodology can be traced back to the multitude of methods and approaches which gradually emerged since the seventies mainly due to unsatisfactory results obtained from application of the conventional methodology to rural development.

In a short period of time, PRA as a methodology has gained in strength through its emphasis on 'participation' in line with the paradigmatic shift which is slowly taking place and has helped to fill the vacuum existing in the sphere of rural development. This has also made for its quick spread.

Participatory Rural Appraisal

Participatory Rural Appraisal (PRA) is a methodology for interacting with villagers, understanding them and learning from them. It involves a set of principles, a process of communication and a menu of methods for seeking villagers' participation in putting forward their points of view about any issue and enabling them do their own analysis with a view to making use of such learning. It initiates a participatory process and sustains it. Its principles and the menu of methods help in organizing participation.

PRA is a means of collecting different kinds of data, identifying and mobilizing intended groups and evoking their participation and also opening ways in which intended groups can participate in decision making, project design, execution and monitoring. It provides an alternative framework for data collection and analysis. Because of its participatory nature, it is an useful methodology to focus attention on people, their livelihoods and their inter-relationships with socio economic and ecological factors.

PRA constitutes a process of involvement with rural people for indigenous knowledge-building exercises. It is a way of learning from and with villagers to investigate, analyze and evaluate constraints and opportunities. It helps to make informed and timely decisions regarding development projects. The participation of rural people can be facilitated through PRA for planning, implementing and monitoring of rural development programmes.

PRA is sometimes known as Participatory Rapid Appraisal where the emphasis is on both 'participatory' and 'rapid'. The emphasis on 'rapid' however, is more in terms of data collection and less in terms of the process of development or even implementation of plans. Other names are also used for describing PRA, some of which are Participatory Rapid Rural Appraisal (PRPA) and Participatory Learning Method (PALM). PRA, as practised in the field has given rise to different schools of PRA with difference in style and emphasis (Chambers: 1991b).

The use of PRA lies in pursuing selected objectives through application of its principles, processes and methods. PRA sessions can be conducted with different objectives in view or there can be a mix of objectives to serve. Some of the objectives are as given below:

(1) for greater and better involvement of villagers by learning about their perceptions, experiences and capabilities;
(2) to generate information and collection of data for immediate or

future use;
(3) for learning about the impacts of earlier or on-going policies and programmes and to frame new ones;
(4) for estimating trends and ascertaining conditions of the issues at hand;
(5) for validation or cross-checking of data collected from other sources;
(6) for training of different categories of persons involved, in the development process, whether from the government, NGOs, banks, donor agencies, researchers, extension agents, scientists etc.; and
(7) for research studies on use of PRA and to suggest improvements in its methodology.

PRA is a process of participation with the villagers in which rapport-building paves the way for them to perform their own analysis and to express themselves whether by means of 'verbals' like narration or 'visuals' such as making a map. The final product of PRA would differ in output and content depending on several factors. The content is in terms of how the process is established and what methods are used and how the analysis progresses. Sometimes an exercise in PRA may not yield the desired results in spite of best efforts. Or it may involve long time logs before anything fruitful happens. Hence, the output of PRA cannot be predicted with any degree of certainty. Sometimes more time is required and better efforts and newer ways can make things happen.

Principles of PRA

The principles guiding PRA are discussed below.

(i) Optimal Ignorance: In order to minimize cost and time, the principle of optimal ignorance is applied by the facilitators which means knowing what is worth knowing and knowing enough to serve the purpose and not knowing the rest or not trying to find out more. Associated with this is seeking appropriate imprecision or avoiding precision that is not necessary (Chambers: 1992).

(ii) Seeking Diversity: PRA is concerned more with analysis of difference rather than looking for representativeness of results or data collected. It is looking for diverse rural events, different processes and forces explaining various relationships in rural communities.

(iii) Offsetting Biases and Triangulating: PRA is essentially a methodology to offset biases of rural development tourism (RDT) and the survey method. It aims at offsetting such biases by being relaxed and not rushing, listening and not lecturing, probing and not speeding indifferently and looking for participation of rural poor and other weaker sections of rural communities (Chambers: 1992).

The process of triangulating is an important part of PRA. For any data generated it is essential to check their reliability and validity by putting them to different tests. Triangulation is cross checking the data in different ways. This is done through use of various methods and by using different sources to validate information. 'Triangulation' is adopted as a principle to improve accuracy. It involves conscious, non-random selection in different dimensions such as (a) team composition, (b) units of observation and (c) PRA methods. Team composition is generally inter-disciplinary and can be constituted in such a manner so as to have the information generated from different perspectives. The units of observation can be changed in order to cross check the information gained and one has the option of going for deeper probing if necessary. Many different groups can be used in combination so as to arrive at views from different angles. Other sources of information such as secondary data sources can also be used. Again, different PRA methods can be used to test and verify a piece of information. For e.g., semi-structured interviews can be supplemented by farm maps, livelihood analysis and flow charts.

(iv) Listening and Learning, Learning Rapidly and Progressively and Learning through Participation: Knowledge of rural people constitutes the base for the socio-economic and agro-ecological information. They have their experiences, their history and culture, their ideas, their priorities and preferences. Listening to rural people helps them in portraying their points of view which otherwise remain unknown. The greater the interaction with rural people in the capacity of a listener rather than a speaker, the greater is the learning achieved. The amount of learning can increase progressively with participation of those who form the subject of enquiry.

These principles make for different features of PRA, some of which are that learning is iterative, methods are innovative and interactive and the process of PRA remains informal so as to facilitate participation.

The Foundations of PRA Behaviour/Attitudes, Methods and Sharing

There are three basic foundations of PRA. These are, (i) attitudes and behaviour, (ii) methods and (iii) sharing, which together determine the nature of PRA. Each of these is incomplete without the other. Since PRA is essentially in a participatory mode, the attitudes and behaviour required are those which are favourable to participation. There are certain kinds of attitudes/behaviour which are not conducive to participation. The attitudes of an outsider as a 'giver' of benefits to the rural masses or the behaviour of that of a 'privileged' outsider can act as a major stumbling block in communication. Without an appropriate mode of behaviour the rural masses can feel left out and be withdrawn and not wish to express themselves. Much of such an exercise can be a lost one.

In this section we shall discuss two foundations of PRA namely attitudes and behaviour and the aspect of sharing.

(i) *Congenial Attitudes and Behaviour*: Generally an outsider's entry in a village raises questions and curiosity in the minds of the villagers. Hence the behaviour of the outsider is essential in removing doubts and in building a rapport with the villagers. The behaviour of an outsider as a listener and a learner together with the quality of embracing errors, if any, reflect the true spirit of PRA. Friendly behaviour can have several advantages. It can help the outsider to gain entry or have acceptance in a village community. However, some kinds of behaviour can make for distortion of impressions of the villagers and can discourage them from expressing their opinions or can even distort the information required.

Not only are the behaviour and attitudes of listening, learning and having respect for rural people are important but also non-verbal behaviour such as the body language is expected to be in the tune with the attitudes and behaviours and should reflect correct signals indicating respect, concern and a serious intention to learn from the villagers.

Some of the beliefs and attitudes which can form a basis for appropriate behaviour so as to elicit participation are as follows:

(a) any knowledge and experience should be respected
(b) rural people generally have a storehouse of indigenous technical knowledge and experience which can be of great use;
(c) the rural people are entitled to have knowledge about rural development programmes, to express their views and to participate in their effective implementation;
(d) the outsider has an opportunity of learning from the rural people about rural life;
(e) the rural people are capable of rational decision-making, implementing, monitoring and evaluating it whether as a community, a group, a household or as individuals.

(ii) *Mutual Sharing*: Direct people's participation is a basic element of PRA. Without such participation, PRA is not feasible, for the outsider is not able to know and understand the systems within which the rural people operate. The outsider can guess, make hunches, try to impute his/her knowledge and values and attribute qualifications in order to understand rural conditions and processes. But an outsider's understanding tends to be far inferior to the one who actually experiences it. Whether it is participation by a community/communities, groups or individuals, the greater the participation the better is the quality of information generated through PRA.

On the one hand, it is important that a villager is willing to participate and share his/her perceptions and problems and, on the other hand, it is equally desirable that the outsider also has the necessary attitudes and communicating skills to evoke the necessary participation from the other side. If a person is not willing to participate then either he/she does it of his own choice or he/she does not find the behaviour of the outsider congenial and a PRA may not be possible. Hence willingness of rural people to share their knowledge and experience and their problems and priorities is equally important.

A PRA experience in a remote tribal village named Thippapur, (Andhra Pradesh) in India became a difficult exercise with the villagers unwilling to participate. The outsiders made gestures to appear friendly yet the villagers were not receptive to them. The villagers were not only apathetic but appeared hostile to the outsiders. Only after repeated attempts to speak to the villagers did the atmosphere slowly become friendly. Repetition of friendly gestures helped in rapport-building which gradually brought more and more villagers to interact with the outsiders. (Kumar Somesh and Kumari Santhi: 1991).

The attributes required in the outsiders are respect for the local people, patience and skills of listening and if these attributes are not reflected in the behaviour of the person conducting PRA then it can become a difficult exercise. The right kind of behaviour facilitates the application of PRA methods. Behaviour can influence the degree of participation and application of the methods. Opportunities for PRA can be conducted with better results when behaviour is congenial. On different occasions, during PRA sessions, villagers may not be willing to participate beyond a point for reasons such as tiredness, fatigue or jobs at hand. If stretched beyond such a point a PRA can become quite unproductive.

The Kinds of PRA

PRA can be of different kinds, namely, (a) exploratory (b) topical (c) deductive (d) research, training and statistics (e) planning and implementing and (f) monitoring and evaluative.

(a) *Exploratory PRA*: A PRA exercise can be undertaken for understanding broad patterns and trends in a rural society. Such exploratory PRAs are quite common to reveal different aspects of rural life and also suggest important issues to be pursued. It can form a basis for further probing into selected areas which appear important and useful. A theme for further analysis can emerge out of such exploration which can help in undertaking either a PRA exercise or help in framing a survey questionnaire on realistic lines.

(b) *Topical PRA*: This has to do with a particular topic which either constitutes the area of investigation by the outsiders or has been suggested by the villagers as a key area to be focussed. For instance, in a theme like 'seasonality' of rural life, PRA can help in exploring different dimensions of the theme under consideration. An exploratory PRA helps in placing the topic in the relevant context. Different hypotheses can be formulated regarding investigation of a topic and can be probed by means of different methods. Or an enquiry through PRA can take its own course without formulation of any specific hypothesis on the issue. A topic can be probed across different groups in a village, across gender, caste, age etc., as a community and over time. Its objective is to find out as much information as possible on a selected topic. It is intensive in its approach and can help in analysis of a particular topic at great length.

(c) *Deductive PRA*: A PRA exercise can be conducted on different aspects of village life which can then provide a basis for having information on themes not directly attempted through PRA. This can help in relating different aspects of the problem to other factors and also help in dealing with sensitive issues. Deductive PRA is especially helpful when used for themes which require tact and cannot be directly probed on account of the nature of the subject concerned such as communal tensions, class struggles, corruption etc. There can be some topics, which are efficiently treated through relating them with different aspects of village life rather than treating them through direct probing. For instance, to learn about the impact of local corruption in a village, direct questions on corruption may not yield much response. PRA sessions on different aspects of village life related to corruption would give indications of its extent and impact.

(d) *PRA for Research and Training*: PRAs can be for the purpose of research in the forms of participation, its processes and methods. PRA can be of a training type for training of different groups of professionals who are likely to use them in their fieldwork or for further training.

(e) *PRA for Project Design and Implementation*: PRA can be conducted for designing projects and implementing them. All stages of a project cycle can be based on PRAs. It can make projects more adaptable to local needs. If village communities or groups are involved in a project right from its initiation, the chances of sustainability of the project increases through people's participation. As shown by experience, if a project is exogeneously set up in a village, the chances of success of that project is low. The risk bearing inclination of the beneficiaries is expected to be higher in all cases where the local people or the intended beneficiaries participate in choosing the projects.

(f) *Monitoring and Evaluative PRA*: PRA can form a basis for monitoring and evaluation of projects and programmes. It can touch upon the problems faced by the community/groups/households in running of projects. With identification of problems, operation of projects can be better informed and solutions to avoid or resolve those problems can be sought through PRA. A 'before and after' comparison of projects can be undertaken for projects which have either involved PRA methods in project formulation and appraisal or those which have not used them at all. In the former case, it becomes easier for the monitoring process to identify the gaps between expected and actual results and improving the working of the project as far as practicable while in the latter case monitoring PRA can bring to light several aspects and areas not considered earlier or taken into account while designing the project and its implementation. However, PRA methods can attempt to provide an opportunity to rectify the defects of the earlier project planning and can suggest scope for possible improvement within the framework of project management.

For monitoring by PRA methods there can be a set of indicators proposed indigenously to guide effective implementation of projects. In case of problematic situations, monitoring through PRA can bring different groups in the villages together for conflict resolution along with other officials such as planners, implementators and other facilitators associated with the programme. Different kinds of impacts of the project such as socio-economic, ecological, and other short-term and long-term impacts can be examined and analyzed by the villagers and outside team for the purpose of monitoring. The flexibility in PRA methods would add to the flexibility in monitoring so as to work towards improving the performance of the project and in the process minimize the adverse consequences.

Participatory Methods and Rural Knowledge

The innovative nature of PRA has helped in adding a large number of methods to its inventory. Such methods have provided rural people with an opportunity to express themselves and have been instrumental in exposing various dimensions of their living which normally remain unperceived or under-perceived. There are different aspects of rural life not all of which can be expressed in quantitative magnitudes. Some of them can be quantified while others are better described qualitatively while some others remain hidden and elusive. Many aspects of rural life can be best expressed through ranking and relative comparisons, for example, ranking of households on the basis of wealth and well being analysis. Some aspects of rural life can also be sensitive and a direct approach to such issues can be a frustrating experience. A relative ranking and scoring of selected issues can enable relative comparisons without directly going into absolute measurements.

Indigenous Knowledge and its Sources

Before discussing the methods it is important to identify the indigenous knowledge sources which are available in rural areas. These sources are a rich repertoire of culture, practices, beliefs and approaches for understanding and appreciating rural people. Learning about rural knowledge base from different sources can be an important aspect of a PRA exercise. It can help to set the context of views expressed by rural people. Much of it is embodied in the art, history and culture of the place concerned. There may or may not exist books to read on local culture and practices but they can be better appreciated through other media of expression such as local art, culture, dance, drama, etc. Some of the sources of rural knowledge base are described below.

(i) *Local History*: Local history, whether found in research reports and books or narrated by villagers can provide background materials and insights for cultural perceptions. These can highlight socio-economic basis and the evolution of legal basis of land ownership and common property resources to explain local people's way of life. Oral history as narrated by rural people can not only be rich in content but can also serve other purposes for a fieldworker. It can be used for dating and putting ages to people as required by different studies, for instance, nutritional studies. It can also be used in trying to put a time scale on local vegetation change and can form an excellent way to break the ice with local people in order to initiate discussion on different topics (Mearns, 1988).

(ii) *Stories, Profiles, Case Studies and Portraits*: These are anecdotal evidences and other real-life experiences narrated by rural people describing different incidents and happenings in the area concerned. They are generally oral when recounted by the villager and they can help in depicting the conditions of livelihood, the major historical events and the coping strategies of the rural people. A study conducted in a village in North-west Pakistan describes how portraits and stories provided colourful descriptions recounted by the local people. These portraits and stories helped to bring to life the conditions of the local people which appeared difficult to be expressed through visual modes (Pretty, 1988).

(iii) *Folk-Lore, Folk Tales, Proverbs and Poems*: Each locality, tribe or community can have its literary and artistic materials which can contain a considerable amount of information depicting its local culture, the legends the rituals, the legendary characters and practices. One can know them from the local people and have them explained. These can depict the conditions, the beliefs, the problems, the perceptions, and the traditions of the community or tribe concerned. They can also form a basis to learn and interpret current conditions in the light of a community's culture and traditions.

Table 1

Indigenous practices and beliefs in Meenakshipuram Village in Kamarajar District, Tamil Nadu, India

The following indigenous practices and beliefs were found from the discussions held with the farmers of Meenakshipuram village by a PRA team. These practices were helping to increase and sustain crop production and in treatment of some common ailments.

* Crushed neem seed extract used for spraying cotton as a pest control mechanism.
* Goat pellet powder mixed with seeds and sown to improve germination.
* Pesticide use has eradicated Striga—a parasitic weed on pearl millet.
* Coriander sown in late karthegai (November) escapes from dew injury and yields more.
* Application of tank silt is very good for crops. It is used to cover manure pits.
* Tying snails shell around neck prevents abortion in goats.
* Sheep penning brings more wealth.
* Goats are primarily kept as economic buffer. They are sold during summer months when the income is low.
* Sorghum fencing: if sorghum is grown in thick stand around cotton fields it saves cotton.
* Growing blackgram in an intercrop is better for the next crop compared with green gram.

Source: Vijayraghavan R., Subramanian S.R., Pretty Jules N., & John K.C. (ed.) (1992), Participatory Rural Appraisal For Agricultural Research At Aruppukotai, Tamil Nadu, Department of Agricultural Economics, Centre for Agricultural and Rural Development Studies, Tamil Nadu Agricultural University. Coimbatore and IIED, London.

(iv) *Sharing Practices and Beliefs*: Sharing of practices and beliefs of villagers with outsiders can improve the level of interaction and can help in de-mystifying village practices and beliefs to the outsiders. The history of beliefs and practices of a community and their rationale, if any, can also be unravelled through group interactions. Table 1 provides an illustration of such practices and beliefs.

(v) *Traditional Management Systems, Farming Practices and Local Resource Inventory*: In order to know more about the background of a village, its traditional management system and local resource inventory can act as sources generating information about the local people, their conditions, their knowledge systems, their perceptions of local resources and their way of resolving problems through their knowledge and management capabilities.

(vi) *Village Analysts or Key Informants* can be found amongst the more knowledgeable persons in a village who can help in analysis of information and in raising issues for further probing. The current issues and problem-areas can be summarized by a village analyst and his or her views can be sought from time to time. However, the reliability and validity of such views can be cross-checked with those of others. There can also exist village organizations of different kinds which can be approached for gaining further insight into the issues concerned.

The PRA Methods

There is perhaps no end to discovery of participatory methods. With each problem there tends to be an appropriate form of expression, to explain a particular issue concerned. It also depends on the user who uses a particular method or methods to express himself or herself. PRA methods can be broadly sub-divided into (a) methods (indirectly or directly) supportive of PRA and (b) methods which involve direct participation of the villagers. In category (a), normally the outsider is active in data generation and collection with little or no involvement of the villager concerned. While in category (b) the villagers are involved right from the beginning and it is they who perform their own analysis and generate data.

The use of different methods mainly depends on the ways of expression which the villagers wish to adopt. The methods aid in participation and expression of views. Much depends on the relevance of the issue and the way in which the villagers wish to present it, their convenience of expression as well as their skills. The methods that can be used on different occasions will be different. Several methods can be combined in different ways in order to analyze issues at hand and conduct an appraisal of the subject under consideration. Some major methods have been described below along with illustrations taken from field situations.

Methods Supportive of PRA

PRA looks for support from different kinds of methods and uses both primary and secondary data review for gaining knowledge of rural situations apart from learning through direct participation. The method of direct observation can also be supportive of the learning process in a PRA exercise.

(a) *Primary and Secondary Data Review*: Before conducting a PRA exercise it is often possible to get some background information on the area to be covered. Such information can help in describing broad features and trends of the area concerned, covering different aspects at different points of time. Sources of such data can be both primary and secondary. The primary source constitutes materials gathered first hand and have a direct relationship with people, situations or events that are being studied such as court records, letters, minutes, memoranda, notes and diaries. They cannot be viewed uncritically which means one has to combine other materials and sources along with the primary sources (Burgess: 1990).

Secondary sources of data can be found in published materials which may include transcript or summaries of primary source materials. Some secondary sources are surveys, books, reports, plans, official records, census records, project reports, maps, aerial photographs, journalistic articles, newspaper cuttings, research papers and data files from computers. The organizations and individuals who are usually associated with collecting such data are government, researchers, statistical agencies, local level educational and technical institutions, non-government organizations, donor agencies, remote-sensing agencies etc. These are generally data collected through the conventional methods and one needs to keep in mind the limitations of such sources, the ways in which materials have been selected, analyzed and presented. For use of all kinds of documentary evidence it is important to guard against problems concerning authenticity, availability, sampling, interpretation and presentation. Documentary evidence provides data link up with other data-obtained through field research (Burgess, 1990).

One of the important secondary sources is aerial photography which can help to know more about the physical features of a certain area. They provide a visual medium to farmers to locate their land and other resources on the ground and explain them (Sandford: 1989). They reduce spatial bias which most field workers tend to encounter on the ground. Experience shows that farmers are quite comfortable with interpreting aerial photographs (Dewees: 1989). Two main field uses of aerial photographs are as aids for mapping boundaries of land and as focus point for discussion in interviews (Mearns: 1989).

It is worthwhile to mention in this context, that the conventional methods support PRA and can also help in evaluation of PRA.

(b) *Direct Observation*: An outsider as a facilitator can directly observe an activity in a village and also observe the effort, skill or knowledge involved in it and can have a first hand appreciation of the activity in question. This helps in forming preliminary ideas about activities or processes observed from close quarters. It is better than guess-work or forming such ideas from a distance or from a remote official headquarter. However, direct observation by itself is generally not enough. It has to be supplemented by other methods of PRA to make it participatory and in the process to enrich the information generated.

Methods with Direct Participation

There are different PRA methods involving direct participation, many of which include diagrams as an integral part. Diagrams help in building consensus and can form a base for resolving conflicts and difference of opinions. They help in cross-checking of information and building up of knowledge on that basis (RRA Notes: 1991). Any discussion is enriched by visual diagrams. They present greater details than what verbal discussions usually are capable of. They help in discussion of related issues important to different villagers, both literate and illiterate. They make the villagers feel interested and involved in discussing different aspects of their own village. They can be more objective than verbal group discussions since any changes to be incorporated in them can take place immediately and any error made can be rectified at once.

It also facilitates exchange of views on the basis of information presented in maps and diagrams. The maps are open for group discussions especially for those who do not have an opportunity to mention their points for discussion and be able to present their views in case of verbal discussions. In case of diagrams, people have the entire set for discussion in front of them and can go into finer details without missing any important point.

Maps can be made with great ease anywhere and they help the

outsider to have a visual impression of the issue under discussion. On many occasions, maps help in rapport-building exercises and in comparison of different views, cultural perceptions and changes over time. They reveal perceptions and preferences which are otherwise hidden and obscure. They form bases for data generation, planning, implementation, monitoring and evaluation.

The use of diagrams, however, has some limitations. Some diagrams drawn are too complicated to be widely understood. This can be avoided through appropriate notes taken as and when diagrams are being explained by the villagers. Sometimes it may become difficult to explain all parts of a diagram due to lack of space. The scope of diagram is limited in case of large gatherings (McCracken, 1989). Diagrams drawn on the ground using local materials, unless translated into paper or photographed, can be easily damaged and destroyed.

The major PRA methods involving direct participation are explained below.

(a) *Semi-structured Interviews*: Semi-structured interviews are partly structured and mostly unstructured depending on the response of the person or group with whom the interview takes place. It is conducted in an informal manner in a relaxed setting where queries emerge according to the responses received. It is a combination of the outsiders initiating interviews followed by discussions of rural people on the topic concerned. The villagers bring in different aspects related to the question. The interviewer being free to probe, frames subsequent questions according to the aspect concerned. The questions are required to be open-ended. Hence the interview can start with a few pre-set questions and further questioning would depend on the answers received. The interviewer generally has a mental checklist. This helps in maintaining a broad framework for the enquiry and for the flow of queries to be an orderly exercise with the progress of the semi-structured interview. Some important aspects of semi-structured interviews are discussed below.

There can be sequencing and a chain of semi-structured interviews. Different methods of PRA can be combined and sequenced such that information on the problems at hand, their causes and the required policy actions can emerge from a PRA exercise. Semi-structured interviews can be repeated as and when required. After presentation of visual diagrams verbal interactions become necessary for explaining the diagrams. Sequencing of semi-structured interviews with other PRA methods (which is discussed in a later section) help in filling gaps, refreshing memories and communicating one's point of view.

Semi-structured interviews can be conducted with different groups in a village or a community. This is one of the forms of group interviews. Apart from meeting casual groups in villages there are permanent groups based on common interests and activities. Permanent groups can be community groups such as those of small farmers or landless labourers, groups of specialist individuals such as rural artisans or silk weavers; and structured groups, involving a mix of individuals according to age, wealth, caste and religion (McCracken, Pretty and Conway, 1988). Outsiders can meet different groups separately or together to know of their problems and opportunities through semi-structured interviews and other methods.

There can be key probes through semi-structured interviews. Probing is continuing to investigate areas perceived as key issues in a PRA exercise. A semi-structured interview can be followed by probing into areas which the villagers perceive as important. Such probing can be through a combination of both visual and verbal methods.

Semi-structured interviews conducted for an evaluation-exercise of a poverty alleviation programme brought to the fore a critical point in loan repayment by beneficiaries. This evaluation was conducted in a few villages in the districts of Hooghly, Midnapore and Purulia in the state of West Bengal, India, for households owning income generating assets through an official credit-subsidy programme. Many of these households had a poor track record on loan repayment, amongst other problems.

The beneficiaries while discussing their problems expressed their views on problems of loan repayment. They pointed out that most of their assets were such that these generated daily income such as bullock/camel carts, rickshaws, selling vegetables, eggs and other commodities whereas there was no official provision for repayment of loans on a daily-weekly basis, in bits and pieces. Hence, even when they were willing to pay off their loans in tiny amounts they were unable to do so at the end of the day due to lack of arrangements for daily repayments. They were unable to save enough money for future repayments for various reasons. The beneficiaries preferred arrangements for loan repayments which would suit their repaying ability and time. This was an 'eye opener' for the outsiders who were under the impression that either the beneficiaries' loan-repaying abilities were poor or they were defaultors out of choice. The semi-structured interviews showed the individual problems of loan repayments which the beneficiaries were facing in an organizational set up which could hardly perceive the capabilities and problems of a poor person.

Concurrent surveys conducted to evaluate the programme indicated the number of loan defaultors, the average period after which they defaulted and the different reasons for default (such as loss of income-generating asset, sale of assets and others). The survey results, however, did not reflect the mismatch between the beneficiaries' convenience and ability to repay as indicated above and the official payment arrangements made by the banks.

(b) *Do-It-Yourself (DIY)*: The activities of rural people can be appreciated better if an outsider who wishes to understand rural realities does them himself or herself. Generally, it appears that such activities involve simple skills of rural people but can be difficult in actual practice. Do-it-yourself gives practical ideas of the complexities involved in rural activities. This can also help in rapport-building with the villagers. For instance, one can plough a field and have a first hand experience of the activities of a farmer or accompany a rural woman to collect fuelwood or fodder and appreciate the difficulties involved in such jobs. Such participation of outsiders in rural activities can often constitute the first step in rapport-building.

(c) *Maps and Models*: Participatory mapping is crucial to PRA and can be on different aspects of rural life such as social issues, resource, health, wealth, literacy, census, livestock, economic activity, social stratification, forms of livelihood etc. Such maps can portray the image of dwellings in a village, of farms and fields, water collections, forests, soils and of many other aspects depending on the topic under consideration. In participatory mapping and modelling, villagers prepare the map model of other village with chalks, colours and other materials either on ground or on paper.

It is a rich tool and is commonly used in PRA. It has enormous potential. Maps by villagers provide a basis for knowing different aspects of a village, for instance, the location of dwellings and buildings and land-use patterns as indicated by a social map showing the position of households in a village and their socio-economic characteristics. A village resource map can also show different kinds of a natural resources and micro environments. In a resource map, the villagers draw the resource profile of the village depicting different kinds of soils, rivers, ponds, trees, crops and micro environments. The problems can be described and discussed on the basis of a resource map along with the opportunities and the constraints. This can also form a basis for a transect walk to be undertaken from a selected point in the village to another or a walk in selected areas of the village. A resource map combined with a social map is shown in Chart 1. Once a social map is made by the villagers it becomes easy for them to describe locations within the village in terms of roads and rivers, the characteristics and conditions of the households, the ownership of dwellings and buildings and land-use patterns. In terms of poor and non-poor households in the villages, social maps visually present the location of such households and their key features. In addition, there is also scope for presenting other kinds of information regarding households such as the heads of households whether a female or a male, the dependency ratios, ownership of assets, cattle, beneficiaries under state programmes, health characteristics and so on.

The social map in Chart 2 shows literacy for each household of village Krishna Rakshit Chak of Midnapore district, West Bengal, India. The map illustrates the position of households regarding literacy and shows that some of them have a combination of both literates and illiterates. Such maps can have a direct bearing on adult literacy programmes.

In any village, social maps form an useful basis for identifying problems in different households, their strengths and characteristics. For example, a social map can form an excellent base for a health map indicating the health problems in different households. Maps can be followed by semi-structured interviews.

Models are an advancement over mapping and represent three-dimensional figures, therefore adding height differences in the landscape. They can be made with local materials. Models are useful for land-use planning and watershed planning, for which the problems, treatment and opportunities can be shown on the model itself. A model or a map can also be historical (representing past shape or form), current or futuristic (showing future shape of a village or area) (Mascarenhas and Kumar, 1991).

(d) *Transect Walk*: Participatory transect walks systematically involve walking with the villagers through an area and discussing about different aspects of land-use and agro-ecological zones in the village observed during the walk. A transect walk is a useful method for knowing rural ecological conditions. A walk from one point of the village to another enables the outsider to observe different aspects of rural ecology and to discuss with rural people about soil conditions, land-use patterns, crops, livestock, micro environments, agro-ecological zones etc.

The importance of a transect lies not only in knowing the agro-ecological zones in rural areas but also in getting an in-depth account

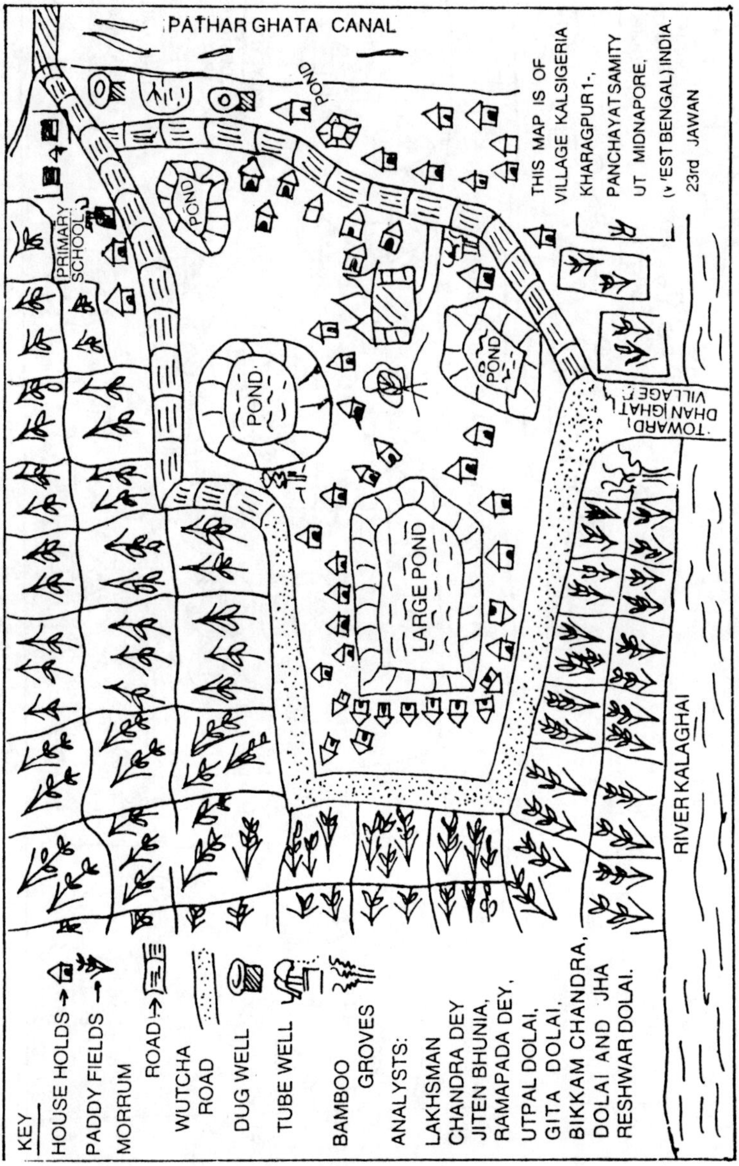

Chart 1 *Resource and social map of a village*

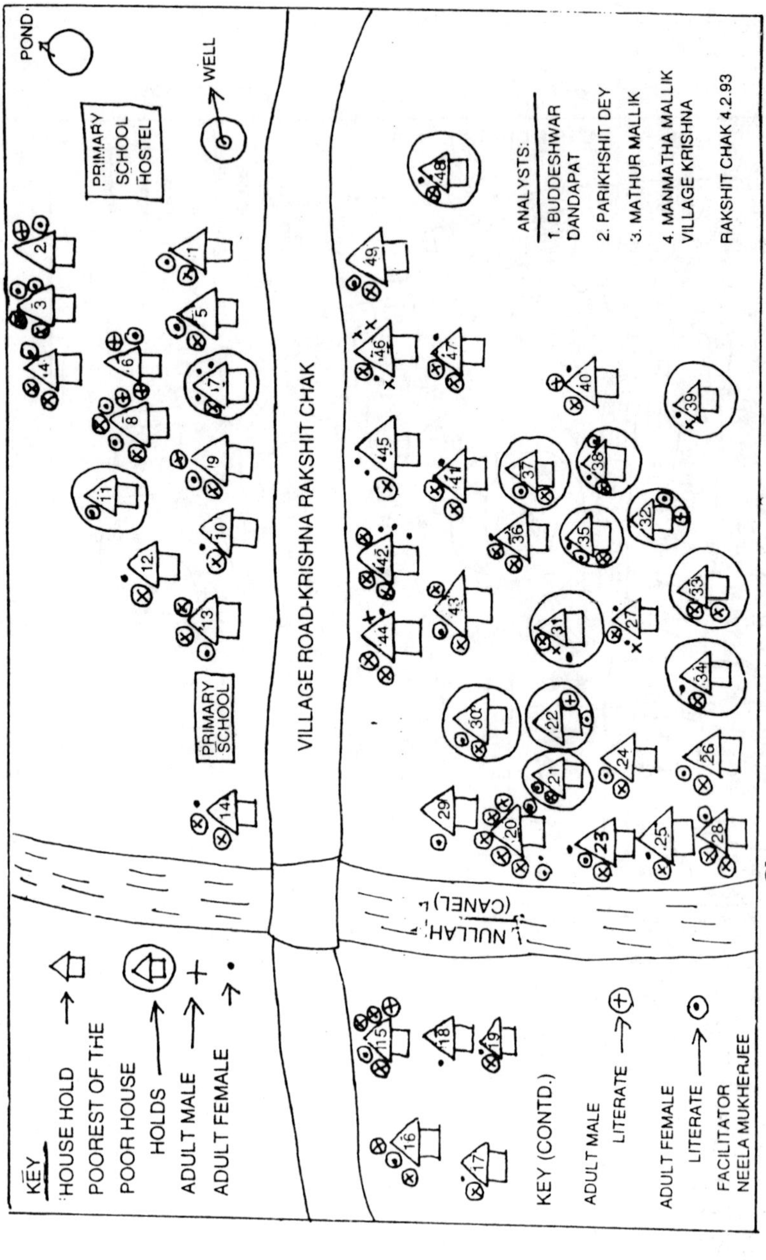

Chart 2 *Literacy map, Krishna Rakshit chak*

from the participating villagers of such zones in the village, their uses, problems and opportunities. One transect walk can be supplemented by other walks so as to enable the outsider to learn more about any village and clarify doubts.

As far as the rural agro-ecosystem of poor people is concerned, the physical variations in the village, the micro-environments and their use can be appreciated better through transect walks which provide visual exposition of the physical features of a village along with local people's interpretations. They help to overcome the 'roadside' bias associated with field visits (McCracken, Pretty and Conway, 1988). Transects help a team to carry out a detailed participatory appraisal of the agro-ecosystem of a village or an area under consideration. It can reveal villagers' perceptions about their natural resources in terms of either a resource-rich or a resource-poor village and the intra-variations in physical resources and agro-ecological conditions existing in the village. However, if a village is large and has considerable variations then it may be difficult to have a full grasp of the village through a single or multiple transect walk/walks. Transect walks across major agro-ecological zones can nevertheless be undertaken which can prove effective in conjunction with drawing of a resource map by the villagers.

The transect shown in Chart 3 is a village of Sidra Kordofan in Sudan. It describes different features of the area covered such as the soil conditions, the landuse, the crops and vegetation grown, the problems and the opportunities. A set of problems have been stated for each agro-ecological zone as described in the transect. The opportunities identified are also in accordance with the zones and different policy actions have been suggested which can be undertaken for the area concerned.

(e) *Seasonal Diagramming*: Rural livelihoods are integrally connected with seasonality. Each season has its own problems and the rural people have different strategies for their livelihoods. The seasons bear heavily on the physical conditions which in turn influence their lives. Seasons bring about differences in climatic conditions, in crops grown, in availability of water, food, fuel and fodder which in turn influence the living conditions in rural areas. Seasonal diagramming can lead to comparisons of related aspects of rural livelihoods such as seasonal variations and their linkages with food, employment, work load, disease etc.

Different aspects of rural life can be reflected through seasonal diagramming. A method which reflects the 'seasonality' aspect of rural

Chart 3

Village of Sidra Korodfan, Sudan. (Source: Theis Jorchim and Grady Heather M (1991), Participatory Rapdi Appraisal for Community Development, A Training Manual Based on Experiences in the Middle East and North Africa, IIED and save the Children Federation, London

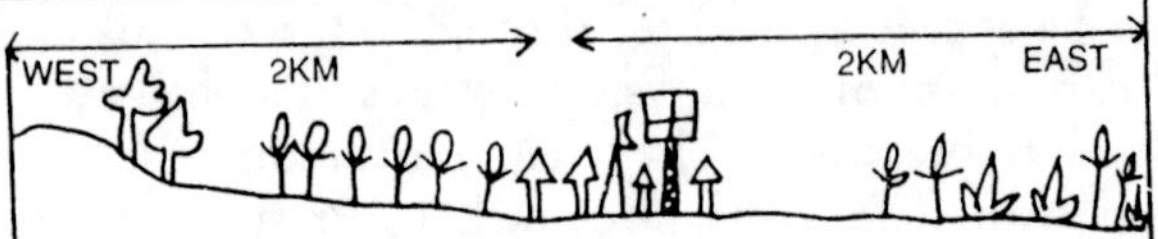

SOIL	.Rocky	Gravel	Gravel	Sand	Clay
LAND USE	Forest	Farmland Village	Village	Farmland Grazing	Farmland
CROPS AND VERATATION	Trees, Bamboo	Grass Shrubs, Middle, Sesame		Sesame, beans hibiscus	Sorghum, groundnuts
PROBLEMS	Erosion	Drought pests		Drought Pests, low Soil fertility	Drought
OPPORTU NITIES	Fuel wood, timber bamboo	Pasture Railfed Farming	Market Transport, Water Credit Health care School	Pasture rainfed farming	Flood Recession Farming

livelihood is a much better method than a picture presented by some other method such as questionnaire survey taken at two different points of a year. In the latter case, the 'seasonality' factor can either be neutralized through 'averaging' or conclusions can be drawn on the basis of a partial picture for one season.

In seasonal diagramming, the villagers prepare diagrams and charts (either with chalks or other materials) either on ground or on paper, of various socio-economic and physical phenomena such as seasonal wages received, food consumed, prices, crops grown, rainfall patterns, sickness and others. In such diagramming, the villagers can make diagrams for seasons/months/days showing the rainfall pattern, employment, labour activity, labour availability, food availability, food intake, disease, fodder, fuelwood availability, livestock disease, need for credit, credit availability and many other aspects.

Chart 4 presents a seasonal calendar of peasants in North Kordofan, Sudan which starts from the month of May. It shows the days of rainfall, crops growing on sand and clay, seasonal labour demand, allied activities like gum tapping, water sources, labour migration and seasonal variations in price of sorghum (Theis and Grady, 1991).

Chart 5 is a seasonal analysis of nine diseases in Udaanampatti village in India. It shows seasonal frequency of diseases of which for e.g., head ache is a frequently occurring disease while the frequency of diarrhoea is largely concentrated in the months of April, October and November. The chart can be directly linked to policy measures in terms of strengthening of primary health care depending on the frequency of a disease and its period concerned.

Food Calendar: Food calendar is a specific use of seasonal diagramming. Seasonal variations in food availability is an integral part of rural life and the PRA method of food calendar can illustrate food availability in different seasons. Both the quantum and the kind of food availability over different seasons or months can be shows through a food calendar.

In a PRA session in Nlaphwane village which is a resource-poor and a drought-affected village near Francistown, Botswana, the villagers made a food calendar as shown in Chart 6 and explained their seasonal food availability in a normal year. They drew a food calendar to describe the availability of food stocks, their staple food in different months and how they supplement it with other kinds of food. They started with the month of July in a normal year with adequate rainfall when they indicated that after the harvest they have 30 bags of staple food. The food availability dwindles slowly over different months and reaches seven bags in June after completion of a full year. It is supplemented through a wide variety of food from the 'wild' and other sources.

(f) *Ranking and Scoring*: The methods of ranking and scoring reveal priorities and preferences. They provide opportunities to rural people to physically rank and re-rank some items or preferences or some uses and explain their reasons for a given ranking. Matrix ranking and scoring is most appropriate when outsiders wish to obtain precise information relationships amongst several different criteria

Chart 4

Seasonal claendar, North Kordofan, Sudan. (Source: Same as in Chart 3)

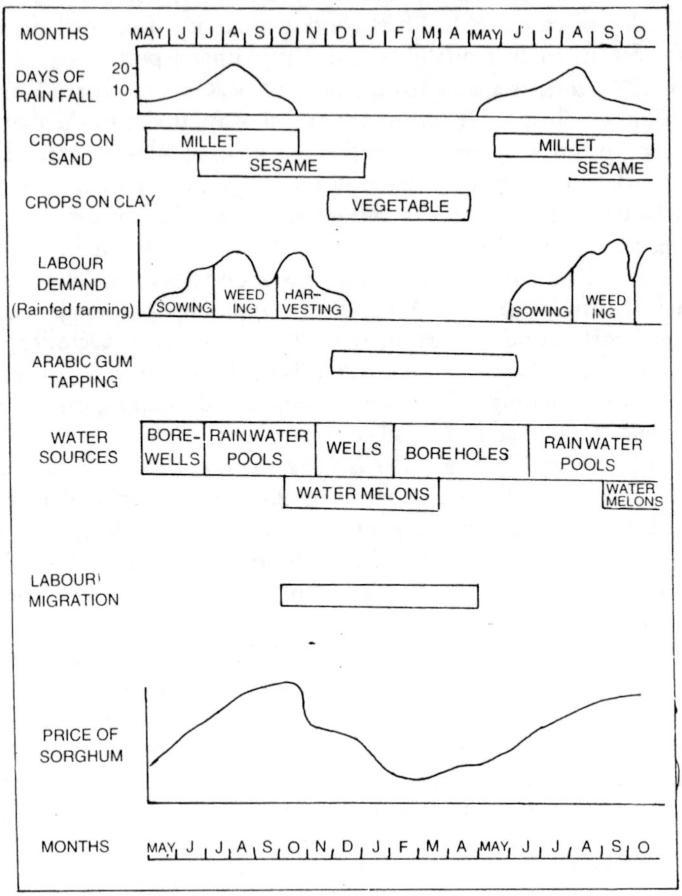

and wish to rank only a few alternatives, related to uses, preferences or priorities. They can help in understanding rural people's criteria for ranking as well as the relative position of their priorities, preferences and choice in matters of occupation, food, fuel, fodder, energy-use etc. They can be used for easy comparisons.

Ranking methods include preference ranking, pair-wise ranking, direct matrix ranking and wealth ranking. Preference ranking involves ranking of a set of problems/preferences/priorities by a group or an individual on the basis of their criteria or perceptions. An illustration

Chart 5

Seasonal health calendar of nine diseases, Udayanampatti village. Villagers used stickers to depict frequency of disease

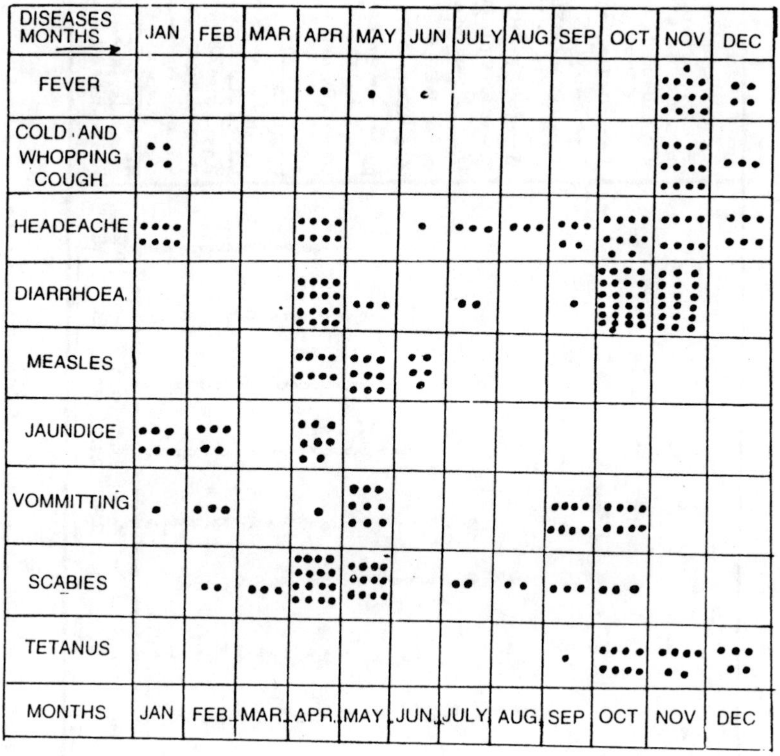

of preference ranking is given in Chart 7 which shows the relative preference for three kinds of cotton varieties with ten criteria. At the end of the matrix, the last row shows that the overall rating is in favour of the third variety of cotton.

Pairwise ranking: Pairwise ranking which uses two items or attributes at a time for ranking can be used to explore rural people's criteria for choosing one alternative over another. A villager or a group of villagers can compare one pair at a time and give reasons for the choice made. At the end, the most favoured choice is identified if

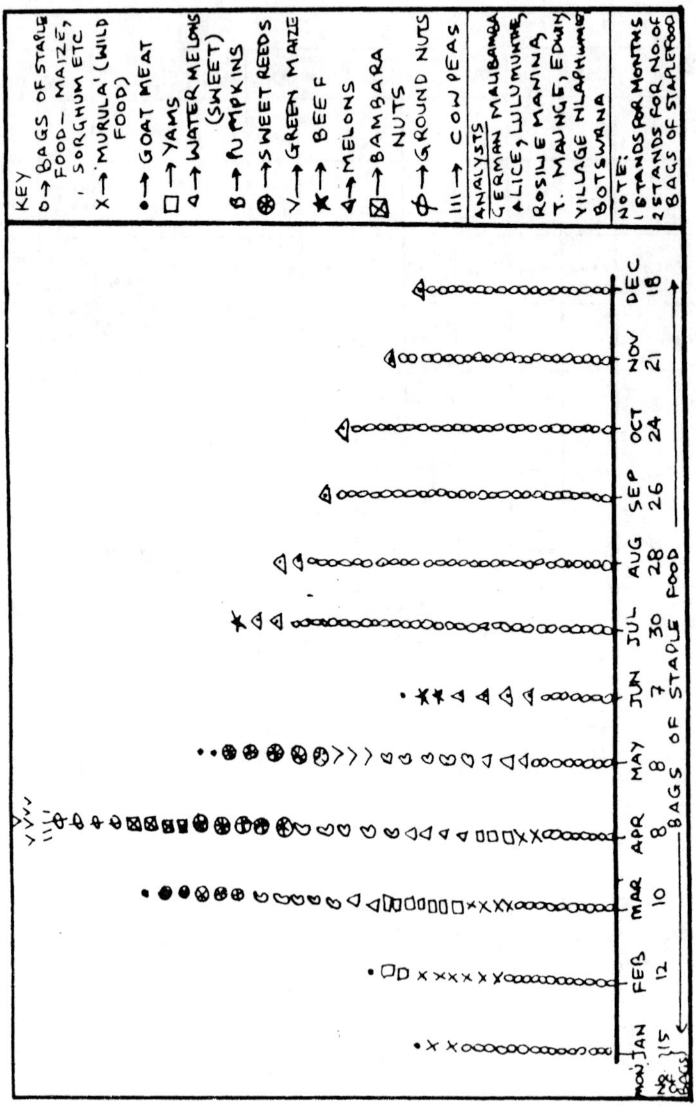

Chart 6 *Food calendar, Village Nlaphwane, Botswana*

Chart 7

Matrix ranking of cotton varieties

VARIETIES / CRITERIA	COTTON VARITIES		
	KARUN GANNI	LAKSHMI	LRA 5166
DURATION	XXXX XXX	XXX XX	XXX X
BOLLS/PLANTS	XXXXXXXX XXXXXXXX XXXXXXXX XXXXXXXXX XX	XXXXX XXXXX	XXXXXXXX XXXXXXXX XXXXX
BOLL WEIGHT	XXX	XXX XX	XXXXX XXXXX
PEST RESISTANCE	XXXXX	X	XX
RESPONCE TO MANURING	XX	XXX	XXXX X
EASE OF BOLL PICKING	X	XXX	XXXX X
POSSIBILITY OF INTER CROPPING	X	X	XXX
PESTICIDE USE	—	X	XXX
YIELD	X	XX	XXXX
NET RETURN	X	XXX	XXXX
OVER ALL RATING	3	2	1

it is a question of choice or, the major problem is identified in case of problems being ranked.

Matrix scoring: In a matrix scoring exercise, different attributes and criteria are listed which are ranked either on the basis of fixed scoring (say scoring out of ten) or free scoring (as many or as less as one wishes) according to their relative importance. An exercise in matrix scoring can illustrate its use in revealing perceptions of rural people.

An exercise on wild trees was conducted in Nlaphwane village in Botswana. The scores are presented in Chart 8. In the matrix scoring exercise, 16 wild trees along with their 16 uses were identified and score for each tree was placed in the matrix, according to its relative use. The villagers used seeds for free scoring. For instance, it can be observed from the matrix that 'Mupani' tree had the following uses (i) firewood, (ii) poles for making houses, (iii) fencing fields, (iv) fibres (v) edible fruits and worms, (vi) shade, (vii) animal fodder and (vii) less harmful insects. Each of these uses had a separated score according to their importance to the villagers.

The exercise of matrix scoring of trees provides a wealth of information. It shows how wild trees play a significant role in the lives of rural people. It also shows how the relative utility of each tree is different to the villager. The rural people are conversant with such uses because they use them in their daily lives.

(g) *Wealth Ranking and Grouping*: Wealth ranking/grouping is a method of ranking/grouping of households on the basis of income, wealth and other local measures of well-being. Different criteria can be used for wealth ranking/grouping based on rural perceptions. Wealth ranking/grouping is based on the presumption that rural people have the necessary knowledge to rank/group households which implies that they have knowledge of kinds and position of household assets other items and attributes of the households concerned.

Grandin's (Grandin, 1988) method of card-sorting is a method for wealth ranking where a list of households is prepared with each household having a separate number. The number of each household together with the name of the head of the household are written on separate pieces of paper which are then ranked by some key informants individually according to their criteria. The different criteria used in ranking by key informants emerges from their discussion on wealth classification which also helps in cross checking of the list and the final wealth classes are computed on that basis. Direct probing of wealth of any household is a sensitive topic. This method helps in ranking of households without any discussion of absolute wealth of the households concerned. Wealth ranking helps in understanding socio-economic disparities amongst households and reveals local criteria for wealth classification. It helps in stratification of a sample according to people's criteria for further study and policy making. It also helps in examining survey data from a rural perspective (Scoones, 1988).

One other way of wealth ranking/grouping is that of wealth map-

Chart 8

Matrix Scoring

	Criteria for scoring	1 Mupani	2 Moso	3 Moroja	4 Murula	5 Mize	6 Mbola	7 Nsunu	8 Mumu	9 Mbgeti	10 Mpawa	11 Swanja	12 Ntamba	13 Nkwag	14 Nthunu	15 Skese	16 Mpanda
		Matrix Scoring of Wild Trees, Village Nlaphwane, Botswana															
1.	Firewood	20	4	2		1	2	1		12					3	12	
2.	Poles for housing	7				12	8	11		11							
3.	Fencing fields	9				5	4	5									
4.	Fencing wells		10							8							
5.	Fencing cattle																
6.	Dashibhoma					10			8	8							
7.	Fibre-making	10														17	
8.	Squeezing beer								15								
9.	Edible	9		12	8				13		13	10	9	10			
10.	Shade	7		6	10				8		7					8	9
11.	To straighten wells									9					8		
12.	To grind seeds				12												
13.	Making of yolks						13									13	17
14.	Medicines				14	6						13					
15.	Less harmful insects	18	12	11	13						13	10	8	9		11	13
16.	Animal fodder	5	4		5		4	3	3		5		5	7	5	4	5

ping which can also be used to generate information on well-being of different households or members of a community through comparison of households or members of a community through comparison of households by different criteria of rural people. In a social map, wealth of different households can be identified by key informants, separately or together, and on that basis, they can be ranked one after another or formed into different groups. This can illustrate the socio-economic disparities within a village according to rural people's criteria. An interesting aspect of wealth mapping is that the points of distinction between households which outsiders' tend to overlook or miss can form an important basis for differentiating between households and their ranking/grouping by rural people (Mukherjee, 1992). As shown in Chart 9, wealth mapping has been presented as done by villagers in a village named Berapal in Sadar block of Midnapore district in West Bengal, India. The village consists mostly of small and marginal cultivators and landless labourers.

On the basis of the village map, the villagers attempted to group the households. They marked the households which were at the lowest strata of poverty according to their perceptions. These included the widowed households which had single widows as heads of households and were maintaining livelihoods with practically no assets, no regular source of income and not enough to eat throughout the year. Others in this group included agricultural labourers having neither any land, nor any regular source of income or food.

Identification of 'poorest of the poor' households was followed by the villagers marking the groups of households above the extreme poor group. They distinguished between these groups on the basis of land ownership. The group of households next identified was described as having better production from land. The production from land helped them in meeting their consumption requirements within the households as well as procuring income through selling a part of their produce.

Wealth ranking/grouping shows the patterns of wealth across households in a community as per local people's perspective. However, such patterns may tell us little about the process of wealth creation, impoverishment, and differentiation. Intra-household dynamics are also not fully reflected in such a method (Scoones, 1992). This however can be overcome by extending wealth mapping to show intra-household differences in a historical perspective.

The method of wealth ranking/grouping becomes cumbersome in villages with large number of households because it may not be feasi-

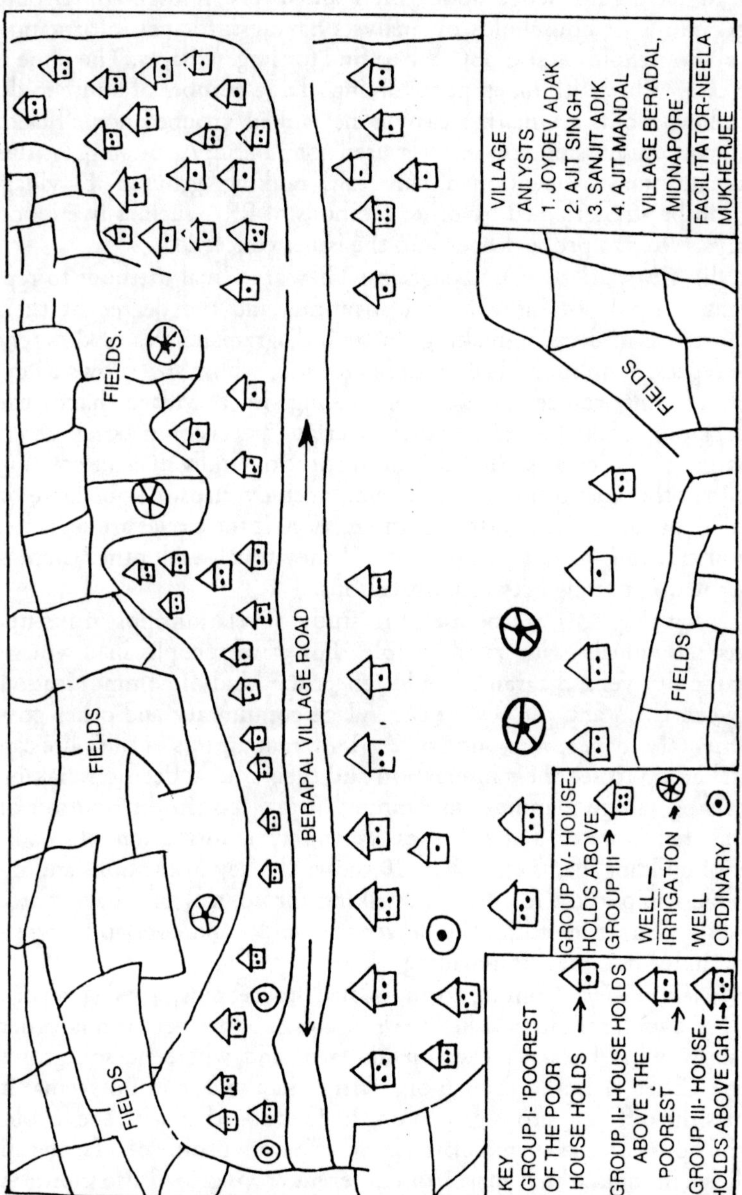

Chart 9 *Wealth mapping, village Berapal*

ble to have knowledge about each and every household. Grouping/ranking of households by analysts having sufficient information on all households is also not easy to find for large villages. The same is the case with wealth mapping involving a large number of households. The households are neither easy to be ranked/grouped nor efficient for group discussions on criteria used for ranking/grouping. In this context, it may be mentioned that wealth ranking/ grouping by villagers can be strengthened by other methods of PRA such as livelihood analysis so as to probe deeper into the issues concerned.

(h) *'Chappati' or Venn Diagrams*: They are visual methods to represent the role of individuals institutions and the degree of their importance in decision-making. In such diagrams circles of different size represent an individual or an institution, whose size shows its degree of importance in decision-making in a village hand the overlapping of circles indicate their overlap in decision making. Overlapping of circles arise due to one institution/individual interacting with another institution or individual. Such overlaps may be large or small depending on the extent of interaction. If the circles are separate, the institutions have no contact and if they touch each other there is information passing between institutions.

Venn diagrams can be useful in study of relationships of institutions/individuals with rural people. For rural people in a village community venn diagrams would reflect the kind of communication between them and the rest of the village community and other governmental organizations and NGOs. Different aspects of their life can be taken up to see their interaction and their role in decision-making involving village planning, in running of projects, in distribution of land, credit, water and other assets and in construction of roads, school building, dams etc. Chart 10 shows the key institutions and individuals important for decision-making for control of village water use in Sudan. It identifies the degree of contact and overlap between them in terms of decision-making.

(i) *Farm Map*: Coming to individual households, a villager with his/her own farm can be asked to draw a map of his/her farm in order to show what he/she grows on his farm and where he/she grows them. Chart 11 is a farm map of a farmer in a village in Botswana. It shows the different crops grown on the field together with the layout of the house on the farm. Chart 12 shows a farm profile of a farmer in a village in India which apart from different crops grown also indicates the soil conditions of the farm. The farm map is an ideal tool for knowing the minute details of a farm, its soil conditions, the vari-

Chart 10

Venn Diagram, village water use control in Sudan.
(Source: Same as in Chart 3)

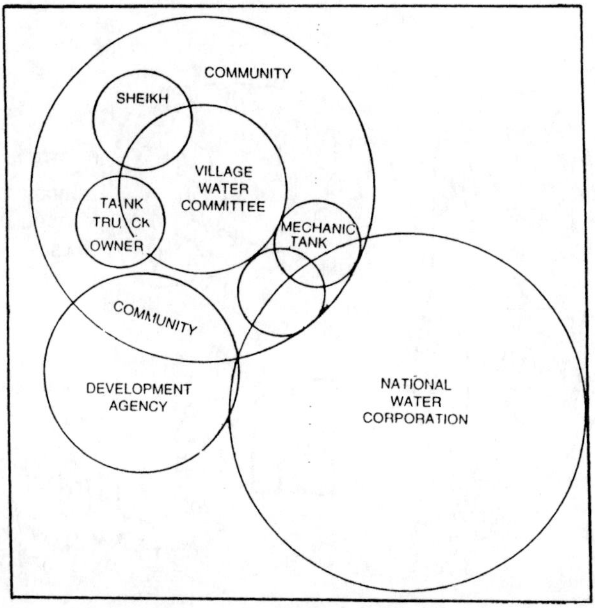

ations, different crops grown, water management, fertilizer use, yields and ownership. A farm map can help in sequencing of seasonal analysis or livelihood analysis to know more about livelihood patterns of resource-poor farmers.

(j) *Case Study*: A case study is a focussed study and can be undertaken either for an individual/household/group/community in relation to one or more events or a phenomenon or alternatively, it can be a study of some socio-economic or political change in relation to an individual, household, group or a community. The difference between the traditional case study method and the case study method of PRA is that in the latter case it is essentially based on a participatory mode along with the principles of PRA as discussed earlier. Case study method can be used effectively for analyzing coping strategies of rural households during say a famine, drought or a disaster.

(k) *Historical Profile*: Both past and future profiles of village and villagers are possible through PRA methods. In a historical profile, the

Chart 11

Farm map of Pai Pandian's farm, T. Meenakshipuram

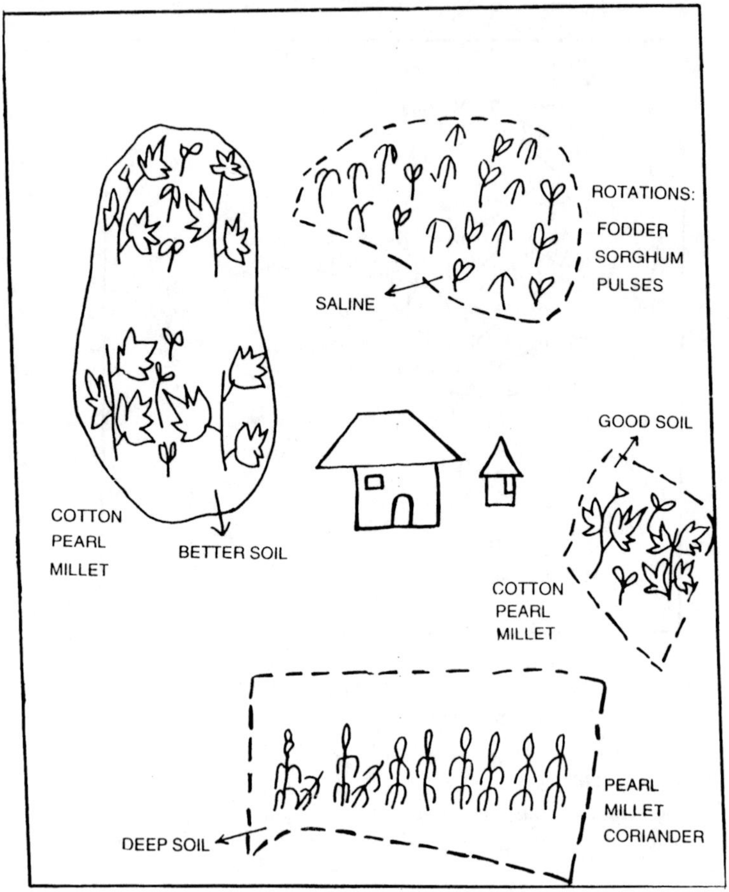

villagers provide an historical account of how different aspects of village life have changed over the years. It can then be used for probing various aspects of quality of life of rural people and the different changes which have taken place over a span of years. A historical transect or a time line are different forms of historical profile.

Historical transect: A historical transect can be done with a group of elderly villagers or with a single elderly person who has knowledge of their village for a long number of years and is able to provide a historical account of the village conditions. It can be done separately

Chart 12

Farm map. (Source: FAO, PRA Workship, Botswana)

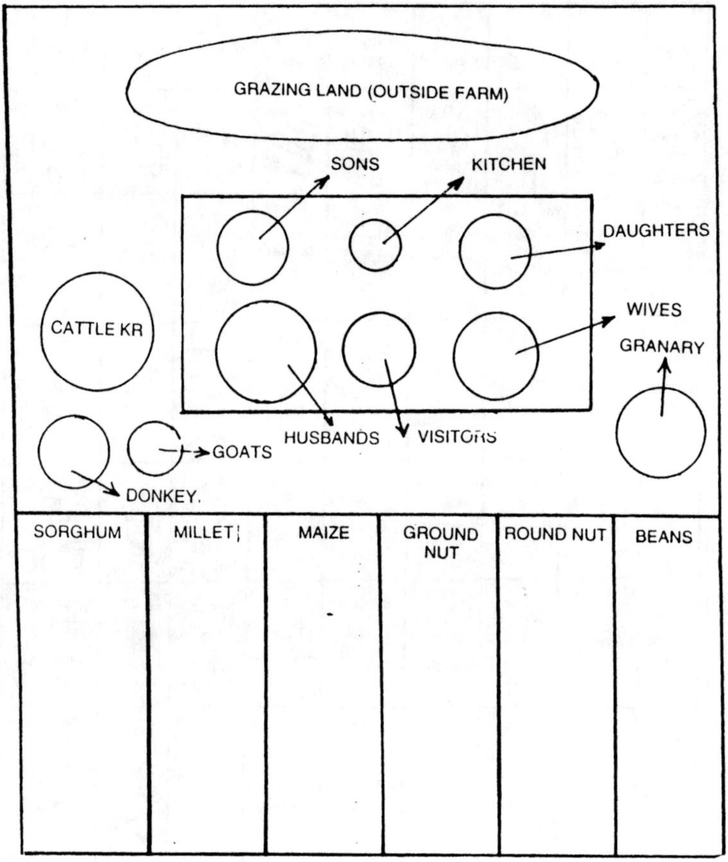

with males and females to bring out the difference in perspectives. The historical context can help in knowing the major events and changes in conditions which have taken place in the past for e.g., changes in cropping patterns of resource-poor farmers, changes in kinds and number of trees in the village, traces of environmental degradation, infrastructural changes in the village and others. Chart 13 depicts a historical transect for crops, animals, farm power and yields in an Indian village for the period 1940 to 1991.

Time line: In the method of time line elderly villagers narrate

Chart 13

Historical transcet for crops, animals, farm power and yield: village T. Meenakshpuram, participants farmers and elephant groups.

	Cotton	Pearl Mille	Sorghum	Finger Millet	Green Grazing	Bullock	Tractor	Yield
Crops. Animals & Power Yield Year							(HIRE)	
1940	Karun-ganni local	Nattu-camby local	Chenj cholan local	Natty kappai local	Poovain local		—	
1970	Karun-ganni local	local	local.	local	local		—	
1979	Lakshmi improved	improved	improved	local	Anjugam			
1989	LRA5166	Maha-rastri W.C.C75 local	Co. 4 K-tall local	local	local Anjugam			
1991	RA 516	W.C C75 X-10 local	K-Tall local	local	local Anjugam			

their life histories. Since it is often difficult to remember the exact dates of important changes, a villager can be facilitated to broadly connect such changes with major events, political regimes and thus, summarize major events and changes that have taken place during his/her life time.

It was through the method of time line, as shown in Chart 14, that information was given by an elderly villager on the historical wages, quality of food and environmental degradation in a village over a period of 70 years. As indicated in Chart 14, wage rate of a poor vil-

Chart 14

Historical transect, village Madhapur, Hyderabad, in Andhra Pradesh

APPROXMATE YEAR	WAGE RATE PER DAY	KIND OF FOOD	TREES
1920	Re. 0.06	CHAPPATI, GOOD QUALITY RICE	
1940-45	Re 0 15	CHAPPATI, GOOD QUALITY RICE, MEAT OCCASIONALLY	
1980	Rs. 1.20	INFERIOR RICE. PULSES, POTATOES	
1985	Rs. 10.00	INFERIOR RICE, DILUTED PULSES POTATOES	
1990	Rs. 15.00	RATION RICE, POTATOES, DILUTED PULSES (PREPARED WITH MORE WATER, LESS PULSES	

ANALYST - SRI ACHAIAH, VILLAGE MADHAPUR, HYDERABAD, (ANDHRA PRADESH), INDIA.

lager named Sri Achaiah of village Madhapur (Andhra Pradesh). India went up from Rs. 0.06 paise (Indian currency) per day in 1920 to Rs. 15.00 per day in 1990 but the value of money had fallen drastically. Hence, even with a considerable rise in wage rate his purchasing power had eroded over the years as a result of which he could purchase lower quantity of food. His quality of food had also deteriorated and he no longer enjoyed the option of having good and nutritious food. On the basis of the time line, he explained his years of hardship which started in the decade of 1980s and continued in 1990s. In these years he did have access to public distribution system to avail of subsidized food prices but he was forced to compromise on the quality of rice and pulses procured from the public distribution system. He was unable to afford meat and also ate less in quantity than earlier periods.

In the time line, he also described ecological degradation of the village over time as witnessed by him. The village and its nearby areas had a rich forest cover with wild life of different kinds which gradually started eroding over the years, and the village at present is full of boulders with almost no trees in sight. One direct impact of the disappearance of forest cover, amongst others, as explained by him was water shortage in the village.

The issue is whether the same information could have been collected through secondary sources. The secondary sources like a questionnaire survey would have provided either an average wage over time, averaged over regions and periods or a range of wages and would have neither indicated any qualitative information nor would have indicated experience of individual well-being and poverty.

(l) *Future Trends* : The future scenario can be visualized by rural people through maps, models and diagrams. The future scenario can be envisaged with regard to the outcome of developmental activities in a village, changes in ecology of a village, population changes etc. They can be explained on the basis of maps and models of a village through which the current position and the future possibility can be visualized and explained. This method can be used by rural people to express their expectations of the future shape of their village and the way in which this can happen, the kind of resources which exist and the size of additional resources required.

(m) *Time Trends*: This method shows quantitative changes over time in different aspects of village life such as yields, population, livestock population, number of trees, area under cultivation, rainfall, time and distance to collect fuelwood and fodder, prices etc. With the help of this method, one can directly or indirectly see the increase or decrease of hardship in poor people's lives. A time trend is different from a historical transect or a time line where the former is more precise in giving indication of change (an increase or a decrease) whereas, the latter can show broad movements of different aspects of village life rather than their precise shifts.

Chart 15 illustrates the trend in sorghum price fluctuations in El Obeid, Sudan. It is a way of visualizing changes over time on the basis of data obtained for a selected period (Theis and Grady, 1991).

(n) *Mobility Map*: This shows the pattern of spatial mobility for different sections of a community with respect to different activities. Patterns of group mobility of rural people can emerge from individual maps. Mobility maps of rural people based on socio-economic aspects, gender, age groups and other criteria can indicate the nature of work, wealth, interaction with outside world and interaction within communities and with other communities in a village. it shows the degree of mobility of rural groups and communities and importance of different areas in terms of their different activities. It also indicates location-specific activity profile.

Chart 16 depicts a mobility map of women from Qarara Area in the Gaza Strip. The map shows that the mobility of women takes place on account of different reasons such as work, health, visiting, shopping and education. The most important reason for mobility is work for which women travel from Qarara to at least 4 places, namely, Gaza city. Noseirat Camp,-Derel Belah, Khan Yunis and Rafah. The women travel to Egypt exclusively for the purpose of education. The map also shows inter-linkages between Qarara and Gaza city and Qarara and Khan Yunis whose links are the strongest in terms of mobility of women. The distance, however, between Qarara and Gaza city is far greater than that between Qarara and Khan Yunis.

(o) *Daily Routine Diagram*: Daily routine diagrams reflect the kind of activities which one does on a daily basis. It can not only show the time spent in different activities but also the size of the work involved. For instance, women spend different hours of day in activities like feeding children, cooking, fetching water, grazing livestock, collecting firewood and fuelwood. It is possible to identify general patterns from daily patterns. The general patterns of different groups can then be compared. Such daily routines can also be depicted on a seasonal basis in order to identify constraints and workloads of different groups related to different activities.

In Chart 17 a typical daily routine diagram of women in the Gaza Strip has been presented. The chart shown three groups of activities of

Chart 15

Time trends. (Source: Same as in Chart 3)

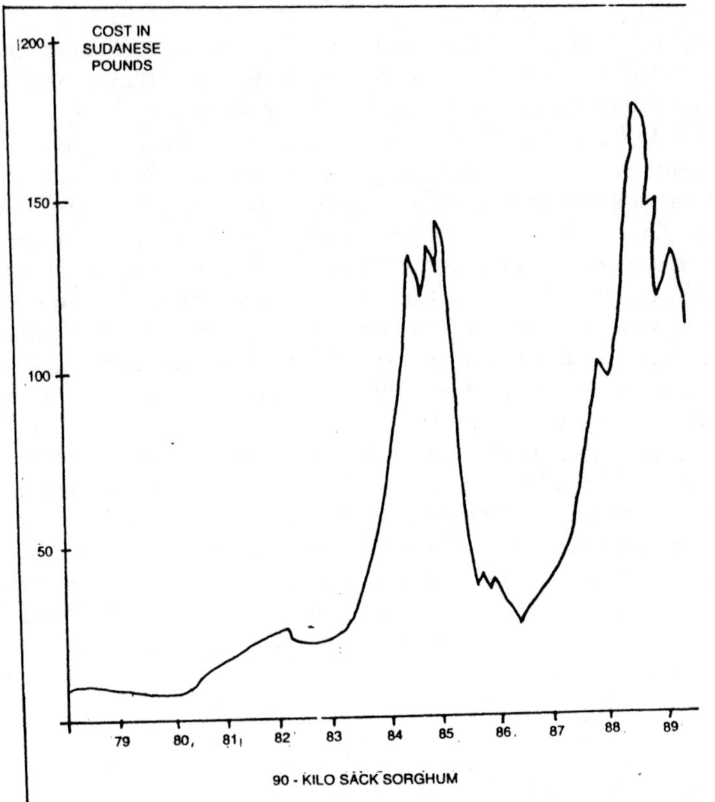

rural and urban women namely work at home, income generation and spare time for self as per different hours of a day. The lower part of the chart shows a typical daily activity profile of women where the time spent on various activities at different hours of the day is indicated.

(p) *Pie Diagrams*: Pie diagrams or pie charts indicate parts of a whole in proportional terms. It can show the use of land, water, credit and patterns of income, consumption and expenditure, sources of

Chart 16

Mobility map of women in Qarara, Gaza. (Source: Same as in Chart 3)

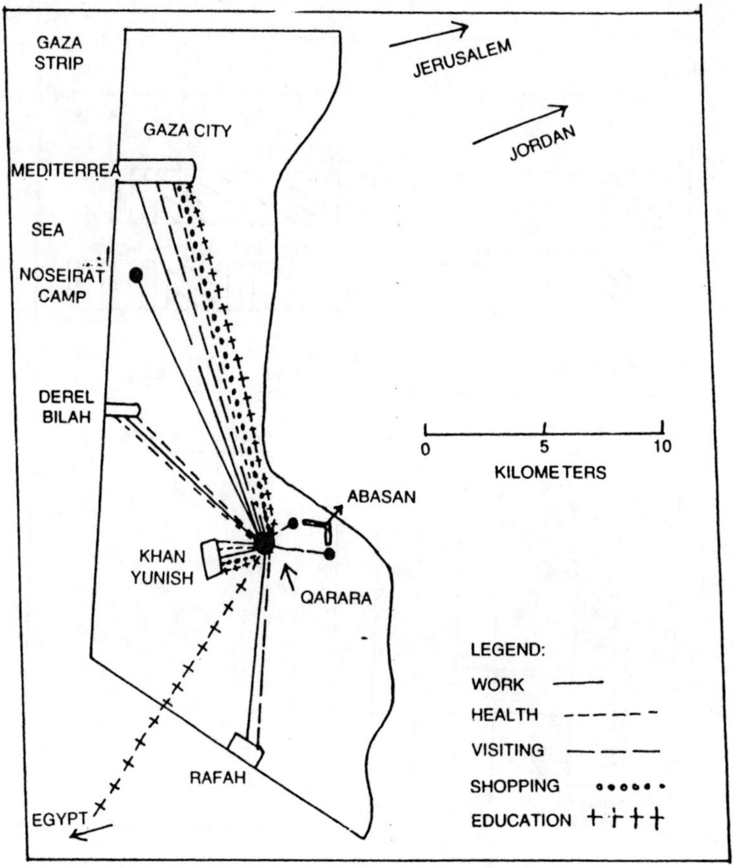

debt, medicines, kinds of trees etc. in lives of rural people. Chart 18 which shows a pie diagram for land utilization gives a rough indication of land-use, where agriculture constitutes 45 per cent of total land, followed by hills and river (35%), barren land (10%), school and panchayat (5%), houses (4%) and forests (1%). The chart also indicates the distribution of agricultural land during different seasons, summer, monsoon and winter, when land utilized for agriculture in the monsoon season is 75 per cent, which is the highest as compared to that in summer which is 10 per cent or the lowest. It shows that the propor-

Chart 17

Typical daily routine of women in Gaza strip.
(Source: Same as in Chart 3)

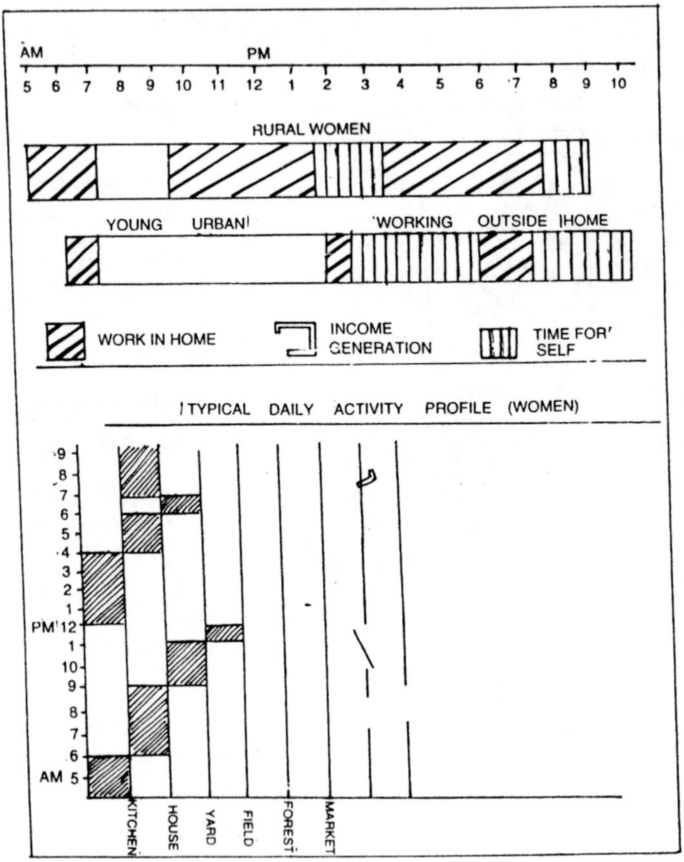

tion of land used for agriculture differs from season to season depending on the climate, availability of water and the nature of crops grown. Pie charts show the importance of relative items in the lives of rural people. In this case, the proportion of land used for agriculture also indicates the seasonal hardship of the farmer in terms of livelihood.

(q) *Livelihood Analysis*: One application of pie chart can be for analyzing livelihood. This depicts the behaviour and adjustment

Chart 18

Pie diagram of land utilization. (Source : Jayakaran Ravi (1991), PRA Camp at Mahilong, Bihar, 21-30 November 1990, Krishi Gram Vikas Kendra, PRA Notes, No. 13, August, IIED, London)

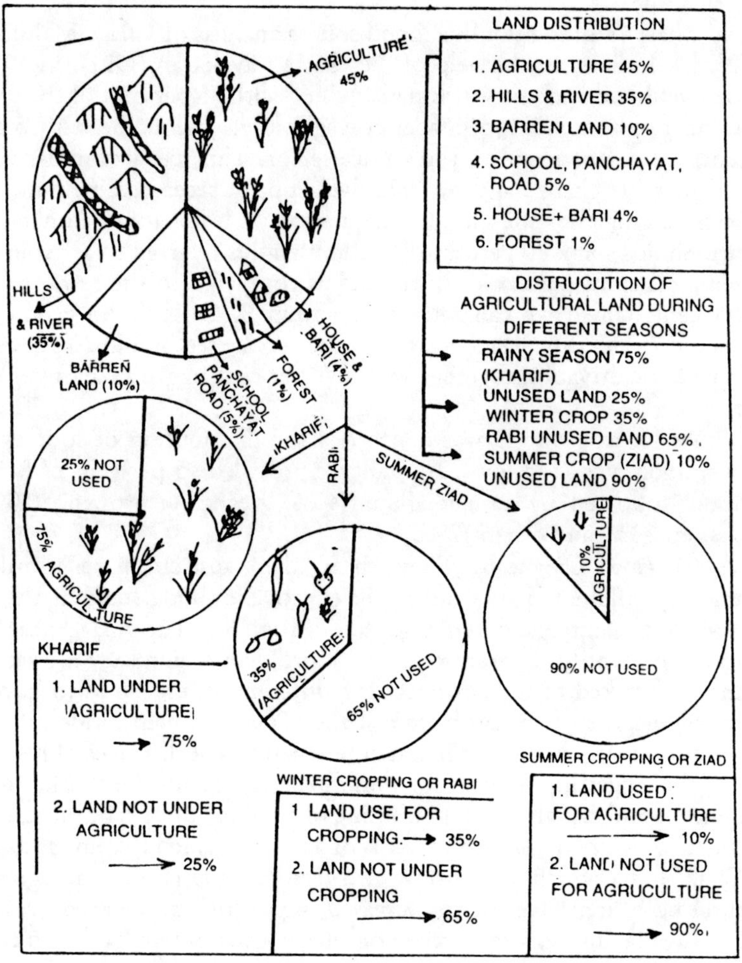

strategies of households with different socio-economic characteristics. Each household has a strategy or strategies to cope with difficult situations which arise from time to time. Such analysis can account for the size of the household, age and gender composition, wealth, assets, livestock, income and expenditure patterns, debt pattern, consumption pattern, seasonality, income by sources, disease and social obligations.

Chart 19 presents a livelihood source analysis of village Mahilong (Bihar), India with the help of pie charts (Jayakaran, 1991). In 1970, the livelihood analysis was less diversified with 75 per cent of the total number of households dependent on agriculture, while the rest (25 per cent) were dependent on the service sector. This scenario underwent considerable change and by 1990 livelihood sources became quite diversified for the households in question. Of the total number of households some 80 percent of the households referred to as group A had a different pattern of livelihood as compared to the rest, i.e., 20 per cent, which we can refer to as group B. Of those in group A, around 75 per cent were engaged in the service sector and 20 per cent in paddy cultivation together with five per cent in growing of vegetables.

As far as group B was concerned the distribution of sources of livelihood was as follows. Agriculture provided 45 per cent of livelihood, followed by casual labour (40%), vegetable growing (10%), business (3%) and others (2%).

(r) *Flow Diagrams*: They show the cause-effect relationship amongst different factors and can be effective for understanding the inter-linkages amongst different aspects of rural life. The villagers can be asked to identify different causes of a problem which they are facing and then asked to inter-connect the different aspects so as to have a causal analysis of the problem at hand. They can help in identifying the problems, the determinants, their nature and linkages. This can help in suggesting policies for minimizing constraints and other bottlenecks and can also help in framing of feasible options. For instance, the flow diagram as in Chart 20, is of a village named Krishna Rakshit Chak, India which shows how two factors, crop failure and agricultural pollution have led to increased impoverishment and decreased food availability in a resource-poor village. Lack of rain has led to crop failure which has lowered the availability of food/income. This, in turn, has led to increased dependence on common property resources, some of which have been affected by agricultural pollution leading to lower availability of food and increased starvation.

Chart 19

Livelihood source analysis, Mahilong. (Source: Same as in Chart 18)

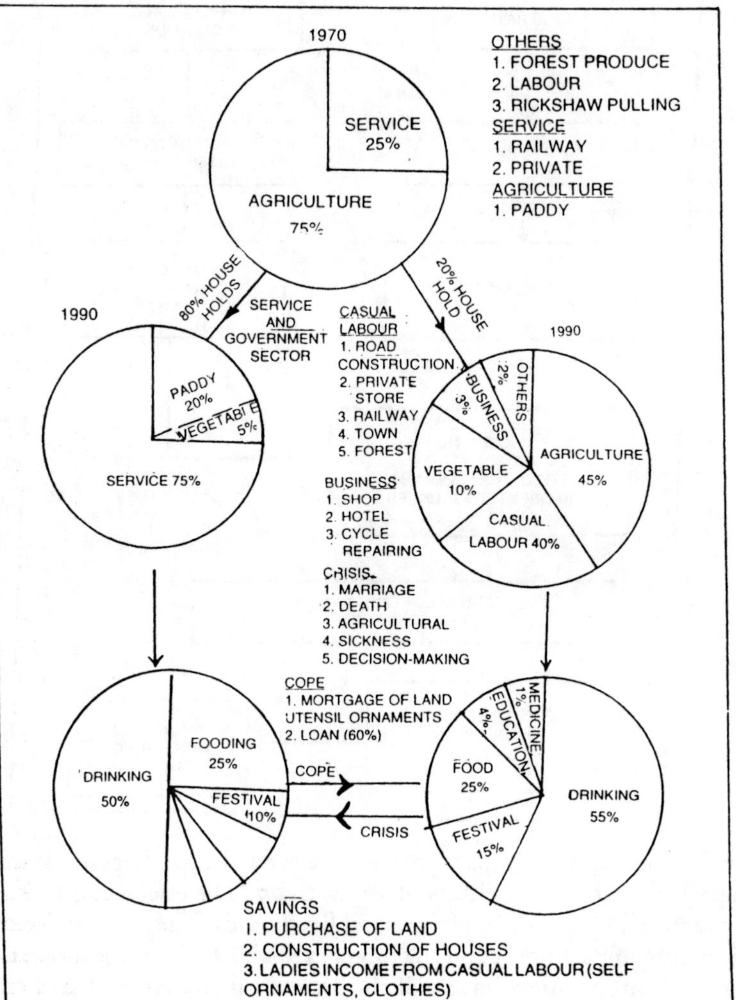

Chart 20

Flowchart village Krishna Rakshit Chak, India. (Source: As narrated by villagers of Krishna Rakshit Chak)

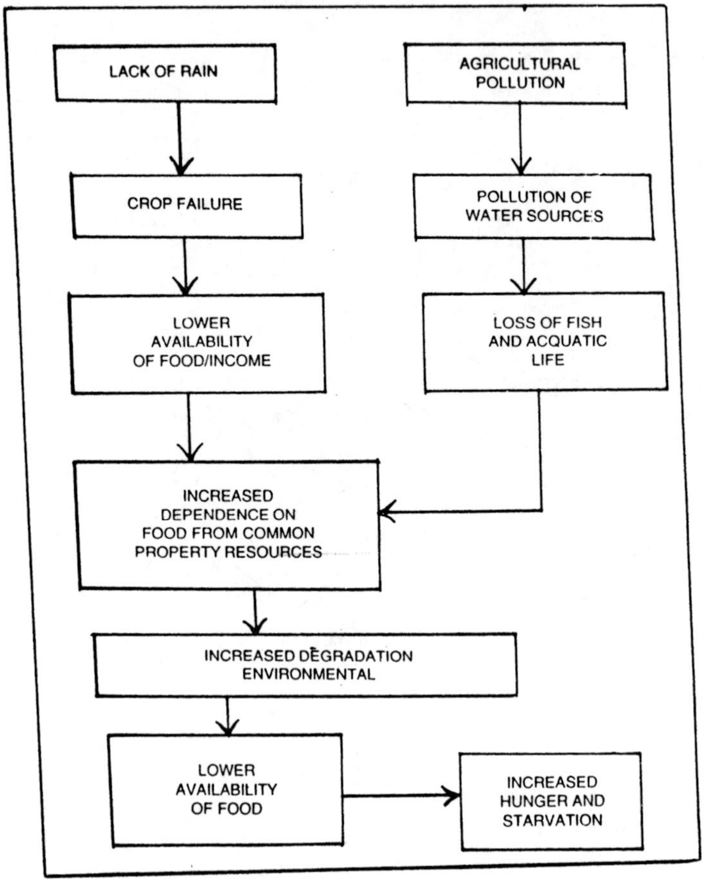

Impact analysis: Impact analysis is a type of flow diagram. It is an impact diagram of the effects of any activity. The effects can be both favourable and unfavourable on rural livelihoods. The impact diagram shows the impact point and the linkages established (or disrupted) as a result of interventions made (Shah, Bharadwaj and Ambastha, 1991). Chart 21 shows the impact diagram of irrigation tank in Gadechi village, India, in which the first-tier and second-tier impacts have been shown. The major impact, is on the fields from a series of socio-economic and other impacts (second-tier impacts) which have taken place

Chart 21

Impact diagram of irrigation tank in Gadechi village. (Source: Shah Parmesh, Bharadwaj, Girish and Ambastha, Ranjit (1991), Farmers analysts and faciliators in participatory rural appraisal and planning, in RPA Notes, Number 13, August, IIED, London)

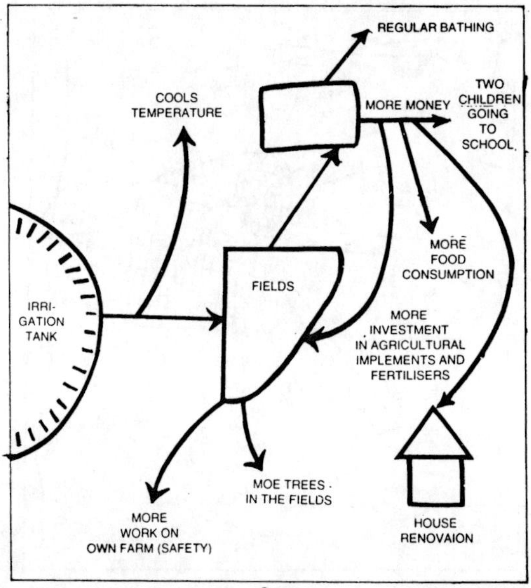

in the livelihood of the farmers, for e.g., increase in food consumption, more children joining school, more income etc.

Systems diagram: A systems diagram depicts a system underlying village life or that of an individual villager and helps in understanding the mechanism and constraints. It is a combination of a farm map with a flow diagram. In Chart 22 systems diagram shows a farm profile and flows of a small farmer in a village in Pakistan. It indicates the relationship between inputs and outputs and flows of output and location of different crops, water bodies and other structures on the farm. The intra-farm flows between each components are also described with the problems involved and the local responses (Guijt and Pretty, 1992).

Sequencing

PRA methods can be used in different sequences for appraising different aspect of rural perceptions. Much depends on the objectives at

Chart 22

Farm profile and systems diagram.
(Source: Guijt, Irene and Pretty, Jules N. (eds.), (1992), Participatory rural appraisal for farmer participatory research in Punjab, Pakistan, Sustainable Agriculture Programme, IIED, London.

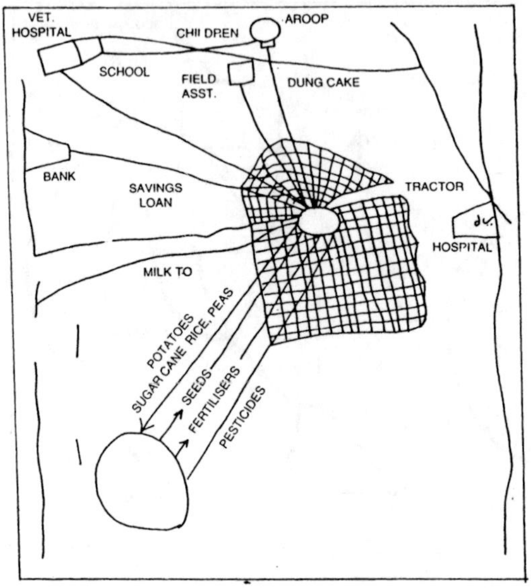

hand, the kind of data required and the use to which the data would be put. There can be different ways of sequencing of methods and using them in different combinations so as to increase their efficiency and utility in the kind of PRA being pursued. The strength of the methods increases with appropriate sequencing and greater information is generated in the process. Different issues can be explored and analyzed with methods used in different combinations. A social map and wealth ranking can be followed by a transect walk in those areas of a village where the poor people are concentrated in order to learn about their problems, opportunities and limitations. This can be followed by farm maps and livelihood analysis so as to know more about the crops grown and the soil conditions and the technology used by rural poor and the kinds of livelihood they have.

This can be followed by seasonality diagrams to have information about various related aspects. All these can help in appropriate interventions by the state or NGO, through project formulation and planning. This sequence can take a couple of days depending on the convenience of the villagers, the rapport-building and the facilitation skills of outsiders.

In another sequence, a resource map can be followed with a food calendar and a matrix scoring and ranking of wild trees. This can lead to placing of wild trees on the resource map so as to locate them in a village. Such matrix scoring can be useful for planning a tree nursery.

In case of planning and implementing programmes for 'poorest of the poor', the villagers can participate in wealth ranking to identify the groups involved. A social map can be drawn followed by wealth ranking so as to know the poor people, their assets and characteristics. Then individual households of the 'poorest of poor' can be approached for their livelihood analysis and the kind of support they look for in terms of the programme to be implemented. The criteria for evaluation of the programme and its monitoring can emerge from the rural people.

Sequences can be both short and long. The length of the sequences would depend on the topic at hand, the willingness, energy and time of the villagers and the information generated. Some topics can take more time than others and can involve sequencing of several PRA methods to reach the core. However, there can never be any hard and fast rule on sequencing since much depends on the situation at hand, the objectives of a PRA exercise and the way in which it takes shape. This is the novelty of PRA where it differs from situation to situation. It is a creative activity whose form and process are difficult to predict beforehand.

References

Burgess, Robert G., (1990), In the Field, An Introduction to Field Research, *Contemporary Social Research Series*, General Editor: Martin Bulmer, Routledge, London.

Chambers, Robert, (1981), '*Rapid Rural Appraisal; Rationale and Repertoire*', *IDS Discussion Paper* No. 155, IDS, Sussex.

Chambers, Robert, (1991a), '*In Search of Professionalism, Bureaucracy and*

Sustainable Livelihoods for the 21st Century', Typescript, I.D.S., Sussex, 28th May.

Chambers, Robert, (1991b) 'Shortcut and Participatory Methods for Gaining Social Information for Projects', in Cernea, Michael M. (ed.), *Putting People First, Sociological Variables in Rural Development*, Published for the World Bank, Oxford University Press.

Chambers, Robert, (1992), *Rural Appraisal: Rapid, Relaxed and Participatory, Discussion Paper*, 311, Institute of Development Studies, October, Sussex.

Conway, G.R., (1985), 'Agroecosystem Analysis', *Agricultural Administration*, 20 (1), 31.

Conway, G.R., (1986), 'Agroecosystem Analysis for Research and Development, Winrock International Institute for Agricultural Development, Bangkok, Thailand.

Conway, G.R., Mian, A., Alam, Z., Yar, M., and Husain, T. (1987), *Agroecosystem Zoning of teh Hunza Valley: First Iteration*-May 1987, Draft Report, International Institute for Environment and Development, London.

Conway, Gordan, (1988), 'Editorial—What's in a name', *PRA Notes*, No. 1, June.

Collinson, M.P., (1981), 'The Exploratory Survey Content, Methods and Detailed Guidelines, for Discussions with Farmers', in *CIMMYT Eastern Africa Economic Programme Farming Systems Newsletter*, April-June.

Dewees, Peter, (1989), '*Aerial Photography and Household Studies in Kenya RRA Notes*, Number 7, September, IIED, London.

Grandin, Barbara, (1988), *Wealth Ranking in Smallholder Communities (A Field Manual*, Intermediate Technology Publications, London.

Guijt, Irene and Pretty, Jules (1992), *Participatory Rural Appraisal for Farmer Participatory Research in Punjab*, Pakistan, IIED, London.

Hildebrand, P.E., (1981), 'Combining Disciplines in Rapid Appraisal: The Sondeo Approach, *Agricultural Administration*, 8 (6), 423.

Jayakaran, Ravi, (1991), '*PRA Camp at Mahilong, Bihar*, 27-30, November, 1990: Krishi Gram Vikas Kendra', RRA Notes, Number 13, August, IIED, London.

Jodha, N.S., (1989), 'Social Science Research on Rural Change: Some Gaps', in Bardhan Pranab (ed.), *Conversations Between Economists and Anthropologists*, Oxford University Press, Oxford.

Khon Kaen University (1987), *Proceedings of 1985 International Conference on Rapid Rural Appraisal*, Rural Systems Research and Farming Systems Research Projects, Khon Kaen University, Khon Kaen, Thailand.

Kumar, Somesh and Kumari, Santhi A., 'The Thippapur Experience: A PRA Diary, *RRA Notes*, No. 11, December, 1991.

Lewis, W. Arthur, (1955), *The Theory of Economic Growth*, Homewood, Richard D. Irwin, Illinois.

Mascarenhas, Jimmy and Prem Kumar, P.D., (1991), 'Participatory Mapping and Modelling: Users' Notes', *RRA Notes*, Number 12, July, IIED, London.

Mathema, S.B. and Galt, D.L., (1987), 'The Samuhik Brahman Process in Nepal: A Multidisciplinary Group Activity to Approach Farmers', *Paper Presented at the Workshop on Farmers and Agricultural Research:* Complementary Methods, Institute of Development Studies, England 26-31 July.

McCracken, Jennifer A., Pretty Jules N. and Conway Gordon R., (1988), *An Introduction to Rapid Rural Appraisal for Agricultural Development Sustainable Agriculture Programme*, IIED, London.

McCracken, Jennifer, (1989), 'Diagrams for Participatory RRA', *RRA Notes*, September, IIED, London.

McCracken, Pretty and Conway Gorlom (1988), *An Introduction to Rapid Rural Appraisal, Sustainable Agriculture Department*, I.I.E.D., London.

Mearns, Robin, (1988), 'On Oral History and Local Calenders: Experiences in the Field in Papua New Guinea', *RRA Notes*, Number 3, IIED, London.

Mearns, Robin, (1989), 'Aerial Photographs in Rapid Land Resource Appraisal, Papua New Guinea' *RRA Notes*, Number 7, September, IIED, London.

Mukherjee, Neela (1992), 'Villagers' Perceptions of Rural Poverty Through the Mapping Method of PRA', *RRA Notes*, No. 15, IIED, London.

Mukherjee Neela (1993), *Participatory Rural Appraisal Methodology and Applications*, Concept, Delhi.

Pretty, Jules, (1988), 'Portraits and Stories', *RRA Notes*, Number 3, IIED, London.

Raintree, J.B. and Young, A., (1983), *Guidelines for Agroforestry Diagnosis and Design, ICRAF Working Paper* No. 6, Nairobi.

Rhoades, R.E., (1982), *The Art of the Informal Agricultural Survey*, International Potato Centre, Lima.

Rhoades, Robert E., (1987), 'Basic Field Techniques for Rapid Rural Appraisal', *Proceedings of 1985 International Conference on Rapid Rural Appraisal, Rural Systems Research and Farming Systems Research Pro-*

jects, Khon Kaen University, Khon Kaen, Thailand.

RRA Notes, (1991), Number 13, August, IIED, London.

Scoones, Ian, (1988), 'Learning About Wealth: An Example From Zimbabwe, *RRA Notes*, Number 2, October, IIED, London.

Scoones, Ian, (1992), 'Wealth Ranking: Insights into Patterns of Rural Differentiation in Southern Zimbabwe', typescript, Sustainable Agriculture Programme, IIED, London.

Sen, Amartya, (1988), 'The Concept of Development' in Chenery H.B. and Srinivasan T.N. (ed), *Handbook of Development Economics*, Volume 1, North Holland.

Shah, Parmesh, Bharadwaj, Girish and Ambastha, Ranjit, (1991), 'Farmers as Analysts and Facilitators in Participatory Rural Appraisal and Planning', *RRA Notes*, Number 13, IIED London.

Shaner, W.W., Philipp P.F. and Schmehl W.R., (1982), *Farming Systems Research and Development: Guidelines for Developing Countries*, Westview Press, Boulder, Colorado.

Standford, Dick, (1989), 'A Note on the Use of Aerial Photographs for Land Use Planning on a Settlement Site in Ethiopia', *RRA Notes* Number 6, IIED, June.

Todaro, Michael P., (1989), *Economic Development in the Third World*, Longman, New York.

Theis, Joachim and Grady, Heather M., (1991), *Participatory Rapid Appraisal for Community Development. A Training Manual Based on Experiences in the Middle East-and North Africa*, IIED and Save the Children Federation.

Warren, Michael D. and Cashman, Kristin (1989), *Indigenous Knowledge for Sustainable Agriculture and Rural Development, Gatekpper Series No. SA* 10, Sustainable Agriculture programme, IIED, London.

Chapter 19

A Model of Economic Base and its Application to the Towns of Uttar Pradesh

H.N. Misra

That a city is always keen on developing its economy is true, for, it has to compete with other cities in a system for its spatial monopoly. A city aims at developing its dimensions in order to stretch its magnitude over a much wider area and thus render its people a strong economic backrest and yield a higher standard of living. The economic activities which are carried out exclusively for people living beyond city limits are known as external activities. Such basic economic activities promote the viability of a town or city over the space. In the absence of this activity the process of growth may be retarded and city's sustenance may be questionable. It may also lead to shrinkage in size of space commanded by a city through its economic linkages. A city also carries on simultaneously the internal functions to fulfil the requirement of local residents. However, 'the basic activities which are also referred to as external activities play a pivotal role in the economic resurgence of a town or a city in a spatial organization. The magnitude of basic activity determines the degree and direction of horizontal dimension i.e., the sphere of influence which is one of the major constituents in explaining the spatial system of towns. As both horizontal and vertical dimensions are interdepend-

Reproduced from Mahadev, P.D. (ed.) *Urban Geography*, Heritage, New Delhi, 1986.

ent, the nature of organization of a city system can also be explained through its basic activities.'[1]

Evolution of the Concept

The idea of economic base permeating as a concept in the urban geographic researches was first given by W. Sombart in 1902.[2] In view of its functional importance in expressing a city's regional relations, it later developed as one of the spatial concepts to analyze the system of cities. Several attempts have been made since then to identify, conceptualize and develop methods and techniques for isolating the basic activity of towns or cities from that of their non-basic activities. Olmstead[3] and Aurousseau[4] attempted to distinguish the two activities in 1920 and 1921 respectively. Otmstead identified the productive functions of a city as primary and ancillary. Aurousseau expressed an identical view. He, however, preferred the term secondary to ancillary. While defining the two terms Aurousseau observes, "The primary occupations are those directly concerned with the functions of the town. The secondary occupations are those concerned with the maintenance of the well-being of people engaged in those of primary nature."[5] Some of the important works in developing the concept of basic and non-basic activities are those by Haig and McCree[6] in 1927; Hartshorne[7] in 1932 and 1936, Hoyt[8] in 1939, Dickinson[9] in 1947; Andrew[10] in 1953, 1954 and 1955; Mattillila[11] and Victor Roterus and Calef[12] in 1955, Charles M. Tiebout[13] and Alexandersson[14] in 1956 and Ullman and Dacey[15] in 1962.

The concept envisages that a city produces two kinds of goods. One is used by local population and the other is needed by non-local population. These two types of activities are referred to as basic and non-basic activities respectively. There are several terms which are alternatively used for basic and non-basic activities, e.g., export, external, non-localized, primary, city-forming, urban-growth, independent and surplus for basic, and local, internal, localized, secondary, city-serving, ancillary, dependent and residentiary for non-basic activities. There are several theoretical objections against this concept. It is said that this is too simple a classification of otherwise too complex a functional system of a city. On account of practical difficulty involved in operationalizing the concept, this is considered to be only an academic exercise which may otherwise be useful as a forecasting technique for predicting the population of a city.[16]

Methods and Approaches

A city in its struggle for its existence has to develop both basic and non-basic activities. But both the activities are so interwoven that it is very cumbersome to identify the two separately, specially in view of the available census data on Indian cities. There are several methods which have been developed to isolate the two activities. These are (1) detailed survey method (2) approximation method and (3) minimum requirement method. Field survey technique, while most appropriate of all the methods, is not possible for a group of cities in view of the practical difficulties involved in it. This is possible only through team work. All the other methods such as residual or macrocosmic, etc., which belong to the group of approximation methods, are rather crude and are based on subjective value judgements. The minimum requirement technique is considered to be the most sophisticated because it attempts to minimize weakness arising out of subjective judgements. This method was first developed by Alexandersson[17] and later modified by Ullman and Dacey.[18]

Methods and Approaches Followed

A modified minimum requirement method has been followed to compute the basic and non-basic population of the towns. This modified approach has been evolved by combining the fifth percentile method of Alexandersson and the minimum requirement method of Ullman and Dacey. The basic, non-basic ratios obtained from these methods have been compared in the later part of the text with that of macrocosmic method and the minimum requirement method in order to test the validity of the modified approach.

The Need for a New Method

The Modified Approach

As it has been pointed out earlier, among the various methods evolved so far to compute the basic population, the minimum requirement method and fifth percentile method are considered to be quite scientific by geographers and economists. In the present analysis, however, the minimum required per cent has been computed by combining the two approaches. It has been done so because both the methods suffer from one or the other weaknesses. For example, Alexandersson considered fifth percentile as the fixed K value for all groups of towns irrespective of their sizes. This is too generalized an approach. Similarly, for an array of towns, the lowest per cent of population in an activity was considered to be the minimum requirement value by Ullman and Dacey. Certainly this method does not suffer from the weakness of fixed K-values as it is the case with Alexandersson's method. In this method, the values so obtained are regressed to assess the minimum required per cent depending on the size of the towns. This is one of the basic advantages of this method, for, it incorporates an element of dynamism by assuming that the minimum requirement value will go on changing with the increasing and decreasing size of towns. But the weakness of this method lies in the fact that very often the lowest per cent value (the first value which was considered by them as the basic per cent) gives a very distorted and absurd picture. Alexandersson tried using the first percentile, but found that this gave a distorted picture, because cities at the lower end of the distribution showed highly abnormal patterns.[19]

In the present method fifth percentile values have been considered as the minimum requirement values and these have been regressed for interpolating the base percent of different size of cities. This is because the fifth percentile cities, however, seemed in fact to exhibit more the characteristics that were expected of most settlements.[20] In the process, thus, therefore, an ideal town at fifth percentile value has been hypothesized for each group of towns under consideration.

The following assumptions have been made while developing the new method of calculating the basic population of towns:

1. The minimum requirement value of a function increases with increasing size of the city.
2. There is a different minimum requirement value for a different group of cities depending on the size.
3. The lowest per cent age of a size-group cannot be considered to be the minimum requirement value because often it is abnormal and absurd and does not represent the characteristics of the majority of settlements.

Data Base

The 1971 Census formed the basis for the economic profile data of towns. The six occupations considered for computing the basic population are, the household industry, manufacturing, construction, trade and commerce, the household industry, manufacturing, construction, trade and commerce, transport and communication and other services. Primary activity or agricultural occupation was considered insignificant from the view-point of basic activity in towns and therefore this was ignored. All the towns having population over 20,000 were taken into account while making application of the new method. In all, thus, 109 towns of the state of U.P. have been selected.

The following steps have been taken for calculating the basic and non-basic population:

Step 1: All the towns are arrayed into 13 groups based on minimum variance method.

Step 2: Towns of each group are arranged from lowest to highest based on the percentage of workers in each category.

Step 3: For each category of workers and also for each group of towns graphs were prepared by cumulating the population of towns. In all, thus, 13x6 graphs were drawn.

Step 4: For each group a town at fifth percentile is interpolated over the graphs which represents the ideal minimum basic requirement value. The values obtained for Household Industry are given below as a case in point (Table 1, Fig. 1).

Table 1

Population of Towns at Fifth Percentile and their Corresponding Minimum Values in per cent in Household Industry for 13 size Groups of Towns

Group no. of towns based	*Population of hypothetical towns at fifth percentile*	*Minimum value in per cent*
1.	14,38,353	4.20
2.	2,62,434	2.83
3.	1,78,743	2.07
4.	1,14,051	2.80
5.	77,373	1.38
6.	71,653	2.90
7.	60,567	1.60
8.	52,861	1.70
9.	42,260	2.02
10.	36,953	2.40
11.	35,121	1.83
12.	31,790	2.50
13.	29,423	1.78

Source: Read from the 13 Groups of Household Industry graphs (Fig. 1).

Similarly, as many as 13x6 ideal towns of different sizes were read for each function. These values, i.e., percentages and population, were then regressed and plotted (Fig. 2). The models based on regression

FIGURE 1

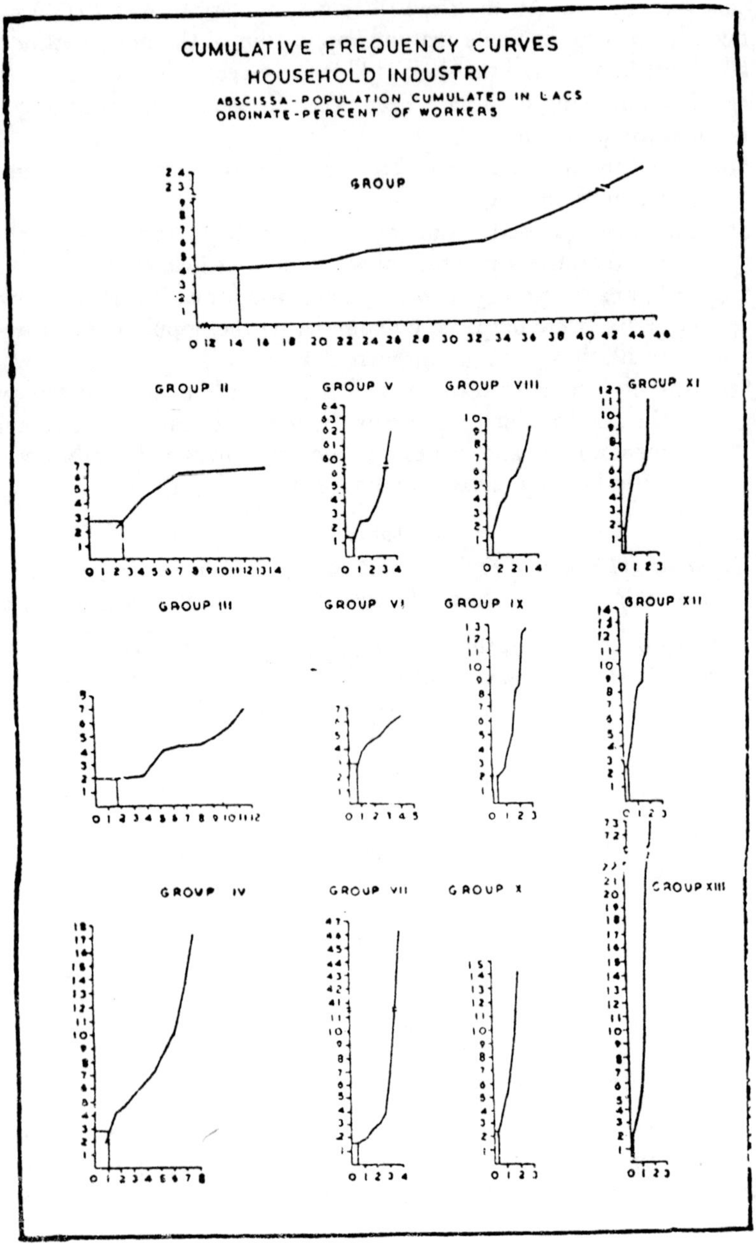
CUMULATIVE FREQUENCY CURVES
HOUSEHOLD INDUSTRY
ABSCISSA-POPULATION CUMULATED IN LACS
ORDINATE-PERCENT OF WORKERS
GROUP
GROUP II
GROUP III
GROUP IV
GROUP V
GROUP VI
GROUP VII
GROUP VIII
GROUP IX
GROUP X
GROUP XI
GROUP XII
GROUP XIII

FIGURE 2

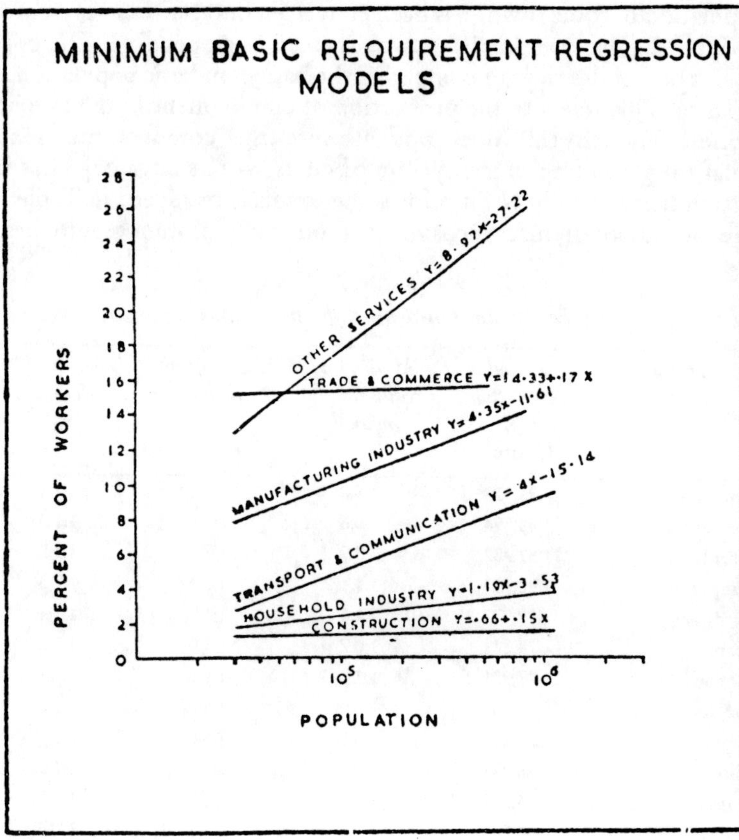

equation are as given below:

For household industry	$Y = -3.53 + 1.19X$
For manufacturing industry	$Y = -11.61 + 4.35X$
For construction	$Y = 0.66 + 0.15X$
For trade and commerce	$Y = 14.33 + 0.17X$
For transport and communication	$Y = -15.14 + 4.00X$
For other services	$Y = -27.22 + 8.97X$

Basic-Nonbasic Ratio

The basic requirement values in percent for the towns under question were read from these regression models (Fig. 2). The basic/non-basic population of some towns has been converted into ratio and presented in Table 2. The ratio for 109 towns is given in Appendix-I. The B/N ratio is one of the ways of comparing the basic-non-basic population at a glance. This refers to the proportion of employment in the two activities. Though this does not measure the complex functional situation prevailing in the system of cities, yet its advantage lies in its simplicity. The B/N ratio for some towns is produced in Table 2. The ratio based on macroncosmic method and minimum requirement

Table 2

B/N ratio based on different methods

Towns	*Actual population based on 1971 Census*	*Minimum requirement method*	*Macro-cosmic method*	*Modified Method*
Sambhal	86,323	1:1.8	1:10.2	1:3.1
Etawah	85,894	1:0.6	1:3.9	1:1.3
Amroha	82,702	1:0.9	1:5.5	1:1.7
Jaunpur	80,737	1:1.1	1:6.4	1:2.3
Hardwar	79,277	1:1.1	1:4.9	1:1.4
Hathras	74,349	1:0.7	1:5.0	1:1.2
Bahraich	73,931	1:1.1	1:6.2	1:2.1
Budaun	72,204	1:0.9	1:5.6	1:1.6
Hapur	71,266	1:0.9	1:6.6	1:1.6
Pilibhit	68,273	1:0.7	1:5.7	1:1.3
Sitapur	66,715	1:0.7	1:4.0	1:1.2
Maunath Bhanjan	64,058	1:0.6	1:1.2	1:0.6
Roorkee	62,456	1:0.5	1:1.2	1:0.8
Bulandshahr	59,505	1:0.7	1:4.7	1:1.1
Fatehpur	54,665	1:2.2	1:9.3	1:4.3
Chandausi	53,393	1:0.7	1:4.7	1:1.4
Gonda	52,662	1:0.8	1:5.2	1:1.3
Haldwani-cum-Kathgodam	52,205	1:0.6	1:4.8	1:1.0
Banda	50,575	1:0.9	1:5.5	1:1.6
Khurja	50,245	1:1.0	1:6.4	1:1.5

Source: Computed for Class II Towns of U.P. from U.P. Census Table, 1971.

FIGURE 3

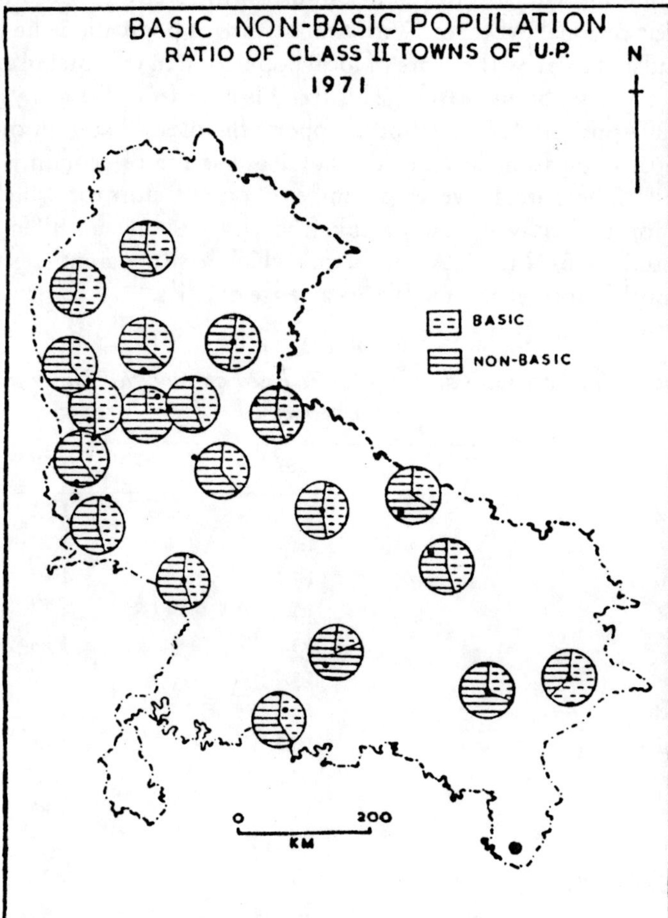

methods are also presented in Table 2 for comparative analysis. A comparative advantage of the three methods may be gauged from the fact that while minimum requirement method underestimates the B/N ratio, macrocosmic method overestimates it. The modified approach shows the value of B/N ratio at the middle range which is neither too high nor too low and, therefore, appears closer to the actual situation. A perusal of Table 2 (column 5) also reveals that the

B/N ratio is not very high. In most of the cases the basic and nonbasic population have almost equal share (Fig. 3). This is simply because these intermediate size towns in the urban hierarchy produce more for their regional existence. With the increase of population the local demand and thereby the share of local population in the total product of the city goes on increasing. This trend is clear from the analysis of table in Appendix 1. It therefore, supports the thesis that with the increase of population in cities the non-basic sector of economy also increases. There are, however, a number of other factors too which directly or indirectly operate within the city system and affect the magnitude of B/N ratio. A few factors which have apparent effect are locational factors, economic factors and age of cities.[21]

Table 3

Changes in B/N ratio during 1961-71 based on Modified Minimum requirement method

Towns	*1961*	*1971*
Sambhal	1:2.7	1:3.1
Etawah	1:1.1	1:1.3
Amroha	1:1.3	1:1.7
Jaunpur	1:1.9	1:2.3
Hardwar	1:1.2	1:1.4
Hathras	1:1.0	1:1.2
Bahraich	1:1.3	1:2.1
Budaun	1:1.3	1:1.6
Hapur	1:1.2	1:1.7
Pilibhit	1:1.2	1:1.3
Sitapur	1:1.0	1:1.2
Maunath Bhanjan	1:1.5	1:0.6
Roorkee	1:0.7	1:0.8
Bulandshahr	1:1.0	1:1.1
Fatehpur	1:1.0	1:4.3
Chandausi	1:1.3	1:1.4
Gonda	1:1.0	1:1.4
Haldwani-cum-Kathgodam	1:0.9	1:1.0
Banda	1:1.1	1:1.6
Khujra	1:1.0	1:1.5

Source: Computed for Class II Towns of U.P. from U.P. Census Tables, 1961 and 1971.

Table 3 has been produced to show the changes in the structure of B/N ratio over a period of ten years (1961-71). From this table it may be observed that the production of non-basic population has increased in all the towns under consideration. It may, therefore, be very useful to find out the possible causes of explanation for the changes which have taken place in B/N ratio in the towns. For this an inter-relationship of as many as four variables has been examined by formulating the following hypotheses:

(i) Total population influences total workers.
(ii) The percentage of basic and non-basic workers is closely correlated with the growth of total workers.
(iii) The growth of population affects the size of basic or non-basic workers.
(iv) Basic and non-basic population are dependent on each other i.e., size of one affects the size of the other.

An intercorrelation matrix by taking into account 109 towns has been presented in Table 4. The four variables considered for the purpose of intercorrelation matrix are:

Var 01 = Per cent growth of total population of towns (1961-71).
Var 02 = Per cent growth of total workers in towns (1961-1971).
Var 03 = Per cent growth of basic workers in towns (1961-71).
Var 04 = Per cent growth of non-basic workers in towns (1961-71).

From this matrix (Table 4) it is clear that except variables three and four all other variables are significantly correlated with each other. Thus all the hypotheses except four are valid, which means that the growth of population affects growth of total workers and basic/non-basic workers and vice-versa.

Table 4

Intercorrelation matrix of four variables for 109 towns of UP

From	*Var 01*	*Var 02*	*To* *Var 03*	*Var 04*
Var 01	0	—	—	—
Var 02	0.64[x]	0	—	—
Var 03	0.40[x]	0.41[x]	0	—
Var 04	0.37[x]	0.56[x]	—0.25	0

[x]Values are significant at .05 per cent confidence level.

FIGURE 4

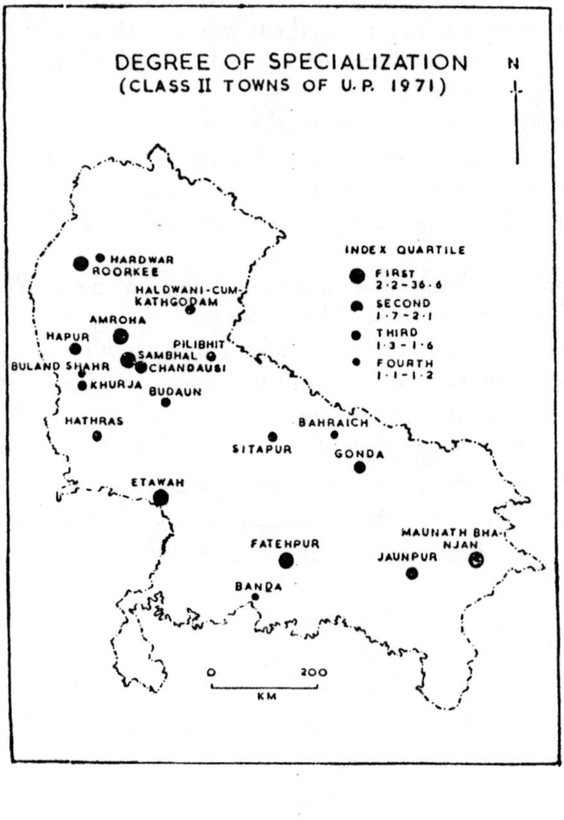

Index of Specialization

The minimum per cent age value computed for obtaining the basic population may also be used fruitfully to assess the specialization characteristics of town in different functions. The index of specialization may be computed by the formula given below:

$$IS = \Sigma_i \left[\frac{(P_i - M_i)^2}{M_i}\right] \div \frac{(\Sigma_i\ P_i - \Sigma_i\ M_i)^2}{\Sigma_i\ M_i}$$

Where, IS is the index of specialization.

i refers to each of the individual industries.

P_i refers to the percentage of total labour force employed in each of the industries.

M_i refers to the minimum requirement for each industry.

E_i refers to the sum of all industries.

Based on the above equation the Specialization Index was computed and results so obtained are presented in Table 5. A map (Fig. 4) showing index of specialization has also been prepared for comparative analysis of some towns.

Table 5

The index of specialization of the towns

Towns	*IS*	*Towns*	*IS*
Sambhal	14.6	Sitapur	1.3
Etawah	2.2	Maunath	36.6
Amroha	2.2	Roorkee	3.6
Jaunpur	2.0	Bulandshahr	1.1
Hardwar	1.3	Fatehpur	2.5
Hathras	1.5	Chandausi	1.9
Bahraich	1.2	Gonda	1.8
Budaun	1.3	Haldwani-cum-Kathgodam	1.6
Hapur	1.7	Banda	1.2
Pilibhit	1.6	Khurja	1.3

The ones having a high index of specialization are Maunath Bhanjan (36.6), Sambhal (14.6) and Roorkee (3.6). While first two specialize in household industry, Roorkee specializes in other services. These towns with high index of specialization may be very sensitive to any change such as change in the economic and industrial policy of government or any economic distress, for example, dirth of raw material. The high index of specialization reduces functional diversity and thereby the centrality on the space. Most of the towns, however, appear to have diversified characteristics and the range of specialization is between 3.0 and 1.0. These towns, on account of their diversified nature, are likely to develop into important central places in the hierarchy of urban settlement system in the near future.

Conclusion

A review of the concept reveals that it is a fairly old one and several techniques have been used to measure the basic-nonbasic employment ratio. But owing to methodological difficulties involved in it, the literature dealing with it is scarce. There is hardly any Indian work to cite as reference in this connection. A new method has been suggested here to measure the basic-nonbasic workers in the population of a city by combining the two methods (fifth percentile and minimum requirement method). It is important to mention that these two methods have been most frequently used to determine the basic-nonbasic ratio. The present method which combines the two approaches is felt necessary to overcome the weakness underlying these two techniques.

Based on B/N ratio, three groups of towns—the dynamic, static and declining—may be identified. The majority of towns, however, are dynamic in the sense that B/N ratio has witnessed a positive change. The economic base measurement also helps in measuring the degree of specialization. The formula of 'Index of Specialization' exposes the diversification of specialization. The degree of diversification declines with the increasing index of specialization. It is important to mention that most of the towns under study are small with a high degree of diversification and low a index of specialization and therefore, there is every possibility for further growth in the functional structure of such towns.

Appendix I

Basic/non-basic ratio of class I, class II and xass III towns of UP, during 1961 and 1971

Towns	*1961*	*1971*	*Towns*	*1961*	*1971*
Kanpur	1:2.6	1:3.1	Ghaziabad	1:1.0	1:1.3
Lucknow	1:2.3	1:2.6	Muzaffarnagar	1:1.2	1:1.4
Agra	1:2.0	1:2.3	Farrukhabad	1:1.3	1:1.5
Varanasi	1:1.9	1:2.4	Faizabad	1:1.5	1:2.0
Allahabad	1:2.1	1:2.4	Mirzapur	1:1.3	1:1.7
Meerut	1:1.8	1:2.0	Sambhal	1:2.7	1:3.1
Bareilly	1:1.7	1:1.9	Etawah	1:1.1	1:1.3
Moradabad	1:1.5	1:1.9	Amroha	1:1.3	1:1.7
Aligarh	1:1.4	1:1.8	Jaunpur	1:1.9	1:2.3
Gorakhpur	1:1.3	1:1.7	Hardwar	1:1.2	1:1.4
Saharanpur	1:1.5	1:1.8	Hathras	1:1.2	1:1.2
Dehradun	1:1.4	1:1.6	Bahraich	1:1.3	1:2.0
Jhansi	1:1.3	1:1.5	Budaun	1:1.3	1:1.6
Rampur	1:1.5	1:2.1	Hapur	1:1.2	1:1.7
Shahjahanpur	1:1.6	1:2.1	Pilibhit	1:1.2	1:1.3
Mathura	1:1.2	1:2.4	Sitapur	1:1.0	1:1.2
			Maunath Bhanjan	1:0.5	1:0.6
Firozabad	1:0.9	1:1.0	Roorkee	1:0.7	1:0.8
Bulandshahr	1:1.0	1:1.1	Rae Bareli	1:0.9	1:1.1
Fatehpur	1:1.0	1:4.3	Unnao	1:1.0	1:1.0
Chandausi	1:1.3	1:1.4	Deoband	1:1.3	1:1.6
Gonda	1:1.0	1:1.3	Deoria	1:1.2	1:1.5
Haldwani-cum-Kathgodam	1:0.9	1:1.0	Nagina	1:1.3	1:1.9
Banda	1:1.1	1:1.6	Shamli	1:0.9	1:1.3
Khurja	1:1.0	1:1.5	Balrampur	1:1.0	1:1.5
Basti	1:1.1	1:2.0	Lalitpur	1:1.5	1:1.4
Balia	1:0.9	1:1.5	Etah	1:0.8	1:1.1
Hardoi	1:1.1	1:1.4	Kashipur	1:0.9	1:1.3
Kasganj	1:1.0	1:1.2	Shahabad	1:2.7	1:3.9
Ghazipur	1:1.3	1:1.3	Kairana	1:1.6	1:5.0
Manipuri	1:0.9	1:1.2	Sultanpur	1:0.8	1:0.9
Lakhimpur	1:1.0	1:1.1	Sikandrabad	1:1.4	1:2.0
Modinagar	1:0.3	1:0.6	Shikohabad	1:0.8	1:1.0
Barabanki	1:1.1	1:1.1.	Baraut	1:1.1	1:1.2

Contd...

Contd...

Bijnor	1:1.4	1:1.6	Mahoba	1:1.6	1:3.1
Najibabad	1:1.0	1;1.2	Vrindaban	1:0.8	1:0.9
Orai	1:1.0	1:1.4	Mughalsarai	1:0.6	1:0.7
Tanda	1:0.7	1:0.9	Konch	1:1.1	1:1.8
Azamgarh	1:1.0	1:1.1	Kannauj	1:1.6	1:2.6
Chandpur	1:1.0	1:1.1	Aonla	1:1.5	1:2.2
Bela Pratapgarh	1:0.7	1:1.0	Gola Gokarannath	1?0.7	1:0.9
Sahaswan	1:3.2	1:5.2	Jahangirabad	1:1.8	1:2.4
Tilhar	1:1.3	1:3.0	Kalpi	1:0.8	1:2.4
Auraiya	1:0.6	1:1.6	Mubarakpur	1:0.3	1:0.4
Mauranipur	1:1.0	1:1.3	Baneri	1:0.8	1:0.9
Rudrapur	1:0.7	1:4.0	Atrauli	1:1.0	1:2.5
Nainital	1:0.4	1:0.7	Almora	1:0.8	1:1.3
Kiratpur	1:1.0	1:2.3	Nahtaur	1:1.0	1:2.5
Mawana	1:1.3	1:1.6	Lahapur	1:1.3	1:1.3
Khatauli	1:0.9	1:1.0	Kandhia	1:1.2	1:4.7
Gangoh	1:1.3	1:1.9	Dhampur	1:1.1	1:0.9
Pilkhuwa	1:0.9	1:1.0	Sandila	1:0.9	1:1.5
Bhadohi	1:1.1	1:1.6	Ujhani	1:1.1	1:1.8
Rath	1:1.4	1:2.0	Sardhana	1:1.3	1:1.7
Seohara	—	1:3.8	Hasanpur	1:0.9	1:1.4

Source: Computation based on Modified Minimum Requirement Regression Model.

Appendix II

Index of specialization of class I, class II and class III towns of U.P.

Towns	*IS*	*Towns*	*IS*
Mubarakpur	39.4	Sikandrabad	3.2
Maunath Bhanjan	36.6	Chandpur	3.2
Tanda	21.2	Hasanpur	2.8
Mogalsarai	12.1	Bhadohi	2.7
Sambhal	14.6	Nainital	2.8
Kairana	12.0	Almora	2.6
Varanasi	9.8	Fatehpur	2.5
Firozabad	8.3	Kanpur	2.4
Kandhla	7.9	Rath	2.4
Modinagar	6.5	Rudrapur	2.4
Sahaswan	4.5	Tihar	2.4
Jhansi	4.3	Vrindaban	2.4

Contd...

Contd...

Sardhana	4.0	Dehradun	2.3
Mahoba	4.0	Etawah	2.2
Nehtaur	3.7	Amroha	2.2
Roorkee	3.6	Pikhuwa	2.2
Jahangirabad	3.5	Konch	2.2
Gorakhpur	3.3	Kashipur	2.2
Gangoh	3.3	Mawana	2.2
Moradabad	2.0	Ghaziabad	2.1
Jaunpur	2.0	Azambarh	2.1
Kiratpur	2.0	Bijnor	2.1
Gola Gokarnnath	2.0	Atrauli	2.1
Kannauj	2.0	Haldwani-cum-Kathgodam.	1.6
Rampur	1.9	Farrukhabad	1.6
Meerut	1.9	Basti	1.6
Chandausi	1.9	Ujhani	1.6
Deoband	1.8	Aonla	1.6
Gonda	1.8	Allahbad	1.6
Lalitpur	1.8	Agra	1.6
Unnao	1.8	Bareilly	1.6
Hapur	1.7	Khatauli	1.5
Kasganj	1.7	Mauranipur	1.5
Sultanpur	1.7	Sandila	1.5
Baraut	1.7	Ballia	1.5
Baheri	1.7	Nagina	1.5
Pilibhit	1.6	Faizabad	1.5
Aligarh	1.6	Hathras	1.5
Deoria	1.6	Najibabad	1.5
Barabanki	1.4	Shahjahanpur	1.5
Orai	1.4	Seohara	1.5
Shahabad	1.4	Mainpur	1.3
Sharanur	1.3	Lakhimpur	1.4
Kalpi	1.3	Shamli	1.4
Lucknow	1.3	Ghazipur	1.4
Muzaffarnagar	1.3	Shikohabad	1.4
Mathura	1.2	Rae Bareli	1.4
Bahraich	1.2	Hardoi	1.4
Banda	1.2	Hardwar	1.3
Etah	1.2	Sitapur	1.3
Bulandshahr	1.1	Budaun	1.3
Bela Pratapgarh	1.1	Balrampur	1.3
Mirzapur	1.1	Khurja	1.3
		Auraiya	1.3

Source: Computation Based on Index of Specialization Formula mentioned in the text.

Notes

1. Misra, H.N., Economic Base of Indian City System, Paper read at the Regional Meeting of A.A.G., University of Michigan, U.S.A., 1977, p. 1.
2. Sombart, N., *Der moderne Kapitalismus*, Vol. 2, 1902 (Leipzig), Quoted in H. Carter, *The Study of Urban Geography*: Edward Arnold, 1972, p. 54.
3. Quoted in R.E. Murphy, *The American City: An Urban Geography*, 2nd ed., McGraw Hill, 1974, p. 86.
4. Aurousseau, M., 'The Distribution of Population: A Constructive Problem', *Geographical Review*, 11, 1921, 563-592.
5. Ibid., p. 574.
6. Haig, R.M. and R.C. McCree, Major Economic Factors in Metropolitan Growth and Arrangement, Vol. I of Regional Survey of New York and Its Environs, New York, 1927.
7. Hartshorne, R., The Twin City District: A Unique Form of Landscape, *Geographical Review*, 22, 1932, 431-442.
   —, A New Map of the Manufacturing Belt of North America, *Economic Geography*, 12, 1936, 45-53.
8. Weimer, A.M. and Hoyt, H., *Principles of Real Estate*, New York, 1939.
9. Dickinson, R.E., *City, Region and Regionalism*, London, 1947.
10. Andrews, R.B., Mechanics of the Urban Base, *Land Economics*, 29, 1953, pp. 161-167, 263-268 and 343-350: 30, 1954, pp. 52-60, 164-172, 260-269 and 309-319: 31, 1955, 47-53, 144-155, 245-256 and 361-171.
11. Mattila, J.M. and W.R. Thompson, The Measurement of the Economic Base of the Metropolitan Area, *Land Economics*, 31, 1955, p. 215.
12. Roterus, V. and Calef, Wesley, Notes on the Basic-Non-basic Employment Ratio, *Economic Geography*, 31, 1955, 17-20.
13. Tiebout, C.M., The Urban Economic Base Reconsidered, *Land Economics* 32, 1956, 95-99.
14. Alexandersson, G., *The Industrial Structure of American Cities*, University of Nebraska Press, 1956.
15. Ullman, E.l. and M.F. Dacey, The Minimum Requirement Approach to the Urban Economic Base, The Regional Science Association: Papers and Proceedings, 1960, 175-194.
16. Johnson, J.H., *Urban Geography*, Pergamon Press, 1969, p. 65.
17. Alexanderson, G., op.cit.
18. Ullman, E.L. and M.F. Dacey, op.cit.
19. Yeats, M.H. and B.J. Garner, *North American Cities*, 2nd ed: Harper and Row, 1976, p. 83.
20. Ibid., p. 83.
21. Northam, R.M., *Urban Geography*, John Wiley and Sons, 1975, p. 154.

Chapter 20

Analytical Techniques for the Study of Regional Structural Change

Kamlesh Misra and Vijai P. Singh

Changes in the structure of regional economy impose severe costs and adjustment problems in a region. In the study of regional structural change an understanding of the developments in the region cannot be acquired without a full investigation of the forces of agglomeration and deglomeration that are at play (Isard, 1975, p. 113). Although the importance of agglomeration economies cannot be ignored, these forces are not well understood by economists and other analysts (Bergsman et al. 1972, p. 265). Without any deliberate disregard to the theoretical importance of agglomeration economies, this paper describes some of the important methodologies and applied empirical tools used by analysts to study regional structural change. A brief discussion of the theory behind each technique is presented followed by its application to the Pittsburgh region. The applications are designed with the objective that they provide some insights to the nature and extent of structural change in the Pittsburgh region.

Forces Driving Regional Growth and Structural Change

A key issue in the analysis of regional growth and structural change is the understanding of the forces that drive such changes. Economists and policy analysts have traditionally viewed regional structure in terms of industrial composition and exports. However, the structure of a regional economy includes more than just these. A detailed understanding of an area's structure might include political and social factors as well as traditional economic variables. Among the economic variables, exports have been considered the primary force that drive regional growth and change. In spite of the importance attached to exports, they, in turn, are to some degree influenced by the mix of industries in a region.

Regional growth and structural change are also dependent on the occupational structure of the region. It is as important to observe changes in the occupational structure as it is important to monitor changes in the industrial structure (Blair, 1991, p. 128). If regional structural change involves movement from goods producing activities to knowledge producing activities, this shift will require a change in the occupational structure. Other factors such as the ownership structure of the local establishments, the nature of the market in which firms buy and sell, the political and social structure of the region, and the demographic structure, including age, gender, and educational composition of the region, can influence economic development prospects in many ways.

Analytical Framework for the Study of Regional Structural Change

Data availability and measurement problems often limit the ability of an analyst to take into account all the factors that have a bearing on regions growth and structural change. Our intent here is to provide a framework that can be used both to demonstrate the use of various tools of regional structural analysis as well as to enhance our understanding of regional structural change in the Pittsburgh region. In order to accomplish these objectives we focus on two key aspects of the regional economy: regional exports and industry composition.

To single out one element of growth such as regional exports for special analysis involves some risk; that too much emphasis may be placed on this element as a casual factor in determining the economic future of the region. Nevertheless exports are, an important element of regional growth. Exports stimulate income and employment which are the primary measure of economic well being (Giarratani, 1989).

Industry composition plays a critical role in regional structural change. A region that has a greater concentration of cyclical industries is affected adversely during periods of recession compared to regions that have a more balanced mix. For instance, the Pittsburgh region dominated by durable manufacturing, was severely affected during the 1970s and 1980s as will be shown later. The understanding of the changing mix of industries over time provides clues not only to what has happened but also to what is likely to happen in the future. In the analysis that follows, we have used these two key regional factors to explain the nature and extent of structural change in the Pittsburgh region.

Employment and Population Shift in Pittsburgh Region

Before we discuss the application of particular methods of regional analysis, a brief description of shifts in employment and population in the Pittsburgh region is presented. This will serve as a context for our discussions on the applicability of particular approaches of economic analysis.

The geographic boundary of the Pittsburgh region is defined on the basis of an integrated economic relationship among various political and administrative jurisdictions. The Pittsburgh region consists of six contiguous counties, namely Allegheny, Armstrong, Beaver, Butler, Washington and Westmoreland. Allegheny County, the largest among them, contains 1.3 million people (57%) and 800,000 (67%) of the region's jobs. The other five counties have their own economic

Table 1

Percentage employed by major sic industries in the Pittsburgh region (1969, 1979, 1989, 1994)

Industry Division	*1969*	*1979*	*1989*	*1994*
	HIST	*HIST*	*HIST*	*FCST*
Total employment	100.00	100.00	100.00	100.00
Goods producing	35.12	30.5	18.87	17.71
Mining	1.07	1.32	0.69	0.62
Construction	5.31	5.59	5.48	6.29
Manufacturing	28.74	23.59	12.7	10.8
Service producing	51.49	56.72	68.89	70.62
Trans and PU	6.12	5.83	5.35	5.59
Wholesale	4.51	4.87	5.04	4.93
Retail Trade	15.4	16.67	18.93	18.31
Fire	5.53	6.42	7.11	7.28
Services	19.93	22.92	32.46	34.51
Government	12.4	11.71	11.06	10.59
Farm employment	0.78	0.79	0.74	0.63

Source: Regional Economic model for the Pittsburgh Region, University of Pittsburgh.

and population base, but there is a high degree of economic, educational and cultural interdependence between the six counties that comprise the region. Certain economic development initiatives are region-wide and there have been discussions of a regional tax to support the infrastructure and cultural resources that serve the interest of the region.

As we examine the long term trends (see table 1), the goods producing industries employed 35 per cent of the total work force or 385,000 persons in 1969 which dropped to 18.87 per cent (221,000) in 1989. The biggest decline occurred between 1979 and 1989 (from 30.50% to 18.87%). A small increase is projected for 1994 at which time there will be 225,000 workers in the goods producing industries in the region. It is important to note that much of this decrease is accounted for by the manufacturing sectors in which employment dropped from a high of 28.74 per cent (315,000) in 1969 to 12.70 per cent (149,000) in 1989. In 1994 it is estimated to drop to 10.80 per cent (137,000). Among the goods producing industries, only the construction industry made some modest gains between 1969 and 1994.

Within the manufacturing sector, primary metals was the largest sector in 1969 (40%) which lost more than 72,000 jobs between 1979 and 1989—a decline of 74 per cent. The rate of decline has slowed and between 1989 and 1994, it is expected to be a little over three per cent. Fabricated metals also declined but not as rapidly. But between 1989 and 1994, it seems to be in a weaker position than the primary metals. Other large employing industries such as electrical equipment, stone, clay and glass, food, printing, chemicals and instruments all experienced employment losses in varying degrees. But for manufacturing as a whole, during 1989-1994, the rate of decline has slowed.

Even though manufacturing employment continued to decline over the past two and a half decades, the total employment in the region grew from 1,094,681 in 1969 to 1,242,419 in 1993—an increase of 13.5 per cent. Clearly this growth occurred in the non-manufacturing sector which accounted for 51.49 per cent of total employment in 1969 but increased to 68.89 per cent in 1989. It is expected to reach almost 72 per cent in 1994. The most rapid growth was in services which consisted of about one third of the total employment in the non-manufacturing sector of the regional economy. Retail trade was another substantial employer followed by fire, transportation and public utilities and wholesale. Government employment has continued to decline at a slow pace but remains at about eleven percent of the total work force. Medical, education, business and non-profit have shown a remarkable and consistent growth in the recent years. The bar chart shown many of these changes at the aggregate levels between 1979 and 1989.

The Economic Base Model

The economic base model provides one of the simplest approaches for identifying and forecasting regional structural change. The basic concept is quite simple: The region's economy is divided into two sectors—a basic (export) sector and a non-basic (service) sector. Those sectors that bring income from outside the region through export of goods and services, are viewed as basic. The sale of goods and services to others within the region takes place in the non-basic sector.

Tiebout (1962, p. 10) described the fundamental relationship posed by the export-base theory:

> Export markets are considered the prime movers of the local economy. If employment serving this market rises or falls, employment serving the local market is presumed to move in the same direction. When the factory (export) closes, retail merchants (local) feel the impact as laid-off factory workers have less to spend. Because of the prime mover role, export employment is considered as "basic". Employment that serves local market is considered adaptive and is titled "non-basic".

The basic sector is the driving force behind all growth in the region and thus the non-basic sector is dependent on the basic sector for its growth. The idea is that if the basic sector is growing then the non-basic sector will also grow in order to fulfill the demand created by the basic sector. The link between the two sectors arises from the linkages and interactions of the export sector and the other business and households in the region. What this implies is that every additional job created in the basic sector will necessitate some job growth in the non-basic sector. To a large extent the growth of the basic sector is dependent on the intensity of demand from outside the region. Thus, the growth of the basic sector is influenced by forces that are external to the regional economy.

In a study of regional economic base the idea is to identify the region's export sector, to forecast the growth in those export sectors, and to assess the impact of additional exports on the region's non-basic sector. These important aspects of the region provide us with clues to the region's growth prospects and structural change (Hoover and Giarratani, 1985).

Figure 1

Economic Structure of the Pittsburgh Region, 1979 and 1989

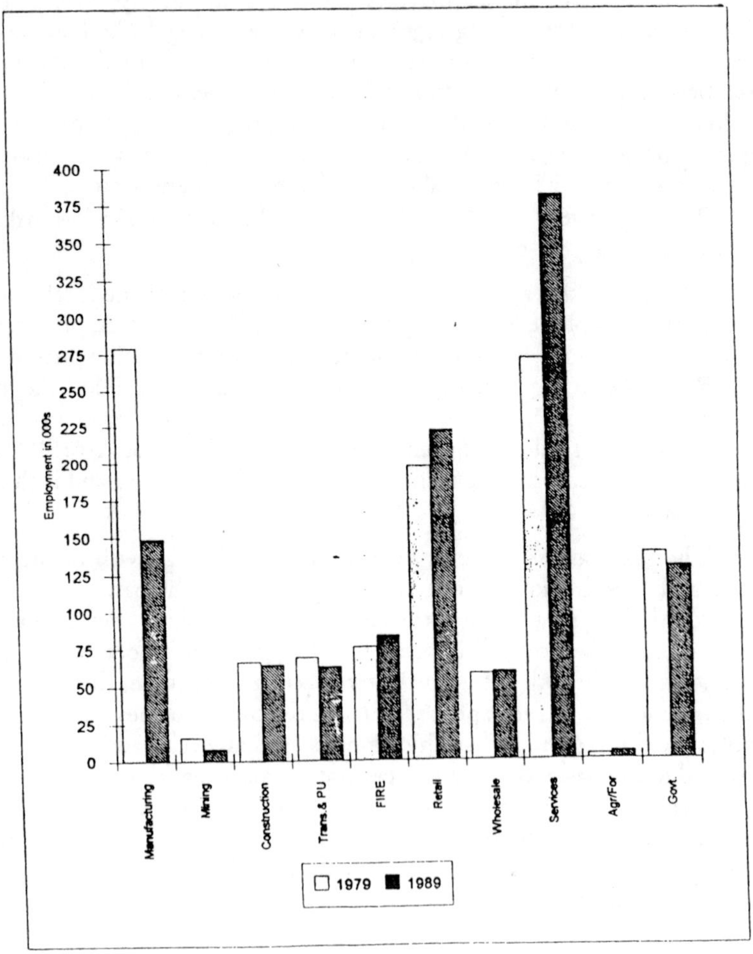

Source: Regional Economic Model for the Pittsburgh Region, UCSUR, University of Pittsburgh.

One of the important elements in using this approach is to make the model operational. This requires that the relationship between the two sectors be clearly defined. The ratio of the total employment to total base employment establishes this relationship and is termed the base multiplier. The multiplier is given by the following expression:

$$\text{BASE MULTIPLIER} = \frac{\text{Total local area employment}}{\text{Total base employment}}$$

Now if the value of the multiplier is four, it means that for each employee in the basic sector, there are a total of four employees in the local economy (3 in the non-basic sector and one in the basic sector). When interpreting the value of the multiplier an analyst has to keep in mind two things: that this is an average multiplier since it takes into account different types of firms/industries in the basic sector, and that it only measures the relationship between the basic and total economy at one point in time and not change in employment over time. This strengthens the argument that it is essentially an average multiplier and should be interpreted with caution.

Measuring the Economic Base

Economic base analysis provides an analyst with the basic insight into the sectors that contribute most to the local economy and aids in identifying the linkages that exist between the basic and non-basic sector. Although there exists a clear and conceptual difference between the basic and non-basic sectors in the economy, it is extremely difficult to determine if the product of an activity is intended for export or for local consumption. The problem gets compounded if the area of study is large and includes several types of industries and export activities. A regional economy is bound to have several industries that serve both local and non-local markets and hence, problems in identifying the level of employment attributable to exports in those industries.

A wide range of techniques are used by analysts to identify and measure the extent of economic activity that can be attributed to the basic sector of the economy. Here we focus only on one such technique, the location quotient approach.

Location Quotient Approach

The location quotient approach can be used to distinguish the proportion of an industry's workers serving local or non-local markets. Location quotients can identify if the local area produces good and services over and above its own requirements and if it sells the excess in non-local markets. It can also be used to identify the types of businesses that are not catering to the needs of the local residents and consequently are a source of consumption leakage from the community (Blair, 1991, p. 120-23).

The location quotient approach was first developed by Hilderbrand and Mace in 1950 and has since been widely used in applied analysis. It assumes that the national economy is self-sufficient. This permits an analyst to compare the regional economy against the standard benchmark of the national economy. According to Ottensmann, "the assumption here is that to meet local needs a region requires a level of economic activity in an industry proportional to the level in the nation as a whole" (Ottensmann, 1985, p. 46). By comparing the activities of each sector of the local economy with that of the national economy it is possible to determine if an individual sector is exporting or importing goods and services.

The location quotient is defined as the ratio of an industry's share of the local economy to the industry's share of the national economy.

$$LQ = \frac{\%\ of\ local\ employment for\ sector\ k}{\%\ of\ national\ employment\ for\ sector k}$$

A location quotient equal to one (1.0) indicates that the local production in the industry is just sufficient to meet the demands of the local residents. A location quotient greater than one (1.0) indicates that the industry or the sector is an export activity and is an important link to the non-local markets and the rest of the outside economy. However, the location quotient should exceed 1.25 in order to represent substantial export activity. On the other hand, if the location quotient is less than one (1.0), then production in these industries is not sufficient to fulfill the local demand, and therefore, goods and services have to be imported to fill that gap. This means that there will be some leakage from the income flow that will result from imports.

Application of the Model for the Pittsburgh Region

Table 2 uses employment data by two digit industry for the US economy and the Pittsburgh region for the year 1990 to illustrate the derivation of the location quotient and its use in identifying industries that can be classified as the basic and non-basic sector. For example, the location quotient for the primary metals industry (SIC 33) is computed by substituting the appropriate values in the above equation.

Table 2

Location Quotient, Basic, and Non-basic Employment Estimates for the Pittsburgh Region

Industry	*1990 Employment (000)*		*LQ*	*Base Employ-ment*	*Non-base Employ-ment*
	United States	*Pittsburgh Region*			
Lumber (24)	852.2	1.883	0.24	0.00	1.88
Furniture (25)	529.2	1.605	0.33	0.00	1.61
Stone clay etc. (32)	626	13.69	2.36	7.88	5.81
Primary metals (33)	757.1	32.233	4.59	25.20	7.03
Fabricated metal (34)	1443.2	12.908	0.96	0.00	12.91
Non-elec machine (35)	2144.6	18.701	0.94	0.00	18.70
Elect. equipment (36)	1696	10.84	0.69	0.00	10.84
Motor veh. (371)	824.7	0.255	0.03	0.00	0.28
Rest trans equi (R37)	1184.9	1.705	0.15	0.00	1.71
Instruments (38)	1004.7	7.203	0.77	0.00	7.20
Misc. manu. (39)	448.9	1.658	0.40	0.00	1.66
Food (20)	1681.2	8.18	0.52	0.00	8.18
Tobacco Manuf (21)	51.5	0	0.00	0.00	0.00
Textiles (22)	704.9	0.17	0.03	0.00	0.17
Apparel (23)	1087.2	1.968	0.19	0.00	1.97
Paper (26)	701.8	2.659	0.41	0.00	2.66
Printing (27)	1717.8	10.238	0.64	0.00	10.24
Chemicals (28)	1099.9	10.971	1.07	0.76	10.21
Petro prod (290	155.7	1.284	0.89	0.00	1.28
Rubber (30)	894.8	5.66	0.68	0.00	5.66
Leather (31)	139.3	0.007	0.01	0.00	0.01
Mining (10,12-14)	931.3	7.571	0.52	0.00	7.57
Construction (15-17)	7226	66.134	0.99	0.00	66.13
Railroad (40)	280	3.983	1.53	1.38	2.60
Trucking (42)	2074.7	16.765	0.87	0.00	16.77
Local/Interurban (41)	427.4	6.727	1.70	2.76	3.97
Air transp (45)	746.6	11.896	1.72	4.96	6.93
Other trsp (44,46,47)	662.268	4.257	0.69	0.00	4.26
Communication (48)	1369	9.333	0.73	0.00	9.33
Public utilities (49)	1009.9	15.121	1.61	5.74	9.38
Banking (60)	1648.8	26.745	1.09	2.15	24.59

Contd...

Contd...

Insurance (63,64)	2616.9	20.302	0.84	0.00	20.30
Credit and fin (61,62,67)	1026.6	8.007	0.84	0.00	8.01
Real estate (65)	3891.3	26.078	0.72	0.00	26.08
Eating/Drinking (58)	7016.6	68.696	1.05	3.55	65.15
Restretail (52-57,59)	15685.2	149.547	1.03	3.92	145.63
Wholesale (50,51)	6624.1	59.67	0.97	0.00	59.67
Hotels (70)	1807	9.376	0.56	0.00	9.38
Per serv/repr (72,76)	3040.5	34.066	1.21	5.84	28.23
Priv. household (88)	1377	9.112	0.71	0.00	9.11
Auto rep/serv (75)	1393.2	12.108	0.94	0.00	12.11
Misc. busi. serv (73)	6931.3	60.746	0.94	0.00	60.75
Amuse and recreation (79)	1916.1	17.861	1.00	0.07	17.79
Motion pictures (78)	592.2	3.146	0.57	0.00	3.15
Medical (80)	8876.3	113.75	1.38	31.34	82.41
Misc prof (81,87,89)	5754.899	59.168	1.11	5.74	53.43
Education (82)	2006.4	37.215	2.00	18.59	18.63
Non-profit (83,84,86)	3877	41.861	1.16	5.86	36.00
Agri/F/F Serv (07-09)	1356.2	5.263	0.42	0.00	5.26
Total	112910	1048.33		125.74	922.58

Source: Regional Economic model for the Pittsburgh Region (REMI), University of Pittsburgh.

$$LQ = \left[\frac{32.233}{1048.325} \Big/ \frac{757.1}{112910.4}\right] = \frac{0.0307471}{0.0067053} = 4.58$$

The location quotient is greater than one (1.0), indicating that the industry's share of the local economy is larger than the industry's share of the national economy. This indicates that the primary metals industry has a greater concentration here and that the local economy specializes in this industry. The primary metals industry in the Pittsburgh region is composed of mainly the steel industry which exports a large volume of its output to areas outside the region. Thus this industry can be assumed to include large basic sector activity. Historically the Pittsburgh region in known for its dominance in the production of steel in the United States. Table 2 also indicates that a large majority of the industries in the Pittsburgh region have a location quotient less than one (1.0), indicating that the industry's share of the local economy is less than that of its national share. Therefore, these industries are assumed not to have any basic sector activity.

The location quotient of 0.97 for Pittsburgh's wholesale sector is almost one (1.0). This suggests that the region is approximately self-sufficient in the wholesale sector. The table also indicates that there exists a substantial variation in the value of the location quotient between industries. An analyst has to use his judgement in assigning any industry to the basic and non-basic sector. For the purpose of analysis, a value between 0.75 and 1.25 probably indicates that the local area is just self-sufficient.

Despite its importance in identifying the basic and non-basic activities, location quotients should be used with skepticism. Sound judgement and familiarity with the local economy are important when interpreting these values. In some situations it will become necessary to assign the activities of a sector to the non-basic sector, regardless of the location quotient value.

Estimates of Basic Employment

Having identified the basic and non-basic sector the question then becomes one of determining the employment attributable to non-local demand. It would be a mistake to assume that all the output and thus all the employment in the basic sector arises due to export activity in that sector. There a very few examples in the real world where an industry exports 100 per cent of its output and that no part of it is consumed locally. The ideal situation in industry is that some part of the output is consumed locally regardless of its export dominance. The job of the analyst is to identify the employment in such industries (with location quotient greater than one) as those resulting from local demand (local consumption) and those from non-local demands (exports).

Based on the notations used by Ottensmann, the location quotient can be used to distinguish the proportion of an industry's workforce serving local or non-local markets. To determine the export employment (basic employment) in industry "i" in time "t", x_i^t the following formula can be used (Ottensmann, 1985):

$$x_i^t = \left(1 - \frac{1}{LQ_i}\right) \textit{ industry } i \textit{ employment}$$

The last two columns of Table 2 present the estimated values of the basic and non-basic employment for each of the two digit industries in the Pittsburgh region. The derivation is fairly simple, for instance by substituting the appropriate values for the primary metals industry in the above equation we get:

$$x_i^t = \left(1 - \frac{1}{4.59}\right) 32.233$$

$$= (1\text{-}0\ .2180793)\ 32.233 = 25.20$$

In this example, 25,200 of the 32,233 jobs in the Pittsburgh region's primary metals industry are directly attributable to the exports from the region. The non-basic employment, then, can be determined by subtracting the estimated basic employment from the total industry employment (i.e., 32,233-25,200 = 703). The above equation should be used to determine the basic employment of those and only those industries that have a location quotient greater than one. Industries that have a location quotient equal to one (1.0) or less than one (1.0) are assumed to fulfill only local demands and their employment is assigned to the non-basic sector only. If the above formula is applied to industries that have a location quotient less than one (1.0), the resulting values will be negative. The negative values, however, can be interpreted as the additional employment that is required in that industry to fulfill local demand. It can also be interpreted as the number of jobs outside the region that are supported by the regional industry. This information can be used by policy makers and analysts who are looking for areas of opportunity to expand production to substitute for imports into the local economy.

The analysis clearly shows that the Pittsburgh region's export activity is concentrated in primary metals, transportation and public utilities, and services (medical and education). It is also evident that primary metals industry still holds an important place in regional exports, accounting for over 78 per cent of its employment related to export activity. Although this analysis by itself is not sufficient to design policies for future course of action, it does enhance our understanding of the adverse effects the decline of the steel industry has had on the region. In order to further understand the causes of economic decline in the Pittsburgh region, it would be appropriate to decompose the shift in the regional economy.

Shift-share Model

According to Hoowver and Giarratani (1985), "Both regional growth and quality of opportunity depends not merely on external influences and location (as discussed in previous section) but also, to a large extent, on the mix of activities that the region has." In order to address the question of the mix of activities in a region and their role in regional growth and change, this section deals with the shift-share technique which is designed to address these types of questions.

Shift-share analysis provides a retrospective view of the causes of growth. It is a technique for dividing an area's growth into three components. First, an area's growth can be attributed to the national growth component. If a region grew at the national average, it would have maintained its share of national employment. This is termed the national share component. Second, an area may grow faster or slower than the national average if it had a disproportionate level of employment in industries that grew fast (or slow) nationwide. Growth that differs from the national average because of the initial composition of a region is termed the mix component. Third, an area may have a competitive advantage (or disadvantage) compared to other areas because its environment is conducive (or impediment) to growth of particular industries. Growth differential due to the nature of the local environment is termed the competitive component.

Other things being unchanged, a given region is likely to grow faster if it specializes in growing industries (Hoover and Giarratani, 1985, p. 371). This decomposition, referred to as shift-share analysis, is a descriptive tool that helps one distinguish those components of the region's economic growth that reflect national and international trends from those that are region specific. The region's policy makers have almost no effect on national and international economic trends. Moreover, in the short run, they have little effect on the region's mix of industries. Hence, inferences about the short run impact of regional policy must generally be made from the performance of particular regional sectors, relative to their national counterparts, that is, from the third, "competitive component" of the shift-share decomposition.

The shift-share method assumes that regional economic change is a function of the sectoral mix in the regional economy. As far as each sector maintains its share of any change in that sector nationally, the model can be used to project future levels of economic activity. In addition, it can be used for the analysis of the strengths and weaknesses in the regional economy, providing an analytical framework for comparing the regional with national economic change (Ottensmann, 1985).

National Share Component: Indicates growth that would occur if local industry "i" grew at the national average rate.

Mix Component: Indicates extra or reduced growth because a particular industry grew more (or less) rapidly than the overall national average growth rate.

Competitive Component: Indicates that the local industry "i" grew more (or less) rapidly than the national rate for industry "i".

Steps in Applying Shift-Share Technique

The first step in using the shift-share model as a tool for economic analysis is to calculate the national growth component. In order to calculate this component, the base year employment in each sector is multiplied by the national average employment growth rate and then they are summed over all the sectors. The result derived from this calculation would show how many new jobs are created in the local economy that can be attributed to the national economic trend. It should be pointed out that in many situations shift-share analysis may not be an appropriate technique, especially if there is reason to believe that the local economy is not representative of the national economy and that the two are structurally different.

The second step is to compute the industrial mix component. The mix component is calculated by multiplying the local employment in each economic sector by the difference in the national growth rate for the whole economy. A positive mix component would indicate that most of the local employment is in sectors growing faster than the national total employment. A negative industrial mix component indicates just the opposite. The negative mix component may be due to the fact that local firms have a declining long-term prospect or that the firms in the local area may be in the grips of the downturn of the business cycle. It also provides a clue to the analysts to investigate if local firms are burdened with inefficient management, outdated technology or shifts and saturation of markets. The analyst has to examine both the total industrial mix as well as the industrial mix for each sector to better understand the nature of change taking place and to suggest appropriate assistance and policy alternatives to shape the future of the local economy.

Lastly, the competitive share component can be derived by multiplying the local employment in each economic sector by the difference in the growth rate of that sector nationally and locally. The results of all the sectors are summed to give the local area's competitive share. A positive share indicates that the local area is more efficient in securing additional employment than the rest of the nation. It indicates that the areas gained employment over and above those attributable to the effect of national growth and its industrial structure. When interpreting the results an analyst has to look at the competitive components for the local area as a whole as well as the individual sectors. They both yield different information and provide different insights.

Application of Shift-Share Technique to Pittsburgh Region

In applying the technique to the Pittsburgh region, our objective is to understand the nature of regional structural change that took place since 1979. The analysis is conducted for the region's major industrial sectors using the data from the Regional Economic Model of the Pittsburgh Region (REMI). Three equal-length, long-term periods, 1979-1983, 1983-1987, and 1987-1991 are selected for analysis. The period 1979-1983 is selected because it was a period of the most intense structural change in the region which resulted in shutdowns of major steel plants and massive job losses. 1983-1987, was a period when the region still continued to loose jobs but was slowly adjusting to the realities of the change. 1987-1991 was a period when major structural adjustments seemed to have been completed and the region was forging ahead of the nation on several economic measures.

Tables 3, 4 and 5 present the results of the shift-share results for the major sectors. The economic change in the region is decomposed into the three components using employment data. We begin by comparing the three tables to highlight the major differences in the behavior of the region's economy.

The raw data on Table 3 for the region shows that Pittsburgh lost about 93,160 jobs between 1979 and 1983, a period of major restructuring and decline in the steel industry in the region. Of this loss in jobs, over 92,000 were in the manufacturing sector of the economy. This performance pales in comparison to more recent periods of 1987-1991 when total jobs increased by 69,790. Only 26,760 of this job difference between the periods reflects variation in the performance of the national economy. The share component column on Table 5 shows that the region's jobs would have increased by 55,910 in the 1987-1991 period compared to only 29,150 in 1979-1983 period had all the sectors grown at the same rate as the composite national economy.

Indeed, the major difference between the 1979-1983 and 1987-1991 is the poor performance in the early period of the region's industries relative to their national counterparts (as evidenced by the large negative competitive component).

Industry Mix and Competitive Component: Key Explanation of Structural Change

The industry mix effect is calculated as the sum across sectors of the initial year employment in each sector times the difference between

Table 3

Shift-share Results for the Pittsburgh Region's Major Sectors 1979-1983 Period

	Pittsburgh		United States		Components			Change
	1979	1983	1979	1983	Share	Mix	Competitive	1979-1983
Total	1035.967	942.811	90667.9	93219.17	29.15	0.00	- 122.31	-93.16
Manufacture	279.37	186.737	21497.19	18920.04	7.86	-41.35	- 59.14	-92.63
Mining	15.611	11.234	1152	1361.1	0.44	2.39	-7.21	-4.38
Cont construction	66.156	54.565	5889.9	5480.1	1.86	-6.46	- 6.99	-11.59
Transport+Pub Ut	69.055	59.546	5618.034	5587.87	1.94	-2.31	-9.14	-9.51
Finance, Ins, + Re	73.037	75.243	8484.752	8943.727	2.14	1.97	-4.91	-0.79
Retail trade	197.405	197.648	17744.06	18580.39	5.55	3.75	- 9.06	0.24
Wholesale trade	57.689	54.811	5677.54	5699.11	1.62	-1.40	- 3.10	-2.88
Services	271.379	298.931	23740.32	27634.83	7.64	36.88	- 16.97	27.55
Agri/for/fish svc	3.265	4.096	864.1	1012	0.09	0.47	0.27	0.83

Table 4

Shift-share Results for the Pittsburgh Region's Major Sectors 1983-1987 Period

	Pittsburgh		*United States*		*Components*			*Change*
	1983	*1987*	*1973*	*1987*	*Share*	*Mix*	*Competitive*	*1983-1987*
Total	942.811	987.185	93219.17	106737.8	136.73	0.00	- 92.35	44.37
Manufacture	186.737	148.406	18920.04	19573.73	27.08	-20.63	-44.78	-38.33
Mining	11.234	9.445	1361.1	1119.2	1.63	-3.63	0.21	-1.79
Cont construction	54.565	63.219	5480.1	6891.3	7.91	6.14	- 5.40	8.65
Transport + Pub Ut	59.546	59.409	5587.87	6125.552	8.64	- 2.91	-5.87	-0.14
Finance, Ins, + Re	75.243	80.496	8943.727	10233.26	10.91	-0.06	-5.60	5.25
Retail trade	197.648	210.203	18580.39	21519.45	28.66	2.60	-18.71	12.56
Wholesale trade	54.811	56.7	5699.11	6331.75	7.95	-1.86	- 4.20	1.89
Services	298.931	354.288	27634.83	33632.38	43.35	21.53	- 9.52	55.36
Agri/for/fish/svc	4.096	5.019	1012	1311.2	0.59	0.62	-0.29	0.92

Table 5

Shift-share Results for the Pittsburgh Region's Major Sectors 1987-1991 Period

	Pittsburgh		*United States*		*Components*			*Change*
	1987	*1991*	*1987*	*1991*	*Share*	*Mix*	*Competitive*	*1987-1991*
Total	987.185	1056.975	106737.8	112783	55.91	0.00	13.88	69.79
Manufacture	148.406	139.091	19573.73	19004.91	8.41	-12.72	-5.00	-9.32
Mining	9.445	7.249	1119.2	967.2	0.53	-1.82	-0.91	-2.20
Cont construction	63.219	65.403	6891.3	6739.1	3.58	-4.98	3.58	2.18
Transport + Pub Ut	59.409	68.272	6125.552	6506.932	3.36	0.33	5.16	8.86
Finance, Ins, + Re	80.496	87.081	10233.26	10822.8	4.56	0.08	1.95	6.59
Retail trade	210.203	218.402	21519.45	22672.6	11.91	-0.64	-3.07	8.20
Wholesale trade	56.7	59.545	6331.75	6581.3	3.21	-0.98	0.61	2.85
Services	354.288	406.47	33632.38	38038.8	20.07	26.35	5.76	52.18
Agri/for/fish svc	5.019	5.462	1311.2	1449.4	0.28	0.24	- 0.09	0.44

Source: Regional Economic Model for the Pittsburgh region, University of Pittsburgh.

the national growth rates for that sector and the overall growth rate in the national economy. Thus, the large negative value of the mix component for manufacturing in the 1979-1983 period (-41.35) supports the conclusion that the region was not well positioned for the change that took place in the national economy and it lost 41,350 manufacturing jobs due to the mix of industries it had. This contrasts with the region's situation during 1987-1991: the mix component for manufacturing (-12.72) indicates that the region's manufacturing sector lost only 12,720 jobs due to its industry mix. The composition of the industry mix effect differs significantly between the two periods. This suggests that the region's industry became more diversified during the 1987-1991 period compared to the 1979-1983 period. As can be seen, the industry mix effect results reflect fewer job losses (relative to what would have happened had all sectors grown at the average rate of the national economy) in sectors with below average national growth rates. Most manufacturing sectors were declining relative to the national average in both the 1979-1983 and 1987-1991 periods, but the Pittsburgh region was harder hit by these relative declines in the early periods of 1979-1983. Moreover, some of the manufacturing sectors that are over represented in the Pittsburgh region, such as steel and fabricated metals, switched from being rapidly declining sectors to moderately declining or no growth sectors between the two periods. Thus, the Pittsburgh region now has a smaller share of manufacturing employment and its current mix of manufacturing employment puts it in a relatively favourable position compared to its past.

The competitive component is large in both periods (1979-1983 and 1987-1991), but with different signs that signify a negative competitive performance in the 1979-1983 period and a positive performance in the 1987-1991 period. By 1983 there were 122,310 fewer jobs in the region than there would have been had all region's sectors grown at sector-specific national growth rates between 1979-1983. This means that with the exception of retail trade and agriculture and forestry, the Pittsburgh region was not even maintaining its share of employment in most of its existing industries. However, this changed dramatically in the years 1987-1991, where the region out-performed the nation in many sectors. Continued growth at rates above national average in sectors such as construction, transportation and public utilities, finance and services led to an additional 13,880 jobs. (Table 5 competitive column). Thus, the analysis indicates a dramatic improvement in the overall competitive position of the region after 1987.

By 1987 Pittsburgh was in a better position to benefit from changes in the national economy. The region's favorable position since 1987 largely reflects the long process of adjustment, a process that gradually and often painfully reduced the region's reliance on the steel industry and other mill-based manufactured goods and increased its reliance on the service sector.

Region's Strong Competitive Performance (1987-1991)

The region's strong competitive performance in 1987-1991 was based on the growth of the sectors such as construction, transportation and public utilities, finance, wholesale trade and services. Trade and construction employment, though important in terms of overall jobs generated, is not the engine of growth; instead, it tends to follow other growth. If productivity growth or increased production of goods exported out of the region generate a growing economy and rising incomes, employment in trade and construction will grow. Otherwise it will not. Thus, the growth of these sectors relative to the national average is fully consistent with the rise in the region's personal income relative to the nation during this period. Hence, the key to the region's economic revival is its outstanding performance in sectors such as transportation and public utilities, finance and services.

The better than national performance in these sectors suggests that the region was doing something right during this period. Before concluding that the performance reflects enlightened regional policies, however, other explanations need to be considered.

Other Explanations of Recent Performance

Growth in Finance and Services: It has become more clear in recent years that employment growth in manufacturing is not the only engine of growth for the region's diversified economy. Rapid growth in financial and business-related services have played an important wealthgenerating role since 1987. Not only did these service sectors grow fast, they also contributed to the region's economic base by bringing new resources into the region. The REMI estimates show that about 40.8 per cent of the employment in private hospitals in the region can be directly attributed to exports, engineering and architectural services which account for 52 per cent of employment that is export related; about 52 per cent of employment in colleges and universities can be attributed to exports. These sectors have shown tremendous growth in recent years. A large part of this growth reflects national trends. With changing modes of production and technological advances in communication and data processing, business and financial services have grown in importance. Thus, the re-development of Pittsburgh, beginning in 1979 with massive structural change which coincided with the changing organization of production to more globally integrated operations, is no coincidence. By 1987, Pittsburgh had once again begun expanding production centers, with production new consisting of the information, communication and coordination functions necessary for firms to compete in the world economy.

Some Growth in High-Tech Manufacturing: Although, manufacturing as a whole has declined in general, there are pockets of growth especially in high-tech manufacturing areas such as non-electrical machinery and instruments. These sectors are the key to growth of the manufacturing in the region. An important factor in the growth in these two sectors has been the agglomeration of research and training institutions in the region. A number of financial institutions and public service institutions in the region have played a key role in financing the region's recent economic growth, though their role is less well documented and has been communicated to us only through interviews conducted by the center on several projects.

Regional Policy Response: An alternative or perhaps complementary explanation for the growth in key sectors of the diversified economy is the role of regional economic policy. The outstanding performance of the region in recent years could possibly reflect a positive response of the business community to the pro-business attitude of regional policy. However, we can only argue that overall regional policies, and not specific policy, in effect, exerted a positive impact on the region's overall business climate and perhaps on economic performance.

Having a much clearer understanding of the industrial composition of the region, its export base, and the knowledge of the factors that may have contributed to the economic decline in the region, it is logical to more to policy questions. In order to demonstrate the impact of a given policy response, we have made use of an important technique of analysis namely the econometric and simulation model for the Pittsburgh region (REMI).

Simulation and Econometric Models

These models combine statistical techniques with economic theory to estimate relationships among variables. These models are widely used in analysis of regional structural change. Econometric and simulation models that fall in this category range from very simple one equation models such as the one used by Weiss and Gooding (1970) to study the growth in Portsmouth area, to high complex models such as the Milwaukee Model developed by Rubin and Erickson (1980) which includes over 97 statistical equations. The purpose of this section is to provide some perspectives on the use of simulation and econometric models as tools for the analysis of regional growth and change. Simulation models are designed to answer "what if" questions and have been traditionally used for policy analysis. Here, however, we focus on the use of one such forecasting and simulation model developed for the Pittsburgh Region by Regional Economic Models, Inc., in Amherst, Mass. A brief description of the model is presented followed by an example of its simulation capability.

According to Giarratani and Houston (1990) the "Pittsburgh REMI model 'calibrates' the vast majority of equations on the basis of cross sectional data available for the national economy. This is in contrast to traditional econometric models which rely on time series data to estimate structural parameters. The model is designed, however, to make use of available information on regional trading and purchase patterns, thus making it unique. While the region is assumed to apply production techniques that characterize the US economy as a whole, each region has a set of trade relationships with other regions that determine the ultimate character of its linkages with the national markets. These linkages map out the nature of policy impacts on regional activities."

The greatest strength of the REMI model is that its structure is very complete with respect to demand and supply relationships underlying regional economics. Because of this, policy questions can be addressed in a consistent way and fundamental economic issues associated with these questions can be exposed for analysis and public debate.

Application of the REMI Model to Pittsburgh

To achieve the objectives of assessing the impact of a policy change several simulations are conducted on the primary metals industry using the Regional Economic Model for the Pittsburgh Region. It should be pointed out that the model does not allow the user to conduct simulations on the steel industry directly. However, simulations can be done on the primary metals industry. Since over 90 per cent of the employment and output of the primary metals industry in the region is in the steel sector, the primary metals industry can be taken as a good proxy for the steel industry.

Selection of Policy Variables

There are several criteria for selecting a policy change to be introduced in the model. However, it is important that any policy change introduced should represent a quantitative change. Policy questions that involve value judgements and are measured on a qualitative scale are difficult to incorporate in the model unless the user is able to find good proxy for that policy question. For instance, it would be difficult to assess the impact of better labour management relations since there are no good statistics available that can capture this variable.

Thus, in this study, the variables selected are those that can be easily incorporated in the model such as cost of production and exports. The REMI estimates show that the cost of production in the primary metals industry in the region is higher than that of the nation. Since cost of production has an impact on the overall competitiveness of the industry both in national and international markets, this variable was considered important in conducting simulations. The competitiveness of the industry also depends on the demand potential which can be captured by changes in exports. Thus, in conducting the simulation, the cost of production which affects the supply side of the market, and the export, which capture the demand side of the market, are considered.

Objective of Simulations

Two types of simulations were conducted to derive some policy conclusions that affect the primary metals industry. The first of these examines the impact of changes in the cost of production in the primary metals industry relative to its national counterpart. The second simulation is designed to show the impact of export shock induced on the industry. There are two ways to shock the model to show the impact of additional exports. A shock can be introduced by directly increasing the export share for the specified industry by changing the EXSMPV variable in the model. An increase in the value of the policy variable implies that the export share of the industry in the region is rising and the industry now accounts for a large share of the total regional exports. The second method to incorporate export shock in the model is through the SALPOL variable. This variable reflects the total sales of the industry. Since over 95 per cent of output of the primary metals industry is exported outside the region, the increase in sales forced onto the model will reflect increases in export sales to the rest of the nation and the rest of the world. We selected the first method to shock the model mainly due to the ease with which it can be accomplished.

For each shock introduced in the model, the results are compared to the baseline forecasts for the Pittsburgh region. The results reported on the accompanying tables show the net impact on the region due to introduced policy change (The reported results are the difference bettern baseline forecast and simulated forecast).

Simulating Change in Cost of Production

The competitive position of the primary metals industry depends largely on the technical aspects of production as specified in its production function, the relative price, and transfer costs (Cassing and Giarratani, 1992). Thus, changes in the competitive position of an industry can be measured by increases or decreases in its cost of production in the region relative to the same industry in the nation. Changes in the cost of production determine the profitability of the local industry and also the extent of external demand for the products of that industry in the region. In order to reach meaningful conclusions on policy questions regarding the competitiveness of the region's primary metals industry, a simulation is conducted to enhance the cost advantage of the industry in the region relative to the nation.

There are several alternative scenarios that can be created to assess the impact on the region of increased cost advantage in the region's primary metals industry. However, two question have to be answered before any cost advantage is introduced in the model. First, what is the magnitude of cost advantage to be introduced? The magnitude of the cost advantage to be introduced has to be based on acceptable logic. Second, can the change introduced in the model be translated into a realistic policy? Any cost advantage introduced should reflect the feasibility of introducing such a change as a policy in a practical situation. Changing the cost advantage of the industry by 25 or 50 per cent will certainly have a large impact on the region, but such a large increase is not only unrealistic but may be impossible through policy instruments.

Considering the two arguments made, a 5 per cent improvement in the cost disadvantage is introduced in the model for the primary metals industry. The history and control forecast data for the region show that Pittsburgh's primary metals industry has a cost disadvantage of about 12 per cent compared to its national counterpart. The average cost disadvantage for all industries in the region is approximately 7 per cent compared to the national counterpart. Thus, in conducting the simulation, the objective is to estimate the impacts on the region if the cost disadvantage in the primary metals industry matches the average for all industries in the region. On the basis of the above information, judgement was made to reduce the cost by 5 per cent. A 5 per cent decrease also seems reasonable and it can be implemented as a policy change in the region.

Table 6 shows the basic results of the relative cost reduction simulation for the Pittsburgh region. It shows that a reduction in relative cost by 5 per cent has the effect of increasing employment and income levels as well as the region's population. Thus, the direction of change is consistent with our expectations that reduction in relative costs should increase the competitiveness of the region as a whole. Total employment increases by 1,942 in 1992, the year the change is introduced (Table 6). If this new cost structure is maintained, total employment would increase by 8,846 by the year 2010. Much of the gain in employment comes from the private non-farm sector of the economy.

The manufacturing sector adds 681 jobs in 1992 and reaches a high of 2,782 by year 2010. However, the non-manufacturing sector has a larger net increase in employment due to its strong linkages to the primary metals industry. As employment in the primary metals industry increases due to reduction in relative costs, employment in industries that supply inputs also increases. This chain reaction increases the employment in all other support industries both in the manufacturing and the non-manufacturing sectors.

Gross regional product, a key measure of the performance of the economy, increases by $82 million in the first year of the change (1992) and increases to about $449 million by year 2010. Personal income, disposable income, and real disposable income also rise showing that there is a general increase in the standard of living of the residents.

The largest impact of the proposed change is on the region's population. A 5 per cent decrease in relative cost in the primary metals industry increases the region's population by 681 in 1992 and by 16,629 in 2010.

Decomposing the total employment of 8,112 in the year 2010 by source of demand shows that 2,429 jobs are created due to an increase in demand for intermediate goods in the region. An additional 2,389 can be attributed to increases in local consumption demand and, 1,833 are a result of increases in exports to the rest of the U.S. and the world. The region also adds approximately $937 million in new output as a result of the change.

Table 6

(Summary Table)

Impact on the Pittsburgh Region of a 5 per cent Reduction in Relative Cost in Primary Metals Industry

	1992	*1995*	*2000*	*2005*	*2010*
	FCST	*FCST*	*FCST*	*FCST*	*FCST*
Total Employment	1.942	5.627	7.612	8.311	8.846
Total Priv. NF Employment	1.914	5.407	7.089	7.627	8.112
Manufacturing	0.681	1.952	2.594	2.73	2.787
Durables	0.67	1.935	2.589	2.724	2.768
Non-durables	0.01	0.17	0.004	0.006	0.019
Non-manufacturing	1.233	3.456	4.495	4.898	5.325
Mining	0.025	0.073	0.098	0.106	0.114
Construction	0.24	0.661	0.734	0.661	0.65
Trans. and PU	0.088	0.245	0.321	0.352	0.385
Fire	0.076	0.208	0.261	0.276	0.311
Retail trade	0.285	0.807	1.1	1.245	1.359
Wholesale trade	0.128	0.365	0.467	0.49	0.517
Services	0.386	1.081	1.492	1.74	1.957
Agr/For/Fish Svc.	0.006	0.016	0.023	0.027	0.031
Employment Decomposed by Source of Demand					
Intermediate	0.566	1.607	2.103	2.267	2.429
Local consumption	0.445	1.283	1.854	2.165	2.389
Government demand	0.004	0.024	0.061	0.09	0.105
Investment activity	0.26	0.7	0.74	0.621	0.576
Exports to US	0.472	1.31	1.671	1.756	1.833
Exports to Multi-region	0.168	0.482	0.661	0.729	0.78
GRP and Income					
GRP 1987 $	0.082	0.245	0.354	0.406	0.449
Personal income	0.069	0.256	0.479	0.663	0.905
Disposable income	0.058	0.215	0.416	0.59	0.807
Real Disp income	0.042	0.129	0.204	0.243	0.267
Population	0.681	5.254	12.213	15.535	16.629

Note: Employment and population in thousands of people, dollar concepts in billions of nominal dollars unless indicated.

Source: Regional Economic Model for the Pittsburgh Region, University of Pittsburgh.

Simulation for Exports

The primary metals industry has lost a large share of its exports since 1979, both in terms of its regional share and the national share. In 1979 the industry accounted for 21 per cent of all regional exports. By 1991 this share had fallen to only 12 per cent, a decline of 9 per cent. In spite of its still being one of the region's largest exporters. In terms of its export sales to the rest of the U.S. and the world, the industry exported $ 6.9 billion of its output in 1979 but it fell to $3.69 billion in 1991, a decline of about $3 billion in export output.

To simulate a change in export scenario, a simulation is carried out for the primary metals industry. The share of the primary metals industry's regional exports is increased by 2 per cent.

Table 7 shows the effect of increasing the industry's share of regional exports by 2 per cent. The total employment would increase by 1,741 in 1992 and by 1,615 in 2010. Gross regional product increases by $81 million in year 2010. In essence, employment, income and population all rise in the region in response to increase in the regional share of the primary metals industry. This response needs to be addressed more clearly. One would think that since there is an increase in the export share of the industry, it has to come from loss of share from other industries which would result in loss of jobs, income and population. How than can we explain the increase in employment, income and population? The answer lies in the nature and strength of the linkages between industries in the region. An industry having stronger ties to other local industries is likely to show a larger impact due to an increase in export share. The primary metals industry in the region has strong linkages to the local industries in the region. It purchases large quantities of its inputs from within the region. Thus, the net impact is an increase in its competitiveness as well as that of the region as a whole.

The largest contribution to total employment comes from exports to the rest of the US and the world (511 jobs in 1992 and 413 in 2010). This seems logical as we are increasing the export share of an industry that is one of the largest exporter in the region. Demand for intermediate inputs generate an additional 438 jobs in 1992 and 386 jobs in 2010. As a result of increased export share, the average wage in the region rises by $180 in 1992 and by $200 in 2010.

Table 7
(Summary Table)
Impact on Pittsburgh Region of a 2 per cent Increase in Export Share Attributed to Primary Metals Industry

	1992	*1995*	*2000*	*2005*	*2010*
	FCST	*FCST*	*FCST*	*FCST*	*FCST*
Total employment	1.741	1.628	1.484	1.537	1.615
Total priv NF Employment	1.716	1.54	1.358	1.402	1.483
Manufacturing	0.611	0.574	0.52	0.507	0.506
Durables	0.602	0.571	0.52	0.504	0.5
Non-durables	0.009	0.003	-0.001	0.002	0.005
Non-manufacturing	1.105	0.966	0.838	0.896	0.977
Mining	0.023	0.021	0.019	0.019	0.02
Construction	0.215	0.177	0.12	0.105	0.108
Trans and PU	0.079	0.07	0.062	0.066	0.072
Fire	0.0688	0.057	0.047	0.05	0.058
Retail trade	0.255	0.231	0.213	0.235	0.254
Wholesale trade	0.114	0.103	0.087	0.088	0.093
Services	0.346	0.303	0.286	0.327	0.366
Agr/For/Fish Svc.	0.005	0.005	0.004	0.005	0.006
Decomposition of Employment by Source of Demand					
Intermediate	0.438	0.389	0.34	0.357	0.386
Local consumption	0.398	0.372	0.366	0.409	0.444
Government demand	0.002	0.009	0.014	0.018	0.019
Investment activity	0.232	0.184	0.114	0.092	0.091
Exports to US	0.511	0.463	0.409	0.405	0.413
Exports to multi-region	0.134	0.124	0.115	0.122	0.129
GRP and Income					
GRP 1987$	0.073	0.071	0.069	0.074	0.081
Personal income	0.062	0.078	0.094	0.12	0.161
Disposable income	0.052	0.066	0.082	0.107	0.144
Real disp income	0.038	0.039	0.042	0.045	0.049
Population	0.61	2.099	2.935	3.072	2.988

Note: Employment and population in thousands of people, dollar concepts in billions of nominal dollars unless indicated.

Source: Regional Economic Model for the Pittsburgh Region, University of Pittsburgh.

The manufacturing sector of the region gains 506 jobs in year 2010 and non-manufacturing gains an additional 977 jobs during the same year. We can also observe the dampening effect on employment in both manufacturing and non-manufacturing over time. This is due to the fact that over the long run there is sufficient time for the market adjustment to take place. However, no dampening effect is seen in total government employment. Because the additions to new jobs will attract new population into the region and thus, the demand for public services will rise.

References

Beeson, P. and Giarratani, F., (1993), Competitive adjustment in the United States steel industry: Some spatial aspects of capacity change by integrated producer. (A working paper), Pittsburgh, PA: University of Pittsburgh, Department of Economics.

Bergman, E., and Goldstein, H.A., (1986), Dynamics, structural change and economic development paths, In E. M. Bergman (Ed.), *Local Economies in Transition: Policy Realities and Development Potentials*, Durham: Duke University Press.

Bergman, J., Greenston, P. and Healy, R., (9 October 1972), The agglomeration process in urban Growth, *Urban Studies*, Vol. 265.

Blair, J.P., (1991), *Urban and Regional Economics*, (Chapter 4, pp. 120-23), Boston: Irwin.

Cassing, S. and Giarratani, F., (1992), An evaluation of the REMI model for the South Coast: A quality management district, *Environment and Planning A, 24*, 1549-1564.

Cassing, S., (1989), *An Evaluation of the Pittsburgh REMI Model*, Pittsburgh, PA: University of Pittsburgh, University Center for Social and Urban Research.

European Communities, (1984), *The Regions of Europe*, Luxembourg: Office for Official Publications of the European Communities.

Giarratani, F., (1990), *An Analysis of Export Activity in Allegheny County: An Application of a Pittsburgh REMI Model*, Pittsburgh, PA: University of Pittsburgh, University Centre for Social and Urban Research.

Giarratani, F., and Houston, D.G., (1991), Simulating sources of uncertainty in policy forecasting with a large scale regional econometric model, *Geographical Analysis*, Volume and pages.

Hoover, E.M. and Giarratani, F., (1985), *An Introduction to Regional Economics*, (3rd ed.0, (Chapter 11, p. 317), New York: Alfred A. Knopf.

Isard, W., (1975), *Introduction to Regional Science* (Chapter 7, p. 113), New Jersey: Prentice-Hall, Inc.

Ottensmann, J.R., (1985), *Basic Microcomputer Programme for Urban Analysis and Planning* (Chapter 4 p. 46), New York: Chapman and Hall.

Regional Economic Model for the Pittsburgh Region, (1993), Regional Economic Models Inc., Amherst, MA.

Rubin, B.M. and Erickson, R.A., (1980), Specification and performance improvements in regional econometric forecasting models: A model for the Milwaukee Metropolitan Area. *Journal of Regional Science*, 20(1), 11-35.

Summers, A.L. and Luce, T.F., (1985), *Economic Report on the Philadelphia Area*, Philadelphia, PA: University of Pennsylvania Press.

Tiebout, C., (December 1962), *The Community Economic Base Study*, New York: The Committee for Economic Development.

Weiss, S.J. and Gooding, E.C., (1970), Estimation of differential employment multipliers in a small regional economy. In H. Richardson (Ed.), *Regional Economics: A Reader* (pp. 55-67), London: Macmillan.

Chapter 21

Some Problems of Interdisciplinary Teamwork and Research in Urban and Regional Planning

K.V. Sundaram

The Interdisciplinary Nature of Planning

The need for interdisciplinary team work and research has been widely stressed in many fields, but nowhere has its importance been so great as in some applied fields like urban and regional planning. Basically this urge towards interdisciplinary efforts in urban and regional planning springs from the increasing awareness of the comprehensive and many-sided character of planning and the complex and specialized nature of its numerous facets. Since the urban and regional planner has to take a broad synoptic view of the future growth and development of the physical environment, he must rely on the findings of various specialized disciplines like architecture, engineering, economics, geography, public administration, statistics and sociology. For example, "an appreciation of the age or condition of buildings demands an understanding of structure, construction and materials; an assessment of mining subsidence requires the acumen of an engineer; the possibilities of reclaiming derelict land merits the knowledge of a soil scientist, botanist or landscape architect and analysis of traffic flow and movement will involve the traffic engineer."[1] A multidisciplinary team of this kind, consisting of specialists in various disciplines, will be able to apply their various techniques in the elucidation of many current problems and would enable the decision-maker to take a wider view aimed at a comprehensive planning approach.

The need for such interdisciplinary exercises in planning has become particularly important in recent years, as planning has shifted its emphasis from an essentially "unitary approach", with its accent on a single invincible scheme, to an "adaptive" one, wherein alternatives are presented from different angles taking several unpredictable elements of change and technology into account.

The urban and regional planning field in India today would seem to be in the early adolescent stage of development. A rather distinctive personality is already emerging. Almost every state government has set up its own town and country planning department under a technical chief. But the organizational structure of their planning teams is yet to take on a multidisciplinary character, without which planning is bound to become a one-sided exercise. The present time therefore, appears to be the opportune moment to reflect on the development of the planning field, the actual and potential relationship of various fields of study to planning and the skills that are needed, other than those of physical planning, to obtain the necessary breadth of vision and depth of focus needed for understanding a problem in all its variety and totality. Against this background, it is proposed to discuss in this paper the various operational problems that are encountered in interdisciplinary team work and research, based on the experience available in the Central Town and Country Planning Organization, where an interdisciplinary team has been functioning for over a decade now.

The Nature of Physical Planning

The physical approach has long dominated the urban and regional planning field, providing its basic concepts as well as its methods of operation. This approach has now yielded place to a more comprehensive approach in which urban and regional planning is regarded as a function of the three fold social, economic and physical aspects of environmental factors (i.e., folk, work and place).

In fact, the expression "physical planning", used to designate town and country planning, is now regarded in some quarters as "an obsolete term reflecting the historical conditions when the methods of economic analysis were not applied to the solutions of urban and regional problems.[2] In the modern approach, it is emphasized that physical growth should be in harmony with well-defined social and economic needs and ends. In the next 50 years or so, the town and country planning profession can be expected to be called upon to use its skills for the planning of social and economic policies, necessitating greater productive involvement with the socio-economic disciplines.[3]

Contributions of Socio-economic Disciplines

Howard remarks: "City planning started as an art with all decisions being made intuitively. It has gradually been equipped with some of the tools of science."[4] It turns for insights to the socio-economic disciplines and for solutions of environmental problems to technology. Among the various socio-economic disciplines which have contributed notably to the advancement of urban and regional planning, special mention may be made of the contributions of geography, economics and sociology.

Geography comes nearer to physical planning than any other social discipline. This great appeal of geography to planning lies in its spatially oriented thinking, its synthetic approach to problems, and its ability to comprehend the totality of phenomena affecting human activity in their environmental setting. With its concept of the region and the techniques it has evolved to study the regional association or distribution of phenomena, geography has made significant contributions to regional planning. In recent years, the emergence of "urban geography" as a separate discipline is a particularly noteworthy event. Among the contributions which this branch of geography has made to urban planning may be mentioned the concept of "urban hierarchy" and "central place analysis", the concept of "umland" and the techniques for the study of city-hinterland relationships. The works of geographers like Walter Christaller, Arthur Smailes, Griffth Taylor, Robert Dickinson, Edward Ullman, Chauncy Harris, Jean Gottmann, and Brian Berry mark significant milestones in the literature on urban geography.[5] The development of various cartographic techniques in the analysis of spatial data, which constitutes another significant line of advance in geography, has also found a wide application in planning. Until recently, geography was basically empirical and lacking in analytical techniques. But in recent years, it has developed a vast literature and skills in quantitative analysis. "Planning has an inescapable geographical basis," says T.W. Freeman. "It is essential to the planners' work, for the planner must understand the existing landscape before he tries to reform it, both in town and country."[6] The modern trends in geography aim to take the science beyond mere analysis and description and to bring into it a concern for prescriptive action. In the words of Dudley Stamp, "the past 50 years have been spent in developing geographical methods of survey and analysis...The time has surely come when those same methods... can be used in helping towards the solution of some of the great problems."[7]

Economics, which is one of the most highly developed among the social sciences, provides a sound theoretical basis for planning. Several investment and programme decisions, for instance, hinge on economics. More recently, econometrics has provided new and refined methods of analysis to several key problems in urban planning. The techniques of cost-benefit analysis, for instance, has now become an invaluable tool in decision-making. In Poland, the choice of an area for further city development is based on a study of comparative cost advantage. The three costs considered here are the cost of preparing terrain for development, the cost of changing the existing land use, and the cost of servicing the land with the various kinds of utility networks.[8] Similarly, there are instances where controversies concerning the location of industrial or communication facilities have been settled by economic calculations. In Krakow, discussion of two possible alternative plans for enlarging the downtown area continued for ten years, until it was resolved by means of economic calculations based on the principle of the economic efficiency of investments.[9]

Economics, until recently, was lacking in the spatial and regional frameworks. Economic theories like production theory, distribution theory, monetary theory, do not ordinarily have a space dimension. But the more recent developments in regional economics have sought to fill this void by incorporating the element of geographic space and economic distance into the formulations. Particular mention must be made in this connection to the emergence of regional science as a specialized discipline with its mathematical and other simulation techniques to study economic base, population, income, multiplier effect, balance of trade, commodity and financial flow, input and output. Equipped with these tools, regional science is able to attempt the analytical solution of difficult policy problems and has become a decision-oriented field.

The relationship between sociology and town and country planning is intimate. Physical planning is essentially homino-centric,[10] as people are always involved both as subjects and as objects of planning. Physical planning influences social life and is itself influenced by existing social conditions. It was not until the time of Ebenezer Howard and Patrick Geddes at the turn of the last century that sociological thinking became an essential part of town planning. For both Howard and Geddes, the city was not merely a physical mechanism and an artificial construction, but essentially a human group, a social organization, and institution.[11] Great architects like Frank Lloyd

Wright, Jean Le Corbusier, Walter Gropius and Siegfried Giedion looked for man in their cities. They introduced the "social criterion" into urban design. The rebuilding of cities undertaken in war-torn Germany and Poland was regarded essentially as a movement in "social rebuilding".

During the last 50 years, notable efforts have been made in social research procedures and techniques to develop instruments that would help standardize and aid in validating professional judgements. An important development is the importation of the ecological approach to the study of the human community with its emphasis on the spatial distribution of interrelated social variables. Among the outstanding contributions of urban sociology may be mentioned the concepts of the "community", "neighbourhood", and "natural area". These concepts advanced studies of the local community. As a result, a series of cultural studies of immigrant communities were made, e.g., Little Italy, China Town, The Ghetto.[12] Studies of natural areas also began to serve as a basis for districting social agency services, e.g., for health districts of New York City and tuberculosis service districts of Chicago. McKenzies' concept of "metropolitan community" marks a milestone in the evolution of the "metropolitan area" concept.[13] The concept of "cominance," emphasized by Donald Bogue[14] and the theory of "concentric zones of city growth" formulated by Burgess[15] furthered ideas about the growth and development of towns. The concept of "rural-urban continuum" stimulated several studies of rural-urban fringe and sub-urbanization. Modern trends in sociology indicate that the sociologist will not remain as a mere investigator of social reality as it is, but will have a more active role to play in policy-making, venturing statements about what should be done.

The degree of collaboration between planners and sociologists and the extent of the impact of sociological thinking on town and country planning differs from one country to another. In some countries like the United States, France and the United Kingdom, "the advice of eminent sociologists is sought and respected by urban planners (here, indeed, they are planners themselves). Among the most important figures are Lewis Mumford in the United States, Paul Chombar de Lauwe in France, and Ruth Glass in England."[16]

The Working Relationship Between Physical Planners and Social Scientists

The above discussion shows that the socio-economic disciplines are fast developing their own frontiers in the applied field of planning. A though their contributions to the general theory and the methods of planning are readily apparent for the most part, several operational constraints come into play, restricting the fuller application of their methods in actual practice. Effective contributions from these specialist disciplines would depend on the nature of the working relationship between physical planners and social scientists and the degree of intellectual and emotional compatibility that exists between them. In fact, a close working relationship between them is yet to come. One of the criticisms levelled against physical planners is that they have failed to involve the sociologists, economists and other social scientists in ways that demonstrate understanding of and respect for their disciplines and their methods. "Putting a sociologist on the team is more of a fashion than a commitment to the problem's definition as a joint one."[17] As Jack Wood remarks: "The planner should not be considered as super-social engineer, but the day has arrived where naive empiricism can no longer be paraded as a scientific approach to planning."[18] It is, therefore, emphasized that the planner must "ground himself in the social sciences much more systematically than in the past and must learn to tolerate, respect and work with those who are as ignorant of the skills of physical planning as he may be ignorant of the skills of social planning."[19] Such awareness has led to the institution of short term courses in Comprehensive Planning,[20] intended to bring specialists in various disciplines together, so as to help them in overcoming the specialized fragmentary ways of their thinking. Of late, there is a tendency in some quarters to regard comprehensive planning as a distinctive discipline and field of study.[21] Their advocates are of the opinion that comprehensive planning contributes to a unique body of knowledge in the same sense in which bio-chemistry or bio-physics produce knowledge beyond what they derive from their parent fields. If a course in comprehensive planning is intended as a sort of inservice training and orientation for achieving better coordination in planning, the institution of such a course would indeed be welcome. But if the idea is to substitute specialists by breeding a class of inter-disciplinarians (i.e., some kind of all-round generalists) by giving them basic training in a number of varied fields without specialization in any, then such a course will have doubtful utility. Herein lies a fallacy of non-specialization.[22] Planning has borrowed extensively from other specialized disciplines and will continue to do so because there is not enough that is sufficiently unique in its substance and methodology to suggest separate intellectual identification. For success in planning, the planner must be a generalist with a speciality, a man who can combine the penetrating insight in his own specialism with an adequate grasp of the wider complex of knowledge upon which various planning activities rest. The professional training for the planner should enable him to "become a highly enlightened consumer of other people's research"[23] and to make him an efficient and close collaborator with researchers in various disciplines.

Problems in Interdisciplinary Teamwork

Interdisciplinary effort which implies joint endeavour is by no means an easy job. It has its own exacting requirements. Though these requirements may be self-evident, it would be useful to reiterate them.

In any teamwork, much depends on the individuals constituting the team, i.e., on the understanding, the good-will and the enthusiasm displayed by the members of the group and the degree of rapport and dialogue which they are able to establish with their counterparts. Every individual of the team must have understanding of, as well as appreciation and respect for, the approaches and contributions of the other planning disciplines. He should learn to see clearly his own contribution as one facet only of a more complex and comprehensive planning programme.

In interdisciplinary situations, problems arise particularly when the members of the team find it difficult to communicate with each other. Undue aggressions, rivalry or unconscious clash of personalities can destroy group effectiveness. Criticisms like the "unscientific nature of the work," the "inability to deliver the goods" or "irrelevance of the study to planning", etc., are sometimes made, particularly when members of a team do not see eye to eye with each other. Such criticisms in their extreme form are neither correct nor helpful. They militate against mutual respect and healthy criticism necessary for progress in a field which cuts across many boundaries, and that is cultivated by various disciplinarians using different implements. In such situations, the tact and ability of the coordinator is brought to test. It is his vision, leadership, and ability to coordinate and direct the specialists under him that ultimately makes or mars any interdisciplinary effort.

In interdisciplinary teamwork, there is no hierarchy among disciplines. The focus is on the specific problem or issue and contribution of every discipline to the central problem is of equal importance. Each collaborator may not only provide a new orientation as to subject matter but may also proceed methodologically in a way which enables him to view certain particular aspects of the functional interrelationship of the various elements. In such an effort, therefore, the individual specialist's status, i.e., the order of his placement in the overall organizational setup, should never come in the way of expression of free opinion in technical matters. Indeed the success of all interdisciplinary endeavour depends on the extent to which the effacement of vertical hierarchy is attained in actual practice. Not infrequently it happens that true interdisciplinary contacts occur not in an institutional setup but primarily on the personal plane.

Some times the specialists in the team are not given sufficient encouragement to use the scientific methods of their disciplines. Constraints are sought to be put on the selection of their problem areas and on their choice of approaches to potential solutions. They become simply tools for doing odd jobs and are made to play only very subordinate roles, virtually becoming "supervised team players"[24] in a game. This tends to kill their initiative and inhibits any effective contribution being made to the common problem. On the other hand, when wide academic freedom is given, the individual disciplinarians tend to drift apart and a compartmentalized instead of a unified effort ensues. A publication of the Town Planning Institute, London drives home this point very well: "Academic freedom is all very well and the researchers should certainly be encouraged to pursue their inquiries by using the methods and concepts that seem to them as professionals to be the most appropriate, but one feels that they need a little more guidance as to what the problems are."[25] The problem in interdisciplinary teamwork is, therefore, essentially one of striking a balance between extreme independence granted to individual workers on the one hand and excessive regimentation on the other. The working relationship among the collaborators in an interdisciplinary team must be as the fingers are to the hand, i.e., separate but united. All these underline the important role of the coordinator in interdisciplinary teamwork.

Problems of a different kind arise when, as sometimes happens, the contributions of individual specialists are ignored. This happens, for instance, when elaborate and time-consuming surveys and studies are undertaken by social scientists; but even as these surveys are halfway through, the planners become impatient and go ahead with their plans, making ad hoc and intuitive decisions, without waiting for the outcome of detailed studies. The planner is also right in a way, as he is responsible for making decisions, often within a legal time limit, on the variety of matters connected with physical planning. This is a situation which the practitioners and proponents of planning must seek to remedy, if the studies undertaken by them are not to end ultimately as mere exercise in futility. It raises an important question as to the time element in socio-economic surveys and studies.[26] Perhaps with the use of electronic computers and other innovations, the analytical capabilities of the social scientist might be further improved and speeded up.

Examples of Interdisciplinary Teamwork in Urban and Regional Planning in India

The Delhi Master Plan may be cited as an example of the outcome of interdisciplinary effort in urban and regional planning in India. In this endeavour, the physical planners numbering 28 in all, collaborated with 17 economists, 4 geographers and 3 sociologists. The Ford Foundation team of experts who assisted in its preparation were also drawn from different disciplines. There were two economists, one sociologist, a traffic specialist, an architect planner, an engineer planner and an expert in public administration. The coordinator of the team was a sociologist planner. The staff engaged in the preparation of the plan were split into project-oriented teams for undertaking various studies such as land use, circulation, site planning, economic base, regional studies, slums, rural planning and landscape architecture and fiscal planning. The composition of each team was based on the nature and requirements of the project. For example, land use, circulation and site planning sections were manned mostly by town planners, architects and engineers. They were assisted in tabulation work by lower staff drawn from socio-economic disciplines. The economic base and regional studies section was primarily a socio-economic team, whose work was coordinated by a town-planner. The present author was associated with rural planning studies. An economist was in charge of the fiscal planning studies. Surveys on slums were undertaken by a socio-economic team comprising sociologists and economists coordinated by a town planner. Integration and coordination were sought to be achieved at all levels, which ensured that no studies or lines of investigation were pursued which did not have a bearing on planning decisions. Whenever differences arose (and such differences arose at the time of preparing a study design or while discussing policy questions), these were sought to be sorted out in a series of integrative work sessions. The effort, on the whole, proved to be stimulating to all concerned and provided a worthwhile cross fertilization of ideas, techniques and research. The team-spirit displayed by the participants was excellent and as a consequence, no major problems had to be faced. Another big interdisciplinary undertaking in urban and regional planning in India is that associated with the preparation of the Calcutta Master Plan. In its initial stages, this work was organized primarily along the lines of individual disciplines. But it became necessary to group and regroup the personnel in various combinations depending on the requirements of particular work projects, so that integration could take place at the level of contributions.

It must be emphasized here that the mere bringing in of various specialized disciplines under one roof does not lead to interdisciplinary teamwork and research. Much depends on the manner of grouping personnel for particular tasks. The various combinations in which the work may be organized depends on the requirements of particular work projects. Some projects like the relocation of offensive trades and callings in a city, for instance, need close collaboration between different planning specialities. In certain other types of work, however, which fall mainly under some particular competence, like budgeting and fiscal analysis for instance, occasional consultation and review by other specialists may be sufficient. Neither extreme fragmentation along the lines of specialized disciplines nor a uniformly patterned staff grouping with an even sprinkling of specialists in every group would be ideal. The grouping, in each case, has to be related to the problem at hand and must take note of the affinity of the respective disciplines to that problem. From this standpoint, perhaps a comparative study of various planning organizations may yield valuable insights.

To sum up, the success of interdisciplinary teamwork in urban and regional planning is largely a matter of organization and depends on the manner in which the work is guided and coordinated by the chief coordinator. It is not always that a successful team could be assembled. The observation of Pask is significant in this context: "You cannot buy a research team. With luck, it grows, making its own common language and thriving on personal interplay which has nothing to do with research."[27]

Note: In this chapter, the term "interdisciplinary" has been used in the same sense as "multidisciplinary".

Notes

1. John N. Jackson, *Surveys for Town and Country Planning*, London, 1963, p. 24.
2. Antoni R., Kuklinski, "Regional Economic Planning for the Development of Satellite and New Towns", United Nations Round Table Conference on the Planning and Development of New Towns, Moscow, 1964.
3. Bernard J. Friedman, "The Changing Prospects for Social Planning", *Journal of the American Institute of Planners*, Washington D.C., Vol. 33, September 1964, p. 311.
4. John T. Howard, "City Planning as a Social Movement, a Governmental Function, and a Technical Profession" in Harvey S. Perloff, (ed.), *Planning and the Urban Community*, 1961, pp. 149-71.
5. See Walter Christaller, *Die Zentralen Orte in Suddeuschland, Gustva Fishcher* (Jena 1933): A.E. Smailes, *The Geography of Towns*, London, 1953; Griffith Taylor, *Urban Geography---- A Study of Site Evolution, Patterns and Classification*, London, 1949; R.E., Dickinson, *City, Region and Regionalism*, London, 1947; R.E. Dickinson, *City and Region: A Geographical Interpretation*, London, 1964; E.L. Uullman, "A Theory of Location for Cities," *American Journal of Sociology, Vol. 46, 1940-41, pp. 853-64; Chauncy D. Harris, Salt Lake City; A Regional Capital*, Chicago, III., 1940; Chauncy D. Harris, "A Functional Classification of Cities in the united States", *Geographical Review*, Vol. 33, 1963, pp. 86-99; Chauncy D., Harris, "Suburbs", *American Journal of Sociology*, Vol. 49, 1943, pp. 1-13; Jean Gottmann, *Megalopolis: The Urbanised North-Eastern Sea Board of the U.S.*, New York, 1961; Brian J.L. Berry, *Commercial Structure and Commercial Blight*, Chicago, III 1963.
6. T.W. Freeman, *Geography and Planning*, London, 1958, p. 13.
7. Dudley Stamp, *Applied Geography*, London, 1960, p. 10.
8. Jack C. Fisher, *City and Regional Planning in Poland*, Ithaca, N.Y. 1966, pp. 67-68.
9. *Ibid*., p. 68.
10. The tendency to consider individuals as a central focus of attention has received, in contemporary sociology, the name "homino-centralism", See H.D. Lasswell and Abraham Kaplan, *Power and Society*, New Haven, Conn 1954, p. 34.
11. Ebenezer Howard, *Garden Cities of Tomorrow*, London, 1945.
12. Howard W. Green, "Cultural Areas in the City of Cleveland," *Ameri-*

can Journal of Sociology, Vol. 38, 1932, pp. 356-67, See Rose Hum, "The Decline of China Towns in the United States", *American Journal of Sociology*, Vol. 54, March 1949, pp. 422-32; Louis Wirth, *The Ghetto*, Chicago, III, 1928.

13. R.D. McKenzie, *The Metropolitan Community*, New York, N.Y., 1933.
14. Donald Bogue, *The Structure of Metropolitan Community*, Ann Arbor, Mich., 1949.
15. Ernest W. Burgess, "The Growth of the City" in Robert E. Park, Ernest W. Burgess, and Roderick D. McKenzie, (eds.), *The City*, Chicago, III., 1925, pp. 47-62.
16. Janusz Ziol Koroski, "Sociological Implications of Urban Planning" in C. Fisher, (ed)., *City and Regional Planning in Poland*, Ithaca, N.Y., 1966, pp. 183-203.
17. Constance Perim, "A Noiseless Secession from the Comprehensive Plan', *Journal of the American Institute of Planners*, Washington D.C. Vol. 33, September 1967, pp. 336-46.
18. Jack Wood, *Town Planning in India: Status and Education*, New Delhi, 1959, p. 26.
19. Town Planning Institute, *Planning Research----1948-1963*, London, 1965, p. xvii.
20. The short-term course conducted by the Institute of Social studies, The Hague, may be cited as an example.
21. In engineering, the term "systems engineering" is employed to describe the effort to encompass in the analysis all elements affecting, for instance, a programme of space exploration or a network of different municipal utilities and services integrated with each other and with the surface routes of the land.
22. Hans Christoph Rieger, "Some Problems of Interdisciplinary Research", *Interdiscipline*, Varanasi, Vol. 3, Spring 1966, p. 12.
23. Donald J. Bogue, "Sociological Research and Urban Planning" in Perloff, (ed.), *Planning and the Urban Community*, p. 60.
24. Rieger, "Some Problems of Interdisciplinary Research".
25. Town Planning Institute, "Planning Research—1948-63."
26. This is also the reason why sometimes executives are less enthusiastic about the formally organized (comprehensive) planning process.
27. Gordon Pask, *An Approach to Cybernetics*, London, 1961, quoted in Rieger, "Some Problems of Inderdisciplinary Research," p. 11.